JOURNAL FOR THE STUDY OF THE NEW TESTAMENT SUPPLEMENT SERIES
183

Sheffield Academic Press

Conflict at Thessalonica

A Pauline Church
and its Neighbours

Todd D. Still

Journal for the Study of the New Testament
Supplement Series 183

For Mom and Dad
(Betty and Willard Still)

Copyright © 1999 Sheffield Academic Press

Published by
Sheffield Academic Press Ltd
Mansion House
19 Kingfield Road
Sheffield S11 9AS
England

Typeset by Sheffield Academic Press
and
Printed on acid-free paper in Great Britain
by Bookcraft Ltd
Midsomer Norton, Bath

British Library Cataloguing in Publication Data

A catalogue record for this book is available
from the British Library

ISBN 1-84127-003-2

CONTENTS

Part I
A TREATMENT OF DISPUTED TEXTS

Part II
THE SOCIAL-SCIENTIFIC STUDY OF DEVIANCE AND CONFLICT

Part III
THE APOSTLE'S ΑΓΩΝ

Part IV
THE THESSALONIANS' ΘΛΙΨΙΣ

PREFACE

This volume is a thoroughgoing revision of a doctoral thesis accepted by the University of Glasgow in June 1996. I conducted my research under the careful and able supervision of Dr John M.G. Barclay. I would like to express my deep gratitude to Dr Barclay for guiding me through the always painstaking and sometimes painful process of PhD work. He is truly a gentleman and a scholar, a man of immense erudition and remarkable goodwill. I am thankful for all that he has taught me both in person and through his publications.

In revising my PhD thesis for publication I have not only sought to make stylistic improvements, but I have also attempted to interact with the most relevant secondary literature that has appeared since I submitted my work for examination in April 1996. Furthermore, I have attempted to address the criticisms of my doctoral examiners, Professor John K. Riches of the University of Glasgow (internal examiner) and Professor Philip F. Esler of the University of St Andrews (external examiner), especially the concerns of the latter who was more critical than the former. To the extent that their critiques have sharpened my thinking and writing, thereby strengthening this volume, I am grateful.

During the writing and rewriting of this book, I have accrued many debts. Institutions and individuals who have supported me and my family financially along the way include: the Overseas Research Scheme, the University of Glasgow, Uddingston Baptist Church, Dallas Baptist University, 'Supper Club I' (the Holts, Middlebrooks, Moffatts and Todds), Dennis and Radene Christian, J.P. and Carolyn Sims and Willard and Betty Still.

A special word of thanks is also due to friends and colleagues who have encouraged me as I have written this piece and its predecessor. Dr Eddie Adams, Dr H. Alan Brehm, Dr Marion Carson, Dr Gary R. Cook, Dr R. Bruce Corley, Dr David E. Garland, Paul and Cheryl Gahm, Dr David and Mary Graham, Mark Nanos, Dr Davey Naugle, Dr Craig S. de Vos, Dr Mike Williams, 'Supper Club I' and 'Supper Club II' (the

Blackburns, Christophers and Plotts) merit special mention. I would also like to thank Professors C.K. Barrett and Beverly Roberts Gaventa as well as Drs David G. Horrell and Craig S. de Vos for allowing me access to their work in a pre-published form.

Most of all, however, I want to express my deep love and appreciation to my wife Carolyn, a budding New Testament scholar in her own right, for her cheerful and sacrificial support of me as I have turned research into a thesis and a thesis into a book. She has been with me every step of the journey, and her constant, encouraging companionship has frequently lightened what I have often perceived to be a heavy load. Now that this project is (finally) complete, I look forward to spending much more time with Carolyn and with our sons Samuel and Andrew.

Finally, I would like to thank my parents, Willard and Betty Still, for loving me, encouraging me and enabling me to pursue my dream of being a student of the New Testament and its world. I am dedicating this volume to them as a sincere token of my abiding appreciation for all they are and for all they do.

Todd D. Still
Dallas Baptist University
Dallas, TX
All Saints' Day, 1998

ABBREVIATIONS

AB	Anchor Bible
ABD	David Noel Freedman (ed.), *The Anchor Bible Dictionary* (New York: Doubleday, 1992)
ABRL	The Anchor Bible Reference Library
AJS	*American Journal of Sociology*
AJT	*American Journal of Theology*
ANRW	Hildegard Temporini and Wolfgang Haase (eds.), *Aufstieg und Niedergang der römischen Welt: Geschichte und Kultur Roms im Spiegel der neueren Forschung* (Berlin: W. de Gruyter, 1972–)
ASoc	*The American Sociologist*
ASR	*American Sociological Review*
ATR	*Anglican Theological Review*
BAFCS	Bruce W. Winter (ed.), *The Book of Acts in its First Century Setting*
BAGD	Walter Bauer, William F. Arndt, F. William Gingrich and Frederick W. Danker, *A Greek–English Lexicon of the New Testament and Other Early Christian Literature* (Chicago: University of Chicago Press, 2nd edn, 1958)
BARev	*Biblical Archaeology Review*
BECNT	Baker Exegetical Commentary on the New Testament
BETL	Bibliotheca ephemeridum theologicarum lovaniensium
BFCT	Beiträge zur Förderung christlicher Theologie
Bib	*Biblica*
BibLeb	*Bibel und Leben*
BibRes	*Biblical Research*
BIS	Biblical Interpretation Series
BJRL	*Bulletin of the John Rylands University Library of Manchester*
BJS	Brown Judaic Studies
BN	*Biblische Notizen*
BNTC	Black's New Testament Commentaries
BR	*Bible Review*
BTB	*Biblical Theology Bulletin*
CA	*Current Anthropology*
CBQ	*Catholic Biblical Quarterly*
CCS	Continental Commentary Series

CCWJCW	Cambridge Commentaries on Writings of the Jewish and Christian World
CD	*Crime and Delinquency*
CII	J.-B. Frey, *Corpus Inscriptionum Iudaicarum* (2 vols.; Rome: Pontifical Institute of Biblical Archaeology, 1936, 1952)
CNT	Commentaire du Nouveau Testament
ConBNT	Coniectanea biblica, New Testament
CPASS	Cambridge Philosophical Association Supplement Series
CPJ	V. Tcherikover and A. Fuks, *Corpus Papyrorum Judaicarum* (3 vols.; Jerusalem: Magnes Press; Cambridge, MA: Harvard University Press, 1957, 1960, 1963 [3rd vol. with M. Stern and D.M. Lewis])
CPNIVC	College Press NIV Commentary
CSHJ	Chicago Studies in the History of Judaism
DB	*Deviant Behavior*
DPL	Gerald F. Hawthorne, Ralph P. Martin and Daniel G. Reid (eds.), *Dictionary of Paul and his Letters* (Downers Grove, IL: InterVarsity Press, 1993)
EB	The Expositor's Bible
EBib	Etudes bibliques
EC	Epworth Commentaries
EKKNT	Evangelisch-Katholischer Kommentar zum Neuen Testament
ETL	*Ephemerides theologicae lovanienses*
ExAud	*Ex Audita*
ExpTim	*Expository Times*
FCGRW	Andrew D. Clarke (ed.), *First-Century Christians in the Graeco-Roman World*
FFNT	Foundations and Facets: New Testament
FFSF	Foundations and Facets: Social Facets
FRLANT	Forschungen zur Religion und Literatur des Alten und Neuen Testaments
GBSNTS	Guides to Biblical Scholarship, New Testament Series
GNS	Good News Studies
HBT	*Horizons in Biblical Theology*
HNT	Handbuch zum Neuen Testament
HNTC	Harper's NT Commentaries
HSCP	*Harvard Studies in Classical Philology*
HTR	*Harvard Theological Review*
HUT	Hermeneutische Untersuchungen zur Theologie
IBS	*Irish Biblical Studies*
ICC	International Critical Commentary
Int	*Interpretation*
ISBS	The International Series in the Behavioral Sciences

IT	Charles E. Edson, *Inscriptiones graeca Epiri, Macedoniae, Thraciae, Scythiae, Pars II. Inscriptiones Thessalonicae et viciniae* (Berlin: W. de Gruyter, 1972)
JAAR	*Journal of the American Academy of Religion*
JBL	*Journal of Biblical Literature*
JCR	*Journal of Conflict Resolution*
JECS	*Journal of Early Christian Studies*
JEH	*Journal of Ecclesiastical History*
JETS	*Journal of the Evangelical Theological Society*
JPP	*Journal of Personality and Psychology*
JProt Theo	*Jährbücher für protestantische Theologie*
JPT	*Journal of Pentecostal Theology*
JRH	*Journal of Religious History*
JRS	*Journal of Roman Studies*
JSI	*Journal of Social Issues*
JSJ	*Journal for the Study of Judaism in the Persian, Hellenistic and Roman Period*
JSNT	*Journal for the Study of the New Testament*
JSNTSup	*Journal for the Study of the New Testament*, Supplement Series
JSOT	*Journal for the Study of the Old Testament*
JSP	*Journal for the Study of the Pseudepigrapha*
JSPSup	*Journal for the Study of the Pseudepigrapha*, Supplement Series
JTS	*Journal of Theological Studies*
MeyerK	H.A.W. Meyer (ed.), *Kritisch-Exegetischer Kommentar über das Neue Testament*
LCBIS	Literary Currents in Biblical Interpretation Series
LCL	Loeb Classical Library
LEC	Library of Early Christianity
MDAIAA	*Mitteilungen des Deutschen Archaeologische Instituts, Athenische Abteilung*
MNTC	Moffatt NT Commentary
NAC	New American Commentary
NedTTs	*Nederlands theologisch tijdschrift*
Neot	*Neotestamentica*
NIBC	New International Biblical Commentary
NICNT	New International Commentary on the New Testament
NIGTC	The New International Greek Testament Commentary
NIVAC	The New International Version Application Commentary
NovT	*Novum Testamentum*
NovTSup	*Novum Testamentum*, Supplements
NTM	New Testament Message
NTR	New Testament Readings
NTS	*New Testament Studies*

NTT	New Testament Theology
NTTS	New Testament Tools and Studies
Numen	*Numen: International Review for the History of Religions*
OTP	James Charlesworth (ed.), *Old Testament Pseudepigrapha*
Proceedings	*Proceedings of the Eastern Great Lakes and Midwest Biblical Societies*
PRS	*Perspectives in Religous Studies*
PSR	*Pacific Sociological Review*
RB	*Revue biblique*
RevExp	*Review and Expositor*
RTR	*Reformed Theological Review*
SBib	Stuttgarter Bibelstudien
SBEC	Studies in the Bible and Early Christianity
SBFLA	*Studii biblici franciscani liber annuus*
SBL	Society of Biblical Literature
SBLDS	SBL Dissertation Series
SBLMS	SBL Monograph Series
SBLSP	SBL Seminar Papers
SBLSS	SBL Semeia Studies
SBT	Studies in Biblical Theology
SCH	Studies in Church History
SEÅ	*Svensk exegetisk årsbok*
SHSG	Sage Human Services Guide
SJT	*Scottish Journal of Theology*
SNTSMS	Society for New Testament Studies Monograph Series
SNTW	Studies of the New Testament and its World
SocAn	*Sociological Analysis*
SocProb	*Social Problems*
SP	Sacra Pagina
SQ	*Sociological Quarterly*
SR	*Studies in Religion/Sciences religieuses*
SSR	*Sociology and Social Research*
ST	*Studia theologica*
SHCT	Studies in the History of Christian Thought
STDJ	Studies on the Text of the Desert of Judah
StudBib	Studia Biblica
SE	*Studia Evangelica*
TDNT	Gerhard Kittel and Gerhard Friedrich (eds.), *Theological Dictionary of the New Testament* (trans. Geoffrey W. Bromiley; 10 vols.; Grand Rapids: Eerdmans, 1964–)
TLZ	*Theologische Literaturzeitung*
TU	Texte und Untersuchungen
TynBul	*Tyndale Bulletin*
TZ	*Theologische Zeitschrift*
UJTS	Understanding Jesus Today Series

USQR	*Union Seminary Quarterly Review*
VC	*Vigiliae christianae*
VT	*Vetus Testamentum*
WBC	Word Biblical Commentary
WC	Westminster Commentaries
WFE	*World Faiths Encounter*
WMANT	Wissenschaftliche Monographien zum Alten und Neuen Testament
WUNT	Wissenschaftliche Untersuchungen zum Neuen Testament
ZB	Zürcher Bibelkommentare
ZKT	*Zeitschrift für katholische Theologie*
ZNW	*Zeitschrift für die neutestamentliche Wissenschaft*
ZPE	*Zeitschrift für Papyrologie und Epigraphik*
ZSNT	Zacchaeus Studies, New Testament
ZTK	*Zeitschrift für Theologie und Kirche*
ZWT	*Zeitschrift für wissenschaftliche Theologie*

INTRODUCTION

1. *Thessalonian Research and the Place of this Study Therein*

Though it has frequently lain fallow,[1] in recent years Thessalonian research has become a fertile Pauline field.[2] In addition to the publication of numerous commentaries[3] and of papers presented to a Leuven

1.   Prior to the publication of Ernest Best's commentary (*A Commentary on the First and Second Epistles to the Thessalonians* [HNTC; Peabody, MA: Hendrickson, 1972]) and Wolfgang Trilling's monograph (*Untersuchungen zum zweiten Thessalonicherbrief* [Leipzig: St Benno, 1972]) in 1972, published scholarly studies on the Thessalonian correspondence were somewhat sparse and sporadic. Important commentators from the late nineteenth to the mid twentieth century include: Gottlieb Lünemann, *The Epistles to the Thessalonians* (trans. Paton J. Gloag; Edinburgh: T. & T. Clark, 1880); George Milligan, *St Paul's Epistles to the Thessalonians* (London: Macmillan, 1908); Ernst von Dobschütz, *Die Thessalonicherbriefe* (MeyerK; Göttingen: Vandenhoeck & Ruprecht, 1909); James E. Frame, *A Critical and Exegetical Commentary on the Epistles of St Paul to the Thessalonians* (ICC; Edinburgh: T. & T. Clark, 1912); Martin Dibelius, *An die Thessalonicher I, II: An die Philipper* (HNT, 11; Tübingen: J.C.B. Mohr [Paul Siebeck], 1937); Béda Rigaux, *Saint Paul: Les Epitres aux Thessaloniciens* (EBib; Paris: J. Gabalda, 1956); and Charles Masson, *Les deux Epîtres de Saint Paul aux Thessaloniciens* (CNT, 11a; Paris: Delachaux & Niestlé, 1957).

2.   On Thessalonian research from 1972–89, see Earl J. Richard, 'Contemporary Research on 1 (& 2) Thessalonians', *BTB* 20 (1990), pp. 107-15. For an extensive annotated bibliography of primarily late-twentieth-century works that are relevant to the interpretation of 1 and 2 Thess., see Jeffrey A.D. Weima and Stanley E. Porter, *1 and 2 Thessalonians: An Annotated Bibliography* (NTTS, 26; Leiden: E.J. Brill, 1998).

3.   Since the publication of Best's commentary in 1972, the following are some of the more important commentaries which have appeared: Wolfgang Trilling, *Der zweite Brief an die Thessalonicher* (EKKNT, 14; Zürich: Benzinger Verlag; Neukirchen–Vluyn: Neukirchener Verlag, 1980); F.F. Bruce, *1 & 2 Thessalonians* (WBC, 45; Waco, TX: Word Books, 1982); I.H. Marshall, *1 and 2 Thessalonians* (NCB; Grand Rapids: Eerdmans; London: Marshall, Morgan & Scott, 1983); Traugott Holtz, *Der erste Brief an die Thessalonicher* (EKKNT, 13; Zürich: Benzinger

colloquium[4] and to the Pauline Theology Group of the SBL,[5] contemporary interpreters have produced volumes focusing upon rhetorical features,[6] theological aspects[7] and pastoral and congregational issues[8] in what is presumably Paul's earliest extant correspondence.

Although publications pertaining to 1 and 2 Thessalonians have proliferated, there remains room in this Pauline field for scholars to sow

Verlag; Neukirchen–Vluyn: Neukirchener Verlag, 1986); Charles A. Wanamaker, *The Epistles to the Thessalonians: A Commentary on the Greek Text* (NIGTC; Grand Rapids: Eerdmans; Exeter: Paternoster Press, 1990); Leon Morris, *The First and Second Epistles to the Thessalonians* (NICNT; Grand Rapids: Eerdmans, rev. edn, 1991); D. Michael Martin, *1, 2 Thessalonians* (NAC, 33; Nashville: Broadman & Holman Press, 1995); Earl J. Richard, *First and Second Thessalonians* (SP, 11; Collegeville, MN: Liturgical Press, 1995); and Beverly Roberts Gaventa, *First and Second Thessalonians* (Interpretation; Louisville, KY: Westminster/John Knox Press, 1998). Karl P. Donfried (ICC), Helmut Koester (Hermeneia), Abraham J. Malherbe (AB) and Jeffrey A.D. Weima (BECNT) are currently composing commentaries on 1 and 2 Thess.

4. Raymond F. Collins (ed.), *The Thessalonian Correspondence* (BETL, 87; Leuven: Leuven University Press, 1990). See also the collection of essays (*Studies on the First Letter to the Thessalonians* [BETL, 66; Leuven: Leuven University Press, 1984]) and the monograph (*The Birth of the New Testament: The Origin and Development of the First Christian Generation* [New York: Crossroad, 1993]) authored by Collins.

5. Jouette M. Bassler (ed.), *Pauline Theology. I. Thessalonians, Philippians, Galatians, Philemon* (Minneapolis: Fortress Press, 1991), pp. 39-85, 183-265.

6. On 1 Thess., Bruce C. Johanson, *To All the Brethren: A Text-Linguistic and Rhetorical Approach to 1 Thessalonians* (ConBNT, 16; Stockholm: Almqvist & Wiksell, 1987), Carol J. Schleuter, *Filling up the Measure: Polemical Hyperbole in 1 Thessalonians 2.14-16* (JSNTSup, 98; Sheffield: JSOT Press, 1994) and Abraham Smith, *Comfort One Another: Reconstructing the Rhetoric and Audience of 1 Thessalonians* (LCBIS; Louisville, KY: Westminster/John Knox Press, 1995). On 2 Thess., Frank Witt Hughes, *Early Christian Rhetoric and 2 Thessalonians* (JSNTSup, 30; Sheffield: JSOT Press, 1989) and Glenn S. Holland, *The Tradition that You Received from Us: 2 Thessalonians in the Pauline Tradition* (HUT, 24; Tübingen: J.C.B. Mohr [Paul Siebeck], 1988).

7. Karl P. Donfried, 'The Theology of 1 and 2 Thessalonians', in *The Shorter Pauline Letters* (NTT; Cambridge: Cambridge University Press, 1993), pp. 1-113.

8. On 1 Thess., Abraham J. Malherbe, *Paul and the Thessalonians: The Philosophic Tradition of Pastoral Care* (Philadelphia: Fortress Press, 1987), and Judith Lynn Hill, *Establishing the Church in Thessalonica* (Ann Arbor, MI: University Microfilms, 1990). On 1 and 2 Thess., Robert Jewett, *The Thessalonian Correspondence: Pauline Rhetoric and Millenarian Piety* (FFNT; Philadelphia: Fortress Press, 1986).

and reap. Paul's repeated reference in 1 Thessalonians to 'affliction' (1.6; 3.3-4), 'opposition' (2.2b; cf. 2.15b, 2.16a, 2.17a) and 'suffering' (2.2a, 14) is an important interpretive issue which has yet to receive adequate scholarly attention and presently requires further investigation (cf. 2 Thess. 1.4-7; Acts 17.1-10a). To be sure, commentators as well as writers of books[9] and articles[10] have noted this terminology and have discussed it with varying degrees of thoroughness and success. However, to the best of my knowledge, no one has carried out a full-length study of θλῖψις in Thessalonica. This volume will fill this lacuna in Thessalonian literature.

Herein, I raise and seek to answer the following question: What does Paul have in mind in 1 Thessalonians when he speaks of 'affliction/ opposition/suffering'? Does the 'affliction' *only* signal a theological *topos*[11] or *merely* suggest psychological *Angst*?[12] I think not. As the title of this work indicates, I am convinced that the θλῖψις to which Paul frequently refers is best conceived as intergroup conflict between Christians and non-Christians in Thessalonica.

Although other interpreters of the Thessalonian letters have concluded similarly, further elaboration and greater precision is required in explaining 'a situation of rather complicated antipathy toward the Christians'.[13] Who opposed Paul and his converts? How were they harried? Why were they harassed? What effects did the conflict have on Paul and the Thessalonian church? These are among the intriguing questions that I will address in this volume.

In what follows, I will substantiate my thesis that Paul and the Thessalonian Christians had discordant relations with outsiders through the exegesis of pertinent passages. Furthermore, I will delineate (with the

9.	E.g. Malherbe, *Paul and the Thessalonians*, pp. 46-52, and Rainer Riesner, *Paul's Early Period: Chronology, Mission Strategy, Theology* (trans. Doug Stott; Grand Rapids: Eerdmans, 1998), pp. 352-62, 371-82.

10.	See esp. the essays by John M.G. Barclay, 'Conflict in Thessalonica', *CBQ* 55 (1993), pp. 512-30, and Karl P. Donfried, 'The Theology of 1 Thessalonians as a Reflection of its Purpose', in Maurya P. Horgan and Paul J. Kobelski (eds.), *To Touch the Text: Biblical and Related Studies in Honor of Joseph Fitzmyer* (New York: Crossroad, 1989), pp. 243-60.

11.	So, e.g., Birger A. Pearson, '1 Thessalonians 2.13-16: A Deutero-Pauline Interpolation', *HTR* 64 (1971), pp. 79-94 (87).

12.	Malherbe, *Paul and the Thessalonians*, pp. 46-48.

13.	Florence Morgan-Gillman, 'Jason in Thessalonica (Acts 17,5-9)', in Collins (ed.), *The Thessalonian Correspondence*, pp. 39-49 (44).

aid of literary parallels, non-literary evidence and the social-scientific study of deviance and conflict) the apparent reasons for and results of this conflict in Thessalonica.

In executing this study, I will also treat other topics of interest to Thessalonian interpreters, including: the integrity of 1 Thess. 2.13-16; the authenticity of 2 Thessalonians; the place of Acts 17.1-10a in the study of Pauline Christianity in Thessalonica; the intention of 1 Thess. 2.1-12; the nature of the relations of Paul with the Thessalonian Christians and of the believers with one another; the contents of Paul's original proclamation in Thessalonica; the composition and formation of the Thessalonian assembly; the apocalyptic and polemical texture of 1 and 2 Thessalonians; and the meaning of and reason for the ethical and eschatological instruction in 1 Thessalonians 4–5 and 2 Thessalonians 2–3.

2. *An Overview of this Volume*

I begin this project by treating texts of disputed authenticity (1 Thess. 2.13-16 [Chapter 1]; 2 Thessalonians [Chapter 2]) and accuracy (Acts 17.1-10a [Chapter 3]). This is a necessary first step because the interpretive conclusions at which I arrive in Part I will determine to what extent these controverted texts will be relevant to this study.

Part II of this project introduces the reader in some detail to the social-scientific study of deviance (Chapter 4) and conflict (Chapter 5). The theoretical insights garnered there will inform and reinforce many of the arguments I set forth in Parts III–IV of this work. Sharp criticism notwithstanding,[14] it has now become commonplace for New Testament scholars to employ the social sciences in their work.[15] Unlike some

---

14. E.g. E.A. Judge, 'The Social Identity of the First Christians: A Question of Method in Religious History', *JRH* 11 (1980), pp. 201-17, and Cyril S. Rodd, 'On Applying a Sociological Theory to Biblical Studies', *JSOT* 19 (1981), pp. 95-106.

15. On the development of social-scientific criticism and an assessment of the discipline, see David G. Horrell, 'Social-Scientific Interpretation of the New Testament: Retrospect and Prospect', in David G. Horrell (ed.), *Social-Scientific Approaches to New Testament Interpretation* (Edinburgh: T. & T. Clark, 1999), pp. 3-27. For a defense of using the social sciences in New Testament interpretation, see, e.g., Philip F. Esler, *Community and Gospel in Luke–Acts: The Social and Political Motivations of Lucan Theology* (SNTSMS, 57; Cambridge: Cambridge University Press, 1987), pp. 12-16. For an introduction to social-scientific criticism with a full bibliography, see John H. Elliott, *What Is Social-*

interpreters who make use of the social sciences, however, I do not focus on any one theorist or theory, nor do I attempt to construct a global or formal 'model' with hypotheses which can be predicted or tested.[16] Rather, I thoroughly survey the social-scientific study of deviance and conflict and then seek to apply relevant theories drawn from these disciplines where they seem to fit.[17] These theoretical perspectives are meant to serve as rudimentary frameworks to supplement, not supplant, careful textual and historical analysis.[18] In this work, I use the social sciences as a sensitizing tool to create original angles of

Scientific Criticism? (GBSNTS; Philadelphia: Fortress Press, 1993). See also Bengt Holmberg, *Sociology and the New Testament: An Appraisal* (Minneapolis: Fortress Press, 1990), and, more succinctly, J. Dorcas Gordon, *Sister or Wife?: 1 Corinthians 7 and Cultural Anthropology* (JSNTSup, 149; Sheffield: Sheffield Academic Press, 1997), pp. 35-58.

16. On the use of models in social-scientific criticism and the advocacy thereof, see, e.g., Philip F. Esler, 'Introduction', in Philip F. Esler (ed.), *Modelling Early Christianity: Social-Scientific Studies of the New Testament in its Context* (London: Routledge, 1995), pp. 1-20 (4-8). For a critique of the model-based approach spiritedly espoused and rigorously employed by Esler and other members of the Context Group (e.g. Bruce J. Malina, Jerome H. Neyrey, John H. Elliott and Richard L. Rohrbaugh), see, e.g., Susan R. Garrett, 'Sociology (Early Christianity)', *ABD*, VI, pp. 88-99 (96-97); David G. Horrell, *The Social Ethos of the Corinthian Correspondence: Interests and Ideology from 1 Corinthians to 1 Clement* (SNTW; Edinburgh: T. & T. Clark, 1996), pp. 9-18; and Richard Bauckham, 'Response to Philip Esler', *SJT* 51 (1998), 249-53.

17. Cf. Wayne A. Meeks, *The First Urban Christians: The Social World of the Apostle Paul* (New Haven: Yale University Press, 1983), p. 6. Although some social-scientific practitioners will object to the eclectic, pragmatic approach I employ here, such a strategy allows one to treat the textual, historical and social-scientific materials in a more nuanced manner. No attempt is made to plug historical holes with social theories. Francis Watson (*Paul, Judaism and the Gentiles: A Sociological Approach* [SNTMS, 56; Cambridge: Cambridge University Press, 1986], p. x) rightly suggests, 'Sociological analysis is not a satisfactory way of filling gaps in our historical knowledge. It is not a substitute for historical evidence, but a way of interpreting evidence.'

18. John M.G. Barclay's ('Deviance and Apostasy: Some Applications of Deviance Theory to First-Century Judaism and Christianity', in Esler [ed.], *Modelling Early Christianity*, pp. 114-27 [125]) remarks in reference to the use of deviance theory in particular are applicable: '[D]eviance theory is no magic wand with which to solve the many intricate problems which confront the historian of early Christianity. It can only be used in conjunction with minute historical analysis of the sources and cannot fill in the gaps which they leave.'

inquiry into particular historical issues and to generate a fresh slate of questions to put to specific texts.

I proceed in Parts III–IV of this work to consider Paul's and his Thessalonian converts' conflict respectively, being mindful all the while of the conclusions drawn and questions raised in Chapters 1–5. Chapters 6–8 focus on the opposition which Paul himself encountered from non-Christians in Thessalonica. Based upon a thorough analysis of various verses in 1 Thessalonians 2 (cf. Acts 17.5-10a, 13), I argue in Chapter 6 that Paul was actively and forcefully opposed in Thessalonica, particularly by Thessalonian Jews who ultimately drove him from the city. In Chapter 7, I address why Paul was maltreated by his Jewish compatriots in Thessalonica and elsewhere. In an effort to discern why Paul experienced frequent conflict with his own people, I consider various Hellenistic-Jewish texts which show how Jews deemed 'apostate' were perceived and treated. Additionally, I examine Paul's own comments about his persecutory activity and about his being opposed by other Jews. I ultimately identify Paul's law-free living and teaching as the primary sources of contention between him and 'stricter' Jews. I then proceed to argue in Chapter 8 that the apocalyptic and polemical texture of the Thessalonian letters may be positively correlated to the hostility which Paul and his converts encountered from non-Christian outsiders.

The final phase of this project, Part IV, considers the Thessalonian Christians' affliction. Chapter 9 deals with the nature and the source of the congregation's conflict. I contend that the church, which Paul depicts as Gentile (e.g. 1 Thess. 1.9; 4.3-8; cf. Acts 17.4), suffered verbal (and perhaps physical) abuse, social ostracism and political sanctions at the hands of their Gentile compatriots (1 Thess. 2.14). Chapter 10 addresses why the congregation encountered such opposition. There I propound that the Thessalonians' conversion coupled with their rejection of their former gods incited the ire of their compatriots. Furthermore, non-Christian opposition was apparently heightened by the assembly's social and ideological separatism, aggressive proselytism and (perceived) subversive character (along familial, religious and political lines). Finally, Chapter 11 considers the consequences of the Thessalonians' conflict with outsiders. Seemingly the hostility the church encountered from without facilitated congregational growth in faith, love and hope.

By way of conclusion, I summarize the study, highlight contributions of this work and offer suggestions for further research. There is, however, much territory to traverse between here and there. So, leaving introductory remarks behind, let us proceed to the study before us.

Part I

A Treatment of Disputed Texts

Chapter 1

1 THESSALONIANS 2.13-16:
A DEUTERO-PAULINE INTERPOLATION?*

1. *Introduction*

1 Thessalonians will serve as the primary source for this study. Two major factors lead to this interpretive decision: (1) References to the subject under discussion occur most frequently in 1 Thessalonians. (2) Virtually all modern commentators have judged the letter to be authentically Pauline.[1] Although scholars affirm the authenticity of 1 Thessalonians, some interpreters aver that 2.13-16, or a portion there-

---

*   I presented an earlier version of this chapter to the Seminar on the Development of Early Christianity in September 1996 at Dallas Theological Seminary. I am grateful to Dr Daryl Schmidt for his formal and cordial response and to other seminar participants for their thought-provoking questions and stimulating discussion.

1.   The only exception in the twentieth century of which I am aware is A.Q. Morton and L. McLeman, *Christianity and the Computer* (London: Hodder & Stoughton, 1964).

2.   For the argument that 2.13-16 is inauthentic, see, e.g., Karl-Gottfried Eckart, 'Der zweite echte Brief des Apostels Paulus an die Thessalonicher', *ZTK* 58 (1961), pp. 30-44; Pearson, '1 Thessalonians 2:13-16'; Hendrikus Boers, 'The Form Critical Study of Paul's Letters: I Thessalonians as a Case Study', *NTS* 22 (1976), pp. 140-58; Helmut Koester, *Introduction to the New Testament. II. History and Literature of Early Christianity* (Philadelphia: Fortress Press, 1982), pp. 112-14; Daryl D. Schmidt, '1 Thess 2:13-16: Linguistic Evidence for an Interpolation', *JBL* 102 (1983), pp. 269-79; John G. Gager, *The Origins of Anti-Semitism: Attitudes toward Judaism in Pagan and Christian Antiquity* (Oxford: Oxford University Press, 1983), pp. 255-56; Norman A. Beck, *Mature Christianity: The Recognition and Repudiation of the Anti-Jewish Polemic of the New Testament* (Selingrove: Susquehanna University Press, 1985), pp. 40-50, 90-92; Lloyd Gaston, *Paul and the Torah* (Vancouver: University of British Columbia Press, 1987), pp. 137, 195; and Claudia J. Setzer, *Jewish Responses to Early Christians: History and Polemics, 30–150 CE* (Minneapolis: Fortress Press, 1994), p. 19. For the suggestion that 2.14-16 is an interpolation, see, e.g., F.C. Baur, *Paul the Apostle of Jesus Christ: His Life*

of, is a post-Pauline interpolation.[2] 1 Thessalonians 2.13-16 reads as follows:[3]

> We also constantly give thanks to God for this, that when you received the word of God which you heard from us, you accepted it not as a human word but as what it really is, the word of God, which is also at work in you believers. For you, brothers, became imitators [μιμηταὶ] of the churches of God in Christ Jesus that are in Judea, for you suffered [ἐπάθετε] the same things at the hands of your own compatriots [ἰδίων συμφυλετῶν] as they [suffered] from the Jews ['Ιουδαίων] who killed the Lord Jesus and the prophets, and drove us out; they displease God and oppose all people by hindering us from speaking to the Gentiles so that they might be saved—so as always to fill up the measure of their sins; but [God's] wrath has come upon them at last [ἔφθασεν δὲ ἐπ' αὐτοὺς ἡ ὀργὴ εἰς τέλος].

Because this pericope speaks specifically of conflict between Christians and non-Christians, it is of obvious import to this study. However, because a number of scholars have called the authenticity of this text into question, interpreters who would employ this passage in their research are obliged to defend its genuineness.

Along with the large majority of New Testament scholars, I think that Paul authored the whole of 2.13-16.[4] Nevertheless, a notable minority

---

and Work, his Epistles and his Doctrine (trans. Allen Menzies; 2 vols.; London: Williams & Norgate, 2nd edn, 1875–76), II, p. 87; Richard, *Thessalonians*, pp. 119-27; and Leander Keck, 'Images of Paul in the New Testament', *Int* 43 (1989), pp. 341-51 (345-46). Cf. Jack T. Sanders, *Schismatics, Sectarians, Dissidents, Deviants: The First One Hundred Years of Jewish–Christian Relations* (London: SCM Press, 1993), p. 7. Meeks (*First Urban Christians*, p. 227 n. 117) doubts the authenticity of 2.15-16 (cf. Bruce [*Thessalonians*, p. 49] who suggests that the authenticity of 2.15-16 remains *sub judice*), as James Moffatt (*Introduction to the New Testament* [Edinburgh: T. & T. Clark, 3rd edn, 1927], p. 73) did 2.16c.

Gehard Friedrich's ('1 Thessalonicher 5,1-11, der apologetische Einschuß eines Späteren', *ZTK* 70 [1973], pp. 288-315) suggestion that 1 Thess. 5.1-11 is an interpolation has won no scholarly support. For a critique of Friedrich's view, see Joseph Plevnik, '1 Thess. 5,1-11: Its Authenticity, Intention and Message', *Bib* 60 (1979), pp. 71-90. Without further discussion, I will presume with other scholars that 5.1-11 is authentic and will employ the passage in this work where deemed appropriate.

3. With some usually minor variations, biblical quotations (including the deuterocanonical books) are from the RSV or NRSV. The Nestle–Aland[27] is the Greek New Testament with which I work.

4. See, among others, Schlueter, *Filling up the Measure*; Johanson, *To All the*

of exegetes are not inclined likewise. F.C. Baur was among the first commentators to suggest that 2.14-16 was un-Pauline.[5] He contended that the statement about the Jews displeasing God (θεῷ μὴ ἀρεσκόντων [2.15c]) 'fits strangely on the lips of Paul' and is 'inconsistent with what we know of Paul's attitude toward his race'.[6] Additionally, Baur thought that the phrase ἔφθασεν δὲ ἐπ' αὐτοὺς ἡ ὀργὴ εἰς τέλος (2.16b) referred to 'the punishment that came upon [the Jews] in the destruction of Jerusalem'.[7] In Baur's estimation, 2.14-16 was composed after 70 CE when both Jewish and Pauline Christianity regarded the

---

Brethren; Jewett, *Thessalonian Correspondence*, pp. 36-42; Collins, *Birth of the New Testament*, pp. 145-46; Smith, *Comfort One Another*, p. 35; Best, *Thessalonians*, p. 123; Marshall, *Thessalonians*, pp. 11-12; Wanamaker, *Thessalonians*, pp. 29-33; Karl Olav Sandnes, *Paul—One of the Prophets?: A Contribution to the Apostle's Self-Understanding* (WUNT, 43; Tübingen: J.C.B. Mohr [Paul Siebeck], 1991), pp. 191-94; George Lyons, *Pauline Autobiography: Toward a New Understanding* (SBLDS, 73; Atlanta: Scholars Press, 1985), pp. 202-207; W.D. Davies, 'Paul and the People of Israel', *NTS* 24 (1977), pp. 4-39 (6-9); G.E. Okeke, 'I Thessalonians 2.13-16: The Fate of the Unbelieving Jews', *NTS* 27 (1980–81), pp. 127-36; Karl P. Donfried, 'Paul and Judaism: 1 Thessalonians 2:13-16 as a Test Case', *Int* 38 (1984), pp. 242-53; John C. Hurd, 'Paul ahead of his Time: 1 Thess. 2:13-16', in Peter Richardson (ed.), *Anti-Judaism in Early Christianity*. I. *Paul and the Gospels* (Waterloo, ON: Wilfrid Laurier University Press, 1986), pp. 21-36; Ingo Broer, ' "Der ganze Zorn ist schon über sie gekommen": Bemerkungen zur Interpolationshypothese und zur Interpretation von 1 Thess 2,14-16', in Collins (ed.), *The Thessalonian Correspondence*, pp. 137-59; J.W. Simpson, Jr, 'The Problems Posed by 1 Thessalonians 2:15-16 and a Solution', *HBT* 12 (1990), pp. 42-72; Jon A. Weatherly, 'The Authenticity of 1 Thessalonians 2.13-16: Additional Evidence', *JSNT* 42 (1991), pp. 79-98; Peter Wick, 'Ist I Thess 2,13-16 antijüdisch?: Der rhetorische Gesamtzusammenhang des Briefes als Interpretationshilfe für eine einzelne Perikope', *TZ* 50 (1994), pp. 9-23; David A. deSilva, ' "Worthy of his Kingdom": Honor Discourse and Social Engineering in 1 Thessalonians', *JSNT* 64 (1996), pp. 49-79; and Simon Légasse, 'Paul et les Juifs d'après 1 Thessaloniciens 2,13-16', *RB* 104 (1997), pp. 572-91.

    5.   Baur, *Paul*, II, p. 87. According to T.J. Baarda ('1 Thess. 2:14-16: Rodrigues in "Nestle–Aland"', *NedTTs* 39 [1985], pp. 186-93), in 1847 (two years after the initial publication of Baur's two-volume work on Paul) A. Ritschl suggested that 2.16c was an interpolation. Baarda also notes that in 1872 P.W. Schmiedel contended that 2.15-16 was an insertion and that in 1876 H. Rodrigues maintained that 2.14-15 (and 16?) was a later addition. Baarda further reports that A. Loisy (1922) and M. Goguel (1925) denied the authenticity of 2.13-16 and 2.14-16 respectively.

    6.   Baur, *Paul*, II, p. 88.

    7.   Baur, *Paul*, II, p. 88.

Jews as enemies.[8] Baur's understanding of 2.14-16 was one of the major factors that led him to reject the authenticity of 1 Thessalonians altogether.[9] Apart from a few scholars,[10] particularly those in the Tübingen and Dutch schools, post-Baurian interpreters have affirmed the Pauline authorship of 1 Thessalonians.[11] However, Baur's ideas about 2.14-16 have influenced a number of subsequent scholars to view these verses as (part of) an interpolation.[12]

Indeed, some writers have questioned the integrity of not only (parts of) 2.14-16 but also the whole of 2.13-16.[13] Birger A. Pearson is the most noted proponent of the interpolation hypothesis of 2.13-16. In an article first published in 1971, Pearson argued against the authenticity of the pericope on historical, theological and form-critical grounds.[14] His carefully crafted essay has thoroughly convinced some scholars.[15]

In this chapter I will attempt to counter the work of Pearson and others who attribute 2.13-16 (or portions thereof) to a later editor.[16] In

8. Baur, *Paul*, II, p. 320.

9. Also noted by Schleuter, *Filling up the Measure*, p. 15.

10. E.g. C. Holsten, 'Zur Unechtheit des ersten Briefes an die Thessalonicher und zur Abfassungszeit der Apocalypse', *JProtTheo* 36 (1877), pp. 731-32.

11. So Hurd, 'Paul ahead of his Time', p. 24.

12. Pearson ('1 Thessalonians 2:13-16', p. 79) acknowledges his indebtedness to Baur.

13. See n. 2 above.

14. Pearson, '1 Thessalonians 2:13-16'. A slightly revised version of this article appears in Birger A. Pearson, *The Emergence of the Christian Religion: Essays on Early Christianity* (Harrisburg, PN: Trinity Press International, 1997), pp. 58-74. In the 'Introduction' to this volume (pp. 1-6), Pearson states in reference to '1 Thessalonians 2:13-16': 'there is one article I wrote many years ago that has, in my present judgment, stood the test of time, and I would not change anything of substance in it' (p. 3). That which follows, then, is a response to Pearson's past and present thinking on 2.13-16.

15. E.g. Boers ('Form Critical Study', p. 152) remarks, 'Although all [of Pearson's] arguments may not be equally compelling, the sum of the evidence is overwhelmingly in his favour. He has produced decisive evidence that the passage is an interpolation.'

16. In her monograph *Filling up the Measure*, Schleuter argues for the authenticity of 2.14-16 on rhetorical grounds. She thinks that the passage is best explained as an instance of polemical hyperbole in Paul. Although Schleuter does note in her study that 'Much stronger structural, stylistic, linguistic, theological and historical evidence needs to be at hand before one can judge what is or is not compatible with Paul's literary structure, style, syntax or theology, and what historical referents to

doing so, I will consider in turn form-critical, grammatical and syntactical, historical and theological arguments which exegetes have forwarded against a text which boasts universal external attestation.[17]

2. *Form-Critical Concerns*

Scholars are in basic agreement that 2.13 marks a transition in 1 Thessalonians. The question is what type of transition. Answers to this query vary. Suggestions concerning the function of 2.13 in the epistle range from the more novel proposals that the verse signals the beginning of a letter[18] or the presence of an interpolator[19] to the less radical suggestions that the verse marks the start of a renewed (or second)

his words are reasonable' (p. 38), she does not seek to defend the genuineness of the passage on such grounds. Therefore, her insightful study in no way renders this chapter redundant. I will be in conversation with Schleuter's important contribution to Thessalonian studies throughout this volume.

17. For similar categories in dealing with the arguments against the authenticity of 2.13-16, see Lyons, *Pauline Autobiography*, pp. 202-207. I have chosen to deal with objections to the non-Pauline origin of the pericope in order of their merit. I will move from the less problematic areas of structure and syntax to the more difficult categories of history and theology.

The textual apparatus of Nestle–Aland[27] indicates that one Vulgate manuscript omits 2.16c. For the argument that there are multiple interpolations in the Pauline Epistles without manuscript attestation, see William Walker, 'The Burden of Proof in Identifying Interpolations in the Pauline Letters', *NTS* 33 (1987), pp. 610-18, and 'Text-Critical Evidence for Interpolations in the Letters of Paul', *CBQ* 50 (1988), pp. 622-31.

18. So, e.g., Rudolph Pesch, *Die Entdeckung des ältesten Paulus-Briefes. Paulus-neu gesehen: Die Briefe an die Gemeinde der Thessalonicher* (Freiburg: Herder, 1984); Walter Schmithals, *Paul and the Gnostics* (trans. John E. Steely; Nashville: Abingdon Press, 1972), pp. 176-81; Jerome Murphy-O'Connor, *Paul: A Critical Life* (Oxford: Clarendon Press, 1996), pp. 105-106; and Richard, *Thessalonians*, pp. 11-17. A compilation theory for 1 Thess. is unnecessary and has been rightly and adequately refuted by, e.g., Werner Georg Kümmel, 'Das literarische und geschichtliche Problem des ersten Thessalonicherbriefes', in W.C. van Unnik (ed.), *Neotestamentica et Patristica: Eine Freundesgabe Oscar Cullmann zum 60. Geburtstag* (NovTSup, 6; Leiden: E.J. Brill, 1962), pp. 213-22; Collins, *Thessalonians*, pp. 96-135; Wanamaker, *Thessalonians*, pp. 29-37; Riesner, *Paul's Early Period*, pp. 404-11; and deSilva, '"Worthy of his Kingdom"', pp. 73-77.

19. E.g. Pearson, '1 Thessalonians 2:13-16', pp. 88-90; Boers, 'Form Critical Study', pp. 149-52; and Schmidt, '1 Thess 2:13-16', pp. 275-76.

thanksgiving,[20] of a thought digression[21] or of a historical recollection.[22] How is the presence of 2.13-16 best explained?

Building upon the work of Robert W. Funk,[23] Pearson contends that 2.11-12 flows naturally into the apostolic parousia which commences in 2.17 and that 2.13-16 interrupts the flow of the text. Additionally, Pearson suggests that the appearance of a second thanksgiving in 1 Thessalonians is a Pauline anomaly and that the epistle reads more smoothly once the interpolated material is removed.[24] Hendrikus Boers also claims on structural grounds that 2.13-16 was not a part of the original composition.[25]

Is 2.13-16 best viewed as an epistolary intrusion as Pearson and Boers claim? Their form-critical arguments against the text's authenticity founder principally upon the fact that there is no typical Pauline epistolary pattern.[26] While Paul's letters may have a similar structure, by no means do his occasional letters rigidly follow a fixed literary pattern. The absence of a thanksgiving in Galatians serves as a well-known example. Even though this is an exception when compared with Paul's other extant writings, the exigencies of the communication offer a satisfactory explanation as to why the thanksgiving is excluded. Similarly, it is entirely plausible that Paul's fond memories of his ministry among his Thessalonian converts prompted him to recapitulate his praise to God for their responsiveness to the gospel.[27] Because Paul's

20. E.g. Lyons, *Pauline Autobiography*, p. 203; Hurd, 'Paul ahead of his Time', p. 28; and Riesner, *Paul's Early Period*, pp. 407-408.

21. Wanamaker, *Thessalonians*, pp. 109-10, and Smith, *Comfort One Another*, p. 36.

22. See Marshall, *Thessalonians*, pp. 76-83, and Johanson, *To All the Brethren*, pp. 94-98.

23. Robert W. Funk, 'The Apostolic *Parousia*: Form and Significance', in William R. Farmer, C.F.D. Moule and R. Richard Niebuhr (eds.), *Christian History and Interpretation: Studies Presented to John Knox* (Cambridge: Cambridge University Press, 1967), pp. 249-68.

24. Pearson, '1 Thessalonians 2:13-16', pp. 89-90.

25. Boers, 'Form Critical Study', pp. 151-52.

26. So also Riesner, *Paul's Early Period*, pp. 406-407.

27. Lyons (*Pauline Autobiography*, p. 177) suggests, 'Whereas Paul's dissatisfaction with the Galatians leads him to omit the thanksgiving period entirely...his satisfaction with the Thessalonians is so complete that the first three chapters of the letter assume the form of thanksgiving.'

extant letters are relatively few in number and because each epistle which has been preserved has distinctive features, talk of a normative Pauline epistolary form is misguided.[28] Furthermore, even if one agrees with Pearson that the transition between 2.12 and 2.13 is unnatural,[29] it need not be thought of as illogical.[30] In fact, one may reasonably view 2.13-16 as a vital communicative link between Paul's recollection of his past ministry among his converts in 1.2–2.12 and his description of his continued concern for his converts in 2.17–3.13.[31]

Karl-Gottfried Eckart has also suggested on form-critical grounds that 2.13-16 is a post-Pauline interpolation. He rejects the authenticity of the passage because of its close resemblance to 1.2-10.[32] Despite Eckart's contention, the similarity between 1.2-10 and 2.13-16 does not necessarily render the latter passage inauthentic. Contrariwise, the affinity in contents and structure between the two passages could well suggest the integrity of 2.13-16. John C. Hurd has observed that it is not unusual for Paul to discuss one point (A), digress to another point (B) and return to the first point (A'). Hurd detects the presence of this A B A' pattern in 1 Thess. 1.2–2.16.[33] He suggests that 2.1-12 (= B) is sand-

---

28. Hurd, 'Paul ahead of his Time', p. 28.

29. Contrast Lyons (*Pauline Autobiography*, p. 203) who remarks, 'From Paul's almost doxological reference to God as the one who calls the Thessalonians to his kingdom and glory in 2:12, the transition to a thanksgiving to God for them in v. 13 is not all that abrupt...' Jewett (*Thessalonian Correspondence*, p. 38) suggests that from a rhetorical perspective the transition between 2.12 and 2.13 is 'smooth and logical'.

30. Smith, *Comfort One Another*, p. 36.

31. Wanamaker (*Thessalonians*, p. 32) perceptively observes, 'Without 2:13-16 it would not be at all clear why Paul was so concerned about his converts. Undoubtedly, 2:13-16 does not tell the whole story, but it would most likely have been adequate for the original readers, who had shared in the untimely separation from Paul implied in v. 17'. Additionally, Weatherly ('The Authenticity of 1 Thessalonians 2.13-16', p. 81) notes that the emphatic ἡμεῖς in 2.17 would be superfluous if 2.13-16 were an interpolation.

32. Eckart, 'Der zweite echte Brief', pp. 32-33. See similarly, Pearson, '1 Thessalonians 2:13-16', p. 91.

33. Hurd, 'Paul ahead of his Time', p. 28. Hurd sees the A B A' pattern not only in 1 Thess. 1.2–2.16, but also in 2.17–3.13 (2.17-20 = A; 3.1-8 = B; 3.9-13 = A'). This leads him to suggest that the first three chapters of 1 Thess. forms a double triptych (p. 30). Hurd also finds what he calls 'the sonata form' in 1 Cor. 8–10 (8 = A; 9 = B; 10 = A') and 12–14 (12 = A; 13 = B; 14 = A').

wiched between two thanksgivings (1.2-10 = A; 2.13-16 = A').[34]
Whether or not 1.2-10 and 2.13-16 are sufficiently similar to posit a
chiastic structure,[35] and whether or not one would label 2.13-16 a
'thanksgiving', when the two passages are compared and Paul's tendency to reiterate himself, albeit with variance, is taken into account,
2.13-16 does not appear to be either un-Pauline or out of place. My
contention, then, is that these verses fit sufficiently well in their present
epistolary context.

34. Hurd ('Paul ahead of his Time', p. 29) outlines the structural similarity of
the two thanksgivings as follows:

1 Thess. 1.2-10:	1 Thess. 2.13-16:
A. We *give thanks to God*	A. We also *give thanks to God*
B. always for you all, *constantly*	B. *constantly*
C. knowing…your election	C. that when you received
D. for *our gospel came* to *you*	D. the *word of God* which *you heard from us*
E. *not* only in *word*	E. you accepted it *not* as the *word* of men
F. *but* also in power	F. *but* as what it really is, the word of God,
G. and in the Holy Spirit and with full conviction…	G. which is at work in you believers.
H. And *you became imitators* of us and the Lord.	H. for *you*, brethren, *became imitators* of the churches…
I. for you received the word in much *affliction*	I. for you *suffered*
J. (The success of the missionaries)	J. (The suffering of the missionaries)
K. You turned to God from idols,	K. hindering us from speaking to the Gentiles
L. to serve a living and true God and to wait for his Son…	L. that they may be saved…
M. who delivers us from the *wrath* to come.	M. But God's *wrath* has come upon them at last.

35. Hurd ('Paul ahead of his Time', p. 30) notes that each panel in the triptych
begins with a formal structural signal and closes with an eschatological climax.
Lyons (*Pauline Autobiography*, p. 203) also sees striking similarities between 1.2-
10 and 2.13-16 but does not suggest a chiastic structure.

3. *Grammatical and Syntactical Issues*

Presupposing that Pearson's conclusions about the form and contents of
2.13-16 were correct, Daryl D. Schmidt sought to strengthen Pearson's
hypothesis by arguing against the text's authenticity on linguistic
grounds.[36] Because Jon A. Weatherly has thoroughly, and to my mind
persuasively, countered Schmidt's article,[37] I will not duplicate his
efforts here. Rather, in this section I will summarize Schmidt's arguments and Weatherly's counter-arguments. At those points where I
think that I can strengthen Weatherly's case against Schmidt, I seek to
do so.

Schmidt begins his syntactical study of 2.13-16 by commenting on
καὶ διὰ τοῦτο. He maintains, 'Nowhere else in 1 Thessalonians is καί
used to connect two matrix sentences [i.e. semantically prominent inde-
pendent clauses], and no other undisputed letter of Paul uses the construction καὶ διὰ τοῦτο (though it is imitated in 2 Thess. 2.11).'[38]
Weatherly notes that there is at least one instance, namely 2 Cor. 1.15,
where Paul uses καί to introduce a matrix sentence and that there are
multiple examples in the undisputed letters of Paul where καί 'introduces and joins cola and even fuller compound sentences'.[39] Thus,
Schmidt's observation regarding καί is accurate but limited to 1 Thessalonians, thereby diluting its strength. Concerning καὶ διὰ τοῦτο,
Schmidt is correct in stating that the construction is used in no other
undisputed letter of Paul.[40] However, Weatherly rightly notes that
Schmidt's explanation of καὶ διὰ τοῦτο in 2 Thess. 2.11 as an imitation
of the phrase in 1 Thess. 2.13 substantially weakens his argument. If the
writer of 2 Thessalonians did indeed copy the phrase from 1 Thess. 2.13,
then the so-called interpolated passage would have had to have been
composed and circulated before the writing of the 2 Thessalonians.

---

36. Schmidt, '1 Thess 2:13-16'.
37. Weatherly, 'The Authenticity of 1 Thessalonians 2.13-16', pp. 91-98.
Rightly recognized by Schleuter, *Filling up the Measure*, p. 34.
38. Schmidt, '1 Thess 2:13-16', p. 273.
39. Weatherly, 'The Authenticity of 1 Thessalonians 2.13-16', p. 92. For
examples of καί introducing and joining cola and compound sentences, Weatherly
lists: Rom. 1.28; 2.27; 3.8; 5.16; 9.29; 11.9; 13.11; 15.10, 11, 12; 1 Cor. 5.2; 6.2,
11; 7.17; 12.16, 26, 28, 31; 13.2; 14.32; 2 Cor. 1.7, 15; 2.3, 16; 7.15; 8.10; 11.14;
12.3, 9; Gal. 6.16; Phil. 1.9, 25; 4.7; and 1 Thess. 1.6.
40. Schmidt, '1 Thess 2:13-16', p. 273.

It therefore appears more likely that καὶ διὰ τοῦτο in 1 Thess. 2.13 is part of the original text of the Epistle, and that 2 Thess. 2.11 is either an 'imitation' of this authentic portion (if 2 Thessalonians is pseudepigraphical) or an example of Paul's own use of the phrase (if 2 Thessalonians is authentic).[41]

Schmidt also maintains that 2.14-16a is 'out of harmony with the pattern of the larger section [i.e. 1.2–3.10]'.[42] In particular, he suggests that the multiple levels of embedded sentences (i.e. dependent clauses) and the separation of κύριον and Ἰησοῦν (2.15a) are at odds with 'typical' Pauline syntax.[43] Schmidt is right to observe that 2.14-16a contains more subordinate clauses than the sentences surrounding it.[44] There are, however, other complex sentences both in 1 Thessalonians (see, e.g., 1.4-6 [five embeds]) and in other Pauline letters (e.g. Rom. 4.16-17 [nine embeds]; 15.15-16 [six embeds]; Phil. 1.12-15 [seven embeds]; 1.27-30 [eight embeds]).[45] With regard to the separation of κύριον and Ἰησοῦν by the participle ἀποκτεινάντων, Schmidt correctly notes that the word order is unusual. Nevertheless, there are occasions in Paul's other Epistles where a verb form separates a noun from an attributive adjective (e.g. 1 Cor. 7.7, 12; 10.4; 12.24; 2 Cor. 7.5; Phil. 2.20).[46] Therefore, 'the particular syntactical combination represented by κύριον ἀποκτεινάντων Ἰησοῦν is not distinctively un-Pauline'.[47]

Recognizing that not all interpolation hypotheses include 2.13-14, Schmidt returns to these verses to find additional linguistic evidence to support Pearson's claim that 2.13-14 as well as 2.15-16 is inauthentic. Schmidt sees the hand of a redactor in two places in 2.14. First, he posits that the phrase τῶν ἐκκλησιῶν τοῦ θεοῦ τῶν οὐσῶν ἐν τῇ Ἰουδαίᾳ ἐν Χριστῷ Ἰησοῦ points to an 'overly-Pauline construction'.[48] Although Schmidt is accurate in saying that Paul does not combine these elements elsewhere in his Epistles, his suggestion that an imitator

41. Weatherly, 'The Authenticity of 1 Thessalonians 2.13-16', p. 93.
42. Schmidt, '1 Thess 2:13-16', p. 273.
43. Schmidt, '1 Thess 2:13-16', p. 273.
44. Schmidt ('1 Thess 2:13-16', p. 273) claims that there are seven embeds. Weatherly ('The Authenticity of 1 Thessalonians 2.13-16', p. 93) disputes this, noting six embeds.
45. Weatherly, 'The Authenticity of 1 Thessalonians 2.13-16', p. 94.
46. Weatherly, 'The Authenticity of 1 Thessalonians 2.13-16', p. 95.
47. Weatherly, 'The Authenticity of 1 Thessalonians 2.13-16', p. 95.
48. Schmidt, '1 Thess 2:13-16', p. 274.

was responsible for the construction does not follow.[49] Paul does join together various aspects of this noun phrase elsewhere, as Schmidt himself observes (see, e.g., 1 Cor. 1.2; 2 Cor. 1.1; Gal. 1.22; Phil. 1.1). It stands to reason, therefore, that Paul was perfectly capable of creating such a construction. Such a suggestion gains credence when one considers the particular components of the phrase. A common Pauline designation for Christian churches (τῶν ἐκκλησιῶν τοῦ θεοῦ) begins the phrase. Then τῶν οὐσῶν ἐν τῇ Ἰουδαίᾳ follows, forming the comparison between Thessalonian and Judean Christians. Finally, ἐν Χριστῷ Ἰησοῦ, which may be taken with τῶν ἐκκλησιῶν τοῦ θεοῦ, identifies the Judean assemblies as distinctly Christian[50] and denotes that it is Christ Jesus who binds the believers together.[51] Because Paul's style is so variable and tends toward verbosity, Schmidt's contention that this construction is overly Pauline carries little weight.

Schmidt also suggests that the separation of τῶν ἐκκλησιῶν from its head noun μιμηταί by the vocative ἀδελφοί in 2.14 is uncharacteristic for Paul.[52] It is true that Paul usually places the vocative ἀδελφοί in front of the head noun which is followed in turn by the genitive. But in light of the syntactical limitations brought on by the multiple modifiers of τῶν ἐκκλησιῶν (cf. Gal. 2.20; 4.28; Phil. 3.17), one may reasonably conclude that the construction is Paul's own.[53]

Lastly, Schmidt suggests that the participial phrase in 2.13 (παραλαβόντες λόγον ἀκοῆς παρ᾽ ἡμῶν τοῦ θεοῦ) 'is an amalgamation of several different Pauline constructions, each one found somewhere in the Pauline corpus, but the final combination itself is not typical of Pauline syntax'.[54] The simple suggestion that τοῦ θεοῦ was a Pauline afterthought added to clarify the origin of the λόγον seems to be as acceptable a solution as positing the presence of an clever redactor.[55] Sometimes Ockham's razor is sufficiently sharp!

---

49. Because Schmidt argues that some parts of 2.13-16 are non-Pauline and other parts are overly Pauline, his hypothesis cannot be disproved. On the weaknesses inherent in this methodological approach, see Hurd, 'Paul ahead of his Time', p. 26.

50. Wanamaker, *Thessalonians*, p. 112.

51. Bruce, *Thessalonians*, p. 45.

52. Schmidt, '1 Thess 2:13-16', pp. 274-75.

53. Weatherly, 'The Authenticity of 1 Thessalonians 2.13-16', p. 98.

54. Schmidt, '1 Thess 2:13-16', p. 276.

55. So also Wanamaker, *Thessalonians*, p. 111.

What then are we to make of Schmidt's linguistic study of 2.13-16? In brief, Schmidt has stacked the investigative cards in his favor to ensure that his conclusions will correlate with his presupposition that the passage is an interpolation. To be sure, Schmidt has made some astute syntactical observations of the passage. However, he 'neglects relevant data from other undisputed Pauline Epistles which suggest that the linguistic phenomena of 1 Thess. 2.13-16 are consistent with Paul's style'.[56] While Schmidt's linguistic arguments against the text's authenticity are weightier than the structural reasons considered above, in the end they do not undercut the integrity of the text. 'Hence Schmidt's arguments are compelling only for someone who has already accepted Pearson's viewpoint.'[57] We may now turn to consider Pearson's historical reconstruction of 2.13-16.

4. *Historical Matters*

Historically speaking, Pearson thinks that 2.13-16 must have been written after 70 CE for two primary reasons. First, he maintains that the aorist verb ἔφθασεν in 2.16c refers to an event in the past, namely the destruction of Jerusalem in 70 CE.[58] Secondly, Pearson asserts that 'there was no significant persecution of Christians in Judaea before the war [i.e. the Roman-Judean War which commenced in 66 CE]'.[59] Under this heading, I will seek to demonstrate that these two contentions are dubious.

a. *The Historical Context of 1 Thessalonians 2.16c*
Although Pearson is correct to translate ἔφθασεν as 'has come',[60] one need not follow his suggestion that 2.16c refers to the sacking of the holy city. Robert Jewett perceptively notes,

> That Christian writers interpreted the destruction [of Jerusalem] as a sign of divine wrath is clear, but there is an unmistakable quality of retrospection in Pearson's argument. From the perspective of those who know

56. Weatherly, 'The Authenticity of 1 Thessalonians 2.13-16', p. 91.
57. Jewett, *Thessalonian Correspondence*, p. 41.
58. Pearson, '1 Thessalonians 2:13-16', pp. 82-83.
59. Pearson, '1 Thessalonians 2:13-16', p. 87.
60. Pearson, '1 Thessalonians 2:13-16', p. 82. So also, e.g., Donfried, 'Paul and Judaism', p. 252, and Hurd, 'Paul ahead of his Time', p. 35. Cf., among others, Weatherly ('The Authenticity of 1 Thessalonians 2.13-16', p. 90) who understands ἔφθασεν to be a prophetic aorist (= 'has drawn near'; 'is coming').

about the Jewish-Roman War, it is surely the most appropriate choice. But to someone who lived before that catastrophe...other events could easily have appeared to be a final form of divine wrath.[61]

Commentators have suggested that Paul could have had in mind, among other things, the expulsion of Jews from Rome in 49 CE (Acts 18.1; Suetonius, *Claud.* 25.4)[62] or the massacre of some twenty to thirty thousand Jews in Jerusalem the same year (Josephus, *Ant.* 20.112; *War* 2.227).[63] While virtually any large-scale catastrophe which befell the Jewish people would suffice, it may be that Paul did not have any major disaster in view when declaring that God's wrath had come upon them.[64] Apocalyptically minded people can detect God's wrath in seemingly insignificant events and are convinced that the final consummation of history is ever close at hand.[65] But even if 2.16c does refer to a specific historical occurrence, it need not be dated 70 CE.

b. *The 'Persecution' of Judean Christians*
'With reference to the alleged persecutions in Judaea', Pearson writes, '1 Thessalonians 2:14 would be the only New Testament text—were it

61. Jewett, *Thessalonian Correspondence*, p. 37. So similarly, Hurd, 'Paul ahead of his Time', p. 35; and Setzer, *Jewish Responses*, p. 18.

62. E.g. Ernst Bammel, 'Judenverfolgung und Naherwartung: Zur Eschatologie des ersten Thessalonicherbriefs', *ZTK* 56 (1959), pp. 294-315 (300).

63. Jewett (*Thessalonian Correspondence*, pp. 37-38) following Sherman E. Johnson ('Notes and Comments [I Thess 2:16]', *ATR* 23 [1941], pp. 173-76) is inclined to this option. For a fuller discussion of potential miseries to which Paul may have been alluding in 2.16c (e.g. the insurrection of Theudas against Rome in 44–46 CE and the famine in Judea in 46–47 CE), see both Jewett and Johnson at the places cited above. See also B.W. Bacon, 'Wrath "unto the Uttermost"', *The Expositor*, Eighth Series 22 (1922), pp. 356-76.

64. Davies ('Paul and the People of Israel', p. 7) suggests that 'it is not necessary to explain the notion that "the wrath has fallen upon the Jews finally and fully" in terms of any extraordinary contemporary event'. So also Best, *Thessalonians*, p. 120, and Hurd, 'Paul ahead of his Time', p. 35. In an effort to explain 2.16c, some scholars have appealed to linguistic similarities in the pre-Synoptic tradition (e.g. R. Schippers, 'The Pre-Synoptic Tradition in 1 Thessalonians II 13-16', *NovT* 8 [1966], pp. 223-34) and in the Matthean eschatological discourse (e.g. J. Bernard Orchard, 'Thessalonians and the Synoptic Gospels', *Bib* 19 [1938], pp. 19-42).

65. For a useful discussion on the apocalyptic worldview and on millenarian groups, see Stephen J. Cook, *Prophecy and Apocalypticism: The Postexilic Social Setting* (Minneapolis: Fortress Press, 1995), pp. 19-84. Cf. Jewett, *Thessalonian Correspondence*, pp. 161-78.

a genuine expression of Paul—to indicate that the churches in Judaea suffered persecution at the hands of the Jews between AD 44 and the outbreak of the war against Rome.'[66] While this statement as it stands is seemingly accurate, the way Pearson frames the issue of the Judean Christians' suffering is misleading. Unlike Pearson, 2.14 does not specify when the Judean churches experienced Jewish opposition.

With the majority of scholars, I think that Paul wrote 1 Thessalonians c. 50 CE[67] and that 2.13-16 is authentic. There is no reason, therefore, for me to consider possibilities for the 'persecution' of Judean congregations post-50 CE. Furthermore, Pearson's claim that Judean Christians were not targets of Jewish opposition from 44 (following the execution of James by Herod Agrippa I [Acts 12.2]) to 50 CE amounts to an *argumentum e silentio*.[68] But what about the conflict between

66. Pearson, '1 Thessalonians 2:13-16', p. 86.

67. For a date of c. 50 CE for the writing of 1 Thess., see, e.g., Best, *Thessalonians*, p. 11; Bruce, *Thessalonians*, p. xxxv; Morris, *Thessalonians*, pp. 13-14; Gaventa, *Thessalonians*, p. 1; and Raymond E. Brown, *An Introduction to the New Testament* (ABRL; New York: Doubleday, 1997), p. 433.

Dating Paul's life and letters is, of course, a notoriously difficult task. I need not enter into the fray of this discussion here. In addition to the standard studies on Pauline chronology by John Knox, *Chapters in a Life of Paul* (ed. Douglas R.A. Hare; London: SCM Press, rev. edn, 1989), Robert Jewett, *Dating Paul's Life* (London: SCM Press, 1979) and Gerd Lüdemann, *Paul, Apostle to the Gentiles: Studies in Chronology* (trans. F. Stanley Jones; London: SCM Press, 1984), see now Riesner, *Paul's Early Period*. For a dialogue between Knox, Jewett, Lüdemann and other New Testament interpreters on Pauline chronology, see Bruce Corley (ed.), *Colloquy on New Testament Studies: A Time for Reappraisal and Fresh Approaches* (Macon, GA: Mercer University Press, 1983), pp. 265-364.

Even if such scholars as Knox (*Chapters in a Life of Paul*, p. 71), Lüdemann (*Paul*, p. 262), Donfried ('The Theology of 1 and 2 Thessalonians', p. 12), Richard (*Thessalonians*, p. 8) and Horrell (*Social Ethos of the Corinthian Correspondence*, pp. 73-74, 77) are correct in dating 1 Thess. to the early to mid 40s CE, my subsequent points stand. Because I think that Paul traveled from Thessalonica to Corinth with rather short intervening stops in Berea and Athens (Acts 17.10, 15; 18.1; cf. 1 Thess. 3.1-6) and because I date Claudius's edict referred to in Acts 18.1 to 49 CE and Gallio's proconsulship spoken of in Acts 18.12 to 50–51 CE, I am inclined to a date of c. 50 CE for 1 Thess. So also, e.g., Riesner, *Paul's Early Period*, p. 322, and Martin Hengel and Anna Maria Schwemer, *Paul between Damascus and Antioch: The Unknown Years* (trans. John Bowden; Louisville, KY: Westminster/John Knox Press, 1997), p. 301.

68. Although explicit New Testament evidence is lacking for conflict between Jews and Christian Jews in Judea between 44–50 CE, based upon Paul's opposition

Jews and Christian Jews in Judea that occurred in the early thirties CE which Pearson cursorily dismisses?[69]

Both Paul and Acts attest that Judean Christians suffered at the hands of their fellow Jews during this period. Despite arguments to the contrary,[70] it is likely that Paul carried out his persecutory activity in Jerusalem and the surrounding vicinity (Gal. 1.13, 22-23; 1 Cor. 15.9; Phil. 3.6; cf. Acts 8.3; 9.21).[71] Additionally, Acts reports that the apostles

to Judean Christians prior to his conversion and his conflict with Jews in Jerusalem thereafter (see, e.g., Acts 9.29-30; 21.15-36; 23.12-15; cf. Rom. 15.31), it seems reasonable to think that things were not as harmonious during these years as Pearson imagines. (On the texts in Acts, see further Torrey Seland, *Establishment Violence in Philo and Luke: A Study of Non-Conformity to the Torah and Jewish Vigilante Reactions* [BIS, 15; Leiden: E.J. Brill, 1995], pp. 256-98.) Okeke ('I Thessalonians 2.13-16', p. 129) suggests, 'Paul's persecution of the Church prior to his conversion is not an isolated case of an eccentric Jew who oppressed the Church while the rest of the Jews welcomed Christianity as a popular sect within Judaism. It seems less probable that the Diaspora Jews had more zeal and persecuted Christians to more or less a degree as Paul personally encountered as a Christian, while the churches of Christ in Judea (in the very heart of Judaism) enjoyed a comfortable and peaceful co-existence with other sects within Judaism.'

See also Robert Jewett ('The Agitators and the Galatian Congregation' *NTS* 17 [1970–71], pp. 198-212 [205-207] and Bo Reicke ('Judaeo-Christianity and the Jewish Establishment, A.D. 33–66', in Ernst Bammel and C.F.D. Moule [eds.], *Jesus and the Politics of his Day* [Cambridge: Cambridge University Press, 1984], pp. 145-52 [148]), who argue that Judean Christians were victims of Jewish zealotism from c. 33 to 54 CE.

69. Pearson ('1 Thessalonians 2:13-16', p. 86 n. 45) notes the 'persecution' of the 'Hellenists' (Acts 8.1) but does not regard this event as relevant since it 'had occurred almost 20 years prior to the writing of 1 Thess'.

70. See, e.g., Knox, *Chapters in a Life of Paul*, p. 22; Schleuter, *Filling up the Measure*, p. 45; E.P. Sanders, *Paul* (ed. Keith Thomas; Past Masters; Oxford: Oxford University Press, 1991), p. 9; Victor P. Furnish, *Jesus According to Paul* (UJTS; Cambridge: Cambridge University Press, 1993), p. 7; and Jürgen Becker, *Paul: Apostle to the Gentiles* (trans. O.C. Dean, Jr; Louisville, KY: Westminster/John Knox Press, 1993), pp. 66-69.

71. So rightly, e.g., Riesner, *Paul's Early Period*, pp. 72-73; Brown, *Introduction to the New Testament*, p. 426; Arland J. Hultgren, 'Paul's Pre-Christian Persecutions of the Church: Their Purpose, Locale, and Nature', *JBL* 95 (1976), pp. 97-111 (105-107); and Martin Hengel, *The Pre-Christian Paul* (trans. John Bowden; London: SCM Press; Philadelphia: Trinity Press International, 1991), pp. 72-79. See further p. 166 nn. 35-36 below.

objects of Jewish persecution and that Stephen (7.58) was martyred in the early thirties CE. Even if Acts exaggerates the severity of the Jewish persecution of Jerusalem Christians, this does not negate the basic fact that not long after 30 CE some Jerusalem believers were opposed by some non-Christian Jews.

Pearson contends that Judean Christians did not encounter 'significant persecution' before the War.[72] If by 'significant persecution' he means some type of pogrom,[73] I would concur. But 1 Thess. 2.14 does not speak of widespread persecution. The verse states that Judean Christians experienced suffering at the hands of their fellow Jews. As demonstrated above, there is sufficient evidence in Paul's Epistles and in Acts to corroborate this claim. Therefore, the need to posit the presence of an interpolator disappears. Paul's first-hand knowledge of the non-Christian opposition that both the Judean and Thessalonian believers encountered enabled him to draw a comparison: the churches in Judea and the church in Thessalonica were opposed in similar ways by their respective compatriots.[74] Pearson's contention notwithstanding, then, 2.14 makes good historical sense coming from Paul.[75]

72. Pearson, '1 Thessalonians 2:13-16', p. 87.

73. This is the clear implication. See Pearson, '1 Thessalonians 2:13-16', p. 87.

74. Convinced that Paul would not have held up Judean Christians as an example for the Thessalonians, Pearson also suggests that the *mimesis* terminology in 2.14 'does not cohere with Paul's usage elsewhere' ('1 Thessalonians 2:13-16', pp. 87-88). While it is true that Paul typically admonishes his churches to imitate himself (see, e.g., 1 Thess. 1.6; 1 Cor. 4.16; 11.1; Phil. 3.17; cf. 2 Thess. 3.9), he does hold up churches as models elsewhere in his Epistles (1 Thess. 1.7; 2 Cor. 8.1– 9.4). Furthermore, as Wanamaker (*Thessalonians*, p. 32) notes, Paul does not exhort the Thessalonians to be imitators of the Judeans; he states that they had already become imitators of them. Despite Pearson's belief that Paul would surely not have praised the Judean churches (one detects the influence of F.C. Baur here), Paul had both freedom and reason to cite the Judean churches as a pattern for the Thessalonian assembly. Jewett (*Thessalonian Correspondence*, p. 39) observes, 'Since a major issue in the congregation was the relation between persecution and faith, it is understandable that Paul should have selected the earliest Christian communities as having experienced the same thing [i.e. suffering] as the Thessalonians.' On *imitatio* terminology in Paul's Epistles in general and 1 and 2 Thess. in particular, see, e.g., Mary Ann Getty, 'The Imitation of Paul in the Letters to the Thessalonians', in Collins (ed.), *The Thessalonian Correspondence*, pp. 277-83; Willis Peter de Boer, *The Imitation of Paul: An Exegetical Study* (Kampen: Kok, 1962); and Jo-Ann A. Brant, 'The Place of *mimesis* in Paul's Thought', *SR* 22 (1993), pp. 285-300.

75. Although Schleuter believes that 2.14 is authentic, she thinks that Paul

5. *Theological Considerations*

The harsh rhetoric directed towards 'the Jews' in 2.15-16 appears to be the primary reason that Pearson and other interpreters consider (a portion of) 2.13-16 to be a deutero-Pauline interpolation.[76] Seemingly embarrassed by this blight on Paul's theology,[77] interpolation advocates seek to explain (away) these vitriolic remarks as incompatible with 'Paul's thought as elsewhere expressed in his epistles', particularly Romans 9–11.[78] While the vituperation of 2.15-16 may well offend modern sensibilities and may appear to be un-Pauline, there are compelling reasons for concluding that these are Paul's words.

To begin, one should note that Pearson and most other scholars who judge 2.13-16 as inauthentic do so based upon Paul's other Epistles. To say that Paul could not have said something in one place because he did

---

exaggerates the Judeans' and Thessalonians' suffering (*Filling up the Measure*, pp. 51-53). This conclusion is based on her (and Pearson's) misconception that severe suffering is to be equated with organized opposition involving martyrdom. 'Persecution' need not be systematic nor physical to be serious. On the nature of the Thessalonians' affliction, see further pp. 208-18 below.

76. Pearson ('1 Thessalonians 2:13-16', p. 85) writes, 'I find it virtually impossible to ascribe to Paul the *ad hominem* fragment of Gentile anti-Judaism in v. 15.' He also remarks that 'the thought that God's wrath has come upon the Jewish people with utter finality (v. 16) is manifestly foreign to Paul's theology...' (pp. 85-86). Cf. Bruce (*Thessalonians*, p. 47): 'Such sentiments are incongruous on the lips of Paul (whose attitude to his fellow-Jews finds clear expression in Rom 9:1-5; 10:1-4; 11:25-32), nor can he be readily envisaged as subscribing to them if they were expressed in this form by someone else.'

77. Steve Mason ('Paul, Classical Anti-Jewish Polemic, and the Letter to the Romans', in David J. Hawkin and Tom Robinson [eds.], *Self-Definition and Self-Discovery in Early Christianity: A Study in Changing Horizons* [SBEC, 26; Lewiston, NY: Edwin Mellen Press, 1990], pp. 181-223 [p. 197 n. 74]) maintains that 'the crucial argument for interpolation is embarrassment...' So, similarly, Jewett, *Thessalonian Correspondence*, pp. 40-41.

78. Pearson, '1 Thessalonians 2:13-16', p. 85. Scholars who affirm the authenticity of 2.13-16 have also compared Paul's statements about 'the Jews' in 2.15-16 with Rom. 9–11 and have concluded that they are more (see, e.g., Donfried, 'Paul and Judaism') and less (e.g. Okeke, 'I Thessalonians 2.13-16') compatible. For a full-length study on the relationship between 1 Thess. 2.15-16 and Rom. 9–11, see J.W. Simpson, Jr, 'The Future of Non-Christian Jews: 1 Thessalonians 2:15-16 and Romans 9–11' (PhD dissertation, Fuller Theological Seminary, 1988).

not say the same thing in another is tenuous. Although there is a basic coherency in Pauline thought, one does not find in his occasional correspondence a static consistency.[79] Therefore, an attempt to harmonize fully Paul's statements about Jewish people in 2.15-16 with remarks he makes about his compatriots in Romans 9–11 may be misguided.[80] That there are tensions in Paul's thinking has become more or less an axiom in Pauline studies. For example, scholars often point out that Paul's instruction on the law is, to say the least, not easily reconciled.[81] It makes good sense, therefore, to allow for some variation in Paul's theologizing about his fellow Jews.

Having said that, it is vital to recognize that the polemic in 2.15-16 is not directed at all Jews. Indeed, scholars have suggested that the word Ἰουδαῖοι, which appears in 2.14 and serves as the antecedent to the participial phrases in 2.15-16, should be translated 'Judeans'.[82] Although one may render the term thus,[83] it appears that the locale of those Jewish people specified in 2.15-16 (namely those Jews who killed the Lord Jesus[84] and the prophets,[85] who drove out Paul and his co-worker[s] and

79. See J. Christiaan Beker's coherence-contingency interpretive scheme in *Paul the Apostle: The Triumph of God in Life and Thought* (Philadelphia: Fortress Press, 1980), pp. 23-36.

80. So Schleuter, *Filling up the Measure*, p. 62.

81. See, e.g., E.P. Sanders, 'Paul', in John Barclay and John Sweet (eds.), *Early Christian Thought in its Jewish Context* (Festschrift Morna D. Hooker; Cambridge: Cambridge University Press, 1996), pp. 112-29 (117, 124).

82. See, e.g., Weatherly, 'The Authenticity of 1 Thessalonians 2.13-16', pp. 86-87, and Hill, *Establishing the Church in Thessalonica*, p. 11.

83. See further M. Lowe, 'Who Were the ΙΟΥΔΑΙΟΙ?', *NovT* 18 (1976), pp. 101-30. On Paul's use of Ἰουδαῖοι elsewhere, see Traugott Holtz, 'The Judgment on the Jews and the Salvation of All Israel: 1 Thes 2,15-16 and Rom 11,25-26', in Collins (ed.), *The Thessalonian Correspondence*, pp. 284-94 (287).

84. Pearson ('1 Thessalonians 2:13-16', p. 85), noting 1 Cor. 2.8, states that Paul 'never attributes the death of Jesus to the Jews'. While the charge of 2.15a is unique in Paul, it should be noted that: (1) Paul does not specify in 1 Cor. 2.8 who 'the rulers of this age' who crucified the Lord actually were. So rightly Furnish, *Jesus According to Paul*, p. 70. *Pace* Pearson (p. 85) who equates the rulers with 'Roman imperial authorities'. (2) At least some early believers were convinced that some Jewish leaders and people were culpable for the death of Jesus (Martin, *Thessalonians*, p. 91). (3) Historically, it is quite probable 'that the Jerusalem ruling elite were guilty of complicity in Jesus' death' (Wanamaker, *Thessalonians*, p. 31).

85. Frank D. Gilliard ('Paul and the Killing of the Prophets in 1 Thess. 2:15', *NovT* 36 [1994], pp. 259-70) argues that the prophets mentioned in 2.15 are

who displease God and oppose all people by hindering Paul and his helper[s] from sharing the gospel with the Gentiles) extends beyond Judea,[86] even if one construes Judea in the broadest way possible so as to include Samaria and Galilee.[87] Nonetheless, the invective in 2.15-16 is best viewed as a polemic directed against particular Jews for opposing those whom Paul believed to be God's messengers (i.e. Jesus, the prophets, himself and his co-worker[s]) and for hindering that which he believed to be God's message (i.e. the gospel).[88] That Paul was not referring in 2.15-16 to Jews in general is supported by the fact the churches in Judea which he praises in 2.14 were comprised primarily, if not exclusively, of Jews. Additionally, Jesus, the prophets and Paul were Jewish! Although it is commonplace for commentators to depict this passage as anti-Jewish,[89] such a description is an anachronism largely prompted, I suspect, by a scholarly sensitivity to the hideous horrors of the Holocaust.[90] Since the sharp attack against 'the Jews' in 2.15-16 arises from an attempt of some (Thessalonian) Jews to hinder Paul from preaching the gospel to the Gentiles,[91] the sardonic statements are better labeled 'anti-oppressor'.[92]

prophets of Jesus, not prophets of the Jews. Note, however, Rom. 11.3.

86. So rightly, Bruce, *Thessalonians*, p. 46.

87. Wanamaker, *Thessalonians*, p. 112.

88. Contra Wayne A. Meeks ('Breaking Away: Three New Testament Pictures of Christianity's Separation from the Jewish Communities', in J. Neusner and E.S. Frerichs [eds.], *'To See Ourselves as Others See Us'*, pp. 93-115 [105 n. 14]); Eduard Verhoef ('Die Bedeutung des Artikels τῶν in 1 Thess 2,15', *BN* 80 [1995], pp. 41-46) and Richard (*Thessalonians*, p. 126) who take 2.15-16 to be a global condemnation of Israel. So rightly Frank D. Gilliard, 'The Problem of the Anti-semitic Comma between 1 Thessalonians 2.14 and 15', *NTS* 36 (1989), pp. 481-502 (498); Davies, 'Paul and the People of Israel', p. 8; and Holtz, 'Judgment on the Jews', p. 285.

89. In addition to those who deny the authenticity of the text on such grounds, see the following interpreters who affirm the integrity of 2.13-16: Best, *Thessalonians*, p. 122; Wanamaker, *Thessalonians*, pp. 48-49; Hurd, 'Paul ahead of his Time', p. 36; Jewett, *Thessalonian Correspondence*, pp. 40-41.

90. Glenn S. Holland (' "Anti-Judaism" in Paul: The Case of Romans', *Proceedings* 10 [1990], pp. 190-203 [191]) issues a needed reminder: 'Paul is not a contemporary Christian addressing contemporary Judaism. He is not speaking of a faith with a history of oppression manifested in ghettos, pogroms, and the Holocaust.'

91. See further pp. 136-37 below.

92. Daniel Patte (*Paul's Faith and the Power of the Gospel: A Structural Intro-*

Pauline polemic is present not only in 1 Thessalonians but also in other letters of Paul.[93] Paul frequently set aside rhetorical courtesies when speaking to his primarily Gentile converts about his Jewish Christian opponents. For example, in Gal. 5.12 he wishes that those who are unsettling the Galatians by preaching circumcision would emasculate themselves! In 2 Corinthians he refers to his rivals as 'false apostles', 'deceitful workmen' and even 'servants of Satan' (11.13-15). And in Phil. 3.2 he tags his Jewish detractors 'dogs', 'evil-workers' and 'mutilators of the flesh'.

Although Paul reserves his harshest words for his Jewish Christian competitors,[94] he also makes caustic remarks about non-Christian Jews in places other than 1 Thess. 2.15-16.[95] For instance, in Romans 9–11, the chapters to which scholars usually appeal when discussing Paul's normative attitude toward the Jewish people, Paul suggests that his unbelieving compatriots are under a curse (9.3) and implies that they are 'vessels of wrath made for destruction' (9.23). In 11.3 Paul recites Elijah's indictment against Israel that 'they killed the prophets' (1 Kgs 19.4; cf. 1 Thess. 2.15a). He also refers to those Jews who do not (yet) believe in Jesus as 'broken off branches' (11.20), 'enemies of God' (11.28) and 'disobedient' (11.31). While it is true that Paul declares that 'all Israel will be saved' (11.26a), to read this statement in its larger epistolary context makes it clear that Paul believes that salvation for Jew and Gentile alike comes through Jesus Christ (9.6-33; 10.3-13; 11.1b-16).[96] Paul, then, is capable of saying unflattering things about

---

duction to the Pauline Letters [Philadelphia: Fortress Press, 1983], pp. 126-27), followed by Lyons (*Pauline Autobiography*, p. 205), followed by Hill (*Establishing the Church in Thessalonica*, p. 13), uses the label 'anti-persecutor'. By inference Paul's polemic in 2.15-16 is also directed toward those Gentiles who oppose his Thessalonian converts. So rightly Wanamaker, *Thessalonians*, p. 114; Schleuter, *Filling up the Measure*, p. 124; and Smith, *Comfort One Another*, p. 36.

93. In addition to 1 Thess. 2.15-16, see the typical Jewish polemic Paul employs against Gentiles in 1 Thess. 1.9 and 4.5. Cf. 1 Cor. 5.1; Rom. 1.18-32; Phil. 2.15.

94. Schleuter, *Filling up the Measure*, pp. 124-95.

95. See further Mason, 'Paul, Classical Anti-Jewish Polemic, and the Letter to the Romans', pp. 192-223.

96. So rightly Mason, 'Paul, Classical Anti-Judaism, and the Letter to the Romans', p. 221; Holtz, 'The Judgment on the Jews', p. 288; and E.P. Sanders, *Paul, the Law, and the Jewish People* (Minneapolis: Fortress Press, 1983), p. 183.

both Christian and non-Christian Jews. Admittedly, 2.15-16 is an especially harsh denunciation of particular groups of Jews; however, such
polemic is not as foreign to Paul as Pearson and others have imagined.[97]

6. *Conclusion*

I have argued in this chapter that there are no pressing form-critical,
syntactical, historical or theological reasons to regard either all or part
of 2.13-16 as a post-Pauline interpolation. Although one cannot 'prove'
the integrity of the text, I have demonstrated above that there are no
compelling arguments against the passage's authenticity. I have also
shown that there is much in the pericope that is plausible in and compatible with a Pauline context.

It may be that 2.15-16 has fostered anti-Jewish attitudes among some
of its readers. And it is indeed deplorable to think that this text has been
illegitimately used to harm Jewish people. However, if my line of interpretation is correct, then it is inappropriate to read 2.15-16 as a piece of
anti-Jewish propaganda. Even though Paul was convinced that those
Jews who refused to accept the gospel and opposed his efforts to share
his message with the Gentiles were subject to God's wrath, he does not
categorically condemn the Jewish people here or elsewhere. One might
think or wish to think that Paul's soteriology is errant, but to accuse him
of anti-Judaism for defending what he believed to be the crux of Israel's
hope seems unfair.[98]

Even if one is embarrassed or offended by 2.15-16, attempts to dismiss the text on such grounds amount to censorship.[99] In short, 'Unless

Pace Krister Stendahl, *Paul among the Jews and Gentiles and Other Essays* (Philadelphia: Fortress Press, 1976), p. 81.

97. Donald A. Hagner ('Paul's Quarrel with Judaism', in C.A. Evans and D.A.
Hagner [eds.], *Anti-Semitism and Early Christianity: Issues of Polemic and Faith*
(Minneapolis: Fortress Press, 1993), pp. 128-50 [131]) remarks: 'it is not at all
historically improbable that Paul could have written this blistering passage.'

98. Holland ('"Anti-Judaism" in Paul', p. 200) notes that Paul's prophetic
proclamations to 'the Jews' were not intended to be 'anti-Jewish' nor can they be
properly read as such. Furthermore, Holland states that Paul may not be rightly
blamed for Christian anti-Judaism 'as if there had been no such thing [as anti-
Judaism] in the Greco-Roman world before Paul, or as if bigotry really needs a
scriptural warrant'.

99. Luke Timothy Johnson, 'The New Testament's Anti-Jewish Slander and
Coventions of Ancient Polemic', *JBL* 108 (1989), pp. 419-41 (421 n. 4). deSilva

and until further [internal and/or external] evidence is forthcoming in support of the interpolation hypothesis, it should be assumed that 2.13-16 formed part of the original text of the letter.'[100] Throughout this study, then, I will draw upon this passage in an effort to comprehend better the contours of the conflict of Paul and the Thessalonians Christians with outsiders.

('"Worthy of his Kingdom"', p. 75) remarks, 'Excising this passage from the letter is not the only way to express our contemporary commitment to respectful dialogue and cooperation rather than vituperation in our relationships with Jews.'

100. Wanamaker, *Thessalonians*, p. 33. Cf. Davies ('Paul and the People of Israel', p. 7) who thinks that 'it is more justifiable to regard it [i.e. 2.13-16] as Pauline than otherwise'.

Chapter 2

IS 2 THESSALONIANS AUTHENTICALLY PAULINE?*

1. *Introduction*

Contemporary scholars studying Pauline Christianity in Thessalonica confront the conundrum of where to place 2 Thessalonians in the discussion. Michael D. Goulder summarizes this scholarly quandary well when he writes, 'We cannot assume it [i.e. 2 Thess.] to be Pauline, since so many scholars dispute that; but we cannot assume it to be irrelevant, when so many of the major commentators have thought Paul to be its author.'[1] To be sure, a few contemporary interpreters have simply

---

* I read an earlier version of this chapter to the Pauline Christianity Group of the Southwest Commission of Religious Studies in Dallas, TX, in March 1997. The presentation and the ensuing conversation helped me in honing this chapter.

1. 'Silas in Thessalonica', *JSNT* 48 (1992), pp. 87-106 (96). Goulder notes (p. 96 n. 1) the following commentators who consider 2 Thess. to be inauthentic: the large majority of scholars (some 90%) contributing to Collins (ed.), *The Thessalonian Correspondence*; Trilling, *Der zweite Brief an die Thessalonicher*; Willi Marxsen, *Der zweite Thessalonicherbrief* (ZB, 11.2; Zürich: Theologischer Verlag, 1982); and Franz Laub, *Erster und zweiter Thessalonicherbrief* (Würzburg: Echter Verlag, 2nd edn, 1988). One could add, among others, Richard, *Thessalonians*; Gaventa, *Thessalonians*; Raymond F. Collins, *Letters that Paul Did not Write* (GNS, 28; Wilmington, DE: Michael Glazier, 1988); Maarten J.J. Menken, *2 Thessalonians* (NTR; London: Routledge, 1994); and Bonnie Thurston, *Reading Colossians, Ephesians, and 2 Thessalonians: A Literary and Theological Commentary* (New York: Crossroad, 1995) to this abbreviated list. Goulder also indicates that until 1980 'almost all commentators held to Pauline authenticity' (p. 96 n. 2). He mentions by name Dobschütz, *Thessalonicherbriefe*; Dibelius, *Thessalonicher*; Rigaux, *Thessaloniciens*; Best, *Thessalonians*; Marshall, *Thessalonians*; and Jewett, *Thessalonian Correspondence*. In this group one could place, among others, Wanamaker, *Thessalonians*; Martin, *Thessalonians*; Morris, *Thessalonians*; David J. Williams, *1 and 2 Thessalonians* (NIBC, 12; Peabody, MA: Hendrickson, 1992); Jon A. Weatherly, *1 & 2 Thessalonians* (CPNIVC; Joplin, MO: College Press, 1996);

assumed the epistle's authenticity[2] or pseudonymity[3] in their work. Goulder correctly maintains, however, that to dismiss prematurely either side of the authorship argument is presumptuous.[4] A more prudent path is to take into account what other New Testament scholars have said about the epistle's genuineness and then in conversation with them to state one's own view. In this chapter, I will follow such a course. To begin, I will note the four factors which lead the majority of contemporary Pauline scholars to judge 2 Thessalonians as inauthentic.[5] Next, I will evaluate these particular arguments raised against the authenticity of the epistle. I will then assess various audience hypotheses for the letter before setting forth what I consider to be the most satisfactory *Sitz im Leben* for 2 Thessalonians. By way of conclusion, I will indicate how I will employ this disputed epistle in this study.

2. *Arguments against Authenticity*

Proponents of the pseudonymity of 2 Thessalonians have marshaled various arguments to support their position. I will not rehearse all of them here.[6] For the purpose of this project, it will suffice to introduce

and Michael W. Holmes, *1 & 2 Thessalonians* (NIVAC; Grand Rapids: Zondervan, 1998).

2. E.g. Bruce W. Winter, '"If a Man Does not Wish to Work...": A Cultural and Historical Setting for 2 Thessalonians 3:6-16', *TynBul* 40 (1989), pp. 303-15.

3. E.g. J. Christiaan Beker, *Heirs of Paul: Paul's Legacy in the New Testament and in the Church Today* (Edinburgh: T. & T. Clark, 1992).

4. So similarly Glenn S. Holland, '"A Letter Supposedly from Us": A Contribution to the Discussion about the Authorship of 2 Thessalonians', in Collins (ed.), *The Thessalonian Correspondence*, pp. 394-402 (395).

5. Marshall (*Thessalonians*, p. 29) observes that since 1970 'the tide of critical opinion has shifted decisively in favour of inauthenticity...'

6. For a fuller discussion and defense of the pseudonymity of 2 Thess. see, e.g., Trilling, *Untersuchungen zum zweiten Thessalonicherbrief*; Holland, *The Tradition that You Received from Us*; Hughes, *Early Christian Rhetoric and 2 Thessalonians*; Collins, *Letters that Paul Did not Write*, pp. 209-45; Menken, *2 Thessalonians*, pp. 27-43; Richard, *Thessalonians*, pp. 19-29; William Wrede, *Die Echtheit des zweiten Thessalonicherbriefs untersucht* (TU, 24.2; Leipzig: J.C. Henrichs, 1903); and John A. Bailey, 'Who Wrote II Thessalonians', *NTS* 25 (1978–79), pp. 131-45. On arguments against the authenticity of the epistle, see also the following commentators who affirm Pauline authorship: Marshall, *Thessalonians*, pp. 28-45; Jewett, *Thessalonian Correspondence*, pp. 3-18; and Wanamaker, *Thessalonians*, pp. 17-28.

the four objections most frequently forwarded against the epistle's authenticity: (1) the epistolary remarks in 2.2 and 3.17; (2) the authoritarian tone of the letter; (3) the eschatological divergence between 1 and 2 Thessalonians; (4) the literary dependence of 2 Thessalonians upon 1 Thessalonians.[7]

a. *Authenticating Comments*
Scholars seeking to establish the pseudonymity of 2 Thessalonians frequently maintain that the letter closing ('I, Paul, write this greeting with my own hand. This is the mark in every letter of mine; it is the way I write' [3.17].) when combined with the mention of a 'letter as if from us' (δι' ἐπιστολῆς ὡς δι' ἡμῶν [2.2]) betrays the work of a forger. Although other universally recognized Pauline letters have postscripts similar to 3.17 (1 Cor. 16.21; Gal. 6.11; and Phlm. 19; cf. Col. 4.18), it is thought that this particular epistolary ending is too emphatic to be authentic. Raymond F. Collins expresses a common scholarly sentiment when he states, 'The modern reader has the impression that the author of 2 Thessalonians, as Hamlet's queen, protests too much'.[8] Moving from such an inference, Collins (among others) contends that 2.2 is another trace of a pseudographer. Although advocates of inauthenticity disagree whether the letter referred to in 2.2 is best understood as an epistle forged in Paul's name[9] or as ([a] portion[s] of) 1 Thessalonians,[10] they agree that this cryptic phrase points to a post-Pauline imitator seeking to authenticate his epistle (cf. 2.15; 3.17).

7.   See, e.g., John A. Bailey, 'Who Wrote II Thessalonians?', pp. 131-45; Collins, *Letters that Paul Did not Write*, pp. 218-24; Thurston, *Reading Colossians, Ephesians, and 2 Thessalonians*, pp. 160-61; Karl P. Donfried, '2 Thessalonians and the Church of Thessalonica', in Bradley H. McLean (ed.), *Origins and Method: Towards a New Understanding of Judaism and Christianity: Essays in Honour of John C. Hurd* (JSNTSup, 86; Sheffield: JSOT Press, 1993), pp. 128-44 (130); Georg Hollmann, 'Die Unechtheit des zweiten Thessalonicherbriefs', *ZNW* 5 (1904), pp. 28-38 (38); and Menken, *2 Thessalonians*, p. 28. Jewett (*Thessalonian Correspondence*, p. 7) notes that these four arguments against the authenticity of 2 Thess. remain at the center of the debate. Cf. also Best, *Thessalonians*, p. 50. I have ordered the arguments for pseudonymity from the weaker to the stronger.
8.   Collins, *Letters that Paul Did not Write*, p. 223. Cf. similarly Bailey, 'Who Wrote II Thessalonians?', p. 138; Menken, *2 Thessalonians*, pp. 35-36; and Richard, *Thessalonians*, p. 394.
9.   So, e.g., Beker, *Heirs of Paul*, p. 74.
10.   So, e.g., Bailey, 'Who Wrote II Thessalonians?', p. 138.

b. *A Detached, Authoritarian Tone*

Numerous exegetes have noted that the cool, formal tone of 2 Thessalonians differs from the warm, personal tone of 1 Thessalonians. Some scholars have employed this distinction to argue against the authenticity of 2 Thessalonians.[11] Interpreters who contrast the letters' tone in an effort to establish the pseudonymity of 2 Thessalonians frequently draw attention to the obligatory thanksgivings of 1.3 and 2.13,[12] the less frequent use of familial terminology in 2 Thessalonians,[13] the lack of emphasis on author and reader relations in the letter[14] and the appeals to apostolic tradition and authority in 2.15 and 3.6-15.[15] In brief, many interpreters think it improbable that Paul would, or even could, write two letters with such contrasting tones to the same congregation within a short space of time.[16]

11. See, among others, Bailey, 'Who Wrote II Thessalonians?', p. 137; Collins, *Letters that Paul Did not Write*, pp. 222-23; Beker, *Heirs of Paul*, p. 73; Richard, *Thessalonians*, pp. 23-24; and Thurston, *Reading Colossians, Ephesians, and 2 Thessalonians*, p. 160.

12. E.g. Menken, *2 Thessalonians*, p. 31.

13. E.g. Collins, *Letters that Paul Did not Write*, p. 222.

14. E.g. Bailey, 'Who Wrote II Thessalonians?', pp. 137-38.

15. Caroline Vander Stichele ('The Concept of Tradition and 1 and 2 Thessalonians', in Collins [ed.], *The Thessalonian Correspondence*, pp. 499-504) argues that the stronger emphasis on tradition in 2 Thess. is un-Pauline. Franz Laub ('Paulinische Autorität in nachpaulinischer Zeit (2 Thess)', in Collins [ed.], *The Thessalonian Correspondence*, pp. 403-17) and A. van Aarde ('The Struggle against Heresy in the Thessalonian Correspondence and the Origin of the Apostolic Tradition', in Collins [ed.], *The Thessalonian Correspondence*, pp. 418-25) suggest that the use of apostolic tradition and authority in 2 Thess. differs from that in Paul's genuine letters.

16. See, for instance, Collins, *Letters that Paul Did not Write*, pp. 222-23. Most scholars who think that 2 Thess. is authentic believe that Paul penned 2 Thess. not long after he had written 1 Thess. See, e.g., Frame, *Thessalonians*, p. 19; Best, *Thessalonians*, p. 59; and Bruce, *Thessalonians*, pp. xl-xlii. Some interpreters who affirm the authenticity of 2 Thess. have suggested that it was written before 1 Thess. See, e.g., J.C. West, 'The Order of 1 and 2 Thessalonians', *JTS* 15 (1913), pp. 66-74; T.W. Manson, 'St Paul in Greece: The Letters to the Thessalonians', *BJRL* 35 (1952), pp. 428-47; Robert W. Thurston, 'The Relationship between the Thessalonian Epistles', *ExpTim* 85 (1973), pp. 52-56; and Wanamaker, *Thessalonians*, pp. 37-45. Most scholars have rejected this theory. As to why, see, e.g., Jewett, *Thessalonian Correspondence*, pp. 26-30. Some exegetes who think that 2 Thess. was written by Paul have sought to explain the relationship between 1 and 2 Thess. by positing that 2 Thess. was intended for a different audience than 1 Thess. For a

c. *Eschatological Inconsistencies*

A number of Pauline interpreters maintain that Paul's instruction on the parousia in 1 Thess. 4.13–5.11 is entirely incongruous with the apocalyptic schema set forth in 2 Thess. 2.1-12.[17] It is maintained that since Paul stressed a sudden and imminent parousia in 1 Thessalonians he would not have taught, at least while in Thessalonica (2 Thess. 2.5), that signs must precede the coming of the Lord. John A. Bailey's remarks are typical:

> These two eschatologies [i.e. the eschatologies of 1 and 2 Thess.] are contradictory. Either the end will come suddenly and without warning like a thief in the night (I Thessalonians) or it will be preceded by a series of apocalyptic events which warn of its coming (II Thessalonians). Paul might have said both things—in differing situations to one church, or to different churches—but he can hardly have said both things to the same church at the same time, i.e. to the Thessalonian church when he founded it.[18]

Bailey and other commentators use what they consider contradictions between the eschatologies espoused in 1 and 2 Thessalonians as a primary piece of evidence in their case against the authenticity of 2 Thessalonians.

d. *Literary Imitation*

The classic studies of William Wrede (*Die Echtheit des zweiten Thessalonicherbriefs untersucht*) and Wolfgang Trilling (*Untersuchungen zum zweiten Thessalonicherbrief*)—both of which sought to establish the pseudonymity of 2 Thessalonians by demonstrating its literary dependence upon, yet divergence from, 1 Thessalonians—have persuaded a number of scholars to conclude, primarily on literary grounds, that 2 Thessalonians is a forged letter.[19] In a volume first published in 1903,

---

review of some of the more well-known theories of separate recipients, see Jewett, *Thessalonian Correspondence*, pp. 21-24.

17. So, e.g., Hughes, *Early Christian Rhetoric and 2 Thessalonians*, pp. 79-83; Holland, *The Tradition that You Received from Us*, pp. 91-127; Beker, *Heirs of Paul*, p. 73; Thurston, *Reading Colossians, Ephesians, and 2 Thessalonians*, p. 160; and Helmut Koester, 'From Paul's Eschatology to the Apocalyptic Schemata of 2 Thessalonians', in Collins (ed.), *The Thessalonian Correspondence*, pp. 441-58.

18. Bailey, 'Who Wrote II Thessalonians?', p. 136.

19. E.g. Donfried, '2 Thessalonians' p. 131. Menken (*2 Thessalonians*, p. 36) remarks, 'Since W. Wrede's...book on 2 Thessalonians, the literary relationship between 1 and 2 Thessalonians counts as the decisive argument for the non-Pauline

Wrede argued that the structural, linguistic and thematic similarities between the two epistles suggest that either Paul slavishly imitated 1 Thessalonians when writing 2 Thessalonians or that a forger liberally drew upon Paul's letter to the Thessalonians when producing an epistle in the apostle's name. For Wrede, the latter option was preferable.[20] He surmises that this Pauline imitator wrote 2 Thessalonians sometime in the first decade of the second century CE.[21] In his influential monograph, Trilling reinforces the work of Wrede by arguing against the authenticity of 2 Thessalonians on stylistic, form-critical and theological grounds. Although Trilling concedes that the vocabulary of 2 Thessalonians is basically Pauline, he contends that the author's style and thought diverges significantly from that of Paul.[22] Trilling's comparative study of 1 and 2 Thessalonians ultimately led him to conclude that 2 Thessalonians was an apocalyptic tract put out in Paul's name by a believer living in Asia Minor sometime between 80 and the early second century CE.[23] While the literary work of Wrede and Trilling has led a significant number of Pauline interpreters to conclude that 2 Thessalonians is pseudonymous, exegetes have not been as eager to endorse their respective proposals for the letter's *Sitz im Leben* (see pp. 55-58 below).

authorship of 2 Thessalonians.' Jewett (*Thessalonian Correspondence*, p. 3) states, 'a substantial shift in critical opinion among leading New Testament scholars has been visible since the publication of Wolfgang Trilling's monograph contesting its authenticity in 1972'.

20. So also Bailey ('Who Wrote II Thessalonians?', p. 136) who thinks that 'it is impossible to conceive of a man as creative as Paul drawing upon his own previous letter in such an unimaginative way'.

21. See Wrede, *Echtheit des zweiten Thessalonicherbriefs*, pp. 95-96.

22. For a response to and refutation of Trilling's work, see esp., Marshall, *Thessalonians*, pp. 32-40; Jewett, *Thessalonian Correspondence*, pp. 10-14; and Wanamaker, *Thessalonians*, pp. 21-28. Daryl D. Schmidt ('The Syntactical Style of 2 Thessalonians: How Pauline Is It?', in Collins [ed.], *The Thessalonian Correspondence*, pp. 383-93) seeks to support the work of Trilling by performing a syntactical analysis of 2 Thess. He concludes that the complex syntactical style of the epistle is closer to that of Col. and Eph., letters which Schmidt also views as pseudonymous. Collins (' "The Gospel of Our Lord Jesus Christ" (2 Thes 1,8): A Symbolic Shift of Paradigm', in Collins [ed.], *The Thessalonian Correspondence*, pp. 426-40) discerns in 2 Thess. a shift away from the kerygmatic language of 1 Thess. and employs this observation to argue against the authenticity of 2 Thess.

23. See Trilling, *Der zweite Brief an die Thessalonicher*, pp. 27-28.

3. Evaluating Objections to Pauline Authorship

The scope of this work precludes a detailed response to the points that scholars have raised against the authenticity of 2 Thessalonians. Nevertheless, a few evaluative remarks are in order here. In regard to the letter mentioned in 2.2 and the closing greeting in 3.17, these verses indicate a forger's ruse only to a person who has already opted for pseudonymity.[24] As noted above, the letter's postscript is not unlike that of other universally recognized Paulines. Moreover, the epistolary ending, although emphatic, is no more so than Galatians, another letter where Paul finds it necessary to reinforce his message and to reassert his authority (cf. also 1 Thess. 5.27 where Paul adjures the church by the Lord to have the letter read to all the believers).[25] Additionally, if Paul had suspected that his previous letter to the Thessalonians had been misconstrued by some of the congregation or that a spurious letter was circulating among the church in his name, thereby distorting his eschatological instruction, then the authenticating signature in 3.17 makes good sense, as does the ambiguous remark about an epistle in 2.2.[26] In reference to 2.2 and 3.17, Judith L. Hill asks with good reason:

24. On this point, the remarks of Menken are particularly revealing. He comments that 2.2 'is best understood on the *presupposition* that Paul was not the author of 2 Thessalonians' (pp. 34-35, emphasis added). After acknowledging that 1 Thess. may have also contained a greeting in Paul's own handwriting, he suggests that 3.17 can be considered 'as an indication against Pauline authorship of 2 Thessalonians *only* in as far as the emphasis on the authenticity is *somewhat* too heavy' (p. 36, emphasis added).

25. Cf. further Phlm. 19 where Paul also seeks to assert his influence, albeit gently. See Peter T. O'Brien, *Colossians and Philemon* (WBC, 44; Waco, TX: Word Books, 1982), pp. 267-68.

26. Wanamaker (*Thessalonians*, p. 239) rightly notes Paul's uncertainty as to what was disturbing the congregation (a πνεῦμα, λόγος and/or ἐπιστολή) and the ambiguity of the phrase ὡς δι' ἡμῶν. Cf. John Knox, 'A Note on II Thessalonians 2:2', *ATR* 18 (1936), pp. 72-73, and Gordon D. Fee, 'Pneuma and Eschatology in 2 Thessalonians 2.1-12: A Proposal about "Testing the Prophets" and the Purpose of 2 Thessalonians', in Thomas E. Schmidt and Moisés Silva (eds.), *To Tell the Mystery: Essays in New Testament Eschatology in Honor of Robert H. Gundry* (JSNTSup, 100; Sheffield: JSOT Press, 1994), pp. 196-215. Does ὡς δι' ἡμῶν refer to ἐπιστολή only? (So, e.g., Bruce, *Thessalonians*, p. 164). Or does the phrase refer to ἐπιστολή, λόγος and πνεῦμα? (So, e.g., Best, *Thessalonians*, p. 278). Either of these readings is possible (as is the reading that takes ὡς δι' ἡμῶν to refer to

'How else would the real author [for her, Paul] have approached such a misunderstanding'?[27]

As to the tone of 2 Thessalonians, scholars have rightly detected that it is more detached and authoritarian than 1 Thessalonians.[28] However, a shift in tone between letters does not necessarily indicate that 2 Thessalonians is the product of a Pauline imitator.[29] When he thought it necessary, Paul could alter his tone, as Gal. 4.19-20 shows. ('My dear children ... how I wish I could be with you now and change my tone [ἀλλάξαι τὴν φωνήν μου], because I am perplexed with you' [cf. 1 Cor. 4.21]). Although Bailey believes that there is no good explanation for the difference in tone between the two letters save the pseudonymous origin of 2 Thessalonians,[30] he fails to recognize that the false rumor circulating among the congregation that the Day of the Lord had arrived and the disruptive behavior of the ἄτακτοι could well have prompted Paul to write to his converts in a cooler, firmer tone.

Concerning the perceived contradictions between the Epistles' eschatologies, I would note that eschatological variation does not necessarily indicate pseudonymity.[31] For some scholars, myself included, the emphasis on the suddenness of the parousia in 1 Thess. 4.13–5.11 is not thought to be wholly incompatible with the various signs which according to 2 Thess. 2.3-12 must precede the parousia.[32] To be sure, the

---

ἐπιστολή and λόγος), but one can say with certainty that ὡς δι' ἡμῶν goes with at least ἐπιστολή.

27. Hill, *Establishing the Church in Thessalonica*, p. 5.

28. Contrast Marshall (*Thessalonians*, p. 34) who thinks that 'it is surely time that the myth of the cold tone of the letter was exploded'. Cf. similarly, Roger D. Aus, 'The Liturgical Background of the Necessity and Propriety of Giving Thanks According to 2 Thes 1:3', *JBL* 92 (1973), pp. 432-38 (438). Although the tone of 2 Thess. is not as severe as (portions of) other Epistles in the Pauline corpus, neither is it as personal and affirming as 1 Thess., as Marshall himself concedes (p. 34).

29. *Pace* Collins (*Letters that Paul Did not Write*, p. 223) who holds, 'The hypothesis of the pseudepigraphical origin of 2 Thessalonians...clearly explains the different relationship [detected in the letters' tone] between the community and the authors of 1 and 2 Thessalonians. The relationships are different because the authors are different.' Cf. the more sober assessment of Menken (*2 Thessalonians*, p. 31) who acknowledges that 'the difference in tone *per se* is not a sufficient reason to deny Pauline authorship but in combination with other factors, it has some weight'.

30. Bailey, 'Who Wrote II Thessalonians?', p. 137.

31. Contrast, e.g., Koester, 'Apocalyptic Schemata of 2 Thessalonians'.

32. This is true among interpreters who argue for (e.g. Marshall, *Thessalonians*,

eschatological outlooks of the two letters have different nuances and emphases, but so do, for instance, Paul's ideas about the resurrection of the dead at the eschaton (cf., e.g., 1 Thess. 4.15-17 with 1 Cor. 15.22-53 and with 2 Cor. 5.1-5).[33] Maarten J.J. Menken, an advocate of inauthenticity, remarks:

> In general, Paul is able to express his ideas in various ways, dependent upon the situation of his audiences and himself...and when it comes to a description of what will happen at God's final intervention in human history, it is only expected that a variety of ideas and images will be used.[34]

Even if one concludes that the eschatological schemes of the letters are inconsistent, a negative verdict regarding Pauline authorship does not automatically follow. John M.G. Barclay, who is inclined to think that 2 Thessalonians is authentically Pauline, remarks,

> Apocalypticists are notoriously slippery characters. Many apocalyptic works present conflicting scenarios of the end and inconsistent theses concerning signs of imminence. That Paul should write both of these apocalyptic passages [i.e. 1 Thess. 4.13–5.11 and 2 Thess. 2.1-12], and do so within a short space of time, is by no means impossible; why should his apocalyptic statements be any more consistent than his varied remarks about the law?[35]

It will not suffice, therefore, to argue against the authenticity of 2 Thessalonians merely on the grounds that its eschatology diverges from or conflicts with that of 1 Thessalonians.

The literary similarity of 2 Thessalonians to 1 Thessalonians is 'the most neuralgic topic in the current scholarly debate [over the authen-

p. 37) and against (e.g. Donfried, '2 Thessalonians', p. 136) the Pauline authorship of 2 Thess. Scholars often note that the Synoptic apocalypses and Rev. also juxtapose the suddenness of the end with premonitory signs. See, e.g., Best, *Thessalonians*, p. 55; Bruce, *Thessalonians*, pp. xlii-xliii; Morris, *Thessalonians*, p. 20; Wanamaker, *Thessalonians*, p. 18; E.J. Bicknell, *The First and Second Epistles to the Thessalonians* (WC; London: Methuen, 1932), p. xxvii; and C. Marvin Pate, *The End of the Age Has Come: The Theology of Paul* (Grand Rapids: Zondervan, 1995), p. 222.

33. So Menken, *2 Thessalonians*, p. 29.

34. Menken, *2 Thessalonians*, pp. 29-30. So similarly, Hill, *Establishing the Church in Thessalonica*, pp. 5-6. Menken (*2 Thessalonians*, p. 30) later concedes that the difference in eschatology between 1 and 2 Thess. 'can only become a reasonable hypothesis [against the Pauline authorship of 2 Thess.] when it is strengthened by other pieces of evidence'.

35. Barclay, 'Conflict in Thessalonica', p. 525.

ticity of 2 Thess.]'.[36] The close correlation between the vocabulary, themes and structure of the two letters is undeniable. What one makes of such a relationship is, of course, the pressing issue. Some interpreters use the leverage of literary arguments to build a case against the authenticity of 2 Thessalonians (see pp. 50-52 above), while other scholars are loath to think that literary arguments are weighty enough to overturn a verdict for Pauline authorship.[37] Regardless of the literary relationship between the letters, advocates both for and against the epistle's authenticity agree that a satisfactory *Sitz im Leben* for 2 Thessalonians is the vital piece to the authorship puzzle.[38] It is to this issue that we now turn.

4. *In Search of a* Sitz im Leben *for 2 Thessalonians*

Earlier in this chapter I noted that even though much of New Testament scholarship has embraced Wrede's and Trilling's work on the literary features of the Thessalonian letters, it has not been as receptive to their respective proposals for the setting of 2 Thessalonians.[39] This is evidenced by the number of suggestions for the epistle's *Sitz im Leben* that have appeared in print. Here I will succinctly present and then critique six audience hypotheses advocating pseudonymity which have been published since Trilling's *Untersuchungen zum zweiten Thessalonicherbrief*.[40] Having done so, I will then offer a *Sitz im Leben* which

36. Donfried, '2 Thessalonians', p. 130.

37. E.g. Frame, *Thessalonians*, p. 53; Murphy-O'Connor, *Paul*, p. 111; and Gordon D. Fee, *God's Empowering Presence: The Holy Spirit in the Letters of Paul* (Peabody, MA: Hendrickson, 1994), pp. 67-68.

38. So, e.g., Jewett, *Thessalonian Correspondence*, p. 18; Marshall, *Thessalonians*, p. 40; Hughes, *Early Christian Rhetoric and 2 Thessalonians*, p. 84; and Donfried, '2 Thessalonians', pp. 131-32.

39. Donfried's ('2 Thessalonians', pp. 131-32) remarks are representative. He writes, 'Although I find the most cogent argument for non-Pauline authorship to be that of literary dependence, I am not persuaded that those critics [in context he mentions Wrede and Trilling by name] have correctly or compellingly described the circumstances that prompted the writing of this letter [i.e. 2 Thess.]...'

40. I have selected what I perceive to be a few of the more important contributions to the discussion. Other interpreters, of course, have also set forth proposals for the setting of 2 Thess. since the publication of Trilling's work in 1972. E.g. Lambertus J. Lietaert Peerbolte ('The KATEXON/KATEXΩN of 2 Thess. 2:6-7', *NovT* 39 [1997], pp. 138-50) has suggested that after Paul's death a pseudonymous writer penned a letter in an intentionally obscure manner to give the readers the

allows for the Pauline authorship of the letter.

In a frequently cited article entitled 'Who Wrote II Thessalonians?', Bailey contends that a Pauline imitator, probably in the 90s CE, wrote a letter for all Christians—though he addressed it to the Thessalonian church—in an attempt to counter gnostic opponents who were asserting that the Day of the Lord had already come and that their spiritual resurrection had already occurred. Bailey imagines that the author was a second or third generation Christian who during a period of apocalyptic resurgence took up 1 Thessalonians as a model to address the concerns of his day, in particular, the delay of the parousia.

While Bailey sees the forger as Paul's friend, Andreas Lindemann views the writer of 2 Thessalonians as Paul's foe.[41] According to Lindemann, the writer seeks to identify 1 Thessalonians as a forged letter (2.2) in order to discredit and to replace its errant eschatology. In Lindemann's view, the epistle mentioned in 2.15 refers to 2 Thessalonians, and the authenticating signature in 3.17 is the forger's attempt to mark 1 Thessalonians as non-Pauline. Lindemann pictures the author of the letter as writing near the end of the first century CE when Christians were being persecuted to oppose apocalyptically minded Christians who believed that the Day of the Lord was at hand.

In *Early Christian Rhetoric and 2 Thessalonians*, Frank Witt Hughes propounds that near the end of the first century CE a 'right-wing' Pauline Christian penned 2 Thessalonians to refute the realized eschatology which had been erroneously attributed to Paul by the authors of Colossians and Ephesians. Hughes contends that the author of 2 Thessalonians was so outraged by the authoritative claims of his adversaries, that is, the writers of Colossians and Ephesians, that he used 1 Thessalonians as a model to craft 'a powerful and well-argued reply...a polished piece of religious rhetoric'.[42]

---

impression that there were reasons for the postponement of the parousia. Peerbolte argues that although the author himself did not know why the Day of the Lord had been delayed, he leads the epistle's recipients to believe that he and the Thessalonian church did.

41. Andreas Lindemann, 'Zum Abfassungszweck des zweiten Thessalonicherbriefs', *ZNW* 68 (1977), pp. 34-47. In this essay, Lindemann is reviving the earlier work of Adolf H. Hilgenfeld ('Die beiden Briefe an die Thessalonicher, nach Inhalt und Ursprung', *ZWT* 5 [1862], pp. 225-64) and Heinrich J. Holtzmann ('Zum zweiten Thessalonicherbrief', *ZNW* 2 [1901], pp. 97-108).

42. Hughes, *Early Christian Rhetoric and 2 Thessalonians*, p. 95.

Glenn S. Holland has also proposed a *Sitz im Leben* for 2 Thessalonians.[43] Holland views the letter as a forged document produced by a second generation Paulinist for the whole Pauline church. For Holland, the imitator was a thoroughgoing apocalypticist, not unlike other Jewish and Christian authors living and writing in the last third of the first century CE. Holland thinks that the author attempts to supplement and to explain the eschatological instruction given in 1 Thessalonians for a Christian generation seeking to cope with the delay of the parousia. Additionally, Holland sees 2 Thessalonians as a direct polemic against advocates of realized eschatology (e.g. the authors of Col. and Eph.), who Holland equates with the ἄτακτοι. The affinities of Holland's thesis with those of Bailey and Hughes are apparent.

Menken's reading of 2 Thessalonians follows in the vein of Holland. In agreement with Trilling, Menken thinks that 2 Thessalonians was written by a Paulinist sometime between 80 and the early second century CE to Christians living in Asia Minor. Menken also avers that the writer opposed realized eschatology by advocating an apocalyptic eschatology similar to Revelation, Mark 13 (and parallels) and *Didache* 16.

While each of the preceding proposals is able, with varying degrees of success, to account for the eschatological upheaval reported in 2.2,[44]

---

43. Holland, *The Tradition that You Received from Us*, pp. 129-58.

44. That realized eschatology is being countered in 2 Thess. is commonly proposed by scholars who accept and reject the authenticity of 2 Thess. It seems unlikely, however, that 'a belief in the present enjoyment of the blessings of heaven could be likely to "shake" Christian believers' (Barclay, 'Conflict in Thessalonica', p. 527). Furthermore, the presence of ταχέως in 2.2 'suggests a sudden turn of events, not a developing theological tendency' (Barclay, 'Conflict in Thessalonica', p. 527 n. 24).

If the author of 2 Thess. is in fact countering a *spiritualized* eschatology, then his appeal to *historical* events which must precede the Day of the Lord makes little sense. Contrast Paul's approach in opposing (over-)realized eschatology in Corinth (see, e.g., 1.5-8; 3.13-15, 17; 4.5, 8-13; 5.5; 6.13-14; 7.26-31; 11.26, 32; 15.24, 51-56; 16.22). Additionally, the fact that 'Day of the Lord' language does not appear in either Col. or Eph. considerably weakens the arguments of Hughes and Holland (so Barclay, 'Conflict in Thessalonica', p. 527 n. 54). To be sure, Col. and Eph. advocate a thoroughly realized eschatology (note, however, Col. 4.6 and Eph. 4.30), but there is no compelling reason to read 2 Thess. as a polemic against such. The recipients of 2 Thess. were convinced that the Day of the Lord had (somehow) come; the writer seeks to redress this misconception by offering a general eschatological timetable. Rightly recognized by Richard (*Thessalonians*, p. 344), an advocate of the epistle's pseudonymity.

other particular features of the letter (e.g. the non-Christian opposition of Thessalonian believers [1.4-9] and the disruptive conduct of the ἄτακτοι in the Thessalonian assembly [3.6-15]) are neither sufficiently explored nor explained. Having effaced some of the specific contours of the letter, these (and other) proponents of pseudonymity are required to offer vague suggestions about when and where the letter was written and about who wrote and received the forged epistle. To my mind, the exceedingly specific nature of the letter argues against such general proposals.[45] For, as Donfried suggests, 'It is difficult to imagine a setting where a letter specifically addressed to the Thessalonians by Paul would be relevant and convincing to a non-Thessalonian church some thirty or more years after the Apostle's death.'[46]

Yet, Donfried's theory is not completely satisfactory either. Convinced that Paul himself is not the author of the letter and that the epistle addresses concrete circumstances in the Thessalonian church, Donfried posits that Timothy (or perhaps Silvanus) penned 2 Thessalonians not long after the first letter had been written and signed it in Paul's name for added authority. While I would agree with Donfried that 2 Thessalonians is directed toward real congregational issues current in Thessalonica, it seems unnecessary to remove Paul from the authorship picture altogether. Although accompanied by Silvanus and Timothy (1.1), Paul is clearly the author of 1 Thessalonians (2.18; 3.5; 5.27; cf. the prescripts of 1 Cor. 1.1; 2 Cor. 1.1; Phil. 1.1; Phlm. 1; and Col. 1.1). The same is seemingly true of 2 Thessalonians (1.1; 2.5; 3.17).[47]

---

45. The letter is addressed to a church experiencing affliction, subject to eschatological confusion and plagued with congregational 'parasites'. It seems unlikely that each of these congregational details was concocted solely for the sake of a forgery, particularly when the issues addressed dovetail so well with what we know of the congregation from 1 Thess. So also Fee, *God's Empowering Presence*, p. 67. If 2 Thess. is inauthentic, one may complement the imitator for being exceedingly clever (or criticize the forger for being thoroughly deceptive). Jewett (*Thessalonian Correspondence*, p. 17) remarks, 'If a forgery occurred, it was remarkably skillful, which presents a major barrier to the acceptance of any forgery hypothesis hitherto proposed.'

46. Donfried, '2 Thessalonians', p. 132.

47. To explain Timothy's signing off in Paul's name, Donfried ('2 Thessalonians', p. 134) appeals to the notion of 'corporate personality'. He overlooks, however, the presence of ἔλεγον in 2.5 (cf. 1 Thess. 2.18; 3.5; 5.27).

5. *A Modest Proposal*

Having concisely considered and countered a number of audience hypotheses for 2 Thessalonians, I will now briefly set out what I believe to be the most convincing *Sitz im Leben* for the letter. Not long after Paul dispatched his first epistle to the Thessalonian assembly (likely from Corinth c. 50 CE), he is informed, perhaps by the courier of 1 Thessalonians, that the assembly was still experiencing hostility from outsiders (2 Thess. 1), that some of his converts (the ἄτακτοι?) were claiming that the Day of the Lord had arrived (2 Thess. 2) and that the ἄτακτοι had stopped working and were now meddling in the affairs of others and living off the goodwill of fellow church members (2 Thess. 3).[48] In response to this report, Paul pens a rather pointed epistle to encourage his beleaguered converts in the throes of affliction, to counter the misconception that the Day of the Lord had come and to counsel the congregation how best to deal with the ἄτακτοι.

While it is true that the tone of 2 Thessalonians is more distant and direct than 1 Thessalonians and that its vocabulary, structure and contents are strikingly similar to the first letter, these factors do not require one to regard 2 Thessalonians as pseudonymous, nor do the seemingly irreconcilable eschatologies. While the limited range of topics addressed in 2 Thessalonians adequately accounts for its close literary relationship with 1 Thessalonians, Paul's effort to redress what he perceived to be potentially disastrous congregational problems sufficiently explains the change in tone and in eschatological tact. Paul likely stresses the necessity of following his verbal and written instructions, as well as his example, to give guidance to the still immature assembly. Paul may well have thought that a fledgling congregation facing external opposition and internal deviation needed both strong affirmation and admonition to stay on spiritual course.[49] While my proposed *Sitz im Leben* for 2 Thessalonians is neither as novel nor as radical as some of the other proposals on offer, it does seem to make good sense of all the evidence at our disposal.

48. Since I will discuss each of these congregational issues in Part IV below, I will not treat them here.

49. Cf. Paul's grave concern in 1 Thess. 3 that his converts stand firm in their newfound faith.

6. *Conclusion*

Although my study of the issues surrounding the authenticity of 2 Thessalonians leads me to conclude that the letter was written by Paul, for the purposes of this project I will treat the letter as a secondary source. I will do so for two primary reasons. First and foremost, 2 Thessalonians contributes only a small amount of data to the topic under consideration. Secondly, it seems unwise to build a case using evidence that most modern interpreters regard as inadmissible. Scholars who think that 2 Thessalonians is authentic might question my decision not to employ the epistle as a primary source in this project. Nonetheless, the widespread skepticism among contemporary commentators regarding the letter's authenticity warrants this concession.[50] I view this interpretive move as tactically advantageous. If 2 Thessalonians is in fact inauthentic, my arguments herein will stand; if 2 Thessalonians is authentic after all, my case will be further corroborated.

---

50. So also Jewett (*Thessalonian Correspondence*, p. 92) who writes, 'Given the problematic status of 2 Thessalonians at the present moment of research, it is prudent to build the picture of the congregational situation primarily on the basis of the clues in 1 Thessalonians.'

Chapter 3

ACTS' ACCOUNT OF THE CONFLICT AT THESSALONICA

1. *Introduction*

Contemporary New Testament interpreters tend to be skeptical of the historical veracity of Acts.[1] It is commonly suggested that Luke's literary, apologetic and theological tendencies compromise the volume's historicity.[2] The not-so-subtle Lukan agendas that permeate (Luke–) Acts prompt some exegetes to devalue greatly[3] or to dismiss totally[4] Acts 17.1-10a when studying Paul and the Thessalonian church.[5] While

1. Jack T. Sanders is among the most critical. He remarks in one article ('Christians and Jews in the Roman Empire: A Conversation with Rodney Stark', *SocAn* 53 [1992], pp. 433-45 [435]) that 'one simply cannot turn to Acts for direct information about Christianity. My own working assumption is not to accept information from Acts at all unless it can be corroborated.' The work of Martin Hengel (*Acts and the History of Earliest Christianity* [trans. John Bowden; London: SCM Press, 1979]), Jacob Jervell (*The Unknown Paul: Essays on Luke–Acts and Early Christian History* [Minneapolis: Augsburg, 1984]), Colin J. Hemer (*The Book of Acts in the Setting of Hellenistic History* [ed. Conrad H. Gempf; WUNT, 49; Tübingen: J.C.B. Mohr (Paul Siebeck), 1989]) and the BAFCS series call such extreme skepticism into question. For an informative, even-handed excursus on the historicity of Acts, see Charles H. Talbert, *Reading Acts: A Literary and Theological Commentary on the Acts of the Apostles* (New York: Crossroad, 1997), pp. 237-54.

2. Throughout this work I will refer to the author of Acts as 'Luke'. This practice is customary among today's commentators and is not meant to prejudge the authorship of this anonymous writing.

3. E.g. Best, *Thessalonians*, p. 7.

4. Richard (*Thessalonians*, p. 6) maintains, 'the Acts account of the mission owes more to Luke's project and remote acquaintance with the Apostle's role than to first-hand data'. Koester (*Introduction to the New Testament*, II, p. 108) contends that 'all of the individual events of Paul's activity in the city [i.e. Thessalonica] are legendary'.

5. Cf. Donfried ('Paul and Judaism', p. 247) who in the course of discussing

I would concur with those scholars who maintain that the Lukan interests present in 17.1-10a should signal caution and that 1 Thessalonians
must be given priority over the second-hand account in Acts,[6] I would
also agree with Raymond F. Collins who remarks that 'one cannot
afford to be hypercritical [of Acts 17.1-10a]. [For,] Luke has not written
his account of Paul's visit to Thessalonica as a simple figment of his
imagination.'[7]

Before rejecting (parts of) the Lukan narrative of Paul's Thessalonian mission as unreliable, then, a critical study of the text itself is in
order.[8] In this chapter I will treat Acts' description of the conflict at
Thessalonica. As necessary, I will anticipate Parts III and IV of this
study by setting Luke's account alongside 1 Thessalonians. I will begin
this chapter by considering in turn the reported origin of and reason for
the opposition. I will then address the purported attack on the house of
Jason and the subsequent accusations lodged before the politarchs.
Next, I will discuss the indicated outcomes of the clash. By way of conclusion, I will assess the value of the narrative for this project.

2. The Proposed Origin of the Opposition

According to 17.5, 'the Jews' (οἱ Ἰουδαῖοι) were responsible for insti-
gating an attack on Jason's house in an effort to bring Paul and Silas
before the assembly (δῆμος). Some scholars have questioned Luke's
claim that Jews sought to hinder Paul in Thessalonica, and a few interpreters have even wondered if there were Jews living in Thessalonica at

Luke's account of Paul's Thessalonian mission comments that 'there must be the
realism that Acts contains much valuable and accurate information about the
Pauline mission even though the writer's theological tendencies are quite apparent'.
Cf. also Malherbe (*Paul and the Thessalonians*, p. 13) who thinks 'the account is
more valuable than has sometimes been thought'.

6.   E.g. Gaventa, *Thessalonians*, pp. 4-5.
7.   Collins, *Birth of the New Testament*, p. 31. So similarly, C.K. Barrett (*The
Acts of the Apostles. II. Introduction and Commentary on Acts XV–XXVIII* [ICC;
2 vols.; Edinburgh: T. & T. Clark, 1998], p. 807): 'There are features of Lucan style
[in this account]... This is not of course to say that Luke made it all up out of his
imagination.'
8.   Riesner (*Paul's Early Period*, p. 343) rightly notes that it is only through
detailed analysis that one can determine whether the particular details of the Lukan
account of Paul's founding visit to Thessalonica are historical or not. He also suggests that one should 'distinguish quite clearly between stylization and invention'.

this point in time.[9] Since there is no other explicit literary evidence indicating that Jews were living in Thessalonica c. 50 CE[10] and since the archaeological record is silent about Judaism in the city during this period, it is suggested that Luke may have erroneously assumed that there was a Jewish community there. While it is true that there is presently no archaeological evidence to support Luke's record of Jews residing in Thessalonica at this time, this comes as no great surprise given that the city has been continuously inhabited since its founding in 316 BCE, thereby preventing thorough excavation.[11] But even if Thessalonica were excavated and no corroborating evidence surfaced, the wide dispersion of Jews throughout the eastern half of the Roman Empire[12]

9.　E.g. Helmut Koester, 'Apocalyptic Schema of 2 Thessalonians', p. 443, and Dieter Lührmann, 'The Beginnings of the Church at Thessalonica', in David L. Balch, Everett Ferguson and Wayne A. Meeks (eds.), *Greeks, Romans, and Christians: Essays in Honor of Abraham J. Malherbe* (Minneapolis: Fortress Press, 1990), pp. 237-49 (239).

10.　See, however, my discussion of 1 Thess. 2.15-16 on pp. 130-35 below.

11.　For an introduction to the archaeological record in Thessalonica, see Holland Lee Hendrix, 'Thessalonians', in Helmut Koester and Holland Lee Hendrix (eds.), *Archaeological Resources for New Testament Study: A Collection of Slides on Culture and Religion in Antiquity*, I (Philadelphia: Fortress Press, 1986), pp. 1-49. See also Helmut Koester, 'Archäologie und Paulus in Thessalonike', in Lukas Bormann, Kelly Del Tredici and Angela Standhartinger (eds.), *Religious Propaganda and Missionary Competition in the New Testament World: Essays Honoring Dieter Georgi* (Leiden: E.J. Brill, 1994), pp. 393-404, and Collins, *Birth of the New Testament*, p. 8. For a discussion of the archaeological material of Jewish origin found in and near Thessalonica dating from around the third century CE onward, see, e.g., Irina Levinskaya, *The Book of Acts in its Diaspora Setting* (BAFCS, 5; Grand Rapids: Eerdmans; Carlisle: Paternoster Press, 1996), pp. 154-57; Sandnes, *Paul—One of the Prophets?*, pp. 187-89; Hill, *Establishing the Church in Thessalonica*, pp. 51-56; Lührmann, 'Beginnings of the Church', p. 239; and Riesner, *Paul's Early Period*, pp. 344-48. Sandnes (*Paul—One of the Prophets?*, p. 189) suggests that such data indicate 'not innovations, but a continuation of what already existed'. According to Levinskaya (*Diaspora Setting*, p. 156) an inscription discovered in 1965 and published in 1994 (see P.M. Nigdelis, 'Synagoge(n) und Gemeinde der Juden in Thessaloniki: Fragen auf grund einer neuen jüdischen Grabinschrift der Kaiserzeit', *ZPE* 102 [1994], pp. 297-306) 'implies that in the third century [CE] there were several Jewish communities in Thessalonica'.

12.　Philo (*Leg. Gai.* 281) notes that there were Jews living in Macedonia. On the dispersion of Jews, see also Josephus, *War* 2.398; *Ant.* 14.115; *Apion* 2.282; and 1 Macc. 15.22-23. Sanders ('Christians and Jews', p. 439) maintains '*there was no place in the eastern Roman Empire where Christianity could expand where there*

makes it likely that in c. 50 CE there would have been a (considerable?) Jewish community in Thessalonica, a strategically located, heavily populated port city.[13]

Even if there were Jews in Thessalonica when Paul visited, some scholars doubt that Paul would have frequented their synagogue. Exegetes sometimes suggest the report that Paul commenced his Thessalonian mission in the synagogue 'as was his custom' (κατὰ τὸ εἰωθὸς, 17:2; cf. 13.5, 14; 14.1; 16.13; 17.10, 17; 18.4, 19; 19.8; Lk. 4.16) is an instance of Lukan stylization which stands in contradistinction to Paul's understanding of himself as the apostle to the Gentiles (see, e.g., 1 Thess. 2.16; Gal. 1.16; 2.7-9; Rom. 1.5, 13-15; 11.13-15; 15.15-21; Col. 1.27; Eph. 3.8).[14] Interpreters also contend that the Gentile composition of the Thessalonian congregation (1 Thess. 1.9; 2.14) renders inaccurate Luke's contention that some of the Jews were persuaded by Paul's preaching and joined him and Silas (καὶ τινες ἐξ αὐτῶν ἐπείσθησαν καὶ προσεκληρώθησαν τῷ Παύλῳ καὶ τῷ Σιλᾷ, 17.4).[15]

It may be that Luke's placement of Paul in the synagogue at the outset of his ministry in a given city is more a Lukan literary convention than a Pauline missionary pattern. Furthermore, Paul does address the

were not Jews already. Jews were simply everywhere' (emphasis his). See also Stephen G. Wilson, *Related Strangers: Jews and Christians 70–170 C.E.* (Minneapolis: Fortress Press, 1995), p. 21.

13. Meeks (*First Urban Christians*, p. 46) remarks, 'There is no reason to doubt the report in Acts of a strong Jewish community [in Thessalonica].' So also Jewett, *Thessalonian Correspondence*, pp. 119-20, and Riesner, *Paul's Early Period*, p. 347. According to Levinskaya (*Diaspora Setting*, p. 154) the earliest epigraphic evidence for Jews in Greece dates to the third century BCE. Karl P. Donfried ('The Cults of Thessalonica and the Thessalonian Correspondence', *NTS* 31 [1985], pp. 336-56 [356 n. 93]) claims, 'There has always been a significant Jewish community in Thessalonica...' Estimates of the city's population at the time of Paul's founding visit range from about 40,000 to 100,000.

14. So Dixon Slingerland, ' "The Jews" in the Pauline Portion of Acts', *JAAR* 54 (1986), pp. 305-21 (312-14); E.P. Sanders, 'Paul's Attitude toward the Jewish People' *USQR* 33 (1978), pp. 175-87 (177); and Meeks, *First Urban Christians*, p. 26. Watson (*Paul, Judaism and the Gentiles*, p. 32) maintains that at an early stage in his Christian activity Paul preached the gospel only to the Jews, but by the time his letters were written 'he was devoting his energies entirely to the preaching of the Gentiles'. Terence L. Donaldson (*Paul and the Gentiles: Remapping the Apostle's Convictional World* [Minneapolis: Fortress Press, 1997], pp. 269-71) has appropriately and adequately critiqued Watson's proposal.

15. So Lührmann, 'Beginnings of the Church', p. 239.

Thessalonian church as though it were comprised of Gentiles.[16] Should one conclude, then, that Paul did not interface with Thessalonian Jews at all and that Luke has added the familiar refrain of Jews opposing Paul?[17] Before surmising such, the following points merit consideration.

Although Gentiles were the primary focus of Paul's missionary endeavors and seem to have constituted the Thessalonian church, 2 Cor. 11.24 indicates that Paul had close contact with at least some Diasporan Jewish synagogues.[18] This verse also shows that some Jews opposed Paul (see also 1 Thess. 2.14-16; 2 Cor. 11.26d; Gal. 5.11; 6.12).[19] Commentators are correct to observe that Acts emphasizes Jewish opposition to Christians in general and to Paul in particular.[20] Nevertheless,

16. See further pp. 218-26 below.

17. So Mason ('Paul, Classical Anti-Jewish Polemic, and the Letter to the Romans', p. 198 n. 77) who states, 'Were it not for Acts 17:5, which thematizes Jewish opposition to Paul...no one would have supposed that his Thessalonian opponents were Jewish.' Cf. deSilva, ' "Worthy of His Kingdom" ', p. 75 n. 45.

18. Rightly noted by, among others, Arland J. Hultgren, *Paul's Gospel and Mission: The Outlook from his Letter to the Romans* (Philadelphia: Fortress Press, 1985), pp. 139-40; Sanders, *Paul, the Law, and the Jewish People*, p. 192; and Meeks, *First Urban Christians*, p. 26. Stanley Kent Stowers ('Social Status, Public Speaking and Private Teaching: The Circumstances of Paul's Preaching Activity', *NovT* 26 [1984], pp. 59-82 [65]) maintains, 'Even though Paul's major mission was to Gentiles, the synagogue must be considered one locus, and perhaps an important one for his preaching where he by birth and heritage would have a recognized although often controversial status as a Jewish Christian.' Note also Paul's statement in 1 Cor. 9.20-21, which does not seem to be mere hyperbole (*pace* Sanders, 'Paul's Attitude toward the Jewish People', p. 177; so rightly, Hultgren, *Paul's Gospel and Mission*, pp. 141-43).

19. For a full treatment of these texts, see Chapters 6–7. Arland J. Hultgren ('The Self-Definition of Paul and his Communities', *SEÅ* 56 [1991], pp. 78-100, [88]) perceptively writes, 'If Paul had lived solely as a gentile among gentiles, or if he evangelized gentiles alone, it is difficult to explain why he would have been persecuted [by his fellow Jews].'

20. See esp. Scott Cunningham, *'Through Many Tribulations': The Theology of Persecution in Luke–Acts* (JSNTSup, 142; Sheffield: Sheffield Academic Press, 1997). I would disagree, however, with Jack T. Sanders (*The Jews in Luke–Acts* [London: SCM Press, 1987]) and Slingerland (' "The Jews" ') who contend that Luke was decidedly anti-Jewish. James D.G. Dunn ('The Question of Anti-semitism in the New Testament Writings of the Period', in James D.G. Dunn [ed.], *Jews and Christians: The Parting of the Ways A.D. 70–135* [WUNT, 66; Tübingen: J.C.B. Mohr (Paul Siebeck), 1992], pp. 177-211 [195]) and Vittorio Fusco ('Luke–Acts and the Future of Israel', *NovT* 38 [1996], pp. 1-17 [17]) also reject the idea

Conflict at Thessalonica

Paul's own epistolary remarks suggest that one should not reject out of hand the possibility that Acts accurately reports Paul's contact and conflict with Thessalonian Jews (see esp. 1 Thess. 2.14-16).[21]

3. The Reason Given for Jewish Opposition

If one may reasonably accept Luke's report that Paul was a target of Jewish hostility in Thessalonica, can one also regard as plausible the reason he gives for the opposition? Acts 17.5 states that jealousy (if construed negatively) or zeal (if understood positively) prompted the Jews to act against Paul (ζηλώσαντες δὲ οἱ Ἰουδαῖοι). Some interpreters understand this remark to be a Lukan redaction (cf. 5.17; 7.9; 13.45).[22] (But cf. also Acts 21.20; 22.3; Gal. 1.14; Rom. 10.2; Phil. 3.6.) To be sure, one can counter Luke's claim that the Jews opposed the Pauline mission because they were jealous (if this is in fact what he is saying). First of all, one might suggest that such a statement betrays Luke's anti-Jewish bias. In contradistinction to Acts, one might also argue that Paul was not in contact with the Thessalonian synagogue.

---

that Luke was anti-Jewish. It is worth noting that although Paul is *frequently* opposed by Jews in Acts, it is not *only* Jews who seek to hinder his mission (see, e.g., 14.5, 19; 17.5; 16.19-25; 19.21-41). See further, Richard J. Cassidy, 'The Non-Roman Opponents of Paul', in Earl J. Richard (ed.), *New Views on Luke–Acts* (Collegeville, MN: Liturgical Press, 1990), pp. 150-62, and Marie-Eloise Rosenblatt, *Paul the Accused: His Portrait in the Acts of the Apostles* (ZSNT; Collegeville, MN: Liturgical Press, 1995), p. xiv. Furthermore, according to Acts, some Jews do respond positively to Paul's message (see, e.g., 13.43; 17.4, 12; 18.4). See further Robert L. Brawley, *Luke–Acts and the Jews: Conflict, Apology, and Conciliation* (SBLMS, 33; Atlanta: Scholars Press, 1987).

21. Hultgren (*Paul's Gospel and Mission*, p. 143) concludes similarly: 'However schematized and idealized the picture in Acts [of Paul's mission is], it cannot be dismissed wholesale.' See also Wanamaker, *Thessalonians*, p. 8, and Goulder, 'Silas in Thessalonica', p. 96. Sanders ('Paul's Attitude toward the Jewish People', p. 177) rightly notes that '1 Thess. 2.14-16 indicates that [Paul] ran into Jews in Thessalonica.' Contrast Ernst Haenchen (*The Acts of the Apostles: A Commentary* [trans. Bernard Noble and Gerald Shinn; rev. trans. R.M. Wilson; Oxford: Basil Blackwell, 1971], p. 513) who supposes that 'Paul was driven out of Thessalonica by a Gentile anti-Christian movement...'

22. So, e.g., Gerd Lüdemann, *Early Christianity According to the Traditions in Acts: A Commentary* (trans. John Bowden; London: SCM Press, 1989), p. 185; Sanders, *The Jews in Luke–Acts*, p. 272; Best, *Thessalonians*, p. 7; and Richard, *Thessalonians*, p. 5.

Furthermore, one might doubt that Paul could have provoked such intense Jewish jealousy or zealousness in such a short period of time. Or, one could question whether a number of God-fearers and leading women left the synagogue to follow Paul and Silas. Having addressed Luke's alleged anti-Judaism and Paul's relationship to the synagogue above, I will now consider the duration of Paul's mission in Thessalonica and the composition of the Thessalonian church. This discussion will place us in a better position to assess Acts' claim that jealousy or zeal caused 'the Jews' to oppose Paul.

Many interpreters maintain that Paul's founding visit to Thessalonica lasted longer than the three Sabbaths that he reportedly preached in the synagogue (Acts 17.2).[23] Paul's Thessalonian mission was at least long enough for him to form an intimate relationship with his converts (e.g. 1 Thess. 2.7-8), to receive aid from Philippi 'once and again' (ἄπαξ καὶ δὶς, Phil. 4.16)[24] and to ply his trade (1 Thess. 2.9; cf. 2 Thess. 3.7-9).[25] It does appear that Luke has compressed his account to focus solely on Paul's entry into (17.1-4) and exit from (17.5-10a) the city.[26] It makes good sense, therefore, to envision some passage of time between Paul's separation from the synagogue and his forced departure from the city.[27]

23. See, among others, William Neil, *The Epistle* [sic] *of Paul to the Thessalonians* (MNTC; New York: Harper & Brothers, 1950), p. xii; Malherbe, *Paul and the Thessalonians*, pp. 13-14; Wanamaker, *Thessalonians*, p. 7; and Lührmann, 'Beginnings of the Church', p. 238. Marshall (*Thessalonians*, p. 5) and Morris (*Thessalonians*, p. 4) suggest that Paul's stay was about a month in duration. Cf. similarly, Donfried, 'The Cults of Thessalonica', p. 356 n. 92.

24. Leon Morris ('ΚΑΙ ΑΠΑΞ ΚΑΙ ΔΙΣ', *NovT* 1 [1956], pp. 205-208) argues, albeit unconvincingly, that καὶ ἄπαξ καὶ δὶς may be read to suggest that the Philippians sent Paul only one gift while he was in Thessalonica.

25. Malherbe (*Paul and the Thessalonians*, p. 13) suggests the Paul's founding mission lasted as long as two or three months. Riesner (*Paul's Early Period*, p. 364) proposes four months or less. W.M. Ramsay (*St. Paul the Traveller and Roman Citizen* [repr.; Grand Rapids: Baker Book House, 1960], p. 228) posits six months. Murphy-O'Connor (*Paul*, p. 102) contends that Paul stayed at least one year in Thessalonica.

26. So also Rudolf Pesch, *Die Apostelgeschichte* (EKKNT, 5.2; Zürich: Benzinger Verlag; Neukirchen–Vluyn: Neukirchener Verlag, 1986), pp. 125-26; Wolfgang Stegemann, *Zwischen Synagoge und Obrigkeit: Zur historischen Situation der lukanischen Christen* (FRALNT, 152; Göttingen: Vandenhoeck & Ruprecht, 1991), p. 226; and Talbert, *Reading Acts*, p. 156.

27. So also Kenneth S. Hemphill, *Spiritual Gifts Empowering the New Testament Church* (Nashville: Broadman Press, 1988), p. 20; Malherbe, *Paul and the*

The seed of jealousy or zeal might have been planted during Paul's stint in the synagogue, but it seemingly blossomed at a later time.

But what could have caused Thessalonian Jews to be jealous of or zealous towards Paul? Acts insinuates it was Paul's success in winning synagogue adherents that incited Jewish envy or zeal. Luke reports in 17.4 that some Jews and a significant number of God-fearers (σεβό-μενοι)[28] and prominent women (benefactresses of the synagogue?) were persuaded by Paul's preaching and joined him.[29] Paul's statement

Thessalonians, pp. 13-14; and Martin, *Thessalonians*, p. 24.

28. Although A.T. Kraabel ('The Disappearance of the "God-Fearers"', *Numen* 28 [1981], pp. 113-26) has argued that Luke invented this category to promote his own theological agenda, virtually all ancient historians maintain that there were indeed God-fearing Greeks who frequented the synagogue, even if they did not always have a particular title. See esp. Joyce M. Reynolds and Robert F. Tannenbaum, *Jews and God-Fearers at Aphrodisias: Greek Inscriptions with Commentary* (CPASS, 12; Cambridge: Cambridge Philological Society, 1987); Paul R. Trebilco, *Jewish Communities in Asia Minor* (SNTMS, 69; Cambridge: Cambridge University Press, 1991), pp. 145-66; and Levinskaya, *Diaspora Setting*, pp. 51-126. See also Louis Feldman, 'The Omnipresence of the God-Fearers', *BARev* 12 (1986), pp. 58-63; Shaye Cohen, 'Crossing the Boundary Line and Becoming a Jew', *HTR* 82 (1989), pp. 13-33 (31-33); Terence L. Donaldson, 'Proselytes or "Righteous Gentiles"?: The Status of Gentiles in Eschatological Pilgrimage Patterns of Thought', *JSP* 7 (1990), pp. 3-27 (5-6 n. 3); John M.G. Barclay, *Jews in the Mediterranean Diaspora from Alexander to Trajan (323 BCE–117 CE)* (Edinburgh: T. & T. Clark, 1996), p. 279 n. 50; Hultgren, *Paul's Gospel and Mission*, pp. 137-143; Wilson, *Related Strangers*, pp. 21-22; Esler, *Community and Gospel in Luke–Acts*, p. 36; Talbert, *Reading Acts*, p. 105; and Meeks, *First Urban Christians*, pp. 207-208 n. 175.

Epigraphical evidence indicates Gentile support of and presence in the Jewish communities in Aphrodisias and Miletus. For the inscriptions and a commentary thereon, see Reynolds and Tannenbaum, *Jews and God-fearers at Aphrodisias*, pp. 48-66. For a survey of the archaeological remains of Diaspora synagogues, see Eric M. Meyers and A.T. Kraabel, 'Archaeology, Iconography, and Nonliterary Written Remains', in Robert A. Kraft and George W.E. Nickelsburg (eds.), *Early Judaism and its Modern Interpreters* (BMI; Philadelphia: Fortress Press; Atlanta: Scholars Press, 1986), pp. 175-210. Although Jewish-Gentile relations were not as cordial in all places as they were in Aphrodisias and Miletus, Diaspora Jews did fraternize with Gentiles, and Gentiles frequented Jewish synagogues. See, e.g., Wilson, *Related Strangers*, p. 22. Luke's report that there were God-fearers present in the Thessalonian synagogue and that they were responsive to Paul's preaching is altogether plausible.

29. This implies that Paul had already established an alternative religious com-

that his converts 'turned to God from idols' (1 Thess. 1.9) combined
with Luke's penchant for highlighting conversions among God-fearers
and the well-to-do[30] has led some commentators to doubt that Jews,
God-fearers and 'leading women' comprised the Thessalonian congregation.[31]

Although 1 Thess. 1.9 (cf. 1.1; 2.14) suggests that Paul wrote exclusively to Gentiles,[32] neither 1 Thess. 1.9 nor any other statement in
1 Thessalonians prohibits one from concluding that there were both
God-fearers[33] and prominent women[34] in the church. If Paul did in fact

---

munity apart from the synagogue, i.e. a church. On the interest of Gentile women in
Judaism, see the following texts from Josephus noted by Talbert (*Reading Acts*, p.
156): *War* 2.20; *Ant.* 18.3; 20.2.

30. On Luke's tendency to call attention to conversion from the upper classes
(cf., e.g., Acts 6.7; 8.27; 10.1; 13.12; 18.8), see Haenchen, *Acts*, p. 507; Luke
Timothy Johnson, *The Acts of the Apostles* (SP, 5; Collegeville, MN: Liturgical
Press, 1992), p. 310; and John Clayton Lentz, Jr., *Luke's Portrait of Paul* (SNTMS,
77; Cambridge: Cambridge University Press, 1993), pp. 98-99. Luke particularly
likes to report the conversion of wealthy women (see, e.g., 16.14-15; 17.4, 12; cf.
Lk. 8.1-3).

31. For a useful discussion on the composition of the Thessalonian church, see
Hill, *Establishing the Church in Thessalonica*, pp. 195-200.

32. Best (*Thessalonians*, p. 82) writes: 'Obviously the Thessalonians were Gentiles before they became Christians for Jews would have not been described as
turning from idolatry.' So similarly Craig S. de Vos, *Church and Community Conflicts: The Relationships of the Thessalonian, Corinthian, and Philippian Churches
with their Wider Civic Communities* (SBLDS, 168; Altanta: Scholars Press, 1999),
pp. 144-47. If Paul's preaching did persuade some Jews to join him and Silas, as
Acts 17.4 maintains, then when Paul wrote 1 Thess. these Jewish believers had
either defected, or they comprised such a small percentage of the church that Paul
thought he could address the assembly as though it were comprised entirely of
Gentiles.

33. Hultgren (*Paul's Gospel and Mission*, pp. 140-41) comments, 'The fact that
Paul speaks of his converts as persons who had turned from idolatry to worship
God does not negate or undermine the view that many of his converts were formerly gentile God-fearers.' Although Paul speaks of his converts' past in 'paganism', Hultgren reasons that 'we need not conclude that the persons never had any
associations with synagogues. Their roots may indeed may have been in paganism
and their idolatry recent.' Furthermore, Hultgren observes: 'God-fearers remained
legally gentiles, had a loose relationship to the synagogue, and did not cut off associations with a larger pagan environment.' Wilson (*Related Strangers*, p. 22) notes
that 'in many synagogues in the diaspora Gentiles were a significant and viable
minority presence, the majority of them intrigued by and compliant with Jewish

have some success in luring God-fearing and well-off Gentiles (like Jason?;[35] cf. Titius Justus [Acts 18.7]) away from the synagogue by his preaching and continued to poach on Jewish preserves even after he had been cut off from the synagogue, then it is reasonable to think that he would have provoked a negative Jewish response.[36] Not only would the Jewish community have viewed Gentile adherents as potential prose-lytes, but they would also have valued their financial and social support. While Jewish jealousy or zeal[37] incited by Paul's missionary activity among synagogue adherents only partially explains Paul's conflict with

ways but unwilling to face the social and physical (i.e. circumcision) disadvantages of full proselytization'. Paul's 'idolaters', therefore, may well be Luke's 'God-fearers'. While Luke seemingly viewed Gentile sympathizers of the synagogue as devout and 'pre-prepared', Paul apparently perceived them as godless 'pagans' who had not or would not turn to God (see also, e.g., 1 Thess. 4.5). This suggests that sympathizers could be viewed from two distinctly different angles.

34. Although Paul writes using masculine terminology and does not mention any of the Thessalonian Christians by name (cf. Phil. 4.2), based on the fact that there were a number of women (some of whom appear to have been wealthy) asso-ciated with the Pauline mission elsewhere (see, e.g., Rom. 16.2, 13, 15-16; Phlm. 1-2; Col. 4.15), it is reasonable to think that the same was true in Thessalonica. So also, Hill, *Establishing the Church in Thessalonica*, pp. 212-13. On women in the Pauline churches, see further Florence Morgan-Gillman, *Women Who Knew Paul* (ZSNT; Collegeville, MN: Liturgical Press, 1992). On Macedonian women, consult Lilian Portefaix, *Sisters Rejoice: Paul's Letter to the Philippians and Luke–Acts as Seen by First-Century Philippian Women* (ConBNT, 20; Stockholm: Almqvist & Wiksell, 1988).

35. While some scholars think that Jason was a Jew (e.g. Riesner, *Paul's Early Period*, p. 348), others consider him a Greek (e.g. Meeks, *First Urban Christians*, p. 63). It is now impossible to know for certain.

36. Barrett (*Acts*, II, p. 812) comments, 'The Jews feared that they were losing control of the synagogue and their appeal to religious non-Jews, and objected to the success of the Christian preachers.' Talbert (*Reading Acts*, p. 135) contends that an overlap in missions was one of the reasons for the hostility between establishment Judaism and the Messianists.

John B. Pohill (*Acts* [NAC, 26; Nashville: Broadman Press, 1992], p. 361) remarks, 'The Gentiles' presence in the synagogue probably gave the Jewish com-munity a degree of acceptance in the predominantly Gentile city and probably also some financial support.' So similarly, Haenchen, *Acts*, p. 509.

37. On zealotism in Judaism, see further pp. 165-70 below. Seland (*Establishment Violence*) has shown how pervasive zealotism was among Pales-tinian and Diasporan (particularly Alexandrian) Jews. Cf. Talbert, *Reading Acts*, pp. 68, 134-35, 157.

Thessalonian Jews,[38] it may well have been a primary reason that Paul encountered Jewish opposition in Thessalonica (and elsewhere).[39]

4. *The Reported Attack*

According to Acts 17.5-6, jealous or zealous Thessalonian Jews sought to oppose Paul and Silas by gathering some ruffians in the marketplaces (προσλαβόμενοι τῶν ἀγοραίων ἄνδρας τινὰς πονηρούς), forming a mob (ὀχλοποιήσαντες) and setting the city in an uproar (ἐθορύβουν τὴν πόλιν). The Jews and their enlisted helpers then stormed the house of Jason (ἐπιστάντες τῇ οἰκίᾳ Ἰάσονος) to locate Paul and Silas so that they could bring them before the assembly (προαγαγεῖν εἰς τὸν δῆμον). Once at Jason's house, however, the Jewish-incited mob discovered that the missionaries were not there.[40] So, they dragged Jason and some other believers before the city authorities instead.

Many details of this reported attack require detailed treatment (e.g. the identity of Jason;[41] Lukan crowd creation and control;[42] the mention of the city assembly [δῆμος][43] and local authorities [πολιτάρχαι][44]). However, in keeping with the purpose of this study, here I will compare Luke's report that non-Christian Jews hindered the Pauline mission

38. See further Chapter 7 below.

39. So also Morton Smith, 'The Reason for the Persecution of Paul and the Obscurity of Acts', in E.E. Urback, R.J. Werblowsky and C. Wirszubske (eds.), *Studies in Mysticism and Religion: Presented to Gershom G. Scholem* (Jerusalem: Magnes Press, 1967), pp. 261-68 (264, 268). Cf. Hultgren ('The Self-Definition of Paul', p. 88) who thinks, 'The most probable explanation of Jewish persecution and flogging was that Paul offended leaders of Jewish communities due to some success in evangelizing Jews and God-fearers.'

40. There has been much speculation as to the missionaries' whereabouts. Had they been placed in hiding? Or, did they just happen to be elsewhere when their opponents arrived at Jason's house?

41. See further Morgan-Gillman, 'Jason'.

42. Consult Collins, *Birth of the New Testament*, p. 229 n. 193.

43. Refer to F.F. Bruce, *The Acts of the Apostles: The Greek Text with Introduction and Commentary* (Grand Rapids: Eerdmans; Leicester: Apollos, 3rd edn rev. and enlarged, 1990), p. 370.

44. On the politarchs, see, among others, Ernest De Witt Burton, 'The Politarchs', *AJT* 2 (1898), pp. 598-632, and G.H.R. Horsley, 'The Politarchs', in David Gill and Conrad Gempf (eds.), *The Book of Acts in its Graeco-Roman Setting* (BAFCS, 2; Grand Rapids: Eerdmans; Carlisle: Paternoster Press, 1994), pp. 419-43.

(either directly or indirectly)[45] with Paul's remarks about affliction in 1 Thessalonians.

At least three interpretive options are available to an exegete examining Acts 17.5-10a alongside 1 Thessalonians. One can contend: (1) Acts has misrepresented the conflict; (2) Luke has conflated Paul's and the Thessalonians' conflict; or (3) Acts does not take into account the church's suffering of which Paul speaks in 1 Thessalonians (1.6; 2.14; 3.3-4; cf. 2 Thess. 1.4-7). I will treat these alternatives in turn.

Some commentators contend that Acts 17.5-10a reveals more about Lukan apology than about Paul's Thessalonian ministry.[46] In discounting the account, critics note that it 'is in keeping with [Luke's] usual style of inculpating the Jews while exculpating the Gentiles'.[47] Interpreters also appeal to 1 Thess. 2.14, where Paul compares the suffering that the Thessalonian Christians had experienced at the hands of their fellow Gentiles to the suffering that Judean Christians had endured from their fellow Jews.[48] I would not deny that Luke tends to focus upon Jewish opposition to Paul both here and elsewhere.[49] Nor would I refute that Paul speaks of Gentile opposition for his Gentile converts in 1 Thess. 2.14. However, it is not necessary to discount Luke's report that Paul was a target of Jewish hostility in Thessalonica, especially in light of Paul's own comments in 1 Thess. 2.15-16.[50]

45. Although it is unclear exactly who is carrying out the attack and making the accusations (see Johnson, *Acts*, p. 307), in Luke's understanding the Thessalonian Jews are ultimately responsible for the riot (so rightly Cunningham, *'Through Many Tribulations'*, pp. 255-56).

46. Collins (*Birth of the New Testament*, p. 36) thinks Luke 'is more interested in the conversion of some Gentiles and the Jews' growing hostility to the gospel than he is in the real situation of the church in Thessalonica'. See also, e.g., Haenchen, *Acts*, pp. 513-14; Lührmann, 'Beginnings of the Church', p. 243; Lüdemann, *Traditions in Acts*, p. 185; and Sanders, *Schismatics, Sectarians, Dissidents, Deviants*, p. 264 nn. 36-37.

47. Chris U. Manus, 'Luke's Account of Paul in Thessalonica (Acts 17:1-9)', in Collins (ed.), *The Thessalonian Correspondence*, pp. 27-38 (36).

48. E.g. Haenchen, *Acts*, p. 513. See further pp. 218-26 below.

49. See Cunningham, *'Through Many Tribulations'*, pp. 257-58. Non-Christian Gentiles presumably played a larger role in Paul's departure from the city than Acts (or, for that matter, 1 Thess.) suggests. Even though Paul's opposition was seemingly Jewish in origin, it was the politarchs' action against Jason and other Thessalonian believers which seemingly necessitated Paul's premature departure from the city.

50. For fuller argumentation, see pp. 130-37 below.

Might it be that Luke has woven disparate conflicts into his condensed account? Some interpreters think so. They propound that although Jews incited the riot against Paul and Silas, it was actually Gentiles who took action against Jason and the believers.[51] This leads this group of commentators to conclude that Luke has combined the apostles' conflict with Thessalonian Jews and the Christians' clash with their Gentile compatriots.[52] Although the Acts account is ambiguous regarding who actually carried out the attack and leveled the accusations against Jason and 'some of the brothers', three observations about 17.5-10a are in order here: (1) Jews are said to be responsible for organizing the opposition (17.5); (2) Paul and Silas were clearly the focus of the attack and accusations (note αὐτούς in 17.5, 6); (3) The Jewish-incited uproar is the reported reason that Paul and Silas had to leave Thessalonica (17.10a). These details seem to suggest that Luke is interested in reporting the Jewish reaction to the missionaries and that he is not thinking of the church's opposition from fellow Gentiles of which Paul speaks in 1 Thessalonians.[53]

It seems best to conclude, then, that either Luke was not informed about the Thessalonian Christians' conflict with their fellow Gentiles or that he was aware of it and was not predisposed (for whatever reason[s])[54] to elaborate upon it. The suggestion follows that Paul was likely not speaking of the events recorded in Acts 17.5-10a when he refers to his converts' affliction,[55] although it is probable that such an

51. See, e.g., C.F.D. Moule, *The Birth of the New Testament* (London: A. & C. Black, 3rd rev. edn, 1982), p. 158; Bicknell, *Thessalonians*, p. 27; Morris, *Thessalonians*, p. 82; Pohill, *Acts*, p. 361; and Morgan-Gillman, 'Jason', p. 44. Each of these commentators is seeking to explain the Acts account in light of Paul's statement in 1 Thess. 2.14.

52. Jewett (*Thessalonian Correspondence*, pp. 116-18) contends that the accusations made and the actions taken against Jason and the believers arose from developments among the Thessalonian church after Paul had departed. Cf. similarly Morgan-Gillman, 'Jason', p. 48.

53. Jason and the other believers appear in Luke's account because of their association with Paul. Haenchen (*Acts*, p. 508 n. 3) rightly notes that the Acts narrative 'deals with the danger in which Paul found himself, and not with Jason or his bail'.

54. Might Luke be interested in demonstrating that it is Jews (in league with the local riff-raff), not Christians (who find allies among the elite), who stir up trouble?

55. So also Dobschütz, *Thessalonicherbriefe*, pp. 109-10, and Bruce, *Thessalonians*, p. 16.

episode would have exacerbated the church's ongoing conflict with Gentile outsiders.[56] (If Paul was thinking of the incident recorded in Acts when he mentions his converts' conflict, then he apparently held Gentiles responsible for the riot and its aftermath.) As for the reported Jewish opposition to Paul in Thessalonica, I am inclined to think that it is historical, even if one does not regard every detail in Luke's narrative to be so. I will argue in Chapter 6 that 1 Thessalonians 2 alludes to Paul's conflict with Thessalonian Jewry.

5. *The Recorded Accusations*

Once Jason and some other believers had been dragged before the politarchs, Luke places on the lips of Thessalonian Jews (and those from the *agora* they had enlisted for support) the following charges: 'These men who have disturbed the empire [οἱ τὴν οἰκουμένην ἀναστατώσαντες οὗτοι][57] have come here also, and Jason has received them; and they are all acting against the decrees of Caesar [τῶν δογμάτων Καίσαρος], saying there is another king [or emperor (βασιλέα)], Jesus.'[58] Although the number of and the nature of the accusations are not altogether clear, it appears that (at least) two charges are leveled against Paul and Silas, and by extension, those people associated with them, that is, Jason and 'some of the brothers'. The missionaries who had been welcomed by Jason into his home[59] are charged, in effect, with disrupting the social order through their ministry (which was now taking place in Thessalonica!) and with defying

---

56. See similarly, Kirsopp Lake and Henry J. Cadbury, *The Acts of the Apostles. IV. English Translation and Commentary* (The Beginnings of Christianity, 1; Grand Rapids: Baker Book House, 1965), p. 206; Harry W. Tajra, *The Trial of St. Paul: A Juridical Exegesis of the Second Half of the Acts of the Apostles* (WUNT, 35; Tübingen: J.C.B. Mohr [Paul Siebeck, 1989), p. 44; and Bruce, *Thessalonians*, p. 16.

57. In support of this translation of οἱ τὴν οἰκουμένην ἀναστατώσαντες οὗτοι see Johnson, *Acts*, p. 307, and H.U. Weitbrecht Stanton, ' "Turned the World upside down" ', *ExpTim* 44 (1932–33), pp. 526-27.

58. Jews level similar charges against Jesus before Pilate in Lk. 23.2, 5 (cf. Jn 19.12, 15).

59. Jason apparently extended hospitality to Paul and the Thessalonian church. It may be that Paul lived at Jason's residence for a portion of his Thessalonian mission.

the decrees of Caesar through their message.[60] Here I will seek to determine if Luke merely creates these charges or if such allegations could realistically have arisen during Paul's Thessalonian mission.

Some commentators aver that the accusations are Lukan inventions which are totally divorced from Paul's ministry in Thessalonica. For example, Wolfgang Stegemann argues that the charges recorded in 17.6-7 are best understood as Luke's attempt to exonerate Christianity of involvement with Jewish insurrectionist movements during Domitian's reign.[61] While Luke may have re-worded the original allegations leveled against Paul *et al.*, I will argue below that Paul's mission and message in Thessalonica provide an adequate *Sitz im Leben* for the basic content of the accusations.

The first charge (i.e. that the missionaries had disrupted the empire) is difficult to interpret.[62] Apparently, the allegation was that Paul and Silas had created social upheaval elsewhere and were now responsible for fomenting public turmoil in Thessalonica, as evidenced by the disturbance at hand.[63] In light of the second, more concrete accusation, the initial allegation might have also been political in orientation.[64] If the

---

60. I take the final clause of 17.7 (βασιλέα ἕτερον λέγοντες εἶναι Ἰησοῦν) to be an explanation of the charge (οὗτοι πάντες ἀπέναντι τῶν δογμάτων Καίσαρος πράσσουσιν). So also Pohill, *Acts*, p. 362, Talbert, *Reading Acts*, p. 157; and Barrett, *Acts*, II, p. 816.

61. See Stegemann, *Zwischen Synagoge und Obrigkeit*, pp. 226-37. For a critique of Stegemann's suggestion, see Riesner, *Paul's Early Period*, pp. 342-44.

62. Pohill (*Acts*, p. 362) describes the charge as 'nebulous'.

63. Could it be that Paul's Jewish detractors in Thessalonica were aware of the trouble that he had created or encountered in Philippi (see 1 Thess. 2.2; cf. Acts 16.19-40) and elsewhere? Tajra (*The Trial of St. Paul*, p. 35) suggests, 'The Jewish leadership is charging Paul with causing disarray and commotion in their communities all over the world.'

64. Pohill (*Acts*, p. 362 n. 59) suggests that 'ἀναστατόω can mean *to stir up sedition, be a political agitator*' (emphasis his). So also Bruce, *Acts of the Apostles*, p. 371. Furthermore, Bruce remarks (p. 371) that outbreaks of Jewish unrest in Judea, Alexandria and Rome around this time might have stood behind such an allegation and that 'The authorities could not be expected to distinguish the militant messianism of the Jewish nationalists from the messianism proclaimed by Paul and Silas.' Cf. Riesner, *Paul's Early Years*, pp. 356-58. E.A. Judge ('The Decrees of Thessalonica' *RTR* 30 [1971], pp. 1-7 [7]) suggests, 'There may have been an imperial edict covering Jewish messianic agitation which the Thessalonian informers invoked.' Judge goes on to state, however, that 'accusations of disturbing the

general nature of the first charge lends credence to the view that the recorded accusations are Lukan inventions, the particular content of the second allegation (i.e. that Paul and the others were 'acting contrary to the decrees of Caesar') suggests that Luke was drawing upon reliable tradition when framing the charges.[65]

The second accusation immediately raises at least two important questions: (1) What are the decrees of Caesar which Paul *et al.* are charged with defying? (2) How were Paul and those associated with him thought to be guilty of violating such decrees? The first question has generated a fair amount of discussion. Some commentators contend that the Christians were charged with sedition (*maiestas*),[66] 'an offense against public law that required no special decree of Caesar to make it illegal'.[67] Other interpreters,[68] following E.A. Judge, think that Paul and his associates were deemed guilty of violating particular decrees, namely oaths of loyalty to the emperor which inhabitants of the empire were required to take.[69] Judge posits that the Thessalonian politarchs would have been responsible for enforcing such decrees on a local level.[70] While Judge may well have pinpointed the type of decrees

peace in general were always a good lever to open a case, which here rests on other grounds'.

65. So also Morgan-Gillman ('Jason', p. 45) who observes that this is a unique charge of which Paul is accused nowhere else in Acts. Judge ('Decrees of Caesar', p. 1) criticizes A.N. Sherwin-White (*Roman Society and Roman Law in the New Testament* [Oxford: Clarendon Press, 1963], pp. 96, 103) for suggesting that the accusation is 'possibly garbled' and 'the most confused of the various descriptions of the charges in Acts...' Judge maintains that Acts is remarkably accurate on legal and political issues and regards the difficulty of the charge as an argument for its authenticity.

66. See, e.g., J.B. Lightfoot, 'The Church of Thessalonica', in *idem, Biblical Essays* (London: Macmillan, 1893), pp. 253-69 (262); Haenchen, *Acts*, p. 510; Stegemann, *Zwischen Synagoge und Obrigkeit*, p. 237; and Tajra, *The Trial of St. Paul*, p. 36.

67. Bruce, *Acts of the Apostles*, p. 371.

68. See, e.g., Donfried, 'The Cults of Thessalonica', pp. 342-44; Morgan-Gillman, 'Jason', pp. 45-46; Manus, 'Luke's Account', pp. 33-34; and Collins, *Birth of the New Testament*, p. 35.

69. Judge ('Decrees of Caesar', pp. 3-5) cites two texts from Dio Cassius (56.25.5-6; 57.15.8) referring to imperial decrees limiting or prohibiting predictions which he thinks might be identifiable with the 'decrees of Caesar'.

70. To support this suggestion, Judge ('Decrees of Caesar', pp. 6-7) refers to a Paphalagonian oath of personal loyalty to Caesar's household (text found in

envisioned in 17.7 and how they were enforced locally, it is now impossible to determine with any degree of certainty the δογμάτα Καίσαρος in view here.[71] Nevertheless, the allegation that Paul and his followers were in one way or another flouting the rule(s) of Caesar would have been a particularly appropriate and serious charge in Thessalonica, a city which at that time had an acute interest in procuring and maintaining Roman favor.[72]

How might such an accusation arise? Some of the eschatological elements in Paul's preaching at Thessalonica may well have given rise to the charge that the Christians were setting up Jesus as a rival to Caesar.[73] If 1 (and 2) Thessalonians are at all indicative of Paul's proclamation in the city, then there are indeed aspects of his message which could have been (mis)construed in an overtly political way.[74] While preaching in Thessalonica, it is likely that Paul spoke of a God who called people into his kingdom (βασιλεία, 2.12; cf. 2 Thess. 1.5) through his Son, the Lord Jesus Christ, who had died and rose again (4.14) and would soon come (παρουσία) from heaven bringing both wrath and salvation (1.9-10; 4.13–5.11; cf. 2 Thess. 1.5–2.12).[75] If

V. Ehrenberg and A.H.M. Jones, *Documents Illustrating the Reigns of Augustus and Tiberius* [Oxford: Clarendon Press, 1949], p. 315) and to a Cypriot oath of allegiance to Tiberius on his assumption of power (for the text, see T.B. Mitford, 'A Cypriot Oath of Allegiance to Tiberius', *JRS* 1 [1930], pp. 75-79). Judge also notes an inscription from Samos where the local magistrates assumed responsibility for administering an oath of loyalty in 5 BCE (text in P. Herrmann, 'Inschriften aus dem Heraion von Samos', *MDAIAA* 77 [1962], pp. 306-27).

71. So also Barrett, *Acts*, II, p. 816.

72. So similarly Riesner, *Paul's Early Years*, p. 357. On Thessalonica's relations with Rome, see esp. the study by Holland Lee Hendrix, 'Thessalonicans Honor Romans' (ThD dissertation, Harvard University, 1984).

73. So also, e.g., Judge, 'Decrees of Caesar', pp. 2-3; Lake and Cadbury, *Acts*, IV, p. 206; Bruce, *Acts of the Apostles*, pp. 371-72; Donfried, 'The Cults of Thessalonica', p. 344; Morgan-Gillman, 'Jason', p. 45; Riesner, *Paul's Early Period*, p. 357; and Pheme Perkins, '1 Thessalonians and Hellenistic Religious Practices', in Horgan and Kobelski (eds.), *To Touch the Text*, pp. 325-34 (328). Lightfoot ('The Church of Thessalonica', pp. 262-63 n. 8) remarks that the correlation between Paul's proclamation as evidenced in Thessalonian letters and the accusation recorded in Acts is 'an undesigned coincidence of a striking kind...'

74. For a fuller reconstruction of Paul's proclamation in Thessalonica, see pp. 233-34. On the political nuances of Paul's proclamation in Thessalonica, see pp. 260-66.

75. In Rev. such eschatological language is indeed politically subversive as

taken out of context, such language could arouse suspicion and prompt the type of accusation recorded in 17.7.[76] Although the eschatological character of Paul's message is not readily apparent from Luke's succinct and stylized summary of his synagogue preaching in 17.3,[77] it is probable that eschatology, not unlike what one finds in Paul's letter(s) to the Thessalonians, would have been a central part of Paul's proclamation to Jew and Gentile alike. It seems likely, then, that the eschatological language of Paul's Gospel in general and the talk of Jesus as Lord in particular would have served as fodder for the accusation that the Christians were defying Caesar's decrees.[78]

Klaus Wengst (*Pax Romana and the Peace of Jesus Christ* [trans. John Bowden; London: SCM Press, 1987], pp. 118-135), among others, rightly notes.

76. We know that Romans were anxious about the activity of 'soothsayers' and 'diviners'. See esp. Ramsey MacMullen, *Enemies of the Roman Order: Treason, Unrest, and Alienation in the Empire* (Cambridge, MA: Harvard University Press; London: Oxford University Press, 1966), pp. 128-62. According to Dio Cassius (56.25.5-6), Augustus prohibited inquiries into and predictions about anyone's death (particularly the emperor's!). Tiberius is reported to have forbidden all divination and to have put to death all foreigners and banished all citizens who practiced the art after he had issued his decree (Dio Cassius, 57.15.8). Tacitus (*Ann.* 2.27-32) records that Libo Drusus was prosecuted for predicting the future. Given the Roman influence on Thessalonica and the city's desire to honor Rome and its rulers, one can imagine that talk of a Lord who had died and rose again, who had a kingdom and who was soon to return to execute justice would not have been embraced enthusiastically by all.

77. Also observed by F.J. Foakes-Jackson, *The Acts of the Apostles* (MNTC; London: Hodder & Stoughton, 1931), p. 161. For a treatment of Paul's preaching based upon 1 and 2 Thess. and Acts 17.2-4, see Dieter Werner Kemmler, *Faith and Human Reason: A Study of Paul's Method of Preaching as Illustrated by 1–2 Thessalonians and Acts 17,2-4* (NovTSup, 50; Leiden: E.J. Brill, 1975).

78. Barrett (*Acts*, II, p. 816) remarks, 'There may not have been a decree specifically to this effect [i.e. a decree prohibiting the proclamation of a rival emperor], but [Christian declaration of an(other) emperor] would hardly be encouraged by the reigning emperor. The charge was one that could readily be used against the Christians; the term βασιλεία τοῦ θεοῦ runs deep into gospel tradition and must have found its way from time to time into Christian preaching, especially in the synagogue. The preachers could hardly deny that they were proclaiming Jesus as βασιλεύς; Lk 23.2 shows how dangerous this could be and Jn 18.36 may reflect explanations that Christians found it necessary to give.'

6. *The Purported Outcomes*

According to Luke, the accusations against the Christians had three effects: (1) They disturbed both the people and the politarchs (17.8); (2) They prompted the politarchs to require Jason and the others to post bond before releasing them (17.9); (3) They led the Thessalonian Christians to send Paul and Silas away from the city immediately (17.10a). As for the first reported outcome of the allegations, it will suffice to say that an agitated response on the part of the people and the politarchs is within the realm of reason.[79] The second and third consequences which Acts records require further comment.

Luke claims that before the politarchs released Jason and the others that they took security from them (ἱκανὸν λαβεῖν = *satis accipere*). Although the narrative details in 17.9 are in all likelihood historical,[80] one is left to wonder precisely what the posting of bail entailed. Presumably, 'By exacting the payment of security, the Politarchs made Jason legally responsible for Paul and Silas. [And they ruled that] the bond would be forfeited and Jason hauled into court anew in the event of any recurring trouble involving the two apostles.'[81]

Commentators often suggest on the basis of Paul's statement in 1 Thess. 2.18 ('We wanted to come to you—I, Paul, again and again—but Satan hindered us') that Jason was ordered by the politarchs to see that Paul and Silas left the city and did not return.[82] However, Paul's remarks in 2.17–3.10 suggest a repeatedly anticipated, yet theretofore thwarted, return to Thessalonica. It is doubtful that Paul would have attempted to return to Thessalonica time and again (καὶ ἅπαξ καὶ δίς, 2.18) if he thought that his visit would have endangered his converts. Therefore, it seems more likely that (an)other now unknown factor(s)

---

79. Riesner (*Paul's Early Period*, p. 357) contends, 'The agitation of the politarchs and of other citizens...was understandable insofar as both this accusation [i.e. 'they are all acting contrary to the decrees of Caesar'] and the mob scene could potentially cost the city its legal privileges as well as its relationships with Roman patrons.'

80. See, e.g., Lüdemann, *Traditions in Acts*, pp. 187-88.

81. Tajra, *The Trial of St. Paul*, p. 43. So similarly Sherwin-White, *Roman Society and Roman Law*, pp. 95-96.

82. So, e.g., Ramsay, *St. Paul the Traveller*, p. 231; Bruce, *Acts of the Apostles*, p. 372; and cautiously Riesner, *Paul's Early Years*, p. 359.

kept Paul from returning to the Thessalonian church.[83]

Interpreters have noted that the action taken by the politarchs was quite mild given the gravity of the charges leveled against the Christians.[84] Might it be that Luke has modified the magistrates' decision in an attempt to preserve the reputation of the Christian movement?[85] I am inclined to think that Luke is correct in reporting the politarchs' response.[86] After all, according to Acts, the persons thought to be directly responsible for the unrest were not even present.[87] 1 Thessalonians indicates that Paul's converts suffered considerable affliction from their fellow Gentiles. It may be, then, that the public accusations resulted in further political sanctions for Paul's converts and heightened Gentile opposition to the church.[88]

The other outcome of the uproar recorded by Luke is the departure of the missionaries from the city. In light of the circumstances, the believers apparently thought that it was unwise for the apostles to remain in the city. Acts reports that the Christians immediately sent Paul and Silas away by night to Berea (17.10a; cf. 1 Thess. 2.15c, 17a).[89] It is likely that Paul also perceived the non-Christian opposition to himself and his converts to be a very real threat. For according to Acts, Paul remains for a substantial amount of time both in Corinth (18.18) and in Ephesus (19.8-10) after having encountered Jewish resistance. This does not appear to have been the case in Thessalonica. Additionally, if Luke may

83. So also D.E.H. Whiteley, *Thessalonians in the Revised Standard Version, with Introduction and Commentary* (London: Oxford University Press, 1969), pp. 49-50; Morris, *Thessalonians*, p. 6; and Morgan-Gillman, 'Jason', pp. 47-48.

84. E.g. Tajra, *The Trial of St. Paul*, p. 44.

85. On politics in Luke–Acts, see esp. Esler, *Community and Gospel in Luke–Acts*, pp. 201-19.

86. Riesner (*Paul's Early Years*, p. 358) wonders if the politarchs' response was not a 'diplomatic measure, first, to assuage the agitated city populace and, second, to keep a potential source of unrest at a distance'.

87. Also noted by Lake and Cadbury, *Acts*, IV, p. 206. Riesner (*Paul's Early Period*, p. 358) suggests that because the charges were in fact false 'Even a complete acquittal by the politarchs would have been possible.'

88. Cf. similarly Tajra, *The Trial of St. Paul*, p. 44, and Bruce, *Thessalonians*, p. 16. Ramsay (*St. Paul the Traveller*, p. 229) writes, 'It would appear that the riot was more serious than the words of Luke at first sight suggest. The language of Paul in his first letter to the Thessalonians, II 14-16 shows that a powerful, dangerous, and lasting sentiment was roused among the classes which made the riot.'

89. Johnson (*Acts*, p. 307) observes that a good amount of activity in Acts takes place at night. See also, e.g., 5.19; 9.25; 12.6; 16.33; 23.31.

be followed in reporting that Thessalonian Jews also caused trouble for Paul in Berea (17.13; cf. 14.19), then this further highlights the intensity of the Thessalonian Jews' hostility toward Paul and his ministry.

7. *Conclusion*

Although Luke's account of Paul's entry into and exit from Thessalonica has been judged as largely unreliable due to its alleged anachronistic and anti-Jewish character,[90] my study of this pericope had led me to conclude that it is likely to be accurate along the following lines: (1) Paul's contact with Thessalonian Jews in their synagogue; (2) Paul's success in converting Gentile sympathizers to Judaism; (3) Paul's conflict with Thessalonian Jews during his stay in that city; (4) Jason's and other Thessalonian believers' appearance before the politarchs due to their association with Paul; (5) The charge leveled against the Christians of defying (by their preaching?) Caesar; (6) Paul's untimely departure from the city due to Jewish opposition.

This is not to suggest that the Acts account is void of Lukan stylization. Luke's hand *may* be detected in: (1) The report that Paul first went to the synagogue according to his custom; (2) The summation of Paul's preaching in the synagogue; (3) The conversion of some Jews; (4) The extent of Paul's success in winning God-fearers and 'leading women'; (5) The motivation for Jewish opposition (i.e. jealousy, if Luke indeed intended ζηλόειν to be construed negatively); (6) The way that the Jews are said to have enlisted support for opposing Paul; (7) The precise wording of the charges; (8) The reaction of the people and politarchs upon hearing the accusations; (9) The departure of the missionaries by night.

In short, Acts' account of the conflict at Thessalonica is not in any way comprehensive. It is a highly condensed and simplified narrative which focuses upon Paul. Despite the fact that Luke's narrative is incomplete and shaped by his own interests, it appears to be accurate in reporting that Paul was forced to leave Thessalonica because of conflict with his fellow Jews. Acts 17.5-10a also points to a likely cause of the Christians' clash with non-Christian Gentiles, namely the suspicion that the believers were politically subversive. Since Paul's banishment from

90. Note, e.g., the remarks of Manus, 'Luke's Account', p. 34.

Thessalonica at Jewish hands and his politically provocative proclamation in Thessalonica (which likely led to [further] conflict between his converts and their Gentile compatriots) is strongly implied in 1 Thessalonians,[91] one may reasonably argue that Luke is *at least* correct on these two issues and that his account may be used to supplement this study at these particular points.

91. I thereby comply with the strict standards of Sanders ('Christians and Jews', p. 435).

Part II

THE SOCIAL-SCIENTIFIC STUDY OF DEVIANCE AND CONFLICT

Chapter 4

THE SOCIOLOGICAL STUDY OF DEVIANCE

1. *Introduction*

Having treated disputed texts in Part I above, I now turn to discuss the social-scientific study of deviance (Chapter 4) and conflict (Chapter 5). In this part of my work I will thoroughly survey these complex disciplines of social study so that I might intelligibly and responsibly employ theoretical insights gleaned from these fields in Parts III–IV below.[1]

Even though I make explicit use of the social sciences in this study, I do not attempt to create a 'model' as a grid through which to run texts.[2]

1. Superficial knowledge and slipshod application of social theory is a glaring weakness in many biblical studies which seek to employ the social sciences. So rightly Bruce J. Malina and Jerome H. Neyrey, *Calling Jesus Names: The Social Value of Labels in Matthew* (FFSF; Sonoma, CA: Polebridge Press, 1988), p. 35. The scope of this project prohibits a review and critique of how exegetes have (mis)used the social sciences. But see Stanley Kent Stowers, 'The Social Sciences and the Study of Early Christianity', in William Scott Green (ed.), *Approaches to Ancient Judaism. V. Studies in Judaism and its Greco-Roman Context* (BJS, 32; Atlanta: Scholars Press, 1985), pp. 149-81. See also Brian S. Rosner, ' "That Pattern of Teaching": Issues and Essays in Pauline Ethics', in Brian S. Rosner (ed.), *Understanding Paul's Ethics: Twentieth-Century Approaches* (Grand Rapids: Eerdmans; Carlisle: Paternoster Press, 1995), pp. 1-23 (14-15).

2. Contrast Malina and Neyrey, *Calling Jesus Names*, and Jerome H. Neyrey (ed.), *The Social World of Luke-Acts: Models for Interpretation* (Peabody, MA: Hendrickson, 1991). See also many of the essays in Esler (ed.), *Modelling Early Christianity*. Sometimes the term 'model' is used interchangeably with or alongside the word 'theory' (so, e.g., Elliott, *Social-Scientific Criticism, passim*). If 'modeling' is conceived as using social-scientific theory to support and supplement exegetical research, then what one encounters in this volume may be described as 'modeling'. However, if by 'model' one means a simplified representation or generalized 'map' of reality used for purposes of control or prediction (see Elliott, *Social-Scientific Criticism*, pp. 40-48), then I would suggest that the way I am seek-

Nevertheless, like those biblical scholars who do engage in model-building, I view the social sciences as heuristic devices that can help interpreters to notice social aspects in texts, to formulate fresh questions to ask of texts and to gain new angles of vision for reading texts. The ensuing survey of the social-scientific study of deviance and conflict is undertaken to gain theoretical tools for an exegetical task.[3]

At this point it is necessary to indicate why I think it is appropriate to apply deviance and conflict theories to this study. In this project I am arguing that Paul and the Thessalonian Christians experienced conflict relations with outsiders. Non-Christian opposition of Paul and his converts suggests that unbelievers perceived them as different and viewed such difference negatively. Deviance theories can shed light on how and why cultures identify individuals as deviants, oppose those considered deviant and enter into conflict over societal norms. Conflict theories allow a fuller understanding of the characteristics and dynamics of discordant social interaction. Theoretical principles drawn from the social-scientific study of deviance and conflict, then, are particularly well-suited for this project.

In this chapter I will discuss the sociological study of deviance.[4] To begin, I will note how other New Testament scholars have employed deviance theory. I will then offer a broad survey of the sociology of deviance before turning to a more detailed discussion of three particular deviance theories. Having done so, I will be in a position to offer a definition of deviance and to explain the deviance process. By way of conclusion, I will pose some questions raised by this survey which I will address as this study unfolds.

---

ing to employ the social sciences herein is not 'modeling'. I seek to use social-scientific theory for descriptive or illustrative purposes, not generative or predictive ones. Although the theories I employ in this project are, of course, modern abstractions, ancient literary and non-literary data contextualize theorizing and curb broad-sweeping generalizations.

3.   On applying general theoretical principles to particular historical contexts and on the relationship between sociology and history, see Horrell, *Social Ethos of the Corinthian Correspondence*, pp. 26-31, and Jack T. Sanders, 'Paul between Jews and Gentiles in Corinth', *JSNT* 65 (1997), pp. 67-83 (76-77).

4.   Although sociologists have dominated the discussion of deviance, anthropologists have begun to show some interest in the subject. See Morris Freilich, Douglas Raybeck and Joel Savishinsky (eds.), *Deviance: Anthropological Perspectives* (New York: Bergin & Garvey, 1991). Here I will focus upon the sociological study of deviance because it has been developed in greater depth and detail.

2. *Deviance Theory in New Testament Studies*

A number of New Testament interpreters have employed insights from
the interactionist or 'labeling' perspective of deviant behavior in their
work.[5] These scholars include Bruce J. Malina and Jerome H. Neyrey,
Anthony J. Saldarini, Jack T. Sanders, John M.G. Barclay and Andrew
McGowan. Malina and Neyrey have applied this particular perspective
to narrative episodes in the Gospels of Matthew and Luke,[6] while Saldarini[7] and Sanders[8] have drawn upon labeling theory to discuss the

---

5.   On labeling theory, see pp. 94-98 below. In a pioneering effort, David E.
Aune ('Magic in Early Christianity', *ANRW* II.23.2, pp. 1507-77 [1514-16]) used
the *anomie* theory of deviance in explaining the phenomenon of magic in early
Christianity.
   Interestingly, there are distinct correlations between Jewett's explanation of why
the Thessalonians were converted and the *anomie* theory of deviant behavior. Jewett thinks that the Thessalonian church was comprised of free artisans and small
traders who were 'suffering from a degree of relative deprivation' (*Thessalonian
Correspondence*, p. 121). According to Jewett, this state of economic dislocation
coupled with the cooptation of the Cabiric cult by the Thessalonian elite led to their
conversion. Stated differently, Jewett believes that the economic and religious woes
of these working class people made Paul's apocalyptic message particularly appealing. The emphasis that Jewett places on economic factors in the Thessalonians'
conversion is akin to the strain (or *anomie*) theory of deviance as developed by
Robert K. Merton (*Social Theory and Social Structure* [New York: Free Press, rev.
edn, 1957], pp. 131-94). Simplistically stated, Merton maintained that lower class
people are more likely to engage in deviant behavior. Sociologists have shown that
Merton's theory is unsustainable. See, e.g., Rodney Stark, *Sociology* (Belmont, CA:
Wadsworth, 5th edn, 1994), pp. 188-89. On the Thessalonians' conversion, see
pp. 229-32 below.
   While Jewett seems to think that the Thessalonian congregation was viewed as
socially deviant, he does not apply deviance theory to his study. Although Jewett
thinks other Thessalonians perceived Paul's converts to be 'politically provocative'
(p. 132), he is not particularly interested in the relations of the Thessalonian Christians with outsiders. Instead, he focuses upon the internal dynamics of the congregation, convinced that there was a significant amount of internal dissension being
created by the ἄτακτοι, Jewett's millenarian radicals.
6.   Malina and Neyrey, *Calling Jesus Names*, chapters 2–3, and 'Conflict in
Luke–Acts: Labelling and Deviance Theory', in Neyrey (ed.), *The Social World of
Luke–Acts*, pp. 97-122.
7.   Anthony J. Saldarini, 'The Gospel of Matthew and Jewish–Christian Conflict', in David L. Balch (ed.), *The Social History of the Matthean Community* (Minneapolis: Fortress Press, 1991), pp. 38-61, and *Matthew's Christian–Jewish*

parting of the ways between Judaism and Christianity.[9] Barclay has applied this approach to deviance in his study of 'apostasy' in the first century CE,[10] and McGowan has viewed accusations of cannibalism against Christians in the second century CE through the lens of labeling theory.[11] Meanwhile, Gerald Harris has utilized other concepts drawn from the sociological study of deviance in exploring Paul's instruction of excommunication in the case of πορνεία in 1 Corinthians 5.[12]

Although these studies differ in their contents, claims,[13] coherence[14] and competence,[15] collectively they illustrate how potentially fruitful

Community (CSHJ; Chicago: University of Chicago Press, 1994), esp. pp. 107-16.

8. Sanders, *Schismatics, Sectarians, Dissidents, Deviants*, esp. pp. 129-49.

9. While Saldarini ('Jewish-Christian Conflict' and *Matthew's Christian-Jewish Community*) focuses specifically on the relations between Christian Jews in Matthew's community and non-Christian Jews, Sanders (*Schismatics, Sectarians, Dissidents, Deviants*) is interested in applying deviance theory to the relations between Jews and Christian Jews in Palestine up until 135 CE.

10. Barclay, 'Deviance and Apostasy', pp. 114-27.

11. Andrew J. McGowan, 'Eating People: Accusations of Cannibalism against Christians in the Second Century', *JECS* 2 (1994), pp. 413-42.

12. Gerald Harris, 'The Beginnings of Church Discipline: 1 Corinthians 5', *NTS* 37 (1991), pp. 1-21.

13. For instance, Sanders (*Schismatics, Sectarians, Dissidents, Deviants*, p. 150) thinks that deviance theory as developed by Kai Erikson (*Wayward Puritans: A Study in the Sociology of Deviance* [New York: John Wiley & Sons, 1966]) provides the answer to the enigma of why there was conflict between early mainstream Judaism and Jewish Christianity in Palestine. On the other hand, Barclay ('Deviance and Apostasy', p. 118) is content to speak of the interactionist perspective as a 'sensitizing concept' and does not attempt to crack little historical nuts with large sociological hammers. Cf. Harris, 'The Beginnings of Church Discipline', p. 12.

14. For example, it remains unclear to me what Malina and Neyrey (*Calling Jesus Names* and 'Conflict in Luke–Acts') accomplish historically by applying labeling theory to the trial narratives of Matthew and Luke.

15. Saldarini ('Jewish-Christian Conflict') does not appear to understand the deviance and labeling process as set forth by Erikson (*Wayward Puritans*). Erikson demonstrates in his study that boundaries are erected by the norm-abiding majority to exclude the norm-breaking minority. Although appealing to Erikson (who Saldarini refers to as 'Ericson') all the while, Saldarini concludes that Jews in Matthew's community remained part of Judaism. This begs the question that labeling theory is meant to address, namely in the perception of whom? While some Jews might have considered Matthew's community within Judaism, other Jews who were not believers in Jesus would have judged the Matthean Christians to be apostate.

deviance theory can be in studying New Testament texts and Christian origins. I have profited from reading my predecessors and hope to build upon their work in this volume. A survey of the sociological study of deviance is an appropriate place to begin.

3. *The Sociology of Deviance*

The following survey will not be and need not be exhaustive. A number of sociologists have written introductions to the study of deviance, and I will not attempt to duplicate their efforts here.[16] Nevertheless, since the sociology of deviance is a complex academic discipline with multiple perspectives,[17] it will be useful to survey the field in enough detail to see where the particular theories upon which I will focus in this project fit in the grand scheme of deviance study.

One may divide deviance theories into three broad theoretical categories: biological, psychological and sociological.[18] My interest is in the sociological study of deviance. Although there seems to be an increased openness among some sociologists to allow for biological and psychological explanations of deviant behavior, sociologists remain justifiably convinced that physical and mental theories of deviance are limited in their explanatory power.[19] Furthermore, given the nature of the data being treated in this project and the inaccessibility of the subjects being studied for observation and testing, we may pass over the biological and psychological theories of deviance with no further comment.

16. Some surveys on deviance which I have found particularly helpful include: Marshall B. Clinard and Robert F. Meier, *Sociology of Deviant Behavior* (New York: Rinehart & Winston, 6th edn, 1985); Larry J. Siegel, *Criminology* (St Paul, MN: West, 4th edn, 1992); Stephen J. Pfohl, *Images of Deviance and Social Control: A Sociological History* (New York: McGraw–Hill, 2nd edn, 1994); and Alex Thio, *Deviant Behavior* (New York: HarperCollins, 4th edn, 1995). Furthermore, most introductions to sociology contain a section on deviant behavior. Two such texts are: J. Ross Eshleman and Barbara G. Cashion, *Sociology: An Introduction* (Boston: Little, Brown & Co., 1983), pp. 148-77, and Stark, *Sociology*, pp. 174-206.

17. Thio (*Deviant Behavior*, p. 4) quips, 'the study of deviant behavior is probably the most "deviant" of all the subjects in sociology'.

18. So, e.g., Eshleman and Cashion, *Sociology*, p. 159.

19. For a succinct survey and critique of the biological and psychological perspectives of deviance, see Edwin H. Pfuhl, Jr, *The Deviance Process* (New York: Van Nostrand, 1980), pp. 38-48.

Sociologists categorize deviance in a variety of ways. Some scholars, like Alex Thio, speak of positivist and humanist theories of deviance.[20] Thio suggests, 'The positivist perspective holds the absolutist view that deviant behavior is intrinsically real, the objectivist view that deviance is observable as an object, and the determinist view that deviance is determined behavior, a product of causation.'[21] Thio places strain theory, differential association theory and control theory in this category. On the other hand, he assigns the labeling, phenomenological and conflict theories to the humanist category, which he describes as follows: 'The humanist perspective consists of the relativist view that the so-called deviance is largely a label given at a given time and place, the subjectivist view that deviance is itself a subjective experience, and the voluntarist view that deviance is a voluntary, self-willed act.'[22]

Other specialists in deviance studies, such as Larry J. Siegel, describe the various deviance perspectives as social structure, social process or social conflict.[23] Siegel maintains that social structure theories such as strain theory 'suggest that people's places in the socioeconomic structure of society influence their chances of becoming [deviant]'.[24] In addition, Siegel suggests that social process theories (e.g. the differential association, social control and labeling perspectives) approach deviance as a result of 'people's interaction with various organizations, institutions, and processes in society'.[25] Lastly, the social conflict perspective as defined by Siegel is the view that deviance is a result of conflict between the classes.[26]

Both positivist and humanist theories of deviance, in Thio's classification scheme, and the social process perspective, in Siegel's categorization pattern, are applicable here. The type of deviance perspectives which are suitable for this study are those processual theories

20. Thio, *Deviant Behavior*, p. 8. Cf. similarly Ronald J. Troyer and Gerald E. Markle, 'Creating Deviance Rules: A Macroscopic Model', *SQ* 23 (1982), pp. 157-69.

21. Thio, *Deviant Behavior*, p. 22.

22. Thio, *Deviant Behavior*, p. 22.

23. Siegel, *Criminology*, p. 213. Although Siegel's work focuses specifically on crime, his discussion is applicable to the study of deviance. In fact, crime may be viewed as a form of deviance. See Clinard and Meier (*Deviant Behavior*) for the same classification scheme.

24. Siegel, *Criminology*, p. 214.

25. Siegel, *Criminology*, p. 249.

26. Siegel, *Criminology*, p. 276.

which consider the social origins of deviance and /or the social reactions to deviance. Along with the large majority of sociologists,[27] I am convinced that deviance cannot be positively linked to one's social class or status. Therefore, I will not employ in this work those conflict and structural theories which attribute deviance to economic factors.[28] Furthermore, I will not attempt to discuss or apply every potentially useful approach to deviance.[29] After having read widely in the sociology of deviance, I have selected three theories for further discussion and application, to wit the differential association, social control and labeling theories. Although these approaches have different theoretical roots, they may be used alongside one another in an attempt to understand deviant behavior more fully.[30] These three theories provide different ways of envisioning and explaining deviance. A discussion of these perspectives of deviant behavior now follows.

4. *Three Approaches to Deviance*

a. *Differential Association Theory*
This perspective of deviance is one of the most popular among sociologists. Its origins and classical expression can be traced to Edwin Sutherland, who, until his death, was considered by many to be the United States' premier criminologist. In his study of criminal behavior,[31] Sutherland suggested that criminal behavior is the product of socialization. Furthermore, he argued that conformity to or deviation from social norms is contingent upon a person's relationships and the frequency and intensity of those relations.

27. See, e.g., Stark, *Sociology*, p. 89.

28. Although deviant behavior is not necessarily caused by one's social economic status, the fact remains that the poor usually lack power and are particularly susceptible to being perceived and treated as deviant. Labeling theorists alert us to this social dynamic. See, e.g., Edwin Schur, *The Politics of Deviance: Stigma Contests and the Uses of Power* (Englewood Cliffs, NJ: Prentice–Hall, 1980).

29. A glance at a textbook on deviant behavior will show that there are a number of deviance theories on offer. Stark (*Sociology*, p. 177) suggests, 'Deviance is one of the most active areas of sociological study.'

30. So also Thio, *Deviant Behavior*; Stark, *Sociology*; and Siegel, *Criminology*.

31. Edwin H. Sutherland, *Principles of Criminology* (Philadelphia: Lippincott, 3rd edn, 1939). Sutherland's associate, Donald Cressey, expanded his mentor's work. See Edwin H. Sutherland and Donald R. Cressey, *Criminology* (Philadelphia: Lippincott, 8th edn, 1970).

Sutherland's differential association theory consists of nine statements.[32] Modified to refer to deviant behavior instead of criminal behavior,[33] the theory unfolds as follows: (1) Deviant behavior is learned. (2) Deviant behavior is learned in interaction with other people in a process of communication. (3) The principal part of the learning of deviant behavior occurs within intimate personal groups. (4) When deviant behavior is learned, the learning process includes both techniques of and rationale for such behavior. (5) The specific direction of motives and drives is learned from definitions of norms as favorable or unfavorable. (6) A person becomes deviant because of an excess of definitions favorable to violation of norms over definitions unfavorable to violation of norms. (7) An individual's interaction with others may vary in frequency, duration, priority and intensity. (8) The process of learning deviant behavior by association with deviant and nondeviant patterns involves all of the processes involved in any other learning. (9) While deviant behavior is an expression of general needs and values, it is not explained by those general needs and values since nondeviant behavior is an expression of the same needs and values.

Although this perspective on deviant behavior is both general and incomplete, it does possess some strengths.[34] First, this theory is broad enough to study both individual and collective deviance of all kinds. Second, this perspective stresses that deviant behavior is learned behavior.[35] Third, the differential association approach describes deviance as a violation of societal norms and conventions.[36] Fourth, it allows for the active decision of an individual to associate with deviant groups and to

32. Sutherland and Cressey, *Criminology*, pp. 77-79.

33. Modified by Clinard and Meier, *Deviant Behavior*, pp. 84-85.

34. In defense of the differential association theory, see Ross L. Matsueda, 'The Current State of the Differential Association Theory', *CD* 34 (1988), pp. 277-306. In this article, Matsueda is countering the work of Ruth R. Kornhauser, *Social Sources of Delinquency* (Chicago: University of Chicago Press, 1978).

35. For the argument that deviance is a role one learns, see Ralph H. Turner, 'Deviance Avowal as Neutralization of Commitment', *SocProb* 19 (1972), pp. 308-21.

36. Some sociologists have suggested that to perceive deviance in such a manner is to superimpose moral categories onto the study of deviant behavior. This critique, however, does not hold. Norms exist in all societies. I will argue in Parts III–IV of this work that Paul and his converts experienced significant opposition because of their (perceived) violation of Jewish and Greco-Roman conventions.

participate in deviant activity.[37] Fifth, this theory is able to account for deviant behavior which is or is not detected.[38] And sixth, this perspective seeks to explain, though in a general way, the cause of deviance.[39]

Despite its strengths, the differential association theory is not without weaknesses. This perspective has been rightly criticized for giving the impression that all deviance is linked to learning and doing.[40] The learning of deviant behavior and the breaking of social norms is not a total explanation for deviance. Some people commit acts considered as deviant with little prior learning, and other individuals are perceived to have done things which they did not do. Differential association theory should be modified, therefore, to allow for individual deviation without the influence of a deviant subculture and for the possibility of unwarranted labeling. Another common criticism of this perspective is that it is tautological. To suggest that deviance is the violation of norms and then consider a norm violation as evidence of deviance does tend toward circular reasoning. However, this logical fallacy can be avoided if adequate proof is given for existing societal norms apart from deviant conduct.[41]

Sutherland's differential association theory continues to exert a significant influence on the study of deviance. Sociologists continue to draw upon and modify Sutherland's seminal work as they seek to understand more fully deviant behavior.[42] The perspective's interest in how group associations can foster and facilitate deviance is valuable for this study. Additionally, the pivotal role that social norms play in the

---

37. Contra Pfuhl (*Deviance Process*, p. 53) who wrongly maintains that the differential association theory is deterministic. The theory does suggest that substantial interaction with deviant groups will lead to deviant behavior. However, this perspective does not contend that a person is passive and pliant in this process.

38. Howard S. Becker (*Outsiders: Studies in the Sociology of Deviance* [New York: Free Press, 1963]) resorts to the category of 'secret deviant' to explain deviance which goes unlabeled.

39. Thio (*Deviant Behavior*, p. 36) thinks that this theory of is little use for explaining individual deviant acts. This is not necessarily the case. The theory contends that deviant behavior is learned through group interaction, not that it is actually carried out in groups.

40. See, e.g., Pfuhl, *Deviance Process*, pp. 53-55.

41. So rightly Clinard and Meier, *Deviant Behavior*, p. 87.

42. See, e.g., Daniel Glaser, 'Criminality Theories and Behavioral Images', *AJS* 61 (1956), pp. 433-44, and Ronald L. Akers, *Deviant Behavior: A Social Learning Approach* (Belmont, CA: Wadsworth, 3rd edn, 1985).

deviance process is a useful insight for this project. Social control theory also emphasizes the importance of social norms.

b. *Social Control Theory*

This particular perspective of deviant behavior has become increasingly influential in sociological circles over the last two decades. Travis Hirschi is the person who is usually associated with this theory.[43] Nonetheless, elements of this conception of deviance may be traced back to Emile Durkheim (1858–1917), one of the founders of modern sociology.[44] This perspective seeks to study deviance from a different angle. Social control theory does not attempt to detect the causes of deviance; rather, this approach is driven by the question 'What causes conformity?'[45] Social control theorists are convinced that if they can explain why people conform to social norms, then they will be able to account for deviations from social conventions.

This approach maintains that people conform to the prescribed norms of a given society because of social bonds. It is argued that strong societal ties produce conformity. Hirschi suggests that there are four ways for individuals to bond to society. One way is through *attachment* to conventional people. When a person is closely associated with norm-abiding others and is concerned about their opinions, the cost of deviant behavior is high, and most people will decide not to run the risk of rupturing such relations. The second way in which one can formulate social ties is through *commitment*. Social control theory suggests that an individual's investments in normative activities (e.g. legitimate acquisition of possessions or earning a good reputation) is a safeguard against deviance. Social bonds can also be created through *involvement* in conventional activities. It is maintained that if one is engaged in norm-conforming activities, then that person will have little interest in or time for deviant acts. The final element in formulating strong ties to society is *belief*. Social control theorists contend that internalization of norms serves as a control against deviance. What one believes, it is suggested,

43. See esp. Hirschi's *Causes of Delinquency* (Berkeley, CA: University of California Press, 1969).
44. So Stark, *Sociology*, p. 191.
45. Becker, one of the foremost labeling theorists, was also interested in this question. Becker (*Outsiders*, pp. 26-27) remarks, 'Instead of asking why deviants want to do things that are disapproved of, we might better ask why conventional people do not follow through on the deviant impulses they have.'

will invariably impact how one behaves.

Hirschi points out in his work that the factors which facilitate social bonding are interrelated. For instance, an individual's belief system is reinforced by their social attachments.[46] Therefore, if those factors which reinforce conventional behavior are strong, then a person is likely to conform to the established norms. However, if an individual's social bonding is weak, then there may be a loosening of social ties, and one may become involved in deviant activity.

Critics of this theory contend that this perspective on deviance has a simplistic view of social control. They suggest that, by focusing upon social control as a preventer of deviance, this approach fails to consider the possibility that control can actually be a cause of deviance.[47] Those who conform to the system also find ways to beat it! Social control theory also fails to note that what is normative behavior for one group may be deviant activity for another. Notwithstanding these short-comings, by highlighting some of the elements that tie a person to conventional behavior, social control theory serves as a helpful tool for studying some of the potential causes of deviance.

c. *Labeling Theory*

While social control theory may be the preeminent perspective of deviance among (American) sociologists in the 1980s and 1990s, labeling theory[48] was undoubtedly the most popular sociological approach (in America) to studying deviant behavior in the 1960s and 1970s.[49]

---

46. Peter L. Berger and Thomas Luckmann (*The Social Construction of Reality: A Treatise in the Sociology of Knowledge* [New York: Doubleday, 1966], p. 158) make a similar point: 'Saul may have become Paul in the aloneness of religious ecstasy, but he could *remain* Paul only in the context of the Christian community that recognized him as such and confirmed the "new being" in which he now located this identity' (emphasis theirs).

47. See Thio, *Deviant Behavior*, p. 42.

48. Erich Goode ('On Behalf of Labeling Theory', *SocProb* 22 [1975], pp. 570-83) argues that the labeling perspective is not a theory at all. Goode is accurate in pointing out that this approach to deviance does not operate with precise definitions or predictive hypotheses. Nevertheless, in a general sense of the term 'theory', that is, abstract speculation or reflection, one may call the labeling approach a theory. In theoretical terms, the labeling approach is actually a version of symbolic inter-actionism. On the labeling perspective, see further, e.g., Edwin Schur, *Labeling Deviant Behavior: Its Sociological Implications* (New York: Harper & Row, 1971).

49. The number of books and articles which have been published on labeling

The origins of labeling theory may be traced to the writings of George Mead,[50] Frank Tannenbaum[51] and Edwin Lemert.[52] This perspective is most often associated, however, with Howard S. Becker and his widely known work *Outsiders*.[53] Unlike the differential association and social control theories, the labeling approach is not concerned with the causes or origins of deviance. Rather, the labeling perspective is interested in the application and amplification of the deviant label (e.g. 'alcoholic' or 'prostitute'). Labeling theorists pose the questions: Who labels whom? And, how are those who are involved in the labeling process impacted?[54]

The main points of the labeling approach may be somewhat simplistically summarized as follows.[55] (1) Deviance is defined socially, not metaphysically. Becker emphasized this point in his now famous words:

> Deviance is not a quality of the act the person commits, but rather a consequence of the application by others of rules and sanctions to an 'offender'. The deviant is one to whom the label has successfully been applied; deviant behavior is behavior that people so label.[56]

(2) People in powerful positions (the so-called 'agents of censure' or 'moral entrepreneurs') are the ones who apply the labels. Labeling theorists argue that those who possess power create deviance when they interpret behavior as deviant, define people as a particular type of deviant and treat them as deviants.[57] (3) A person is stigmatized when

---

theory is staggering. In discussing this perspective, I have tried to include the most important literature.

50. George Mead, 'The Psychology of Punitive Justice', *AJS* 23 (1918), pp. 577-602.

51. Frank Tannenbaum, *Crime and Community* (Boston: Ginn, 1938).

52. Edwin Lemert, *Social Pathology* (New York: McGraw–Hill, 1951).

53. Although Becker is the most renowned labeling theorist, he is not the only important pioneer of this perspective, nor was he the initial one. See also, e.g., the seminal articles of John I. Kitsuse ('Societal Reaction to Deviant Behavior: Problems of Theory and Method', *SocProb* 9 [1962], pp. 247-56) and Kai T. Erikson ('Notes on the Sociology of Deviance', *SocProb* 9 [1962], pp. 307-14).

54. Thio, *Deviant Behavior*, p. 47.

55. I am indebted to Leonard Broom, Charles M. Bonjean and Dorothy H. Broom (*Sociology* [Belmont, CA: Wadsworth, 1990], pp. 100-101) for the points that follow.

56. Becker, *Outsiders*, p. 9.

57. On this process, see further Schur, *Politics of Deviance*.

labeled deviant.[58] (4) When a person is labeled deviant and thereby stigmatized, a deviant identity may be formed and a deviant career may be set in motion.

At this point I digress to note that some sociologists such as Kai T. Erikson[59] and Nachman Ben-Yehuda[60] have skillfully combined insights from labeling theory and Durkhemian functionalism.[61] Although functionalism is a flawed theoretical orientation that must be used with considerable caution,[62] it can be usefully applied to simpler forms of community where norms and roles are more clear-cut and well-defined than in most modern industrialized societies. In their respective studies, Erikson and Ben-Yehuda have demonstrated that communities characterized by mechanical solidarity (i.e. groups which use little energy or information) tend to possess a collective conscience or agreed-upon norms.[63] These conventions give such groups a sense of cohesion and serve as boundary markers.[64] A community's boundaries provide a group with a sense of stability and identity. In more homogeneous communities, when these markers of accepted normality are perceived to be threatened, then there may be a reaction from those who are interested in preserving the status quo. In cases where behavior is deemed to be particularly odd or to touch upon sensitive societal nerves, then a reaction, perhaps even a violent one, is likely to occur. Deviant acts, then, serve to reinforce a community's boundaries and to

58. See William D. Payne, 'Negative Labels: Passageways and Prisons', *CD* 19 (1973), pp. 33-40.

59. Erikson, *Wayward Puritans*. Note also Robert A. Dentler and Kai T. Erikson, 'The Functions of Deviance in Social Groups', *SocProb* 7 (1959), pp. 98-107.

60. Nachman Ben-Yehuda, *Deviance and Moral Boundaries: Witchcraft, the Occult, Science Fiction, Deviant Sciences and Scientists* (Chicago: University of Chicago Press, 1985).

61. Note also Lewis A. Coser, 'Some Functions of Deviant Behavior and Normative Flexibility', *AJS* 68 (1962), pp. 172-81.

62. As to why, see pp. 109-10 n. 9.

63. The differences between mechanical and organic (i.e. groups that use a great deal of energy and information) societies is helpfully discussed and illustrated by Yehudi A. Cohen, 'Social Boundary Systems', *CA* 10 (1969), pp. 103-17.

64. Erikson (*Wayward Puritans*, pp. 9-10) describes a community's boundaries as 'a specific territory in the world as a whole, not only in the sense that it [i.e. the community] occupies a defined region of geographical space but also in the sense that it takes over a particular niche in what might be called cultural space and develops its own "ethos" or "way" within that compass'.

refocus a group's energies by excluding those who are seen to challenge such symbolic markers. This is not to suggest, however, that deviance is automatically boundary-maintaining; it may play a boundary-changing role.[65] Regardless of the ultimate outcome, deviant behavior 'creates a sense of mutuality among the people of a community by supplying a focus for group feeling'.[66]

Following this important theoretical excursus, we come to consider a few of the criticisms which have been leveled against the labeling perspective. Critics of the labeling theory frequently point out that the theory fails to address the etiology or origin of deviant acts.[67] This often leads to the corresponding criticism that labeling theorists portray the labeled person as passive and innocent, thereby absolving deviants of any responsibility for their actions.[68] While these related critiques appear cogent, one should recognize that the labeling perspective is not concerned with the causes of deviance as such, nor is the approach necessarily interested in attaching blame. Rather, this perspective is concerned with how, why and under what circumstances a certain group selects particular people from within the group and labels them as deviant. Labeling theorists are also interested in the social ramifications of a person's status degradation. Others have criticized the labeling perspective for being relativistic to an extreme[69] and for being imprecise in identifying who is doing the labeling, what labels are being used, who is considered deviant and what the results of being labeled actually are.[70] The fact that labeling theorists insist that deviant behavior is contingent upon place, time, the activity at issue, the people involved and so on, creates the impression of imprecision. And at a high level of abstraction, the labeling perspective, like other theories of deviance, is quite blunt. However, when applied to particular people, places and

65. Ben-Yehuda, *Deviance and Moral Boundaries*, p. 20.

66. Erikson, *Wayward Puritans*, p. 4.

67. See, e.g., Stark, *Sociology*, p. 203.

68. So Frances Fox Piven, 'Deviant Behavior and the Remaking of the World', *SocProb* 28 (1981), pp. 489-508, and Paul G. Schervish, 'The Labeling Perspective: Its Bias and Potential in the Study of Political Deviance', *ASoc* 8 (1973), pp. 47-57.

69. Jack P. Gibbs, 'Conceptions of Deviant Behavior: The Old and the New', *PSR* 9 (1966), pp. 9-14.

70. See, e.g., Alexander Liazos, 'The Poverty of the Sociology of Deviance: Nuts, Sluts, and Perverts', *SocProb* 20 (1972), pp. 103-20, and John Hagan, 'Labelling and Deviance: A Case Study in the "Sociology of the Interesting"', *SocProb* 20 (1973), pp. 447-58.

events (e.g. 'apostasy' among Jews and Christians in the first century [Barclay], the witch hunts in Europe in the fifteenth, sixteenth and seventeenth centuries [Ben-Yehuda]; the Quaker invasion among the Puritans of seventeenth-century New England [Erikson]; and marijuana smokers in the United States in the 1960s [Becker]), labeling theory becomes a useful conceptual tool. In combination with the differential association and social control theories, the labeling perspective of deviance will be a sharp instrument in enabling me to dissect more precisely the socio-historical complexities of the conflict relations which Paul and his Thessalonian converts experienced with outsiders. Having discussed the three theories of deviance upon which I will draw in this work, I will now offer a definition of deviance.

5. Defining Deviance

Deviance is a difficult to define. In fact, Edwin Lemert maintains that the term is better left undefined.[71] Despite the fact that no one definition of the term will be satisfactory for all interested parties, it will be useful to offer a working definition. In doing so, I will draw upon the preceding theoretical discussion.

There is a plethora of definitions of deviance on offer. When the dust of debate settles, however, four basic understandings of deviance emerge.[72] The first is the statistical. This view maintains that deviance is anything that departs from the norm. This view is not adequate for the obvious reason that to be different from the majority does not necessarily constitute deviance. For instance, a person may stand seven-feet tall, and while this is unusual, it is certainly not socially deviant. Another conception of deviance is the absolutist perspective. This view maintains that there are universal values that are operative in all places at all times, and violation of these values constitutes deviance. This view fails to take into account that different cultures have different understandings of what is and is not deviant. For example, it is considered inappropriate to consume alcoholic beverages in most Texas Baptist Church circles, and those church members who do drink alcohol,

---

71. Edwin Lemert, 'Issues in the Study of Deviance', *SQ* 22 (1981), pp. 285-305.

72. So Clinard and Meier, *Deviant Behavior*, p. 4. Becker (*Outsiders*, pp. 3-8) mentions five views of deviance: the statistical, pathological, functional, relativistic or normative and labeling or reactionist.

especially in social settings, run the risk of being viewed by fellow Baptists as 'sinful'. On the other hand, many Scottish Baptists drink in moderation in both private and public settings, and such behavior is generally considered acceptable. This example drawn from personal observation shows that an absolute definition of deviance is inadequate.

To my mind, deviance is best defined by combining the last two conceptions of deviance, namely the normative and the relativist views. While the normative perspective highlights the fact that deviance is 'behavior that does not conform to the prevailing social norms',[73] the reactionist conception stresses the relative nature of conduct deemed deviant. Becker combines these two views of deviance when he writes: 'In short, whether a given act is deviant or not depends in part on the nature of the act (that is, whether or not it violates some rule) and in part on what other people do about it.'[74]

Deviance, then, is any behavior or belief that is perceived by a particular social group as a violation of their given norms or conventions. This definition, however, should not lead to the erroneous conclusion that social scientists believe that all deviance is of the same ilk. Students of society usually differentiate between higher-consensus or 'hard' deviance (e.g. murder, rape and robbery) and lower-consensus or 'soft' deviance (e.g. drug and alcohol [ab]use and prostitution). [75] Traditionally, positivists have studied the former type of deviant behavior, while humanists have investigated the latter kind. Having offered a working definition of deviance, I will now consider the deviance process.

73. Broom, Bonjean and Broom, *Sociology*, p. 349.

74. Becker, *Outsiders*, p. 14. Jack D. Douglas and Frances C. Waksler (*The Sociology of Deviance: An Introduction* [Boston: Little, Brown & Co., 1982], p. 10) also combine the normative and reactionist perspectives in defining deviance. The comments of Erikson (*Wayward Puritans*, p. 6) on the meaning of deviance are also instructive at this point. He writes, 'the term "deviance" refers to conduct which the people of a group consider so dangerous or embarrassing or irritating that they bring special sanctions to bear against the persons who exhibit it. Deviance is not a property *inherent in* any particular kind of behavior; it is a property *conferred upon* that behavior by the people who come into direct or indirect contact with it. The only way an observer can tell whether or not a given style of behavior is deviant, then, is to learn something about the standards of the audience which responds to it' (emphasis his).

75. See, e.g., Thio, *Deviant Behavior*, p. 22, and Ben-Yehuda, *Deviance and Moral Boundaries*, p. 10.

6. *The Deviance Process*

As indicated above, one may classify the three perspectives of deviance which I am employing in this project as processual theories. That is to say, these theories focus on the influence that social instruction and interaction have on individuals.[76] It will strengthen this study to consider the deviance process. In doing so, I will clarify and expand upon the definition of deviance given above. We will begin by considering social norms and social control.

a. *Social Norms*

In essence, norms are cultural values which guide behavior in particular places at specific times.[77] Norms serve two basic functions.[78] First, they clarify what type of behavior is and is not deemed appropriate. Prescriptive norms inform a person what to do, whereas proscriptive norms guide an individual concerning what not to do. Second, norms indicate what type of behavior is anticipated in a particular culture. While norms may be formal rules or laws, they may also be traditions or customs. In any event, norms are shared and observed by a given society or community. This is what makes norms distinctly social.

Communities pass along their norms from generation to generation in codified and uncodified form. Frequently, social norms are as much 'caught as they are taught'. The impact that a community's written and unwritten norms has on an individual's perception of reality and behavioral patterns is immense.

What is normative is contingent upon the given cultural context. To this extent, norms are relative. As a result, deviance is also relative and must be viewed through the spectacles of the social audience which interprets a given act. It is true that some acts (e.g. murder) are almost always considered deviant.[79] Nevertheless, many acts are left open for cultural interpretation. For example, while polygamy is a criminal offense in the United States, it is lawful, indeed honorable, among some Muslims in some Arab countries.[80]

76. See Siegel, *Criminology*, p. 222.
78. So similarly, Broom, Bonjean and Broom, *Sociology*, p. 45.
78. See further Robert F. Meier, 'Norms and the Study of Deviance: A Proposed Research Strategy', *DB* 3 (1981), pp. 1-25.
79. So Ben-Yehuda, *Deviance and Moral Boundaries*, pp. 10-11.
80. I am indebted to Stark (*Sociology*, p. 177) for this example.

How can one determine the existence of a norm in a given cultural context? The qualitative approach to studying normative behavior suggests that norms are so woven into the fabric of a given group that they can only be analyzed within a particular community. The inferential strategy maintains that a negative reaction to a behavior is proof positive that a norm has been violated.[81] New Testament interpreters depend upon ancient texts and artifacts in an effort to understand more fully the norms of the ancient peoples and cultures they study.

b. *Social Control*

How groups respond to and deal with norm-violating behavior is known as social control. There are both internal and external aspects to social control. The internal facet is linked to the socialization process. Peter L. Berger and Thomas Luckmann define socialization as 'the comprehensive and consistent induction of an individual into the objective world or a sector of it'.[82] While primary socialization introduces an individual into society, secondary socialization introduces a person into different spheres of social life.[83] Resocialization, or alternation, involves reorienting one's social world and revisioning one's symbolic universe.[84] It is during these different phases of the socialization process that a person is taught to comply with or to deviate from societal norms. Internalization of a culture's customs, beliefs, values, attitudes and traditions is a perpetual process that often occurs in a rather unstructured and unconscious fashion.

Sanctions comprise the external aspect of social control and are used to accomplish compliance to norms. Sanctions can be both formal or informal and positive or negative. Positive formal sanctions (e.g. bonuses) and informal sanctions (e.g. verbal encouragement) reward and reinforce norm-conforming conduct. On the other hand, negative formal sanctions (e.g. imprisonment) and informal sanctions (e.g. verbal harassment) are meant to discourage what is viewed as deviant behavior. Each type of sanction can have a powerful effect on an individual's identity and conduct.[85]

81. Clinard and Meier (*Deviant Behavior*, p. 12) mention these two strategies for studying norms.
82. Berger and Luckmann, *Social Construction of Reality*, p. 130.
83. Berger and Luckmann, *Social Construction of Reality*, p. 130.
84. Berger and Luckmann, *Social Construction of Reality*, p. 157.
85. The differential reinforcement theory as developed by Akers (*Deviant*

c. *Becoming Deviant*

How does a person become deviant or assume a deviant identity? As indicated above, a person learns how to act and to react socially as a result of socialization. In this continuous process one acquires the ability to perform certain roles. A role involves the various behaviors and duties learned by and expected of a given person.[86] Social roles are inextricably linked to social rules. How people behave is contingent upon how they understand their roles. For instance, teachers and students, employers and employees, parents and children all know their respective roles and are anticipated to behave accordingly. If these roles were reversed, chaos could occur. Social roles make social control possible.

The sum of a person's prescribed roles is known as a 'role set'. Role prescriptions and norm requirements are learned through social interaction. The roles one performs are based upon the individual's attachments and involvements. A person's roles will vary from group to group. Any group, be it a family, business, sports team or church, is comprised of various role relations and has particular behavioral expectations. Often role behavior differs from prescribed roles. This may be due to any number of reasons, including role confusion, role strain or role conflict.

If an individual fails to fulfill a prescribed role and deviates from a community's norms, at some times and in some places this person may be labeled as deviant and treated as an outsider. Labeling occurs when a particular characteristic of a person or a specific aspect of one's behavior or belief is brought to the fore by (a) community member(s) who desire(s) to condemn, control or censure that individual. For example, in some communities a person who engages in extra-marital relations is called an 'adulterer'. Or, an individual who fails to complete a formal course of study is spoken of by some as a 'drop-out'. A label, then, is a tag that highlights a 'negative or unfavorable' aspect of a person while down-playing or ignoring their 'positive or favorable' features. After an individual is labeled, it is possible that a pattern of deviant behavior or

---

Behavior) highlights the important role of positive and negative reinforcement in the development of a person's behavioral patterns. John Braithwaite (*Crime, Shame and Reintegration* [Cambridge: Cambridge University Press, 1989]) emphasizes the effects that the largely informal sanction shame can have on an individual.

86. Broom, Bonjean and Broom, *Sociology*, p. 351.

belief will set in.[87] Those people who restructure their lives and reorient their behavior around a given label are known as secondary deviants.[88] When secondary deviance occurs, deviance amplification often follows (i.e. the gradual isolation of the labeled individual from former social networks and the reiteration of one's social role and identity as a misfit).

d. *Responding to Labeling*

Being labeled deviant is neither certain nor automatic. When an individual is accused of or caught in an act considered deviant, there are various ways that this person can respond to negative sanctions and stigma. Sociologists have noted several ways individuals seek to avoid and /or neutralize deviant labels.[89] A list and description of seven of the more common 'management techniques' follows.[90]

1. *Secrecy*. If a deviant act is not public knowledge, negative sanctions and stigma will not follow. Some deviants, therefore, will keep their activity under wraps in an effort to avoid negative labeling.

2. *Manipulating the physical environment*. Those deemed deviant will sometimes try to alter their behavior in a particular setting in an effort to convince others that there is nothing different about them.

3. *Rationalization*. People considered deviant may attempt to explain away their deviance. This may be done by denying responsibility for the act, by maintaining that their behavior or

---

87. Becker (*Outsiders*, p. 101) refers to such a pattern as a 'deviant career'.

88. Primary deviance is a norm violation that may go unnoticed and have little influence on the actor.

89. Neutralization theory is frequently identified with David Matza and Graham Sykes, 'Techniques of Neutralization: A Theory of Delinquency', *ASR* 22 (1957), pp. 664-70. See also Matza's *Delinquency and Drift* (New York: John Wiley & Sons, 1964).

90. The first five management techniques are found in Gregory C. Elliott, Herbert L. Ziegler, Barbara M. Altman and Deborah Scott, 'Understanding Stigma: Dimensions of Deviance and Coping', *DB* 3 (1982), pp. 275-300. The last two neutralization devices are located in Pfuhl, *Deviance Process*, pp. 65-68. See further Turner, 'Deviance Avowal'; Joseph W. Rogers and M.D. Buffalo, 'Fighting Back: Nine Modes of Adaptation to a Deviant Label', *SocProb* 22 (1974), pp. 101-18; and Teresa E. Levitin, 'Deviants as Active Participants in the Labeling Process: The Visibly Handicapped', *SocProb* 22 (1975), pp. 548-57.

beliefs harmed no one and/or by claiming that their actions or
attitudes are justified given the circumstances.

4.   *Altering behavior.* Some folks who are labeled deviant attempt
     to counter this stigma by changing their roles in an effort to
     alter the perception of others.

5.   *Deviant subcultures.*[91] Becoming a part of a deviant subculture
     may help one to avoid negative sanctions and stigma. The less
     one relates to others outside a particular group the less one
     risks outsiders' disapproval. All the while, however, deviant
     subcultures facilitate and reinforce deviant activity and tend to
     be labeled by outsiders.

6.   *Condemnation of the condemners.* A technique often utilized
     by those who are regarded as deviant is to lash back verbally
     at the enforcers and labelers in an effort to blunt the blow of
     negative sanctions and stigma. Instead of passively allowing
     deviance amplification to occur, some people attempt to resist
     being labeled.

7.   *Appeal to higher authorities.* When tagged with a label, people
     may also appeal to a higher level norm or to a higher authority
     figure. This is an attempt on the part of those thought deviant
     to clarify the rationale for their behavior or beliefs.

Having surveyed the sociological study of deviance, some concluding
remarks and questions are in order.

7. Conclusion

Although some biblical scholars remain skeptical of employing social-
scientific insights in the exegetical task and label those who use the
social sciences as 'determinists' or 'reductionists', social theory can be
a useful tool when used appropriately. While general social theories
cannot, of course, answer specific historical questions, they can help an
interpreter to raise interesting questions of the historical material under
investigation.

The sociology of deviance is suggestive for this study. In light of the
fact that Paul and his Thessalonian converts differed from most of their

---

91. On deviant subcultures see the pioneering work of Albert Cohen, *Delinquent Boys* (New York: Free Press, 1955), and Albert Cohen and James Short,
'Research on Deviant Subcultures', *JSI* 14 (1958), pp. 20-35.

respective compatriots in both behavior and beliefs, it stands to reason that deviance theory can aid this investigation. In fact, given that Paul and his converts were considered by their compatriots as different in a threatening way, one may rightly conclude that they were viewed by not a few people as deviant.

Some theoretically informed questions have arisen from this survey of the sociology of deviance. I will address the following queries, though not sequentially or systematically, in Parts III–IV below.

1. How did outsiders react to Paul and the Thessalonian Christians? What type of negative sanctions and stigma did these believers encounter? (Chapters 6, 9)

2. How were the boundary lines drawn in the various communities under consideration? Was there much tolerance? At what point did tolerance give way to resistance and why? (Chapters 7, 10)

3. What norms were Paul and his converts thought by non-Christian outsiders to have violated? Did the deviance of Paul and his converts from the status quo create and perpetuate their conflicts with outsiders? In what important ways did Paul's and the Thessalonian believers' behavior and beliefs differ from their respective compatriots? (Chapters 7, 10)

4. Why did some Jews oppose Paul? (Chapter 7)

5. Why did the Thessalonian Christians encounter opposition from their fellow Gentiles? Why would these Pauline Christians have been viewed as a dangerously deviant subculture? Was movement into and/or out of the Thessalonian congregation encouraged or discouraged? (Chapter 10)

6. How did the Thessalonian Christians' compatriots view their conversion? How did their conversion affect their attachments, commitments, involvements and beliefs? (Chapter 10)

7. How did Paul and the believers in Thessalonica react to the negative sanctions and stigma they incurred? What impact did external opposition have on Paul's communication with the Thessalonians and on the church's internal relations? (Chapters 8, 11)

The questions posed here illustrate how useful deviance theory will be for this study. Granted, some of these queries might have been raised without assistance from the sociology of deviance. Nevertheless,

drawing upon the social study of deviant behavior not only aids in formulating interesting questions, but it also allows for greater precision of
expression. Before addressing the questions raised above, however, I
will first discuss another field of social theory fruitful for this study.

Chapter 5

THE SOCIAL-SCIENTIFIC STUDY OF INTERGROUP CONFLICT

1. *Introduction*

Having surveyed the sociological study of deviance in Chapter 4, I will now overview the social-scientific study of conflict.[1] Conflict theory, I propose, will allow for a fuller comprehension and a clearer articulation of the conflict relations between Christians and non-Christians in Thessalonica. In this chapter I will garner useful insights regarding intergroup conflict from theorists in the fields of sociology, social psychology and cultural anthropology.[2] To be sure, a general discussion

1.   These two fields are compatible, for 'Conflict represents a clash of interests instigated by some sort of deviance from accepted norms, often resulting in specific kinds of countermeasures' (Seland, *Establishment Violence*, p. 6).

2.   In sociology, conflict theory is but one of several theoretical perspectives. Although conflict theory is often associated with Karl Marx, it is not in any way coterminous with Marxism. (On Marxian thought, see, among others, Lewis A. Coser, *Masters of Sociological Thought: Ideas in Historical and Social Context* [New York: Harcourt, Brace, Jovanovich, 1971].) Theorists other than Marx (e.g. Georg Simmel, Max Weber, William G. Sumner, Gaetano Mosca, Roberto Michels, Lewis A. Coser, C. Wright Mills and Ralf Dahrendorf) have contributed to the development of conflict theory, and the theoretical underpinnings of conflict theory are broader than Marxism. For an overview of conflict theory and theorists, see James T. Duke, *Conflict and Power in Social Life* (Provo, UT: Brigham Young University Press, 1976).

In social psychology, the study of intergroup conflict is one area of specialization within the field of intergroup relations. Two collections of essays on intergroup relations from which I have profited are: Stephen Woschel and William G. Austin (eds.), *Psychology of Intergroup Relations* (Chicago: Nelson–Hall, 2nd edn, 1986), and John C. Turner and Howard Giles (eds.), *Intergroup Behavior* (Chicago: University of Chicago Press, 1981).

In cultural anthropology, I have drawn upon three studies that address the issue of group conflict, namely Victor Turner, *Schism and Community in an African Society* (New York: Humanities Press, 1957); Alan R. Beals and Bernard J. Siegel,

of the social-scientific study of conflict cannot serve as a substitute for the thorough investigation of a given conflict situation. Nevertheless, theoretical principles drawn from the social-scientific study of conflict can assist one in interrogating particular texts which speak of conflict and in offering fresh observations about such texts.

I am not the first New Testament interpreter to see the potential of applying conflict theory to the study of relations between Christians and non-Christians. John G. Gager,[3] John H. Elliott,[4] Graham N. Stanton[5] and Jack T. Sanders[6] have all preceded me.[7] However, these exegetes have focused upon the *functional outcomes* of conflict on the given Christian communities under investigation. Furthermore, these scholars have relied heavily, if not exclusively, upon Lewis A. Coser's *The Functions of Social Conflict*, which is essentially a commentary on the earlier work of Georg Simmel (1858–1918).[8] To be sure, Coser's book

Divisiveness and Social Conflict: An Anthropological Approach (Stanford, CA: Stanford University Press, 1966); and Robert A. LeVine and Donald Campbell, *Ethnocentrism: Theories of Conflict, Ethnic Attitudes and Group Behavior* (New York: John Wiley & Sons, 1972). See also the work of the political anthropologist Marc Howard Ross, *The Culture of Conflict: Interpretations and Interests in Comparative Perspective* (New Haven: Yale University Press, 1993). De Vos (*Church and Community Conflicts*) utilizes Ross's 'culture of conflict' theory to explain why some Pauline Christians (i.e. the Thessalonian and Philippian churches) experienced conflict in their given cultural contexts and why other Pauline converts (i.e. the Corinthians) did not.

Political scientists (e.g. S. Touval and I.W. Zartman, *International Mediation in Theory and Practice* [Boulder, CO: Westview, 1985]) and economists (e.g. T.C. Schelling, *Strategy of Conflict* [Cambridge, MA: Harvard University Press, 1960]) have also furthered our knowledge of conflict.

3. John G. Gager, *Kingdom and Community: The Social World of Early Christianity* (Englewood Cliffs, NJ: Prentice–Hall, 1975).

4. John H. Elliott, *A Home for the Homeless: A Sociological Exegesis of 1 Peter, its Situation and Strategy* (Philadelphia: Fortress Press, 1981).

5. Graham N. Stanton, 'Matthew's Gospel and the Damascus Document in Sociological Perspective', in *idem, A Gospel for a New People: Studies in Matthew* (Edinburgh: T. & T. Clark, 1992), pp. 85-107.

6. Sanders, *Schismatics, Sectarians, Dissidents, Deviants*.

7. Seland (*Establishment Violence*) has recently used conflict management theory in his study of establishment violence in Philo and Luke.

8. Lewis A. Coser, *The Functions of Social Conflict* (New York: Free Press, 1956), and Georg Simmel, *Conflict and the Web of Group-Affiliation* (trans. Kurt H. Wolff; New York: Free Press, 1955). Sanders (*Schismatics, Sectarians, Dissidents, Deviants*, pp. 128-29) does mention, albeit briefly, the work of Louis Kriesberg,

is a classic in the field of conflict studies. However, his seminal contribution is now dated, and the theoretical study of conflict has marched forth unabated. Even though subsequent publications on conflict relations have not completely discredited the work of Coser, his conclusions have been significantly modified, especially the functionalistic assumptions which undergird his observations.[9]

The Sociology of Social Conflicts (Englewood Cliffs, NJ: Prentice–Hall, 1973). Each of the scholars mentioned in the text above also notes the work of Simmel (*Conflict*), but with the partial exception of Elliott (*Home for the Homeless*, p. 113), who actually quotes another person's evaluation of Simmel, none of them attempts to understand Simmel on his own terms.

   9.   Functionalism, which was once the dominant theoretical orientation in sociology, must be used with caution. Functionalism is frequently critiqued for the following reasons. (1) Functionalism is thought to be circular in its argumentation. Functionalists frequently assume that the existence of X (let X = a social system) explains the appearance of Y (let Y = manifest and/or latent functions and/or dysfunctions) which in turn perpetuates the existence of X. (2) Functionalism has also come under sociological fire for its illegitimate teleological orientation, i.e. the erroneous assumption that consequences create causes. (3) Another common criticism of functionalism is its reification of society and its tendency towards determinism. In the functionalist perspective social processes are personified; the social system is thought to have needs and wants. Understanding society in such a reified fashion underestimates human initiative and involvement. (4) Critics maintain that functionalism wrongly assumes commensurability between radically different societies.

   Coser does manage to avoid some of the pitfalls of extreme functionalism, like speaking of societal needs or functional prerequisites. Nevertheless, Coser's work on conflict is analytically one-sided. In an attempt to underscore the potential benefits (or 'functions') of conflict, he significantly down-plays the harmful effects (or 'dysfunctions') of conflict. A balanced conception of social conflict takes into account both constructive and destructive aspects. So, rightly, Jack Nusan Porter and Ruth Taplin, *Conflict and Conflict Resolution: A Sociological Introduction with Updated Bibliography and Theory Section* (Lanham, MD: University Press of America, 1987), p. 6. John Rex (*Social Conflict: A Conceptual and Theoretical Analysis* [London: Longmans, 1981], p. 74) rightly observes that 'the theory of the "functions of social conflict" is a part, but only a small part, of the total theory of conflict'.

   As one might expect, Simmel (*Conflict*) also focused on the positive outcomes of conflict. Duke (*Conflict and Power*, p. 105) notes, 'Simmel's optimism did not allow him to dwell long on the negative side of conflict. He gained no pleasure himself in describing and analyzing the seamier side of social life as Marx seemed to do, so Simmel contented himself with discussions of the benefits to be derived from social conflict.' On Simmel's contribution to conflict theory see Jonathan H.

In what follows I will discuss the social-scientific study of conflict under the following headings: factors affecting conflict; classifying conflict; defining intergroup conflict; characteristics of intergroup conflict; causes of intergroup conflict; the cycle of intergroup conflict; consequences of intergroup conflict; and coping with intergroup conflict. At the conclusion of this chapter, we will know a good deal more about the social-scientific study of conflict, and we will have ample theoretical resources upon which to draw in executing this study. Furthermore, this chapter will broaden and update the previous work of New Testament interpreters who have employed concepts from the sociological study of conflict. As I result, I hope that the ensuing discussion will serve as a resource for biblical interpreters employing conflict theory in their research.

2. *Factors Affecting Conflict*

The place to begin studying a given conflict is, of course, with the particular details of that conflict. Morton Deutsch, a leading conflict theorist in social psychology, suggests that one should do the following when studying conflict relations:[10]

1. Identify the characteristics of the parties in conflict (e.g. their values and motivations; their aspirations and objectives; their physical, intellectual and social resources for waging or resolving conflict; and their beliefs about conflict, including their conceptions of strategy).

2. Investigate the prior relations of the parties in conflict. Explore their attitudes, beliefs and expectations regarding one another.

3. Study the nature of the issue(s) giving rise to the conflict. Consider the scope, rigidity, motivational significance, formulation and periodicity of the conflict issue(s).

4. Examine the social environment within which the conflict occurs, including the nature of the social norms and the way the culture tends to respond to conflict.

5. Consider the interested audiences to the conflict, particularly

Turner, *The Structure of Sociological Theory* (Homewood, IL: Dorsey Press, rev. edn, 1978) pp. 121-42, and Coser, *Masters of Sociological Thought*, pp. 176-215.

    10. Morton Deutsch, *Resolution of Conflict: Constructive and Destructive Processes* (New Haven: Yale University Press, 1973), pp. 5-7.

their relationships to the parties in conflict and their interests in the outcomes of the conflict.

6. Explore the strategy and tactics employed by the parties in the conflict.

7. Observe the consequences of the conflict to each of the participants and to other interested parties.

I will bear these factors in mind in Parts III–IV of this study. In this way, we will gain a more comprehensive understanding of the conflict in Thessalonica.[11]

3. *Classifying Conflict*

a. *Personal and Group Conflict*

Conflict can occur at both an individual and a group level. In addition, conflict can take place both within and between people and groups. Conflict within a person is known as 'intrapersonal', and conflict between at least two people is referred to as 'interpersonal'. When conflict exists within a group it is called 'intragroup', and conflict experienced between groups is labeled 'intergroup'.[12] Although it is easy to classify conflict in theory, in reality it is rather complex. In the study I am undertaking it is difficult to know how best to describe the conflict relations of Paul and the Thessalonian church with outsiders. It seems likely that conflict took place on multiple levels.[13] In any event, one may perceive the conflict in Thessalonica as intergroup conflict, with Paul and his converts comprising one group and their respective opponents forming another.[14] To conceive of the conflict as intergroup is in keeping with Paul's dualistic perspective as set forth in his letter(s) to the Thessalonians. Therein, he places people into one of two categories. The following are among the bipolar pairs which appear in the Thessa-

11. One might suggest that these factors affecting conflict could be dealt with intuitively. I would not dispute this claim; however, it is useful to spell out explicitly the variables which shape social conflict.

12. For these (and a few other) categories of conflict, see Deutsch, *Resolution of Conflict*, p. 10.

13. Ronald J. Fisher (*The Social Psychology of Intergroup and International Conflict* [New York: Springer, 1990]) observes that conflict can and often does occur simultaneously at the individual, group and intergroup levels.

14. Additionally, one may divide either group into sub-groups: Paul (and his co-worker[s]) and the Thessalonian church on the one hand and their Jewish and Gentile opponents on the other.

lonian correspondence: 'those who know God'/'those who do not know God'; 'insiders'/'outsiders'; 'children of light'/'children of darkness'; 'us'/'them'.[15]

b. *Real and Imagined Conflict*

Social scientists also make a distinction between real and imagined conflict. Conflict which is concrete and involves incompatibilities between the concerned parties is known as realistic conflict. Conflict which occurs primarily or solely in the mind is called unrealistic conflict. While realistic conflict is based on objective differences and requires social interaction between the involved parties, unrealistic conflict arises from perceived problems and does not, at least at the outset of the psychological discomfort, demand social intercourse with the other party.[16] I understand the conflict relations in Thessalonica as primarily realistic conflict.[17]

Because I view the conflict in Thessalonica as for the most part realistic, I will draw upon insights from the Realistic Conflict Theory (RCT) in this study.[18] The basic thrust of this social psychological theory is that real conflict of interest leads to intergroup conflict.[19]

15. See further pp. 196-97 below. N. Ross Reat ('Insiders and Outsiders in the Study of Religious Traditions', *JAAR* 51 [1983], pp. 459-76 [459]) contends, 'Every religious tradition, by its very existence and regardless of its claims to universality, divides the world into two sets: insiders of the tradition and outsiders to the tradition.'

16. Fisher, *Conflict*, p. 31. For an understanding of realistic conflicts as 'Conflicts which arise from frustration of specific demands within the relationship and from estimates of gains of the participants...', and of unrealistic conflicts as interaction for the purpose of 'tension release', see Coser, *Functions of Social Conflict*, p. 49.

17. Contrast Malherbe (*Paul and the Thessalonians*, pp. 46-48, and 'Conversion to Paul's Gospel', in Abraham J. Malherbe, Frederick W. Norris and James W. Thompson [eds.], *The Early Church in its Context: Essays in Honor of Everett Ferguson* [Leiden: E.J. Brill, 1998], pp. 230-44 [234-37]) who tends to psychologize the Thessalonian Christians' affliction. Although I view the conflict in Thessalonica as primarily realistic, I would not necessarily maintain that Paul and his converts perceived and responded to the conflict objectively.

18. For an overview of RCT, see Donald M. Taylor and Fathali M. Moghaddam, *Theories of Intergroup Relations: International Social Psychological Perspectives* (New York: Praeger, 1987), pp. 33-57. See also, Fisher, *Conflict*, pp. 22-28.

19. RCT has its intellectual roots in the work of William G. Sumner, *Folkways* (Boston: Ginn, 1906).

Some conflict theorists (e.g. Muzafer Sherif [20] and Morton Deutsch[21]) are interested not only in how conflicts arise but also in the course that conflicts take and how group conflicts can be resolved.[22]

c. *Morton Deutsch's Typology of Social Conflict*
When categorizing conflict, social theorists often seek to differentiate between conflict and competition and between constructive and destructive (or beneficial and detrimental) conflict.[23] Such distinctions are extraordinarily difficult to make, and these perspectival differentiations need not detain us here. Instead, we will move on to consider a summary of Deutsch's typology of social conflict.

Deutsch suggests that there are six types of conflict: veridical, contingent, displaced, misattributed, latent and false.[24] He describes these kinds of conflict as follows. *Veridical conflict* is conflict which 'exists objectively and is perceived accurately'; 'It is not contingent upon some

20. Muzafer Sherif, *In Common Predicament: Social Psychology of Intergroup Conflict and Cooperation* (ISBS; Boston: Houghton Mifflin, 1966).

21. Morton Deutsch, *Resolution of Conflict*, and 'Constructive Conflict Resolution: Principles, Training, and Research', *JSI* 50 (1994), pp. 13-32.

22. While RCT is a useful theoretical perspective, it is not a complete theory of intergroup conflict. It may be usefully combined, however, with Social Identity Theory (SIT) to form a more comprehensive theory of intergroup conflict. This theory, developed by the late Henri Tajfel (see, e.g., *Human Groups and Social Categories: Studies in Social Psychology* [Cambridge: Cambridge University Press, 1981]), focuses on 'conditions in which people will feel motivated, individually or collectively, to maintain or change their group membership and their intergroup situation' (So Taylor and Moghaddam, *Intergroup Relations*, p. 59). For an attempt to integrate RCT and SIT, see Fisher, *Conflict*, pp. 87-115.

23. See further Fisher, *Conflict*, p. 32, and Deutsch, *Resolution of Conflict*, pp. 10, 17.

24. Deutsch, *Resolution of Conflict*, pp. 11-15. Herb Bisno (*Managing Conflict* [SHSG, 52; Newbury Park, CA: Sage, 1988], pp. 30-33) also offers a sixfold typology of conflict. Bisno speaks of the following conflict types: interest/commitment, induced, misattributed, illusionary, displaced and expressive. Bisno and Deutsch share in common the categories misattributed and displaced conflict. Bisno's interest/commitment category of conflict is analogous to Deutsch's veridical type, and his illusionary type is equal to false conflict in Deutsch's paradigm. Bisno also speaks of two types of conflict not addressed by Deutsch, namely induced and expressive. By induced conflict, Bisno is referring to 'conflicts intentionally created in order to achieve other than explicit objectives' (p. 31). When referring to expressive conflicts, Bisno means 'conflicts characterized by a desire to express hostility, antagonism, or other strong feelings' (p. 31).

easily altered feature of the environment.'[25] *Contingent conflict* is conflict which can be easily resolved if the involved parties are willing to opt for readily available alternatives. *Displaced conflict* occurs when an underlying conflict gives rise to a surface conflict. Presumably, if the underlying conflict were resolved, then the manifest conflict would not occur. A *misattributed conflict* takes place when parties engage in conflict over wrong issues or erroneous assumptions. This type of conflict begins when a previously uninvolved party is drawn into a conflict by a faulty attribution or perception of another party. The fifth type of conflict in Deutsch's schema is *latent conflict*. Latent conflict is conflict which is 'brewing under the surface' and could 'explode' at any time. *False conflict* is the last conflict type which Deutsch identifies. This type of conflict occurs when there is no objective reason for it. Deutsch is careful to point out in his work that more than one type of conflict may be present in any given conflict situation.[26] I suspect that such was the case with Paul's and his converts' conflict with outsiders.

4. *Defining Intergroup Conflict*

Having considered some of the factors affecting conflict and various types of conflict, I will now attempt to define intergroup conflict. There is, of course, a plethora of definitions of conflict on offer. This is due largely to the fact that conflict is such an ambiguous, elastic concept. Raymond W. Mack and Richard C. Snyder remark, 'In its broadest sense it [i.e. conflict] seems to cover everything from war to choices between ice-cream sodas or sundaes.'[27] Some conflict theorists attempt

25. Deutsch, *Resolution of Conflict*, p. 12.
26. Deutsch, *Resolution of Conflict*, p. 15.
27. Raymond W. Mack and Richard C. Snyder, 'The Analysis of Social Conflict: Toward an Overview and Synthesis', *JCR* 1 (1957), pp. 212-48 (212). Interestingly, Mack and Snyder do not attempt to offer a definition of conflict; instead, they seek to describe conflict by highlighting its essential elements. They suggest that conflict: (1) requires at least two parties, units or entities; (2) arises from position or resource scarcity; (3) involves behaviors designed to destroy, injure, thwart or otherwise control the other party; (4) requires interaction among parties in which actions and counteractions are mutually opposed; (5) involves the attempt to acquire or to exercise power; (6) constitutes a fundamental social interaction process having important consequences; (7) represents a temporary tendency toward disjunction in the interaction flow between parties; (8) does not represent a breakdown in the regulated conduct, but rather a shift in the governing norms and expectations (pp. 218-19). I will use the work of Mack and Snyder below when

to account for this broad range of meaning when defining 'conflict'. For example, Deutsch describes conflict as existing 'whenever incompatible activities occur'.[28] Because this definition is so broad, it is also, at least for our purposes, too blunt. Greater specificity is desired.

Other authors such as Louis Kriesburg emphasize the perspectival character of conflict. Kriesburg writes, 'Social conflict is a relationship between two or more parties who (or whose spokesmen) believe they have incompatible goals.'[29] In discussing deviance, the importance of perspective was stressed. I will argue in Chapters 7 and 10 below that incompatible perceptions and goals led to external clashes between Christians and non-Christians. Kriesburg rightly stresses the perspectival nature of conflict. It is possible, however, to expand upon and to hone his definition.

In his work on group dynamics, D.R. Forsyth observes that the Latin *conflictus* suggests a 'striking together with force'.[30] Applying the meaning of this word to group interaction, Forsyth suggests that group conflict occurs when 'the actions or beliefs of one or more members of [a] group are unacceptable—and hence are resisted by—one or more of the other group members'.[31]

Building upon Kriesberg, Forsyth and others, I offer the following definition of intergroup conflict: *disputatious social interaction between groups which results from the fact that the behaviors and beliefs of one*

noting some of the characteristics of intergroup conflict.

28. Deutsch, *Resolution of Conflict*, p. 10.

29. Kriesburg, *Social Conflicts*, p. 17. See similarly D.G. Pruitt and J.Z. Rubin, who define conflict as 'a perceived divergence of interests or a belief that the parties' current aspirations cannot be achieved simultaneously' (*Social Conflict: Escalation, Stalemate, and Settlement* [New York: Random House, 1986], p. 4). Cf. Fisher (*Conflict*, p. 6), who describes conflict as 'A social situation involving perceived incompatibilities in goals or values between two or more parties, attempts by the parties to control each other, and antagonistic feelings by the parties toward each other'.

30. D.R. Forsyth, *Group Dynamics* (Pacific Grove, CA: Brooks/Cole Publishing, 2nd edn, 1990), p. 353.

31. Forsyth, *Group Dynamics*, p. 353. Cf. Susan K. Boardman and Sandra V. Horowitz ('Constructive Conflict Management and Social Problems: An Introduction', *JSI* 50 [1994], pp. 1-12 [4]) who define conflict as 'an incompatibility of behaviors, cognitions (including goals), and /or affect among individuals or groups that may or may not lead to an aggressive expression of this social incompatibility'. I will argue that in Thessalonica the divergent behaviors and beliefs of Christians and non-Christians did lead to 'aggressive expression' of 'social incompatibility'.

or more members of one group are deemed incompatible with the beha-
viors and beliefs of one or more members of another group.

5. Characteristics of Intergroup Conflict

Although it is not possible to predict precisely when and with whom
conflict will occur, social theorists have noted some characteristics or
conditions which accompany intergroup conflict. In this section I will
discuss three factors which facilitate intergroup conflict. First of all,
there must be *interaction* or contact between the two groups.[32] As
Seneca (*Ep.* 103.5) once observed, 'People collide only when they are
traveling the same path.' Where there is no social interaction, there is
little potential for friction. Alternatively, contact with another party,
especially if it is consistent, can sow seeds of discord. Although this
point may appear trite, it is of some significance for this study. It was
Paul's contact with Thessalonian Jews that created his poor relations
with some of them.[33] Additionally, the fact that Paul's Gentile converts
would probably have had little sustained contact with Jews, at least subsequent to their conversion, renders unlikely the view that the Thessalonian Christians were subjected to Jewish opposition. Instead, it
appears that they were harassed by their fellow Gentiles.[34]

   In order for intergroup conflict to occur there must also be a degree of
collective identity.[35] That is to say, 'the outgroup must be visible and in
some way distinguishable from the ingroup'.[36] As with deviance,
boundaries play an important role in the creation and perpetuation of
conflict.[37] Furthermore, the research of Sherif and Sherif[38] and Tajfel[39]
has shown that the tendency of a group to glorify itself and to vilify

32. See, among others, Mack and Snyder, 'Analysis of Social Conflict', p. 218.

33. In Chapter 3 I concluded that Luke's report of Paul frequenting the synagogue in Thessalonica and of his being driven from the city by unbelieving Jews
appears to be accurate. See further pp. 130-35 below.

34. See further pp. 218-26 herein.

35. Kriesburg, *Social Conflicts*, p. 99.

36. Deutsch, *Resolution of Conflict*, p. 68.

37. See John G. Holmes, John H. Ellard and Helmut Lamm, 'Boundary Roles
and Intergroup Conflict', in Worchel and Austin (eds.), *Intergroup Relations*, pp.
343-63.

38. E.g. Muzafer and Carolyn W. Sherif, *Groups in Harmony and Tension: An
Integration of Studies on Intergroup Relations* (New York: Harper & Row, 1953).

39. Tajfel, *Human Groups*.

other groups can and frequently does lead to conflict.

Opposition (or competition) is the final component of intergroup conflict I will note. As we will see directly below, a number of factors can prompt one group to oppose or to compete with another. More often than not, however, the group with influence and power is able to prevail over the weaker other.[40] Students of society have been and continue to be interested in the (ab)use of power.[41] The absence or presence of power has certainly shaped the relations of Christians and non-Christians across the centuries[42] and probably shaped the conflict between believers and unbelievers in Thessalonica.

6. *Causes of Intergroup Conflict*

Conflicts and snowflakes are similar to the extent that no two are exactly alike. Nevertheless, social scientists who study conflict suggest that there are some common causes or sources of conflict. Some of the proposed causes of conflict are so all-encompassing that they are not particularly illuminating. For example, Alan R. Beals and Bernard J. Siegel suggest that conflict can be traced to internal strains and external stresses.[43] But this is not saying much. More helpful is the work of Daniel Katz who contends that there are three basic reasons for conflict between groups: economics, ideology (i.e. values or beliefs) and power.[44] Although these suggested causes of conflict are also rather broad, most intergroup conflicts may be linked to at least one of these

40. This is one of the foundational principles of conflict theory. See esp. the discussion of Duke, *Conflict and Power*, pp. 235-54. On the issues of influence and power, see also Bisno, *Managing Conflict*, pp. 40-45, and Deutsch, *Resolution of Conflict*, pp. 84-93.

41. In fact, Thio (*Deviant Behavior*, pp. 75-81) seeks to explain deviant behavior on the basis of power.

42. R.I. Moore (*The Formation of a Persecuting Society: Power and Deviance in Western Europe, 950–1250* [Oxford: Basil Blackwell, 1987]) highlights this fact in his fascinating study.

43. Beals and Siegel, *Divisiveness and Social Conflict*, p. 157.

44. Daniel Katz, 'Nationalism and Strategies of International Conflict Resolution', in Herbert C. Kelman (ed.), *International Behavior: A Social-Psychological Analysis* (New York: Holt, Rinehart & Winston, 1965), pp. 356-90 (373-74). Mack and Snyder ('Social Conflict', pp. 220-21) maintain that there are two primary sources of conflict: ideology and culture.

three sources.[45] Economic conflict arises over competition for scarce material goods and resources,[46] while value conflict 'revolves around incompatible preferences, principles, or practices that people believe in and are invested in with reference to their group identity'.[47] Power conflicts occur when one party attempts to extend its influence by controlling another party.

Three additional remarks are in order concerning the causes of conflict. First of all, when trying to assess the source(s) of a conflict, one should take into account the personality and interactional styles of a given group.[48] Although it is impossible to measure such dynamics, there is little doubt that they help to create and to shape intergroup conflicts.[49] Secondly, although a conflict may be realistic in nature, unrealistic factors (e.g. misperception) are frequently present as well.[50]

45. Mack and Snyder ('Social Conflict', p. 221) observe, 'Most social scientists now accept the principle of multiple causality; hence, there is no one basic source of conflict.'

46. Karl Marx (*Capital* [New York: Vintage Books, 1977], and Marx and Friedrich Engels, *The Communist Manifesto* [New York: Pantheon Books, 1967]) maintained that economics is *the* source of conflict. Surely this is too simplistic. Bisno (*Managing Conflict*, pp. 28-29) helpfully expands the category of economic conflict to structural conflict. While including economic elements, structural conflict also addresses the struggle for non-material advantages and rewards, such as honor and status. On conflicts over status and honor, see further Max Weber, *The Theory of Social and Economic Organization* (New York: Free Press, 1947), esp. pp. 132-35.

47. Fisher, *Conflict*, p. 34. On value conflict, see further Ralph H. Turner, 'Value Conflict in Social Disorganization' *SSR* 38 (1954), pp. 301-308. Deutsch (*Resolution of Conflict*, pp. 15-16) makes a distinction between conflicts over values and conflicts over beliefs. He suggests that values represent what 'should be' (i.e. the ideal), whereas beliefs mirror that which 'is' (i.e. the real). In practice, there tends to be more of an interplay between values and beliefs than Deutsch suggests.

48. So Bisno, *Managing Conflict*, p. 28. Although groups do not possess a personality or interactional style as such, the members of groups do, and people formulate their impressions of a group by interacting with the group's members.

49. Robert A. Wortham ('The Problem of Anti-Judaism in 1 Thess 2:14-16 and Related Pauline Texts', *BTB* 25 [1995], pp. 37-44) suggests that Paul's feelings of inadequacy and insecurity were partly responsible for his vituperative outburst against his fellow Jews in 1 Thess. 2.14-16.

50. R.M. Williams, Jr. (*The Reduction of Intergroup Tensions* [New York: Social Science Research Council, 1947], p. 39) thinks that the combination and mutual reinforcement of realistic and unrealistic conflict elements perpetuate intergroup hostility.

Finally, one should note that a given conflict results from a combination of causes, and in the ebb and flow of social interaction these sources of conflict can meld to the extent that they become indistinguishable.[51] Furthermore, as Fisher notes, 'It is not uncommon for a conflict to originate from one source and then proliferate to include other sources and issues and to escalate through a combination of realistic and unrealistic factors.'[52] I will consider the reasons for Paul's and the Thessalonian believers' conflict with outsiders in Chapters 7 and 10 respectively. I will argue that a variety of factors precipitated their conflict with non-Christians.

7. *The Cycle of Intergroup Conflict*

Different disputes have different dynamics. As a result, the only way one can pinpoint the particulars of a given conflict is to study it carefully.[53] This project is an attempt to describe in as much detail and with as much precision as possible the complex conflict situation between believers and unbelievers in Thessalonica. Notwithstanding the need to spell out the specifics of a given conflict, conflict theorists have been able to detect general stages of conflict. In this section we will consider two proposed patterns of conflict relations.[54]

Victor Turner likens conflict to a four-act social drama.[55] According to Turner, the first act of a conflict is the occurrence of a breach of regular norm-governed relations. Act two is typified by a period of mounting crisis (i.e. the intensification of conflict). In the third stage of

51. See Katz, 'Conflict Resolution', p. 374. Fisher (*Conflict*, p. 34) remarks, 'Typologies of conflict, like all categorization systems, have the appeal of simplifying social reality through analysis, thus initially increasing our understanding. However, none can do total justice to the complexity of social life.' So similarly, Bisno, *Managing Conflict*, pp. 29-30.

52. Fischer, *Conflict*, p. 34.

53. So rightly Beals and Siegel, *Divisiveness and Social Conflict*, p. 170.

54. There are, of course, other proposed patterns of conflict relations which we will not consider here. See, e.g., Alan C. Filley, *Interpersonal Conflict Resolution* (Glenview, IL: Scott, Foresman & Co., 1975), pp. 7-18. Filley suggests that conflict unfolds as follows: antecedent conditions, perceived and felt conflict, manifest behavior, conflict resolution or suppression and resolution aftermath. See also de Vos, *Church and Community Conflicts*, pp. 11-26, for a useful discussion on the development of conflict.

55. Turner, *Schism and Community*, p. 92.

the conflict, various attempts are made by the concerned parties to contain or to resolve the crisis. Then, in the fourth act, there is either the restoration of ruptured relations or a breach between the groups.

Kriesburg has also proposed a cycle of social conflict.[56] His model has five stages. According to Kriesburg, a conflict begins with parties having conflicting goals. These rival aims, which are not always recognized at first, constitute the objective grounds for conflict between the concerned entities. The second stage of conflict occurs when the involved parties become aware that an incompatibility exists, and they seek some way to contend with the other. The third phase of the conflict cycle centers upon the pursuit of contradictory goals by the respective sides. During this stage the conflict will often escalate (i.e. will increase in magnitude). Prior to the fourth aspect of conflict, the so-called termination stage, there will be a de-escalation of the conflict. However, in a prolonged conflict there may be a recurrence of escalation and de-escalation. Once a conflict is terminated, then the last stage is reached: the outcome stage.[57]

8. *Consequences of Intergroup Conflict*

How can conflict with an outgroup impact the ingroup? This is the question with which I will deal in this section. At the outset it is necessary to note that I am not seeking to determine the 'functions' of intergroup conflict like Coser and those biblical scholars who have followed in his functionalist footsteps. (As noted above, social theorists have significantly revised Coser's one-sided analysis of conflict.) Rather, I want to enumerate some of the potential outcomes of social conflict on groups thus engaged.[58]

First, *intergroup conflict may lead to ingroup hostility toward the outgroup*. While not denying the possible influence of other factors (e.g. a given cultural context), the presence or absence of hostility is

56. Kriesburg, *Social Conflicts*, p. 19.
57. Due to the paucity of data, it is now impossible to run Paul's and the Thessalonian Christians' conflict with non-Christians through these proposed cycles. My purpose for considering these potential patterns of conflict is to observe how conflicts can unfold.
58. The insights of Coser (*Functions of Social Conflict*) are, in fact, helpful here. Unlike Coser, however, I am not seeking to demonstrate that social conflict fulfills 'a number of determinative functions in groups and other interpersonal relations' (p. 8).

often linked to the (perceived) reason(s) for the conflict[59] and the opportunity for social interaction between the involved parties.[60]

Intergroup conflict may also result in ingroup solidarity,[61] *enhanced awareness of ingroup identity*[62] *and tightening of group boundaries.*[63] Frequently, though by no means always or automatically, groups huddle together in the midst of conflict to weather the cold winds of disapproval blowing from outside.[64] On the other hand, when intergroup conflict is minimal or non-existent, there is a tendency for groups to be less unified, for member loyalty to be low and for a group to break up into smaller units.[65]

When a group is experiencing conflict with another party, *there is also the possibility that the ingroup will exaggerate its virtues and will magnify outgroup vices.*[66] Frequently, conflict with an outgroup heightens ingroup bias[67] and results in a stereotypical perception and portrayal

59. Muzafer Sherif *et al.* (*Intergroup Conflict and Cooperation: The Robber's Cave Experiment* [Norman, OK: University of Oklahoma Press, 1961]) have observed that the more important the values at stake in the intergroup conflict, the greater the possibility for hostility.

60. Coser (*Functions of Social Conflict*, pp. 67-72) suggests that the closer the relationship between the parties in conflict the greater the conflict will be. Stark (*Sociology*, p. 296) writes, 'Contact accompanied by inequality and competition breeds contempt. It can even turn former friends into strangers.'

61. On this ubiquitous principle in conflict studies, see, among others, Simmel, *Conflict*, pp. 92-93; Coser, *Functions of Social Conflict*, pp. 87-95; LeVine and Campbell, *Ethnocentrism*, p. 31; and Filley, *Conflict Resolution*, pp. 6-7.

62. Coser, *Functions of Social Conflict*, pp. 104-10.

63. Coser, *Functions of Social Conflict*, pp. 95-104, and Deutsch, *Resolution of Conflict*, p. 76.

64. Dorwin Cartwright ('The Nature of Group Cohesiveness', in Dorwin Cartwright and Alvin Zander [eds.], *Group Dynamics: Research and Theory* [New York: Harper & Row, 3rd edn, 1968], pp. 91-109 [103-105]) suggests the following outcomes of group cohesiveness: increased member loyalty, increased participation in group activities, greater conformity to group norms and a greater sense of security for group members.

65. So Deutsch, *Resolution of Conflict*, p. 76. For the presence and absence of conflict and the impact that such had on the Pauline congregations in Thessalonica and Corinth, see John M.G. Barclay, 'Thessalonica and Corinth: Social Contrasts in Pauline Christianity', *JSNT* 47 (1992), pp. 49-72, and de Vos, *Church and Community Conflicts*.

66. See LeVine and Campbell, *Ethnocentrism*, p. 32, and Deutsch, *Resolution of Conflict*, pp. 75-76.

67. The term 'ethnocentrism' is appropriate here, if by ethnocentrism one means

of outsiders by insiders.[68] That is to say, ingroup glorification and out-group denigration are common dynamics of groups engaged in conflict.

A final potential consequence of intergroup conflict which merits mentioning is that *conflict can cause a group to 'crack down' on those who would seek to deviate from group norms.*[69] When in the throes of conflict, ingroups tend to be less tolerant of deviance than they are when relations with outgroups are harmonious.[70] Furthermore, some conflict theorists have observed that conflict relations tend to reduce group defection.[71] This tendency is usually linked to the increased internal solidarity of a group engaged in conflict.

Having said that, conflict with an outgroup can also divide and destroy an ingroup. It appears that the way a group responds to conflict is based in large measure on how it interprets (or is led to interpret) a given conflict. If a group perceives a conflict as (ultimately) beneficial (e.g. a labor strike), then it may well be unified in and through conflict (and vice versa). The Thessalonians' conflict with their Gentile compatriots seems to have solidified their faith and their fellowship—both one with another and with Paul.[72] An overview of how (leaders of) groups attempt to manage conflict with other groups will conclude our survey of the social-scientific study of intergroup conflict.

a 'cultural narrowness' in which an individual or group rigidly accepts those who are culturally similar and rigidly rejects those who are culturally dissimilar. On ethnocentrism, see further Summer, *Folkways*; Fisher, *Conflict*, pp. 22-24; and esp. LeVine and Campbell, *Ethnocentrism*.

68. So Louise H. Kidder and V. Mary Stewart, *The Psychology of Intergroup Relations: Conflict and Consciousness* (New York: McGraw–Hill, 1975), pp. 26-35.

69. See further, Pat Lauderdale, Jerry Parker, Phil Smith-Cunnien and James Inverarity, 'External Threat and the Definition of Deviance', *JPP* 46 (1984), pp. 1058-68.

70. So, e.g., Coser, *Functions of Social Conflict*, pp. 70-71; Deutsch, *Resolution of Conflict*, p. 76; and Levine and Campbell, *Ethnocentrism*, p. 33. For an interesting study of how the Amish—an Anabaptist group which defines itself over against culture—deal with deviance, see John A. Hostetler, *Amish Society* (Baltimore: The Johns Hopkins University Press, 3rd edn, 1980), pp. 292-312.

71. E.g. Coser, *Functions of Social Conflict*, pp. 95-104, and LeVine and Campbell, *Ethnocentrism*, p. 33. On the dynamics of disaffection, see further Hans Toch, *The Social Psychology of Social Movements* (New York: Bobbs–Merrill, 1965), pp. 157-81.

72. See further pp. 272-80 below.

9. *Coping with Intergroup Conflict*

How do groups, or representatives thereof, who are engaged in conflict seek to deal with it? The correct response to this query is: variously. Here, I will note and comment upon four possible ways that groups cope with conflict.[73] One common approach to managing conflict is to *compete* with or fight against the other party with a view to imposing the ingroup's aims onto the outgroup. Such an strategy, sometimes called the 'win–lose' approach, usually results in either victory for one party and defeat for the other or in a stalemate typified by continual tension. Those groups which opt for this particular conflict management style tend to have a strong ingroup bias.

Another tactic for dealing with conflict is *avoidance or withdrawal*. This modus operandi for managing conflict concludes that a degree of isolation, be it physical or psychological, is preferable to and/or safer than attempting to counter the opposition.

Seeking to *accommodate* the opposing group is also a way of dealing with conflict. This approach assumes that expediency is the best policy and reasons that it is wise to limit one's losses by acceding to the demands of the other and by trying to smooth over strained relations.

A fourth strategy for coping with conflict is to enter into *dialogue* with the other group. This course of conflict management assumes that the other party is willing to discuss the reason(s) for conflict and hopes that creative alternatives to the conflict can be found. Such social inter-action requires a degree of trust and respect between the involved par-ties. Nevertheless, the ingroup is not opposed to converting the out-group to its own perspective while in the course of the negotiations! It remains to be said that there may be a combination of responses on the part of a group to a given conflict.

10. *Conclusion*

In this chapter I have explored the social-scientific study of intergroup conflict relationships. I have noted various aspects of conflict, defined intergroup conflict and considered proposed classifications, characteris-

73. In formulating this section I have drawn upon the following resources: Kriesburg, *Social Conflicts*, pp. 206-208; Bisno, *Managing Conflict*, pp. 60-98; Fisher, *Conflict*, pp. 187-91; and Filley, *Conflict Resolution*, pp. 48-59.

tics, causes and consequences of intergroup conflict. Furthermore, we have seen how intergroup conflict can unfold and how groups engaged in conflict may seek to deal with it. As a result of this discussion, we have gained a good grasp of the characteristics and dynamics of intergroup conflict. I have been and will be cautious not to allow the general to take precedence over the particular in this study. Nevertheless, it stands to reason that one should take a careful look at conflict in general if one desires to understand more thoroughly the specifics of a given conflict. General observations about conflict do not dictate the conclusions at which one arrives; rather, the social-scientific study of conflict assists one by suggesting possible directions in which to look and helpful questions to ask.

The preceding discussion will be particularly informative in addressing the following questions below:

- How and by whom were Paul and his converts opposed? (See Chapters 6, 9).
- Why did Paul and the Thessalonian believers encounter conflict with outsiders? (See Chapters 7, 10).
- What impact did the conflict have on Paul and on the church? How did the Christians seek to cope with their 'afflictions'? (See Chapters 8, 11).

Having set forth in some detail the social-scientific concepts which I will employ in this study, we may now turn to consider the contours of Paul's and the Thessalonians' conflict with outsiders. In the chapters which follow, I will return to the preceding discussion of deviance and conflict time and again in an attempt to understand better the particular texts under investigation and the social realities which stand behind them.

Part III

THE APOSTLE'S ΑΓΩΝ

Chapter 6

NON-CHRISTIAN OPPOSITION TO PAUL
AND HIS THESSALONIAN MISSION*

1. *Introduction*

In this chapter, I will treat verses in 1 Thessalonians which indicate non-Christian opposition to Paul and his ministry in Thessalonica. The verses upon which I will focus are located in 1 Thessalonians 2, the chapter where Paul reflects upon his initial visit to Thessalonica (2.1-16) and begins to express his deep desire to see his converts again (2.17-20). At the outset of this chapter, I will examine 2.2. I will then consider portions of two other verses, namely 2.15b and 2.16a. Lastly, I will discuss 2.1-12 with a view to discovering why Paul penned this pericope.[1] By way of conclusion I will summarize my findings regarding Paul's troubles in Thessalonica.

2. *Opposition in Thessalonica*

In 1 Thess. 1.2-10 Paul gives thanks to God for the Thessalonian congregation. In particular, he offers thanksgiving for his converts' faith, love and hope (1.3) as well as for their election (1.4-5), imitation (1.6-8) and conversion (1.9-10). Paul's reflection on his mission to Thessalonica and the results thereof prompts him to remind the church in 2.1

---

* I presented a portion of this chapter (section 5) in an earlier form to the Southwestern Regional Group of the Institute for Biblical Research in March 1998. I would like to thank the group for its supportive response.

1. Did Paul intend this passage to function as an apology against actual or potential accusations and/or as parenesis for the Thessalonian congregation? If there is validity to the view that 2.1-12 is a Pauline apology, is it possible to detect the source(s) of and the reason(s) for the slander?

that the missionaries'[2] coming (εἴσοδος) to them was not in vain (οὐ κενὴ γέγονεν).[3]

At this juncture a reader might anticipate Paul to give additional reasons why he thought his sojourn in Thessalonica was successful (note 2.13). Instead, he proceeds to speak of the circumstances surrounding the apostles' initial visit to the city and to remark upon the character of their message and ministry while there (2.2-12).[4] In 2.2 Paul maintains

2.   It is now impossible to know precisely who assisted Paul in Thessalonica. While it is clear enough that Silvanus (or Silas) was present with Paul when the church was founded (Acts 17.10a), it remains an open question whether or not Timothy was with them at this point. Although Timothy is included in the address of 1 Thess. (1.1; cf. 2 Thess. 1.1) and had been to Thessalonica by the time Paul wrote the epistle (3.2, 6), Paul does not explicitly state that Timothy was with him and Silas in Thessalonica. Furthermore, Acts does not indicate Timothy's presence.

Although scholars tend to assume that Timothy was in Thessalonica when the church was founded (e.g. Bruce, *Thessalonians*, p. xxii; Haenchen, *Acts*, p. 512; Collins, *Birth of the New Testament*, p. 20; J. Peter Bercovitz, 'Paul and Thessalonica', *Proceedings* 10 [1990], pp. 123-35 [123]), there may be validity in Schmithals's suggestion (*Paul and the Gnostics*, p. 181) that he was not present when Paul initially visited the city. Could it be that Paul sent Timothy to Thessalonica because he had not previously been there and had not experienced the controversy with outsiders which Paul and Silas had?

Because Timothy's presence in Thessalonica when the church began is unclear, when referring specifically to Timothy's presence during the founding visit, I will use qualifiers such as 'perhaps' and 'maybe'. When the reader encounters co-worker(s), colleague(s) or helper(s), it should be taken as shorthand for Silvanus and perhaps Timothy (and for all we know other Pauline associates as well!). Since my interest revolves around Paul himself and the conflict that he encountered, at times I will simply speak of Paul without reference to his coworker(s). For a treatment of Paul and his helpers see, E. Earle Ellis, 'Coworkers, Paul and His', *DPL*, pp. 183-89.

3.   I render κενή in 2.1 'in vain', emphasizing results, instead of 'insincere', emphasizing motives, for the following reasons: (1) this translation coheres with Paul's usage of the term in 3.5 and elsewhere (1 Cor. 15.10, 58; 2 Cor. 6.1; Gal. 2.2; Phil. 2.16); (2) it fits well with what Paul has said in 1.9-10 regarding the results of the apostles' visit. So similarly, Wanamaker, *Thessalonians*, p. 92, and Holmes, *Thessalonians*, p. 61 n. 6. Cf. otherwise, Marshall, *Thessalonians*, pp. 62-63, and Jeffrey A.D. Weima, 'An Apology for the Apologetic Function of 1 Thessalonians 2.1-12', *JSNT* 68 (1997), pp. 73-99 (94 n. 58).

4.   So rightly, Paul Ellingworth and Eugene A. Nida, *A Translator's Handbook on Paul's Letters to the Thessalonians* (New York: United Bible Societies, 1976), pp. 19-20.

that the Thessalonian believers knew of the fact (καθὼς οἴδατε) that even though[5] the preachers 'had already suffered [προπαθόντες] and been shamefully treated [ὑβρισθέντες] in Philippi, [they] had courage [ἐπαρρησιασάμεθα] in [their] God to declare to [the Thessalonians] the gospel of God in spite of great opposition [ἐν πολλῷ ἀγῶνι]'.

Interpreters debate the meaning of ἀγών in 2.2. While some think that ἀγών refers to Paul's intrapersonal psychological conflict and anxiety,[6] others contend that Paul uses the term to describe the exertion entailed in the proclamation of the gospel.[7] Still others suggest that ἐν πολλῷ ἀγῶνι refers to the non-Christian opposition which the missionaries experienced in Thessalonica.[8] I hold to the latter view.[9]

5.   I take the participles in 2.2a to be circumstantial participles denoting concession or opposition. See also, e.g., J.B. Lightfoot, *Notes on the Epistles of St. Paul (1 and 2 Thessalonians, 1 Corinthians 1–7, Romans 1–7, Ephesians 1:1-14)* (Winona Lake, IN: Alpha Publications, n.d.), p. 19; Victor C. Pfitzner, *Paul and the Agon Motif: Traditional Athletic Imagery in the Pauline Literature* (NovTSup, 16; Leiden: E.J. Brill, 1967), p. 114; and Morris, *Thessalonians*, p. 59 n. 7.

6.   So Dobschütz, *Thessalonicherbriefe*, p. 85; Rigaux, *Thessaloniciens*, p. 405; Malherbe, *Paul and the Thessalonians*, p. 48; and, albeit cautiously, Frame, *Thessalonians*, p. 94. If Paul had intended to indicate that he overcame anxiety in order to declare the gospel in Thessalonica, one is left to wonder, despite the position of these commentators, why he did not employ the term μέριμνα (cf. 2 Cor. 11.28). Below I will offer further and weightier objections to this interpretation.

7.   E.g. Lightfoot, *Notes*, p. 20, and Dibelius, *Thessalonicher*, p. 7. Holtz (*Thessalonicher*, p. 70) maintains that the conflict of which Paul speaks is that which exists between the gospel and the world.

8.   See, among others, Milligan, *Thessalonians*, p. 17; Best, *Thessalonians*, p. 92; Marshall, *Thessalonians*, p. 64; Wanamaker, *Thessalonians*, p. 93; Morris, *Thessalonians*, p. 61 n. 12; Pfitzner, *Paul and the Agon Motif*, p. 114; and Weima, 'Apologetic Function', pp. 94-95 n. 59.

John Chrysostom (*Homilies*, 13.329) seemingly thought that Paul was struggling with both internal and external conflict. This could conceivably have been the case (cf. 2 Cor. 7.5). However, in 2.2 Paul is in all likelihood maintaining that he and his helper(s) were facing external pressure. Bruce J. Malina (*The New Testament World: Insights from Cultural Anthropology* [Atlanta: John Knox Press, 1981], pp. 32-33) contends that Mediterranean culture was and is an *agonistic* culture characterized by conflict over and competition for a much sought after but limited good: honor.

9.   Apparently Paul was thought of and treated as dangerously deviant by some in Thessalonica. Seemingly there were people in positions of civil/religious power (the so-called 'agents of censure' interested in protecting and perpetuating the status

Contextual considerations support this position. Although ἀγών can connote spiritual or internal striving,[10] the fact that Paul links the apostles' declaration of the gospel in Thessalonica with their suffering (προπαθεῖν) and shameful treatment (ὑβρίζειν) in Philippi strongly suggests that the missionaries met external resistance in both locales.[11] Furthermore, Paul's claim that they had courage (παρρησιάζεσθαι) in God to speak the gospel in spite of considerable affliction indicates a conflict situation.[12] Ernest Best suggests that the apostles' 'preaching can only be described as courageous if there is external opposition'.[13]

---

quo) who sought to thwart the ministry of the apostle by means of negative informal (e.g. verbal harassment) and perhaps even formal sanctions (e.g. religious and political bans). On how Paul might have been opposed by unbelievers in Thessalonica, see pp. 137, 149 below. As to why Paul encountered conflict with Jews in Thessalonica (and elsewhere), see Chapter 7.

10. Bruce (*Thessalonians*, p. 25) and Frame (*Thessalonians*, p. 94) maintain that ἀγών carries this meaning in Col. 2.1. See otherwise, Pfitzner (*Paul and the Agon Motif*, pp. 109-13, 126-29) who thinks that external circumstances are in view.

11. So rightly, Barclay ('Conflict in Thessalonica', p. 513) who contends, 'The parallel with Philippi suggests vigorous, possibly physical, opposition.' On Paul's troubles in Philippi, see Phil. 1.30, where Paul once again uses the term ἀγών to describe conflict with outsiders. Cf. Acts 16.19-40.

12. So also C.E.B. Cranfield, 'A Study of 1 Thessalonians 2', *IBS* 1 (1979), pp. 215-26 (220). Pfitzner (*Paul and the Agon Motif*, p. 112) observes, 'In Acts the word [παρρησιάζεσθαι] designates the joyful and fearless courage which accompanied the early proclamation of the Easter message in the face of opposition (Acts 9:27f., 13:46, 14:3 and 19:8; also Eph 6:20).'

Abraham J. Malherbe (' "Gentle as a Nurse": The Cynic Background to 1 Thessalonians 2', *NovT* 12 [1970], pp. 203-17, and 'Exhortation in First Thessalonians', *NovT* 25 [1983], pp. 238-56) views Paul's παρρησία against a Cynic backdrop. While Malherbe marshals some striking parallels from the writings of Dio Chrysostom (40–c. 120 CE), he does not adquately address the external obstacles which Paul faced when preaching in Thessalonica (and elsewhere). Furthermore, he neglects to note that Cynics also encountered opposition. See pp. 139-43 below. As a result, Malherbe's Paul emerges looking more like an ideal Cynic philosopher than a Jewish apostle to the Gentiles (cf. 1 Thess. 2.6, 16), despite his qualifications in 'Paul: Hellenistic Philosopher or Christian Pastor?', *ATR* 68 (1986), pp. 3-13. Bruce W. Winter ('The Entries and Ethics of Orators and Paul [1 Thessalonians 2:1-12])', *TynBul* 44 [1993], pp. 55-74 [73 n. 73]) critiques Malherbe's placement of Paul in a philosophical frame.

13. Best, *Thessalonians*, p. 92. Pfitzner (*Paul and the Agon Motif*, p. 113) adds, '[I]t is hard to understand how Paul could have spoken of the boldness of his preaching in one breath, and of his fear and anxiety in the other—unless one avoids

Paul's remarks in 1.6 also need to be considered here. In this verse he states that his converts 'became imitators of [the missionaries] and of the Lord, for [they] received the word in considerable affliction [ἐν θλίψει πολλῇ], with joy inspired by the Holy Spirit'. Paul is maintaining in 1.6 that the Thessalonian believers imitated their apostles and Lord in that they too experienced suffering.[14] It is conceivable that Paul had his own troubles in Thessalonica in mind when commending his converts.[15]

My view that Paul is referring in 2.2 (and 1.6) to external opposition which he and his co-worker(s) encountered from unbelievers in Thessalonica becomes even more persuasive when viewed alongside other remarks in the epistle. Another statement indicating the ministers' conflict in Thessalonica appears in 2.15b.

3. *Expulsion from Thessalonica*

In 2.15b Paul contends that certain Jews ἡμᾶς ἐκδιωξάντων. This cryptic phrase, which occurs in the context of Paul's polemic against some Jewish people (2.15-16), immediately raises at least three interpretive questions: (1) What is the meaning of the New Testament *hapax legomenon* ἐκδιώκειν? (2) To whom does ἡμᾶς refer? (3) Who are the Ἰουδαῖοι who ἡμᾶς ἐκδιωξάντων? I will treat these closely related queries in reverse order.

a. *Identifying the* Ἰουδαῖοι
I indicated in Chapter 1 that one may translate Ἰουδαῖοι in 2.14 as either 'Judeans' or 'Jews'. I concluded that the latter rendering is more probable. Nevertheless, I emphasized that Paul was not referring to all Jews, but to those particular Jews who Paul saw as opposing the work of God by causing Judean Christians to suffer, by killing the Lord Jesus

the obvious contradiction by an artificial distinction between his external behaviour and inner feelings!'

14. So also de Boer, *Imitation of Paul*, p. 114, and John S. Pobee, *Persecution and Martyrdom in the Theology of Paul* (JSNTSup, 6; Sheffield: JSOT Press, 1985), p. 70.

15. It appears that ἐν θλίψει πολλῇ (1.6) and ἐν πολλῷ ἀγῶνι (2.2) are more or less synonymous expressions. Wanamaker (*Thessalonians*, p. 93) remarks, 'Since 1:6 (cf. 2:13-17; Acts 17:5-9) makes it clear that the gospel was delivered in a situation of opposition in Thessalonica, it seems probable that Paul is recollecting that opposition here [i. e. in 2:2].'

and the prophets, by banishing or persecuting Paul and his co-work-ers(s) and by hindering the Pauline mission. I suggested in Chapter 1, therefore, that the Jews to whom Paul refers did not necessarily share a common locality. Rather, they shared an ethnicity as well as a similar hostility toward those people (i.e. the Judean Christians, Jesus, the prophets, Paul and his helper[s]) and/or things (i.e. the gospel message and its proclamation to τοῖς ἔθνεσιν) that Paul perceived to be from or of God. This interpretive decision leaves open for discussion the specific cross-section of Jews about whom Paul was thinking when he wrote ἡμᾶς ἐκδιωξάντων.

Detlef von Dobschütz thinks that Paul is speaking in 2.15b of his expulsion from Jerusalem by zealous Jews who belonged to what Dob-schütz calls the 'Thorapolizei', that is, a corps of young men that existed in Jewish communities both in Palestine and the Diaspora and took (forceful) action against non-conforming Jews. Dobschütz main-tains that prior to his conversion Paul was closely affiliated with such a group and that subsequent to his Damascus experience was strenuously opposed by the same, particularly in Jerusalem.[16] I find this suggestion unconvincing. Dobschütz's proposal is open to criticism on various grounds.[17] I need only to observe here, however, that Dobschütz neglects to consider the all-important first person plural personal pro-noun in 2.15b: ἡμᾶς. Before one can determine the group of Jews who ἡμᾶς ἐκδιωξάντων, it is necessary to determine the referent of ἡμᾶς.

b. *To Whom Does ἡμᾶς Refer?*
There are at least three possible ways to construe the 'us' of 2.15b.[18] The pronoun may either refer to Paul and his co-worker(s), to Paul and other apostles in general or to Paul and the Thessalonian Christians.

---

16. Detlef von Dobschütz, 'Paulus und die jüdische Thorapolizei' (Inaugural dissertation, Friedrich Alexander Universität, Erlangen, 1968), p. 102.
17. For a fuller summary and critique of Dobschütz's work, see Seland, *Estab-lishment Violence*, pp. 29-30.
18. So Schlueter, *Filling up the Measure*, p. 70. Holmes (*Thessalonians*, p. 84) offers a fourth option. He holds that by 'us' Paul means Judean Christians who were forced to leave Jerusalem (noting Acts 8.1, 4, 23-25, 29-30). It seems highly unlikely in writing to the Thessalonians, however, that Paul would use 'us' in such a way so as to exclude himself. In any event, according to Acts 8.1b-3, Paul was not driven out of Jerusalem; rather, he was among those who were ravaging the church thereby forcing Christians to flee the city for safety (cf. 9.23-25)!

Against the last of these options[19] is the fact that it was seemingly Gentiles, not Jews, who opposed the Thessalonian believers.[20] Furthermore, if ἐκδιωξάντων is best understood as 'to drive out' or 'banish' (see pp. 133-35 below), then this was clearly not the case for Paul's converts who remained in Thessalonica.

Could it be that Paul uses 'us' in reference to Christian apostles in general? Schlueter thinks so. To support this position, however, Schlueter offers the dubious suggestion that when Paul speaks of 'apostles of Christ' in 2.7 he possibly had in mind the Jerusalem apostles who, unlike himself, received financial support from the believers to whom they ministered (cf. 1 Cor. 9.3-14)![21] Furthermore, she turns to 'parallels' in Matthew and Luke where she finds 'us' referring to 'us apostles' (see Mt. 23.34-36; Lk. 11.49).[22]

One need not go this far afield to discover the referent of 'us'. Time and again in 1 Thessalonians 2 (2.1, 2 [twice], 3, 4 [twice], 5, 6 [twice], 7, 8 [three times], 9 [four times], 10, 11, 13 [twice], 15, 16, 17 [twice], 18 [twice], 19 and 20), Paul employs the first person plural to refer to himself, Silvanus and possibly Timothy. While it is true that Paul can use the first person plural to refer to all Christians (1.10; 4.7; 5.5-10) and perhaps only to himself (3.1, 2, 6),[23] his predominate pattern in 1 Thessalonians is to refer to himself and his co-worker(s) in the first person plural and to the Thessalonian Christians in the second person plural. This is clearly the case in the immediate context of Paul's statement in 2.15b. It seems best, then, to understand the 'us' of 2.15b as a reference to Paul, Silvanus and possibly Timothy.[24] The high probability that ἡμᾶς is to be understood here as it is throughout (practically) all of the epistle, that is as shorthand for Paul, Silvanus and Timothy(?), leads me to take the phrase ἡμᾶς ἐκδιωξάντων as a reference to an experience that Paul and his co-worker(s) had with some Jews in Thes-

---

19. Contra Rigaux, *Thessaloniciens*, p. 78.

20. See further, pp. 218-26 below.

21. Schlueter, *Filling up the Measure*, p. 72.

22. Schlueter, *Filling up the Measure*, p. 72.

23. So Karl P. Donfried, 'War Timotheus in Athen? Exegetische Überlegungen zu 1 Thess 3,1-3', in Johannes Joachim Degenhardt (ed.), *Die Freude an Gott für unsere Kraft. Festschrift zum 65. Geburtstag Otto Bernhard Knoch* (Stuttgart: Katholisches Bibelwerk, 1991), pp. 189-96.

24. So also Frame, *Thessalonians*, p. 112; Best, *Thessalonians*, p. 116; and Marshall, *Thessalonians*, p. 79.

salonica.[25] Although the meaning of 2.15b is not immediately clear to belated readers of the letter, it would not have been lost on the epistle's original recipients.[26] The Thessalonian Christians would have readily recalled the apostles' clash with Jews in their city which necessitated their leaders' premature departure.

c. *Interpreting* ἐκδιώκειν

The term ἐκδιωξάντων is an aorist participle. The verb from which it is derived is the compound ἐκ-διώκειν. Interpreters disagree on how to translate this term. Best prefers the translation 'persecuted'.[27] In support of this rendering he writes: 'in the Greek of this period prepositions had lost much of their value when attached to verbs and served only to intensify their meaning'.[28] Furthermore, Best maintains that ἐκδιωξάντων should be taken 'as a real past tense referring to the persecutions Paul and his companions (and perhaps the Thessalonians also) suffered on their visit to Thessalonica and which were instigated by Jews (Acts 17.1ff)'.[29] Drawing upon the work of Best, Schlueter also opts for the translation 'persecuted', although she does not think it necessary to conceive of a particular episode of opposition.[30]

Alternatively, other scholars contend that ἐκδιώκειν is better rendered 'to drive out, banish or expel'.[31] In arguing for the translation 'to drive out', Charles A. Wanamaker appeals to the term's 'literal' mean-

---

25. So also, e.g., Craig C. Hill, *Hellenists and Hebrews: Reappraising Division within the Earliest Church* (Minneapolis: Fortress Press, 1992), p. 37 n. 69. Cf. Weatherly, *Thessalonians*, p. 88.

26. Marshall (*Thessalonians*, p. 79) maintains that the readers of the letter would have picked up on this allusion. Cf. Lightfoot, *Notes*, p. 33, and Frame, *Thessalonians*, p. 112.

27. Best, *Thessalonians*, p. 116. So also Morris, *Thessalonians*, p. 84.

28. Best, *Thessalonians*, p. 116. Note similarly Lünemann, *Thessalonians*, p. 69, and Cranfield, '1 Thessalonians 2', p. 225 n. 9.

29. Best, *Thessalonians*, p. 116. See similarly, Lightfoot, *Notes*, p. 33, and cautiously, Frame, *Thessalonians*, p. 112.

30. Schlueter, *Filling up the Measure*, pp. 68-70.

31. Dobschütz, 'Paulus', p. 102; Bruce, *Thessalonians*, p. 47; Malherbe, *Paul and the Thessalonians*, p. 62; Marshall, *Thessalonians*, p. 79; Richard, *Thessalonians*, p. 121; Wanamaker, *Thessalonians*, p. 115; and Holmes, *Thessalonians*, p. 84. A.T. Robertson (*Word Pictures in the New Testament* [6 vols.; Nashville: Broadman Press, 1931], IV, pp. 21-22) suggests that the verb means 'to drive out or banish, to chase out as if a wild beast'.

ing and to the aorist tense of the participle.[32] Two additional observations strengthen this interpretation. First, in 2.17a Paul speaks of being torn away or orphaned from (ἀπορφανίζεσθαι) the Thessalonian Christians. Paul employs the aorist participle here to connote an enforced separation between the missionaries and their converts. Given the tense and voice of the participle and the immediate context in which it occurs (i.e. where Paul is referring to the Jewish opposition of himself and his Gentile mission), it makes good sense to understand the participial phrase (ἀπορφανισθέντες ἀφ' ὑμῶν) metaphorically and as a further allusion to the expulsion of Paul and his coworker(s) from Thessalonica by some Jews.[33]

In further support of translating ἐκδιώκειν as 'to drive out', one may note that this is the typical meaning of the term both in the LXX (e.g. Deut. 6.19; 1 Chron. 8.13; 12.15; Ps. 36.28; Jer. 27.44; 29.19; Joel 2.20) and in other Greek literature (e.g. Thucydides, 1.24; Demosthenes, *Or.* 32.6; Josephus, *Apion* 1.292). Even though ἐκδιώκειν can occasionally mean 'to persecute' (e.g. Ps. 115.15; Sir. 30.19), lexical and contextual evidence suggests that the term is best rendered in 1 Thess. 2.15b as 'to drive out, banish or expel'. Such a translation allows the preposition ἐκ to carry a strong sense and preserves the full value of the past participle as referring to a single event.

Although I disagree with Best's translation of ἐκδιωξάντων, he rightly suggests that Paul was thinking of a particular event when writing ἡμᾶς ἐκδιωξάντων. In fact, I would contend that Paul was referring to the occasion when he, Silvanus and Timothy (?) were driven from Thessalonica by some unbelieving Jews.[34]

---

32. Wanamaker, *Thessalonians*, p. 115. Dobschütz ('Paulus', p. 102) writes, 'Gelegentlich kann aber auch die Vorsilbe ἐκ bei διώκω die Intensität einer Verfolgung ausdrücken. Gegen die Bedeutung "heftig verfolgen" spricht hier jedoch der Aorist ἐκδιωξάντων, der auf eine einmalige Handlung weist.'

33. Wanamaker (*Thessalonians*, p. 120) reasons, 'Since the passive form of the participle would require Paul to be portraying himself as an orphaned child, it seems better to understand the participle in a metaphorical sense as referring to the sudden and violent loss of the Thessalonians, which the apostle had experienced as a result of Jewish intervention (see 2:15f.).' So also Marshall, *Thessalonians*, pp. 79, 84-85, and Malherbe, *Paul and the Thessalonians*, p. 62.

34. If Acts 17.13 can be followed, then Paul was also driven out of Berea by some Thessalonian Jews. Holtz ('Judgment on the Jews', p. 285) reckons, 'This [detail] is not likely to have been a free invention by Luke.' Contrast Lüdemann, *Traditions in Acts*, p. 186.

The apposite remarks of Claudia J. Setzer reinforce my position. Although she concludes that 1 Thess. 2.13-16 is not authentically Pauline, in her discussion of 2.15b she astutely observes:

> The idea of Christian missionaries being driven out of a particular place meshes with Paul's testimony about himself (1 Cor 15:9; 2 Cor 11:26; Gal 1:13; 5:11; 6:12; Rom 15:31) as well as with the image of him in Acts as a perpetrator and victim of mob actions (8:1-3; 11:19 [?]; 13:45, 50; 14:2-5, 19; 17:5-9). It also harmonizes with Josephus' report of revolutionaries making life unbearable for more moderate members of the community in Judea in the midst of general anarchy and intolerance [see, e.g., *Ant.* 20.5; *War* 2.13; 4.5].[35]

My contention that Paul and his co-workers(s) were driven out of Thessalonica by some Jews is supported, then, not only by Paul's statements in 2.15b and 2.17a but also by Paul's remarks elsewhere,[36] by the multiple reports in Acts of Paul being harassed by unbelieving Jews (in spite of the fact that some of these episodes may be stereotyped and/or exaggerated)[37] and by the willingness of some less-tolerant Jews in some places (e.g. the zealous Judean Jews spoken of by Josephus[38]) to oppose, sometimes even violently, those with whom they disagreed.[39]

35. Setzer, *Jewish Responses*, p. 21.

36. For a fuller treatment of a number of the Pauline texts cited by Setzer, see Chapter 7.

37. A.J. Goddard and S.A. Cummins ('Ill or Ill-Treated?: Conflict and Persecution as the Context of Paul's Original Ministry in Galatia (Galatians 4.12-20)', *JSNT* 52 (1993), pp. 93-126 [120]) maintain, 'The record of Acts is unlikely to have totally fabricated the numerous accounts of Paul's physical suffering and persecution.' So similarly Smith, 'Persecution of Paul', p. 261.

38. Jewett ('Agitators') argues that there was an increase of zealotic activity in Judea in the late forties and early fifties CE which spread to surrounding regions.

39. It is precisely at this point where Dobschütz's study ('Paulus') is most convincing. See also the work of Seland, *Establishment Violence*. Seland argues that Philo (*Spec. Leg.* 1.54-57, 315-318; 2.225-254) and Acts (6.8; 7.60; 21.15-26, 27-36; 23.12-15) indicate the presence of Jews, both in Jerusalem and in the Diaspora, who stood ready to perform zealotic vigilante actions against non-conformers to the Torah. Conflict theorists have observed that ideological conflict between parties who interact closely and frequently can be particularly intense. See p. 121 above.

4. *Prohibited from Preaching to the Gentiles*

In 2.16a Paul contends that some Jews ('Ιουδαῖοι of 2.14b is still serv-
ing as the subject) were responsible for 'hindering us from speaking to
the Gentiles in order that they might be saved [κωλυόντων ἡμᾶς τοῖς
ἔθνεσιν λαλῆσαι ἵνα σωθῶσιν]'. This participial phrase is best taken
as an explanatory participle (note the absence of καί) of at least 2.15d
(καὶ πᾶσιν ἀνθρώποις ἐναντίων)[40] and in all likelihood of 2.15c as
well (καὶ θεῷ μὴ ἀρεσκόντων).[41] In 2.15c-16a, then, Paul maintains
that the Jews who hinder him and his coworker(s) from proclaiming the
gospel to the Gentiles displease God and oppose people. But who were
the Jews doing the hindering? Precisely whom were they hindering?
And how were they preventing whomever from speaking to the Gentiles?

I argued above that Paul, Silvanus and possibly Timothy were driven
out of Thessalonica by some of the Jews residing there (2.15b, 17a). I
also noted that Paul frequently experienced conflict with his fellow
Jews. Given the two other allusions to Jewish opposition of Paul's
Thessalonian mission in the immediate context, I would suggest that it
is likely that Paul is once again referring to his experience in Thessalonica in 2.16a.[42] If this is indeed the case, then it also seems likely that
the ἡμᾶς of 2.16a should once again be understood as referring to Paul,
Silvanus and Timothy (?). As I demonstrated above, ἡμᾶς typically
refers to Paul and his colleague(s) throughout 1 Thessalonians and
clearly does so throughout chs. 1–2.

The present tense participle (κωλυόντων) in 2.16a, however, seems
to indicate that Paul is referring not only to the missionaries' experience
in Thessalonica but also to continued Jewish opposition of the Pauline
mission. Unfortunately, Paul does not indicate in 1 Thessalonians or
elsewhere in his extant letter corpus the other places where he felt himself hindered by Jews. If one gives credence to Acts and if one places
the writing of 1 Thessalonians in Corinth c. 50 CE, then Paul could have
been thinking in 2.16a of previous controversial encounters with his
compatriots in Pisidian Antioch (13.44-45), Iconium (14.2-5), Lystra

40. Thus Frame, *Thessalonians*, p. 112, and Marshall, *Thessalonians*, p. 79.
41. So Lightfoot, *Notes*, p. 34; Best, *Thessalonians*, p. 117; Wanamaker, *Thessalonians*, p. 115.
42. So also Marshall, *Thessalonians*, p. 79. Cf. similarly Sanders, *Paul, the
Law, and the Jewish People*, pp. 190-91.

(14.19) and Berea (17.13) as well as his present conflict with Corinthian Jews (18.5-6, 12-17; cf. 1 Thess. 3.7; 2 Thess. 3.2). However, even if one dates 1 Thessalonians differently and/or is highly skeptical or completely dismissive of the reports of Jewish opposition of Paul in Acts, there is enough evidence in Paul's own letters to conclude that Thessalonica was not the only place that Paul ran into trouble with non-Christian Jews (see esp. 2 Cor. 11.24, 26d; Gal. 5.11; 6.12). Paul's caustic denunciation of some of his kin in 2.16b, then, appears to have been prompted by his experience of Jewish resistance to his Gentile mission, particularly in Thessalonica.[43]

How was it that non-Christian Jews prevented Paul and his co-workers from speaking to the Gentiles? Based on Paul's statements in 2.15b and 2.17a, I am led to conclude that the Thessalonian Jews hindered Paul's ministry by forcing him to leave the city.[44] Beyond this it is impossible to know what Paul had in mind in 2.16a. Was he referring to Jewish attempts to incite Gentile political opposition against him (cf. Acts 17.5-10a; 18.12-17)? Could Paul be thinking of being excommunicated from particular Jewish synagogues, thereby being prohibited from reaching God-fearers with the gospel? Unfortunately, we simply cannot say. Nonetheless, thus far I have positively concluded that Paul and his colleague(s) encountered Jewish opposition in Thessalonica which resulted in their expulsion from the city. We now turn to consider one final question: Do non-Christian charges stand behind Paul's self-presentation in 2.1-12?

5. 1 Thessalonians 2.1-12: Apology and /or Parenesis?

a. *An Overview of the Passage*
Following Paul's claim that the apostles' visit to Thessalonica was not in vain and that they declared the gospel with God-given courage

---

43. See further pp. 200-205 below. Frame (*Thessalonians*, pp. 110-11) writes, 'The past experiences in Thessalonica and Beroea (Acts 17:1-15), the insinuations alluded to in vv. 1-12, and the present troubles in Corinth (3:7; cf. Acts 18:5ff.) explain sufficiently [the] prophetic denunciation of the Jews [in 2.15-16] (cf. Phil. 3:1ff.).'

44. Contra Schlueter, *Filling up the Measure*, p. 69. So rightly Colin G. Kruse, 'The Price Paul Paid for a Ministry among Gentiles: Paul's Persecution at the Hands of the Jews', in Michael J. Wilkins and Terence Paige (eds.), *Worship, Theology and Ministry in the Early Church: Essays in Honor of Ralph P. Martin* (JSNTSup, 87; Sheffield: JSOT Press, 1992), pp. 260-72 (261-62).

despite external opposition (2.1-2), Paul rehearses, in language which is strikingly negative and antithetical, the nature of their ministry among the Thessalonian believers (2.3-6). Paul contends that their appeal was not made from error, uncleanness or guile (ἡ γὰρ παράκλησις ἡμῶν οὐκ ἐκ πλάνης οὐδὲ ἐξ ἀκαθαρσίας οὐδὲ ἐν δόλῳ, 2.3). Moreover, he maintains that they did not attempt to please people when sharing the gospel (οὐχ ὡς ἀνθρώποις ἀρέσκοντες, 2.4), nor did they use words of flattery or try to mask greed while in Thessalonica (οὔτε γάρ ποτε ἐν λόγῳ κολακείας ἐγενήθημεν ... οὔτε ἐν προφάσει πλεονεξίας, 2.5). He also states that they did not seek glory from the Thessalonian believers or others (οὔτε ζητοῦντες ἐξ ἀνθρώπων οὔτε ἀφ' ὑμῶν οὔτε ἀπ' ἄλλων, 2.6). On the contrary, Paul appeals to his converts (καθὼς οἴδατε, 2.5; cf. 1.5; 2.1, 2, 9, 10, 11; 3.4; 5.2) and even to God (θεὸς μάρτυς, 2.5; cf. 2.10) to attest that as apostles of Christ (ὡς Χριστοῦ ἀπόστολοι, 2.7) they 'have been approved by God to be entrusted with the gospel' (δεδοκιμάσμεθα ὑπὸ τοῦ θεοῦ πιστευθῆναι τὸ εὐαγγέλιον, 2.4) and that they aim to please God, the one who tests their hearts (οὐχ ὡς ἀνθρώποις ἀρέσκοντες ἀλλὰ θεῷ τῷ δοκιμάζοντι τὰς καρδίας ἡμῶν, 2.4). In 2.3-6, then, Paul is denying that the missionaries are guilty of error (πλάνη), uncleanness (ἀκαθαρσία), deceit (δόλος), 'buttering people up' (ἀνθρώποις ἀρέσκοντες), using flowery speech (ἐν λόγῳ κολακείας), greed (πλεονεξία) and seeking glory from people (ζητοῦντες ἐξ ἀνθρώπων). This is quite a collection of denials!

The tone of 2.7-12 is more positive. In these verses Paul maintains that while in Thessalonica the missionaries were gentle (ἤπιοι)[45] to

---

45. Contra Nestle–Aland[27] and UBSGNT 3rd rev. edn which read νήπιοι. *Pace* also Stephen Fowl, 'A Metaphor in Distress: A Reading of ΝΗΠΙΟΙ in 1 Thessalonians 2.7', *NTS* 36 (1990), pp. 469-73; John Gillman, 'Paul's ΕΙΣΟΔΟΣ: The Proclaimed and the Proclaimer (1 Thess 2,8)' in Collins (ed.), *The Thessalonian Correspondence*, pp. 62-70 (63 n. 4); Weima, 'Apologetic Function', p. 96 n. 64; Morris, *Thessalonians*, p. 69; and Gaventa, *Thessalonians*, pp. 27-28. Although manuscript evidence may favor the reading νήπιοι (P[65] ℵ* B C* D* F G I Ψ* 104*. 326[c]. *pc* it vg[cl.ww] sa[ms] bo), 'only ἤπιοι seems to suit the context, where the apostle's gentleness makes an appropriate sequence with the arrogance disclaimed in ver. 6' (Bruce M. Metzger, *A Textual Commentary on the Greek New Testament* [New York: United Bible Societies, 1971], p. 630). See also Helmut Koester ('The Text of 1 Thessalonians', in Dennis E. Groh and Robert Jewett [eds.], *The Living Text: Essays in Honor of Ernest W. Saunders* [Lanham, MD: University Press of America, 1985], pp. 219-27 [225]) who rather dogmatically asserts: 'Considering context and subject matter, there cannot be the slightest doubt that νήπιοι is wrong.'

their converts (2.7), shared their very selves with them (2.8) and cared for them like a nursing mother (2.7) and an encouraging father (2.12). Nevertheless, even in vv. 7-12 Paul calls upon his converts and God to bear witness (ὑμεῖς μάρτυρες καὶ ὁ θεός) to the apostles' 'holy and righteous and blameless' (ὁσίως καὶ δικαίως καὶ ἀμέμπτως) behavior among them (2.10; cf. 1.5b). On the surface, 2.1-12 appears readily intelligible: Paul is reviewing with his converts the character and conduct of the missionaries in their presence. But why did Paul pen this pericope? The answer to this query is a source of scholarly contention.

b. *The Function of 1 Thessalonians 2.1-12*
Scholars tend to take one of two basic positions with regard to Paul's motivation for writing 2.1-12. Some hold that Paul is presenting an apology for his ministry in these verses and that his defense is occasioned by actual or potential accusations made against him in Thessalonica. Others assert that Paul's self-presentation in this passage is meant to serve as a model for the Thessalonian Christians to emulate, not to counter slanderous charges. In this section I will argue, against the majority of contemporary interpreters, that the pericope under consideration has an apologetic function.[46]

Although trends in Pauline studies are often difficult to detect, a discernible shift has occurred in recent years regarding the reading of 1 Thess. 2.1-12.[47] Due in large measure to the influential work of Abraham J. Malherbe,[48] the preponderance of modern-day Thessalonian scholars now stand persuaded that Paul's purpose for writing 2.1-12 was purely parenetic.[49] That is to say, these interpreters contend that

46. So also Weima in his recently published article, 'Apologetic Function'.
47. After a thorough survey of the state of the discussion, Weima ('Apologetic Function', pp. 79-80) concludes that a 'a truly dramatic shift has taken place'. He observes, '[W]ith a couple of notable exceptions [Traugott Holtz is noted by name], the widespread consensus of interpreters today is that the autobiographical statements of 1 Thess. 2.1-12 have an exclusively parenetic function and that the apologetic function is no longer a realistic option but is indeed now "off the table" [a quotation from an unpublished article by Johannes Schoon-Janssen].'
48. See esp. Malherbe's ' "Gentle as a Nurse" '. In this article Malherbe appeals to the earlier work of Dobschütz (*Thessalonicherbriefe*, pp. 106-107) and Dibelius (*Thessalonicher*, pp. 7-11). These German exegetes also concluded that Paul was not countering accusations in 2.1-12.
49. One sees the mark of Malherbe's work on, e.g., Wanamaker, *Thessalonians*, p. 91; Holmes, *Thessalonians*, p. 61; Gaventa, *Thessalonians*, pp. 25-26; Lyons,

Paul's intent in this passage is to place before the Thessalonian believers an ideal example which they are to imitate. This line of interpretation signals a departure from the traditional view that in 2.1-12 Paul is
defending himself.[50]

In a 1970 essay entitled '"Gentle as a Nurse": The Cynic Background
to 1 Thess ii', Malherbe maintains that it cannot be determined from
Paul's self-description in 2.1-12 that he was defending himself against
accusations.[51] He seeks to support this interpretation by observing verbal and formal parallels between Paul's statements in 2.1-12 and Dio
Chrysostom's *Orations*, particularly *Oration* 32. Malherbe persuasively
demonstrates that there are distinct similarities between the negative
and antithetical language employed by the Cynic philosopher Dio in his
Orations and the Christian preacher Paul in 2.1-12. He also usefully
highlights in his discussion the fact that accusations against philosophical charlatans were common in antiquity. While I would concur with
Malherbe that there are striking parallels between Paul and Dio in the
particular passages he examines and that wandering philosophers were
frequently lambasted in Paul's and Dio's day, I do not endorse his thesis that 1 Thess. 2.1-12 is purely parenetic. I now turn to explain why I
think our exegetical predecessors had a better argument than Malherbe
and his contemporary followers.

Pauline Autobiography, pp. 190-201; Boers, 'Form Critical Study', p. 150; deSilva,
' "Worthy of his Kingdom" ', p. 69; Earl J. Richard, 'Early Pauline Thought: An
Analysis of 1 Thessalonians', in Bassler (ed.), *Pauline Theology*, I, pp. 39-51 (48);
Helmut Koester, '1 Thessalonians: Experiment in Christian Writing', in F.F.
Church and Timothy George (eds.), *Continuity and Discontinuity in Church History*
(Leiden: E.J. Brill, 1979), pp. 33-44 (41); Daryl W. Palmer, 'Thanksgiving, Self-
Defence, and Exhortation in 1 Thessalonians 1–3', *Colloqium* 14 (1981), pp. 23-31;
Steve Walton, 'What Has Aristotle to Do with Paul? Rhetorical Criticism in
1 Thessalonians', *TynBul* 46 (1995), pp. 229-50, (esp. 230, 244); David E. Aune,
The New Testament in its Literary Environment (LEC, 8; Philadelphia: Westminster
Press, 1987), p. 206; and J.W. Simpson, Jr, 'Thessalonians, Letters to the', *DPL*,
pp. 932-39 (936).

50. Weima ('Apologetic Function', p. 74) notes in the late 1960s Schmithals
(*Paul and the Gnostics*, p. 151) could justifiably write, 'On this point [i.e. that Paul
is responding to charges in 2.1-12] the exegetes from the time of the Fathers down
to the last century have never been in doubt.'

51. Malherbe, ' "Gentle as a Nurse" ', p. 217.

c. *1 Thessalonians 2.1-12 as an Apology*

In his *Orations* 32 Dio attempts to paint a portrait of an ideal philosopher, someone remarkably like himself! Not only does Dio describe such a person as an individual who defies the ὕβρις of the crowd and gets involved in the ἀγών of life (32.8, 20), but he also asserts that the bona fide philosopher does not speak in vain (32.9), nor for the sake of glory or personal gain (32.11). The genuine philosopher, like Dio, is divinely directed to speak (ὑπὸ δαιμονίου τινὸς γνώμης, 32.12) and does so with boldness and purity of mind and without guile (32.11). In the course of describing the ideal philosopher, Dio laments the fact that there are numerous so-called Cynics who

> achieve no good at all, but rather the worst possible harm, for they *accustom thoughtless people to deride philosophers in general*, just as one might accustom lads to scorn their teachers, and, when they ought to knock the *insolence out of their hearers*, these Cynics merely increase it (*Or.* 32.9, emphasis added).

This passage from Dio indicates that it was not uncommon for people, whom he depicts as 'thoughtless', to slander philosophers. Despite Malherbe's claims that Dio himself was not being maligned,[52] given the widespread derision and criticism of philosophical types in antiquity[53] there is good reason to think that Dio's own self-presentation was influenced to a considerable extent by concrete accusations which he himself had encountered. Furthermore, in light of the fact that charges often flew around wandering sophists in antiquity, it would come as no surprise to find people trying to affix negative labels to Paul, nor would it seem unusual for Paul to attempt to defend himself and his mission against harmful accusations.[54] Additionally, the sociology of deviance alerts us to the fact that it is not unusual for those who are viewed and labeled as deviant (perhaps Paul was perceived as a 'third-class' philosopher and was being accused accordingly) to defend themselves (see pp. 103-104 above). Dio's statements about the philosophical life in *Oration* 32, then, can actually be used against Malherbe's conclusion that Paul's purpose for penning 2.1-12 was merely parenetic.[55]

---

52. Malherbe, ' "Gentle as a Nurse" ', pp. 214-15, 217.

53. See further, e.g., Lucian's (c. 125–180 CE) *Peregr.*

54. So also Holtz, *Thessalonicher*, p. 94, and Riesner, *Paul's Early Period*, p. 369. After a careful sifting of the evidence, Weima ('Apologetic Function', p. 96) maintains that Paul's integrity and sincerity were being called into question.

55. Riesner (*Paul's Early Period*, p. 369) remarks, 'It would be astonishing if

There are yet further reasons to conclude that Paul wrote these verses primarily for apologetic purposes, not the least of which is the great intensity of Paul's self-presentation in this pericope.[56] Having mentioned the considerable external opposition which the apostles had encountered in Thessalonica (2.2), Paul immediately begins in 2.3 to mount a thorough defense. In 2.3-6 Paul seeks repeatedly to exonerate the missionaries from any alleged wrong doing. On the charges of error (πλάνη), uncleanness (ἀκαθαρσία), deceit (δόλος), people pleasing (ἀνθρώποις ἀρέσκοντες), flattery (ἐν λόγῳ κολακείας), greed (πλεονεξία) and glory seeking (ζητοῦντες ἐξ ἀνθρώπων), Paul pleads not guilty. It is extremely unlikely that Paul would list so many negatives at the outset of his self-presentation for purely parenetic purposes. Unless Paul were seeking to respond to specific accusations which had been, were being or might potentially be leveled against him and his colleague(s), why would he sense the urgent need to review so explicitly the ministry of the missionaries among the Thessalonians? If Paul merely intended in 2.1-12 to exhort and encourage his converts, then he miserably missed the mark. It is hard to imagine how his Thessalonian converts would be in danger of becoming like this or behaving in these ways![57]

My argument that 2.1-12 is primarily apologetic is further buttressed by the fact that Paul emphatically and repeatedly denies charges against the preachers' character and conduct by appealing to the Thessalonians (2.1, 2, 5, 9, 10, 11) and to none other than God (2.5, 10; cf. Rom. 1.9; 2 Cor. 1.23; Phil. 1.8). Such an emphatic defense is paralleled in Paul only in Gal. 1.1–2.14 (note esp. 1.20: ἃ δὲ γράφω ὑμῖν, ἰδοὺ ἐνώπιον τοῦ θεοῦ ὅτι οὐ ψεύδομαι) where, notwithstanding the arguments of George Lyons to the contrary,[58] Paul is responding to the agitators' contention that his gospel had a human /Jerusalem origin.[59]

the apostle of Christ (1 Thess. 2:7) had compared himself to a philosopher merely for reasons of admonition. The text becomes immediately comprehensible as coming from the hand (or dictation) of Paul if he is thinking of very real or at least potential accusations...'

56. Also noted by Sandnes, *Paul—One of the Prophets?*, p. 198.

57. Marshall (*Thessalonians*, p. 61) correctly observes, '[T]he comments [in 2.1-12] are more concerned with the characteristics of missionaries and pastors than of ordinary members of the congregation.'

58. Lyons, *Pauline Autobiography*, pp. 75-176.

59. So rightly John M.G. Barclay, *Obeying the Truth: Paul's Ethics in Galatians* (Minneapolis: Fortress Press, 1988), p. 41 n. 10. See also Barclay's 'Mirror-

When these foregoing observations are coupled with the fact that talk of the apostles' external conflict in Thessalonica permeates 1 Thessalonians 2 (note again 2.2, 15, 16, 17; cf. 1.6), the scales are tipped decidedly to the side of 2.1-12 being a Pauline apology.[60] Paul's primary purpose in penning this passage, then, was to defend himself against actual (or at least potential) accusations, not to exhort his converts. Whatever parenetic intentions Paul had in writing 2.1-12, they should be judged secondary.

d. *The Origins of and Reasons for Accusations against Paul*

Having established that Paul is responding to slanderous statements in 2.1-12,[61] I will now consider the possible origins of and reasons for such verbal assaults. Suggestions abound concerning whom Paul is seeking to counter in 2.1-12. Some scholars, most notably Walter Schmithals,[62] have contended that Paul directed his apology toward Christian opponents who had infiltrated the Thessalonian congregation. Schmithals suggests that Paul was attempting to counter Gnostic

Reading a Polemical Letter: Galatians as a Test Case', *JSNT* 31 (1987), pp. 73-93, esp. pp. 86-90. Weima ('Apologetic Function', p. 91) describes Paul's apology in 2.1-12 as 'muted' in comparison to Gal. 1.1–2.14. He reasons that Paul's apology is so forceful in Gal. because is responding to internal attacks and is seeking to defend his apostolic status whereas his defense is less angular in 1 Thess. because he is countering external attacks and is trying to uphold his apostolic character. 1 Thess. 2.1-12 and Gal. 1 are nevertheless parallel to the extent that in both passages Paul is seeking to exonerate himself before God and others.

60. Although a minority view, some contemporary interpreters still espouse this position. E.g. Holtz, *Thessalonicher*, p. 94; Bruce, *Thessalonians*, pp. 27-28; Marshall, *Thessalonians*, p. 61; Williams, *Thessalonians*, p. 36; Riesner, *Paul's Early Period*, pp. 369-70; Sandnes, *Paul—One of the Prophets*, p. 198; Fee, *God's Empowering Presence*, p. 41; Weima, 'Apologetic Function'; Barclay, 'Conflict in Thessalonica', p. 513; and Kruse, 'Paul's Persecution', p. 261.

61. It is possible that Paul is responding to accusations made against him in 2.17-20 as well. In this pericope Paul stresses that he misses the Thessalonians and indicates that he had attempted repeatedly to return to them but had been hindered from doing so by Satan. Perhaps some outsiders were suggesting that Paul's prolonged absence proved that he did not care about his converts. Weima ('Apologetic Function', pp. 82-83) notes that older commentators (e.g. Frame, *Thessalonians*, pp. 14, 17, 140) thought of 2.1-12 (or 2.1-16) as Paul's defense of his past ministry among the Thessalonians 'apologia pro vita sua et labore suo' and of 2.17-3.10 as Paul's defense of his present absence from Thessalonica 'apologia pro absentia sua'.

62. Schmithals, *Paul and the Gnostics*, pp. 123-218.

intruders in 1 Thessalonians. To arrive at such a position, Schmithals argues that Gnosticism stands behind Paul's statements in 1.2–2.12; 4.3-8; 4.9-12; and 5.12-14. Almost all scholars have rejected this exotic theory.[63] In addition to the fact that Schmithals's conception of a fully developed Gnosticism in the first century CE is highly unlikely,[64] there is not a trace of evidence in 1 Thessalonians that Christian interlopers had invaded the congregation (cf. Gal., 2 Cor. 10-13 and Phil. 3).[65]

Another line of interpretation suggests that Paul was seeking in 1 Thess. 2.1-12 to counter opposition which had arisen from within the congregation. Interpreters such as Wilhelm Lütgert[66] and Robert Jewett[67] have labeled these Pauline dissidents as 'spiritual enthusiasts' and 'millenarian radicals' respectively. Karl P. Donfried is also convinced that Paul's apology in 1 Thess. 2.1-12 'is in response to criticisms received from that Christian community'.[68] Whereas Lütgert and Jewett think that Paul is combating theological problems among his converts, Donfried believes that Paul is contending with congregational criticism which had arisen as a result of the Christians' continued affliction and prolonged separation from Paul. I will not enter into a detailed discussion of the work of these three scholars at this juncture. However, I will offer some reasons as to why I disagree with the notion that Paul is responding to internal criticism in 2.1-12.[69]

First of all, the tone of 1 Thessalonians is that of affirmation, not correction (see, e.g., 2.20; 4.1, 9-10; 5.11). Secondly, it is not likely that Paul would have referred to the Thessalonian church as an exemplary assembly (τύπος, 1.6; cf. 2 Thess. 1.4) and as his 'glory and joy' (2.20; cf. 3.9-10) if they were critical of him and his ministry![70] Thirdly, there is no explicit talk in the letter of divisions within the congregation

63. Wolfgang Harnisch (*Eschatologische Existenz: Ein exegetischer Beitrag zum Sachanliegen von 1 Thessalonicher 4,13–5,11* [FRLANT, 110; Göttingen: Vandenhoeck & Ruprecht, 1973]) is the only scholar of whom I am aware to embrace Schmithal's proposal.

64. So Marshall, *Thessalonians*, p. 18.

65. Also noted by Wanamaker, *Thessalonians*, p. 54.

66. E. Wilhelm Lütgert, 'Die Volkommenen im Philipperbrief und die Enthusiasten in Thessalonich', *BFCT* 13 (1909), pp. 547-654.

67. Jewett, *Thessalonian Correspondence*, esp. pp. 175-78.

68. Donfried, 'Cults of Thessalonica', p. 351.

69. See further pp. 272-75 below.

70. Contrast 1 Cor. 3.1-3 where Paul contends that the Corinthians are babes in Christ and still of the flesh.

(contrast, e.g., 1 Cor. 3.3; Phil. 2.1-4; 4.2). When Paul wrote 1 Thessalonians, Timothy had just returned to him from Thessalonica. Upon his return, Timothy indicated to Paul that the Thessalonians 'remember[ed] [them] kindly and long[ed] to see [them]' (3.6). This does not sound like a relationship in tension. While there was, of course, potential for strained relations between Paul and the church in Thessalonica, as 2 Thessalonians indicates, there is no clear evidence in 1 Thessalonians to support the supposition that Paul was countering criticism from his converts.[71]

My contention, then, is that Paul crafted 1 Thess. 2.1-12 in response to verbal abuse that he had received, was receiving and/or anticipated receiving from non-Christians in Thessalonica. Timothy may have reported to Paul that the slander which he and his coworker(s) had experienced from unbelievers during their sojourn in Thessalonica was continuing and perhaps even escalating.[72] In the (unlikely) event that the charges against Paul and his helper(s) were neither actual nor public, Paul might have thought it prudent to remind his converts of the ministers' upright character and continued concern lest their faith falter in the prolonged absence of the apostles and in the protracted presence of affliction (see esp. 2.17–3.12).[73]

Interestingly, anthropologist Bernard Siegel has observed that leaders of groups that are exposed to external threats over an extended period of time but are unable or unwilling to combat directly their opposition (see 3.12; 4.11-12; 5.15; cf. 2 Thess. 1.5-12) frequently attempt to help members cope with such 'environmental stress' by countering (potential) criticism and by offering (additional) instruction.[74]

Can we be more precise regarding the source of the slander to which Paul was seemingly subjected? Not a few interpreters have suggested that Paul is responding in 2.1-12 to accusations from Thessalonian

71. After having offered similar arguments against the idea of that Paul was responding to internal criticism in 2.1-12, Weima ('Apologetic Function', p. 89) concludes that it is 'impossible to believe that Paul was facing attack from believers inside the church. There is no justification, therefore, for seeing 2.1-12 as Paul's response to criticisms raised by Judaizers, Gnostics, Spiritual Enthusiasts, Millenarianists or any other yet-to-be-identified group within the Thessalonian church.'

72. Cf. Gillman, 'Paul's ΕΙΣΟΔΟΣ', pp. 68-69.

73. See similarly Weima, 'Apologetic Function', p. 98, and Holtz, *Thessalonicher*, p. 94.

74. Bernard Siegel, 'Defensive Structuring and Environmental Stress', *AJS* 76 (1970), pp. 11-32.

Jews.[75] In support of this position exegetes have appealed to the Septuagintal background of Paul's vocabulary in 2.1, 3 (particularly the terms κενός, παράκλησις, πλάνη, ἀκάθαρτος and δόλος)[76] as well as to the opposition of Thessalonian Jewry alluded to by Paul in 2.15-16.[77] While I am in basic agreement with those scholars who seek to understand Paul's apology against a primarily Jewish backdrop, I would hasten to add that the particular vocabulary Paul employed in his defense may have been his own mode of expression and not actual charges brought against him by his Jewish opponents in Thessalonica. Nevertheless, it is possible that the charges which Paul seeks to deny in 2.3-6 would be similar to those brought against him by his fellow Jews in that city and elsewhere.[78]

I have argued above that some Jews drove Paul and his associate(s) out of Thessalonica. If this interpretation is correct, then it makes good sense to envision Jews maligning Paul both while he was in Thessalonica and after he had departed. In all likelihood, however, Paul would have also encountered Gentile criticism as well. Throughout 1 Thessalonians Paul characterizes the congregation as converted Gentiles (1.1, 9; 2.14; 4.5) who continued to experience θλῖψις at the hands of their own συμφυλεταί (1.6; 2.14; 3.3-5; cf. 2 Thess. 1.4-5; 2 Cor. 8.1-2).[79] It seems probable, therefore, that Paul would have been opposed by his converts' compatriots as well.[80] But why would some Jews and Gentiles have slandered Paul?

75. E.g. James Denney, *The Epistles to the Thessalonians* (EB; New York: Hodder & Stoughton, n.d.), p. 70; Frame, *Thessalonians*, p. 90; Williams, *Thessalonians*, p. 36; and Holtz, *Thessalonicher*, p. 94.

76. See esp. William Horbury, 'I Thessalonians ii.3 as Rebutting the Charge of False Prophecy', *JTS* NS 33 (1982), pp. 492-508. Cf. A.-M. Denis, 'L'apôtre Paul, prophète "messianique" des gentils. Etude thématique de 1 Thess. II,1-6', *ETL* 33 (1957), pp. 245-315; Bartholomäus Henneken, *Verkündigung und Prophetie im ersten Thessalonicherbrief: Ein Beitrag zur Theologie des Wortes Gottes* (SBib, 29; Stuttgart: Katholisches Bibelwerk, 1969); and Sandnes, *Paul—One of the Prophets?*, pp. 199-211

77. See Horbury, 'I Thessalonians ii.3', p. 493, and Denney, *Thessalonians*, p. 70.

78. Cf. Acts 21.28, 24.5 for the types of charges Paul's compatriots brought against him.

79. See further Chapter 9.

80. Cf. Weima ('Apologetic Function', p. 91): 'Given the fact, then, that a number of the citizens of Thessalonica [i.e. the συμφυλεταί] were harassing and perse-

Charges may have been mounted to explain away the success of Paul's Thessalonian mission. Although we know have no way of knowing how many people responded positively to 'the gospel of God' (2.1, 8, 9; cf. 3.2),[81] one is given the impression that the church was a vital congregation (1.5-10; 2.13; cf. 2 Thess. 3.1; Acts 17.4), despite its experience of severe affliction and the loss of some group members to death (4.13). One way Paul's detractors could have accounted for his accomplishments in Thessalonica would have been to accuse him of crafting a message designed to please people (ἀνθρώποις ἀρέσκοντες) and of presenting his message in an enticing way (ἐν λόγῳ κολακείας). Although Paul was no silver-tongued orator in the estimation of his Corinthian opponents (2 Cor. 10.10), his presentation in Thessalonica was apparently persuasive enough to win some people over and provocative enough to incite unfavorable criticism from those he failed to convince (2.1-2).

An attempt on the part of outsiders to undercut the Thessalonian Christians' claim that they had found the truth is another reason that Paul could have been criticized. Non-Christians in Thessalonica might have reasoned that if they could defame the messenger and thereby lessen his converts' admiration for and trust in him (3.6), then they might also be able to discredit the message and even put an end to this new-fangled cult which had arisen in their midst.[82] Seeking to discredit leaders with the intent of altering the opinions of followers was a common strategy in antiquity (and remains so until today).

A careful reading of Galatians and 2 Corinthians suggests that this was precisely what was happening to Paul in Galatia and Corinth. Paul's Christian opponents attempted to undermine his message and ministry by maligning him. Similarly, the Matthean Jesus remarks, 'If they [i.e. outsiders, particularly Jews] called the master of the house Beelzebul [see Mt. 9.34; 12.27], how much more will they malign those of his household' (Mt. 10.25b). Regardless of the precise *Sitz im Leben*

cuting members of the local church, it seems only natural to conclude that these attacks would also be aimed at the church's leader, Paul, who was in the minds of some unbelievers in the city the source of the problem.'

81. Hill (*Establishing the Church in Thessalonica*, pp. 247-48) surmises that 30 to 75 comprised the Thessalonian church. De Vos (*Church and Community Conflicts*, p. 171) suggests that 20 to 25 members made up the congregation.

82. Holtz (*Thessalonicher*, p. 94) writes, 'Denn mit dem Boten steht und fällt die Botschaft.'

of this statement, it is clear that non-believers sought to unsettle believers by slandering Jesus. We should probably understand Mt. 11.19 in a similar way, where Jesus is described as 'a glutton and a drunkard, a friend of tax collectors and sinners' (φάγος καὶ οἰνοπότης, τελωνῶν φίλος καὶ ἁμαρτωλῶν).

Such a slanderous strategy was also utilized by Gentiles against Jews in antiquity. Josephus reports that 'pagan' detractors of Judaism

> partly through ignorance but mainly through malevolence, have made statements about our lawgiver Moses and his laws which are neither just nor true, slandering the former as a charlatan and cheat and alleging that the laws have instructed us in vice and not in any virtue (*Apion*, 2.145).[83]

These parallels support my argument that Paul's apology in 2.1-12 is best understood as a response to his being verbally abused by Jews and Gentiles in Thessalonica. It is likely that Paul's non-Christian opponents asserted that he was a slick-talking, money-hungry, glory seeking charlatan who peddled a second-rate message which could not be trusted. Such slander was probably an attempt on the part of unbelievers to explain away the success of Paul's Thessalonian mission and to undercut his converts' confidence in him and in the Lord.[84]

6. *Conclusion*

In this chapter I have argued from various texts in 1 Thessalonians 2 that Paul experienced considerable opposition from non-Christians both during and after his Thessalonian mission. Furthermore, based upon my reading of 2.15b, 16a and 17a, I have maintained that Paul encountered conflict with some Thessalonian Jews. Paul reports that he and his co-worker(s) were driven out of the city by some Jews (2.15b) and were thereby prematurely torn away from the Thessalonian congregation (2.17a). Paul understood this particular episode of Jewish opposition as well as his continued conflict with his compatriots as a hindrance to his preaching the gospel to the Gentiles (2.16a).

Unfortunately, Paul does not indicate how Thessalonian Jewry sought to hinder him or how they actually expelled him from the city. However

83. Molly Whittaker (trans.), *Jews and Christians: Graeco-Roman Views* (CCWJCW, 6; Cambridge: Cambridge University Press, 1984), p. 60.
84. Note well the grave concern Paul expresses for his converts' continuance in the faith in 3.1-13.

else some Jews in Thessalonica opposed Paul, the apostle's apology in 2.1-12 suggests that slander was one way in which they (and unbelieving Gentiles) sought to undo him. In all likelihood, then, Paul experienced at least verbal harassment and possibly physical violence from non-Christian outsiders (Jews in particular) during his Thessalonian mission and continued to be maligned after his forced departure.[85]

Lastly, I would note that the conclusions arrived at in this chapter are based upon my exegesis of portions of 1 Thessalonians 2. It may now be observed, however, that there is a direct correlation between Paul's remarks and Luke's narrative concerning who forced Paul and Silas to leave Thessalonica (cf. Acts 17.5-10a). Even if one is loath to accept as historical Luke's depiction of how the missionaries' expulsion took place, it is probable, especially in light of the corroborating evidence in 1 Thessalonians 2, that Acts is at least correct in reporting that Paul and Silas were objects of Jewish opposition and that Jewish hostility cut short their stay in the city. Acts 17.1-10a, then, provides a commentary, if tendentious at points, on Paul's cryptic comments about his being 'banished', 'hindered' and 'orphaned' at the hands of some Thessalonian Jews. Conflict with his fellow Jews was apparently a common experience for Paul. In the following chapter I will explore why this was the case.

---

85. From all appearances, Paul was thoroughly deviantized by his opponents. Some Jewish outsiders seemingly considered Paul to be a threat to the stability and integrity of their community, and some Gentile unbelievers seemingly thought that Paul's presence was having a negative effect on the city of Thessalonica and its inhabitants. Accordingly, Paul's detractors apparently attacked his credibility in an effort to undermine his ministry. From the perspective of the non-Christian opponents of Paul, his forced exit from the city signaled that their stigmatization and degradation of the apostle was successful. On the deviance process, see pp. 100-105 above.

Chapter 7

WHY DID SOME JEWS OPPOSE PAUL?*

1. *Introduction*

In the previous chapter I argued that Paul, a Jewish apostle to the Gentiles (see, e.g., 1 Thess. 2.16; Gal. 1.16; 2.8-9; Rom. 11.13; 15.16), experienced opposition in Thessalonica both during and after his founding visit. Paul's cryptic comments about his conflict in Thessalonica, however, provide us with few details as to how he was hindered.[1] Putting together the pieces of information we do find in 1 Thessalonians, I concluded that Paul was verbally harassed and physically banished from the city by some Thessalonian Jews (cf. Acts 17.5-10a). Concerning why Jews in Thessalonica opposed him, Paul is silent.[2]

*   Earlier versions of this chapter were presented to a Glasgow–St Andrews postgraduate seminar (November 1994) and to the Seminar on the Development of Early Catholic Christianity (February 1998). Questions raised and criticisms offered by Dr Joel Marcus and Professor Richard Bauckham at the initial presentation and Professors William Farmer and Everett Ferguson at the second one were especially helpful.
    1.   This is typical of Paul. Although he frequently speaks in his extant letters of having suffered and of having been opposed, afflicted and persecuted (e.g. Rom. 8.35b; 1 Cor. 4.9-13; 15.32; 16.9; 2 Cor. 1.3-11; 4.7-12; 6.3-10; 11.23-29; 12.10a), he seldom elaborates upon the source of, the nature of and the reasons for his conflict. Despite Paul's tendency to speak of his suffering in generalities, there is no good reason, as we will see below, to dismiss all such statements as a product of Pauline paranoia.
    2.   Luke maintains in Acts 17.5 that the Jews resisted Paul because they were jealous or zealous of his missionary success. In Chapter 3 above I concluded that jealousy or zeal may well have been a reason for the Jewish opposition of Paul. I would reiterate here that it makes good sense to think that Thessalonian Jews could have been envious or zealous of Paul's poaching people from their synagogue, particularly if Paul experienced some success among Gentile sympathizers as Acts 17.4 indicates. Although a zealous response on the part of Thessalonian Jewry to

However, even if Paul had explicitly stated why he was harassed, the foregoing discussion of deviance and conflict has alerted us to the perspectival nature of social interaction. And given the relativity of social reality, one should be reluctant to reach a definitive conclusion as to why a conflict occurred based upon any one party's perception. Nevertheless, a subjective Pauline view would certainly be better than what we presently possess!

Since Paul does not indicate why Thessalonian Jews opposed him in 1 (or 2) Thessalonians, to address the conundrum before us we will have turn to other ancient literature, Pauline and otherwise. My working presupposition in this chapter is that controversies between Jews in other social-historical contexts may shed light on Paul's conflict with Thessalonian Jews.[3] Although the literary parallels I will consider here

Paul's subversively successful ministry has an a priori plausibility, it is likely a partial explanation of why Paul clashed with Jews in Thessalonica and elsewhere. The social-scientific study of conflict suggests that conflict relations tend to be complex and multi-causal (see p. 119 above).

In 1 Thess. 2.16 Paul does comment on what he considers to be one of the practical outcomes of his conflict with his Jewish compatriots, namely the hindrance of his Gentile mission.

3.   This is not to suggest, of course, that the reasons for conflict would be precisely the same in any two particular settings. Robert Jewett ('A Matrix of Grace: The Theology of 2 Thessalonians as a Pauline Letter', in Bassler [ed.], *Pauline Theology*, I, pp. 63-70 [67]) maintains that when Paul wrote the Thessalonian letters 'the obligation to obey the Torah still remains intact, and it appears perfectly consistent that no hint of an antithesis between law and gospel is given'. If Jewett's contention is correct, then it is not likely that the reasons for Jewish opposition of Paul which come to light in Galatians (i.e. Paul's stance on circumcision and dietary laws) are applicable to Paul's conflict with Thessalonian Jewry. Despite Jewett's suggestion, it is probable that Paul already perceived a tension between law and gospel by the time he wrote the Thessalonian Epistles and that his thought and practice were already shaped by this understanding. See in particular the work of Terence L. Donaldson, 'Zealot and Convert: The Origin of Paul's Christ-Torah Antithesis', *CBQ* 51 (1989), pp. 655-82, and *Paul and the Gentiles*, esp. pp. 169-73, 284-92.

Paul's pre-Christian persecution of the church suggests that he detected a conflict between Torah and Christ prior to his conversion. (On Paul's persecuting activity, see section 3 below.) It stands to reason that other Jews, perhaps even some in Thessalonica, could have reasoned similarly. If so, they would have perceived Paul as a threat to the law and would have sought to oppose him before the crisis in Galatia arose. I am assuming with Jewett and most other New Testament scholars that Paul wrote 1 Thess. prior to Gal. If Paul penned Gal. first, as some interpreters

cannot provide a definitive answer as to why Paul came into conflict with Jews in Thessalonica, at the very least this chapter will highlight the kinds of activities and attitudes that provoked disagreement among Jews in antiquity.[4]

I will begin this chapter by noting six reasons why various Hellenistic-Jewish writers looked upon fellow Diaspora Jews askance and even as 'apostates'.[5] I will then consider Paul's persecution of the church prior to his conversion. Next I will turn to the interpretation of Pauline texts (except those already treated in Chapters 3, 6 above) which indicate conflict between Paul and his fellow Jews. Having considered some causes of discord between different stamps of Jews in antiquity, I will offer some concluding remarks concerning Paul's troubled relations with his compatriots.

As I conclude this introduction, I should explicitly state some of the previously discussed social-scientific principles upon which I will draw in responding to the question at hand: (1) Behaviors and beliefs are learned through social interaction and intimate association with others (see pp. 91-93, 100-101 above). (2) Strong ties to a given community enhance the probability of conformity to that particular group's norms (see pp. 93-94 above). (3) When an individual fails to comply with a

contend, then one may be even more confident that Paul saw the law and his gospel as incompatible prior to his sojourn in Thessalonica.

4.   E.P. Sanders ('Paul on the Law, His Opponents, and the Jewish People in Philippians 3 and 2 Corinthians 11', in B. Richardson [ed.], *Anti-Judaism in Early Christianity*, I [Waterloo, ON: Wilfrid Laurier University Press, 1986], pp. 75-90 [86]) remarks, 'One would like to understand better just what it was about the Christian movement which some Jews found offensive enough to require punishment.' One aim of this chapter is to further understanding along these lines.

5.   I am indebted to John M.G. Barclay ('Who Was Considered an Apostate in the Jewish Diaspora', in Graham N. Stanton and Guy Strousma [eds.], *Tolerance and Intolerance in Early Judaism and Christianity* [Cambridge: Cambridge University Press, 1998], pp. 80-98) for references to and commentary upon the majority of the Hellenistic-Jewish texts which I will treat below. I have chosen to concentrate on Hellenistic-Jewish texts because they provide the closest parallels possible to the situation in Thessalonica and to other places in the Diaspora where Paul came into conflict with his Jewish compatriots.

Unless indicated otherwise in the footnotes, texts and translations (with occasional variations) of Greek and Latin authors are from the LCL (Cambridge, MA: Harvard University Press; London: Heinemann). The LXX text with which I work is A. Rahlf (ed.), *Septuaginta* (Stuttgart: Deutsche Bibelgesellschaft, 1982). Quotations of *OTP* are from Charlesworth (ed.).

community's conventions, at some times and in some places such a person may be perceived and treated as deviant by some group members (see pp. 94-98, 102-103 above). (4) When deviant behavior and /or belief threatens a community's boundaries, those who are committed to preserving and protecting a group's *ethos* may seek to condemn, control and/or censure those who disregard the behavioral and /or ideological norms (see pp, 96-98, 101-102 above). (5) Social conflict occurs when two (or more) parties disagree about what behaviors and beliefs are acceptable (see pp. 114-16 above). (6) Social conflict is complex and is often multi-causal (see p. 118 above). (7) Particularly intense social conflicts may be unresolvable and may ultimately result in a breach between the involved parties (see p. 112 above). (8) Those who are thought of as deviant and /or are engaged in conflict respond in a variety of ways (see pp. 103-104, 123 above).

2. *Transgressing Judaism in the Diaspora*

What kinds of actions and attitudes would have been judged by Diaspora Jews as unacceptable?[6] In this section I will offer an answer to this question by focusing upon what Philo, Josephus and the authors of *3, 4 Maccabees* say about those people they viewed as (likely to become) apostates.[7] Below I will enumerate six things that Diaspora Jews did and/or thought that one or more of these Hellenistic-Jewish writers denounced as (leading to) apostasy from Judaism.[8]

---

6.   On Diasporan Jews, see John J. Collins, *Between Athens and Jerusalem: Jewish Identity in the Hellenistic Diaspora* (New York: Crossroad, 1986), and esp. Barclay, *Jews in the Mediterranean Diaspora*.

7.   On apostasy as a 'blatantly judgmental term employed by "insiders" in excluding others', see John M.G. Barclay, 'Paul among Diaspora Jews: Anomaly or Apostate?', *JSNT* 60 (1995), pp. 89-120 (111). See also Barclay's *Jews in the Mediterranean Diaspora*, pp. 83-88; 'Who Was Considered an Apostate?', pp. 80-83; and esp. 'Deviance and Apostasy'. Barclay draws upon the labeling theory of deviant behavior (pp. 94-98 above) in insisting that 'apostasy, like beauty, is in the eye of the beholder' ('Who Was Considered an Apostate?', p. 81).

8.   In his colossal work *Jew and Gentile in the Ancient World: Attitudes and Interactions from Alexander to Justinian* (Princeton, NJ: Princeton University Press, 1993), Louis Feldman gives terse treatment to 'apostasy' from Judaism. In his brief section on the subject, he attempts to differentiate between 'apostasy' and non-observance of the commandments. As we will see, such a distinction is not always detectable in our sources. See further Barclay, *Jews in the Mediterranean*

a. *Abandoning Jewish Ways*

In our sources, the most common charge leveled against those Diaspora Jews thought to be apostate is the general accusation that they forsook their Jewish ancestral customs. At the outset of his work, the writer of *3 Maccabees* (first century BCE) speaks of one Dositheos, the son of Drimylus, who foiled an attempted assassination of Ptolemy IV Philo-pator, king of Egypt (221–204 BCE). Dositheos, who may be the same individual spoken of as the eponymous priest of Alexander and the deified Ptolemies (*CPJ* 127, from 222 BCE),[9] is depicted by the author of *3 Maccabees* as a Jew by birth who later 'renounced the law and was estranged from his ancestral traditions' (μεταβαλὼν τὰ νόμιμα καὶ τῶν πατρίων δογμάτων ἀπηλλοτριωμένος, 1.3). In the estimation of *3 Maccabees*, Dositheos had rejected the Jewish way. Seemingly the author thought Dositheos's intimate association with Egyptian authori-ties (and deities) to be tantamount to apostasy.[10]

Philo (c. 15 BCE–45 CE) also emphasizes observing the ancestral customs as an essential part of being Jewish. In *Jos.* 254, Philo reports that Joseph's father, Jacob, was both grateful for and fearful of his son's success in Egypt. According to Philo, Jacob was thankful to God for Joseph's safety and prosperity. Nevertheless, he was afraid that his young son, being surrounded by people who are blind towards the true God, being tempted by the lures of riches and renown, being separated from the support network of his family and being cut off from good teaching, would depart from his own customs and adopt foreign ones.

In another place, Philo contrasts transformed Jewish proselytes with those Jews he depicts as 'rebels of the holy laws' (τοὺς τῶν ἱερῶν νόμων ἀποστάντας) who have 'sold their freedom' (ἐλευθερίαν πεπρακότας) for 'delights of the belly and the organs below it' (*Virt.* 182). For Philo, such sensual rebellion flies in the face of divine

---

Diaspora, pp. 84-87. In Feldman's opinion, 'apostasy' from Judaism was not com-mon. In fact, he maintains that the only two 'apostates' from Judaism of whom we can be certain are Dositheos and Antiochus of Antioch. Contrast E. Mary Small-wood, *The Jews under Roman Rule from Pompey to Diocletian: A Study of Political Relations* (Leiden: E.J. Brill, 2nd edn, 1981), pp. 204; 234 n. 59; 258; 281, n. 84; 359; 360 n. 16; 361-63; 378; 380-81; 385; 391; 473, and Stephen G. Wilson, 'The Apostate Minority', *ST* 49 (1995), pp. 201-11 (201 n. 2).

9.   So Barclay, *Jews in the Mediterranean Diaspora*, p. 32-33, 104; Barclay, 'Who Was Considered an Apostate?', p. 83.

10.   Barclay, 'Who Was Considered an Apostate?', p. 84, and Collins, *Athens and Jerusalem*, p. 20 n. 49.

instruction. One other passage from Philo, a text to which we will return below, is worth noting here. In the course of his commentary on Moses' instruction on marriage, Philo maintains that Moses commands Israelites not to marry a person from another nation lest they succumb to opposing customs. Philo is particularly concerned that the sons and daughters of exogamous marriages will be enticed to set aside genuine customs for spurious ones (*Spec. Leg.* 3.29). In Philo's opinion, then, neglect of Jewish customs places one on a slippery slope toward apostasy. In fact, one may reasonably conclude that Philo would regard as apostate those Jews who defied the holy laws and disregarded the Jewish way with no visible signs of repentance.[11]

Turning to Josephus (37/38–?CE), one discovers at least four instances of 'apostasy' outside of Palestine, all of which involved the rejection of Jewish traditions and the adoption of Gentile ones.[12] Antiochus of Antioch was one individual whom Josephus considered an

---

11. So Harry A. Wolfson, *Philo: Foundations of Religious Philosophy in Judaism, Christianity, and Islam* (2 vols.; Cambridge, MA: Harvard University Press, 1948), I, pp. 75-76, and Seland, *Establishment Violence*, p. 95. Cf. Feldman, *Jew and Gentile*, p. 80.

12. So Barclay, 'Who Was Considered an Apostate?', pp. 86-88. Josephus also considered Menelaus and the sons of Tobias to be apostate on the same score. Josephus reports that these men 'abandon[ed] the ancestral laws and the way of living according to them...to follow the king's [i.e. Antiochus IV Epiphanes' (ruled 175–164 BCE)] laws and adopt[ed] the Greek way of life' (τοὺς πατρίους νόμους καταλιπόντες καὶ τὴν κατ' αὐτοὺς πολιτείαν ἔπεσθαι τοῖς βασιλικοῖς καὶ τὴν Ἑλληνικὴν πολιτείαν ἔχειν, *Ant.* 12.240; cf. 1 Macc. 1.11). In reference to Menelaus and the sons of Tobias, Josephus reports that they petitioned Antiochus to build a gymnasium in Jerusalem. Once granted permission, Josephus maintains that they sought to cover up their circumcision 'in order to be like Greeks even when unclothed'. Then he adds that these deserters of Judaism were guilty of 'giving up whatever other ancestral traditions they had' in order to imitate 'the practices of foreign nations' (τά τε ἄλλα πάνθ' ὅσα ἦν αὐτοῖς πάτρια παρέντες ἐμιμοῦντο τὰ τῶν ἀλλοεθνῶν ἔργα, 12.241).

In *Ant.* 4.100-115, Josephus records a story which further demonstrates the significance of Jewish ancestral traditions in his eyes. He reports that the tribes of Reuben, Gad and Manasseh were charged of sedition and idolatry by the other tribes. In response to such accusations, Josephus has representatives of the tribes under investigation remark: 'Have a better opinion of us and cease to accuse us of any of these crimes, for which all would justly deserve to be extirpated who, being the stock of Abraham, *embark on newfangled ways that are perversions of our customary practice*' (4.113, emphasis added).

156 *Conflict at Thessalonica*

apostate (see *War* 7.46-53). Josephus indicates that hatred of the Jews was widespread at the outset of the Roman–Judean War (7.46-47). According to Josephus, this was when Antiochus, a Jew who was highly regarded because his father served as the chief magistrate of the Jews in Antioch, came before a city assembly and accused his father and other Jews of plotting to set Antioch aflame (7.47). Furthermore, Josephus reports that Antiochus offered proof of his conversion and of his detestation of Jewish customs by sacrificing according to Greek custom (περὶ μὲν τῆς αὐτοῦ μεταβολῆς καὶ τοῦ μεμισηκέναι τὰ τῶν Ἰουδαίων ἔθη τεκμήριον ἐμπαρέχειν οἰόμενος τὸ ἐπιθύειν ὥσπερ νόμος ἐστὶ τοῖς Ἕλλησιν) and by recommending to the Antiochenes that the rest of the Jews be compelled to do likewise (7.50-51). Additionally, Josephus records that Antiochus gained the aid of Roman military troops to oppress further his people by abolishing the Sabbath rest (7.52-53). In Josephus's opinion, Antiochus's betrayal of his people, his departure from Jewish customs and his conversion to Greek ways rendered him apostate.

According to Josephus, Tiberius Julius Alexander (born c. 15 CE) was another individual who abandoned Judaism.[13] Alexander, the son of a devout, wealthy man who had once served as an alabarch in Alexandria (*Ant.* 20.100; see also 18.159-160, 259; 19.276-277) and the nephew of Philo, was extremely successful in Roman administration. Over the course of his career, Alexander held such posts as: procurator of Judea (c. 46–48 CE; *Ant.* 20.100), army officer under Corbulo in Armenia (63 CE; Tacitus, *Ann.* 15.28), governor of Egypt (66–69 CE; *War* 2.309, 487-98; 4.616) and chief of the general staff of Titus at the siege of Jerusalem in 70 CE (*War* 5.45-46; 6.237). Although Alexander's administrative positions would have required him to honor Egyptian and Roman gods,[14] Josephus does not present him as an apostate in *The Jewish War* which he composed in the late seventies CE (see, e.g., the laudatory remarks about Alexander in *War* 2.220). In his *Antiquities of the Jews* (published 93 CE), however, Josephus suggests that Tiberius Alexander was inferior to his father in 'piety toward God' (πρὸς τὸν θεὸν εὐσεβείᾳ) because he 'did not abide by his ancestral practices' (τοῖς πατρίοις οὐκ ἐνέμεινεν οὗτος ἔθεσιν, *Ant.* 20.100). It

13. For a fuller treatment of Alexander, see E.G. Turner, 'Tiberius Julius Alexander' *JRS* 44 (1954), pp. 54-64. See also Barclay, *Jews in the Mediterranean Diaspora*, pp. 105-106, and 'Deviance and Apostasy', pp. 119-21.
14. Barclay, 'Who Was Considered an Apostate?', pp. 87, 95 n. 26.

seems clear enough that Josephus ultimately considered Tiberius Alexander to have renounced Judaism. Why, then, did Josephus speak of Alexander's 'apostasy' only in his *Antiquities*? He probably thought it politically prudent not to offend a powerful Roman official during his lifetime. In all likelihood, Alexander was dead by the time Josephus's *Antiquities* was published.[15]

Josephus reports two other cases of 'apostasy' among Diaspora Jews that merit mention here. The first involves the children of another Alexander who had married a non-Jewish princess named Jotape (*Ant.* 18.138). According to Josephus, Alexander's offspring (who were descendants of Herod the Great and reared in Rome) were apostates for they 'abandoned from birth the observance of the customs of the Jews and changed over to the ways of the Greeks' (ἅμα τῷ φυῆναι τὴν θεραπείαν ἐξέλιπε τῶν Ἰουδαίοις ἐπιχωρίων μετατάξαμενοι πρὸς τὰ Ἕλλησι πάτρια, *Ant.* 18.141). As with Antiochus and Tiberius Alexander, Josephus regarded the children of Alexander to be outside of Judaism because they adopted a Greek way of life. Another individual that Josephus presents as an apostate is the Cilician king and Jewish proselyte Polemo. In order to marry Berenice, Polemo converted to Judaism (i.e. he was circumcised). Shortly thereafter, however, Berenice deserted Polemo. As a result, he was released from the marriage and from further adherence to the Jewish customs (τοῖς ἔθεσι τῶν Ἰουδαίων ἐμμένειν ἀπήλλακτο, *Ant.* 20.147; cf. *Apion* 2.123).

The writer of *4 Maccabees* (late first century CE [?]) is another author who understood as apostate those individuals who abandoned the Jewish customs for a Greek way of life. In an attempt to persuade his fellow Diaspora Jews to hold fast to their ancient traditions and to resist the temptation of assimilation, the author of *4 Maccabees* showcases the self-control, courage, justice and piety (5.23-24) of nine devout Jews (an aged priest Eleazar, seven unnamed brothers and their unnamed mother). According to *4 Maccabees*, these exemplary Jews were tortured and martyred by Antiochus IV Epiphanes for their stubborn refusal to renounce Judaism. For the author of this pseudo-philosophical tract, faithful Jews (represented by the praiseworthy martyrs) must overcome the pressure 'to deny the ancestral laws of [their] national life [ἀρνησάμενοι τὸν πάτριον ὑμῶν τῆς πολιτείας θεσμόν]...by adopting the Greek way of life and by changing [their] manner of life' (μεταλα-

15. So Turner, 'Alexander', p. 63, who is followed by Barclay, 'Deviance and Apostasy', p. 120, and *Jews in the Mediterranean Diaspora*, p. 106 n. 8.

βόντες Ἑλληνικοῦ βίου καὶ μεταδιαιτηθέντες ἐντρυφήσατε ταῖς νεότησιν ὑμῶν, 8.7-8). As we will see below, the litmus test of Jewish fidelity for the author of *4 Maccabees* is the willingness to refrain from eating forbidden, defiling foodstuffs (1.33; 4.26), particularly pork and food sacrificed to idols (5.2).

b. *Worshipping Other Gods*
In addition to the general charge of abandoning Jewish ways, one finds in Philo, Josephus and *3, 4 Maccabees* the accusation of apostasy for more specific offenses. The worship of other gods (i.e. 'idolatry') is one activity frequently understood by our sources to signal desertion of Judaism.[16]

In the historical novel *3 Maccabees*, it is reported that Egyptian Jews were rounded up by the command of Ptolemy IV Philopator and pressured to offer sacrifice to Dionysus. According to the author, the 'majority acted firmly with a courageous spirit and did not abandon their religion' (οἱ δὲ πλεῖστοι γενναίᾳ ψυχῇ ἐνίσχυσαν καὶ οὐ διέστησαν τῆς εὐσεβείας, 2.32). However, we are told that some three hundred Jewish men 'willfully transgressed against the holy God and the law of God' (7.10). The author believed that those Jews who attained Alexandrian citizenship by worshipping Dionysus did so to gain a good reputation with the king (2.31) and to satisfy their stomachs (7.11). Those Jews who compromised themselves are, according to *3 Maccabees*, to be detested, ostracized and thought of as profane enemies of the Jewish nation (2.33; 7.15). The climax of the book is the destruction of these 'defiled' people at the hands of their 'holy' compatriots (7.10-15). The spirit of hostility which the writer displays toward those Jews who became Alexandrian citizens by embracing 'idolatry' and neglecting Jewish food laws makes it clear whom and what he considered to be outside of Judaism.

In the course of their commentaries on the 'seduction' of Israelite men by Midianite women (Num. 25.6-15), both Philo and Josephus seem to equate idolatrous worship with defection from Judaism. Philo comments on this story in three places: *Vit. Mos.* 1.295-305, *Spec. Leg.* 1.54-58 and *Virt.* 34-44. Philo viewed as converts to paganism the young men of Israel who participated in the worship of Midianite gods

---

16. On the rejection of alien, pluralist and iconic cult by most all Diasporan Jews, see Barclay, *Jews in the Mediterranean Diaspora*, pp. 429-34.

in return for sexual pleasures (*Vit. Mos.* 1.298). Furthermore, Philo thought the sacrifices and libations offered by the Israelites to foreign gods 'estranged them from the service of the One, the truly existing God' (ἀλλοτριοῦσι τῆς τοῦ ἑνὸς καὶ ὄντως ὄντος θεραπείας θεοῦ, *Virt*. 40).[17]

In his treatment of this story (*Ant.* 4.126-155), Josephus includes dramatized speeches of the Midianite women and of Zambrias. Josephus reports that the Midianite women told their Israelite suitors that if they wanted to live with them (and with the rest of the world for that matter!), then they needed to set aside their strange customs (i.e. eating and drinking in a particular way and worshipping a peculiar god). Josephus indicates that the Israelite youths succumbed. Not only did they offer sacrifice to their companions' gods, but they also partook of foreign foods in order to please their Midianite lovers. Josephus depicts these men as transgressors of the ancient customs (παρέβησαν τὰ πάτρια, 4.139).

In the mouth of one 'apostate', Zambrias, Josephus puts a scathing attack on the tyrannical rule of Moses (4.145-149). During his speech, Zambrias asserts his free will by flaunting the facts that he had married a foreign wife, Chosbia, and that he had offered sacrifice to her gods (4.149). For Josephus, Zambrias's devotion to Chosbia's religion and his neglect of the decrees of Moses placed him outside of Judaism (Ζαμβρίας...κελευσθεὶς ὑπὸ τῆς γυναικὸς πρὸ τῶν Μωυσεῖ δοχθέντων τὸ πρὸς ἡδονὴν αὐτῆ γενησόμενον ἐθεράπευεν, 4.141). Josephus also judged Antiochus of Antioch (see pp. 155-56 above) as a deserter of Judaism because, among other things, of his willingness to renounce Jewish customs and to convert to worshipping in a Greek manner (*War* 7.50).

c. *Disregarding Dietary Laws*

For the writers of *3* and *4 Maccabees* in particular, worshipping foreign gods and eating forbidden foods are closely correlated. In their thinking, faithful Jews were not to participate in such 'base' activities. One of the reasons given by the author of *3 Maccabees* for the 'apostasy' of

---

17. In his writings, Philo also instructs his readers to avoid involvement in the mysteries (*Spec. Leg.* 1.319-321) and to exercise extreme caution in joining clubs and associations (*Ebr.* 20-21, 95). Seland (*Establishment Violence*, pp. 96-97) maintains that Philo viewed the mysteries and associations as inducements to apostasy.

more than three hundred men was their desire to satisfy their stomachs (7.11).[18] This, of course, is a reference to the 'apostates'' willingness to abandon Jewish food laws. In *4 Maccabees* infidelity to Jewish dietary laws is synonymous with rejection of Judaism. Those who eat defiling foods are thought by this author to have renounced Judaism (4.26; 5.3). On the other hand, the writer conceives of those Jews who remain faithful to the food laws (e.g. Eleazar, the seven brothers and their mother) as models of Jewish piety.[19]

Philo and Josephus also comment upon the harmful effects of laxity toward the Jewish dietary laws. Although neither Philo nor Josephus seem to have regarded a neglect of dietary laws as apostasy per se, both authors appear to think that a compromised position on the food laws is characteristic of those who abandon Judaism. While contrasting 'rebels from the holy laws' with proselytes, Philo remarks that the former 'sold their freedom' for, among other things, food and drink (*Virt.* 182). Philo believes that enjoyment of such sensual pleasures ultimately inflicts severe injury both to body and soul (ὧν τὰ τέλη βαρύταται ζημίαι σώματός τε καὶ ψυχῆς ἐισι, *Virt.* 1.2). For Philo, such behavior is harmful and paves a path leading away from Judaism. In his commentary on Numbers 25 (*Ant.* 4.126-155), Josephus mentions the willingness of the Israelite youths to set aside their 'peculiar' stance on food and drink at the request of their Midianite companions (4.139). Josephus's narrative suggests that abandonment of dietary requirements played a role in their apostatizing process.

One probable reason that these Hellenistic-Jewish sources stress fidelity to dietary laws is that they made a valuable contribution to Jewish communal life.[20] Despite the fact that the Jewish dietary laws were often misconstrued and maligned by outsiders (e.g. Strabo, *Geo.* 16.2; Tacitus, *Hist.* 5.4; Diodorus 34.1.2), these regulations erected a social boundary between Jews and non-Jews and strengthened the soli-

---

18. As noted above, these men are also considered by the author as 'enemies of the nation' (2.33) for participating in the Dionysiac cult and for pursuing Alexandrian citizenship (2.30).

19. Wolfson (*Philo*, I, p. 75) rightly sees that in *4 Macc.* dietary laws 'are treated as a symbol of any law for which a Jew is to give up his life if forced openly to violate it'.

20. See further Esler, *Community and Gospel in Luke–Acts*, pp. 71-109. See also the discussion on community boundaries at pp. 96-98 above.

darity of Jewish communities living in the Diaspora.[21] A general reluctance to marry foreigners seems to have operated in a similar way.

d. *Marrying Other Peoples*

Although the Mosaic law prohibited Israelites from marrying certain Gentile nations (e.g. Exod. 34.15-16; Deut. 7.1-4; 23.3; cf. Josh. 9.3-27; 11.19; Judg. 3.5-6; Ezra 9.1-2; Neh. 10.30), Philo and Josephus interpreted such Pentateuchal prohibitions as a general ordinance forbidding exogamy.[22] Philo maintains that Moses says 'do not enter into the partnership of marriage with a member of a foreign nation' (*Spec. Leg.* 3.29), and Josephus writes that Moses 'prohibited marriage with persons of other races' (*Ant.* 8.191-192). Although neither Philo nor Josephus states that exogamy is apostasy per se, they were both aware (and afraid) that intermarriage could lead Jewish spouses and/or their progeny away from their customs and ultimately from their God.[23]

According to Philo, Moses prohibited intermarriage because of the inherent conflict between Jewish customs and those of other nations and because of the tendency of those Jews who did intermarry to forsake their ancestral traditions. Philo thinks that even if a Jew who marries a non-Jew is able to stand firm in Judaism, it is probable that their children will prefer 'spurious customs' and will 'unlearn the honor due to the one God' (*Spec. Leg.* 3.29). Elsewhere Philo illustrates the perils of

21. Wolfson, *Philo*, I, p. 74. Barclay (*Jews in the Mediterranean Diaspora*, p. 437) remarks, 'Even if not every Jew maintained this demarcation [i.e. separatism at meals], it typically served to bind the Jewish community together in distinction from others and thus to solidify Jewish ethnic identity on a daily basis.'

22. While some Jewish writings take a 'hard line' against intermarriage (see, e.g., *Jub.* 30.7, 14-17; *Ps.-Philo* 9.5; 18.13-14; 21.1; 30.1; 44.7; 45:3; Tob. 4.12), others display a more liberal attitude (see, e.g., Ruth, *Jos. Asen.*). The writer of *Jos. Asen.* seemingly advocates conversion of Gentiles to Judaism prior to marriage. Cf. also Josephus, *Ant.* 20.139. For an unsympathetic Roman perspective on the Jewish practice of endogamy, see Tacitus, *Hist.* 5.5.

Though exogamy was generally discouraged and probably not widespread, it did occur. In addition to the examples given below, note Acts 16.1 where Luke reports that Timothy's mother, a Christian Jew, was married to a Greek man. Furthermore, Acts indicates that Timothy was uncircumcised (16.3). This marital relationship between a Jewish woman and a Gentile man is a prime example of why many Jews denounced intermarriage. By not having her son circumcised, Timothy's mother failed to follow the Jewish way.

23. Seland (*Establishment Violence*, p. 95) maintains, 'Philo condemns [intermarriage], explicitly pointing to the inherent danger of apostasy.'

exogamy on the offspring. He tells of a man whose mother, a Jewess, married an Egyptian. Philo reports that this 'base-born' man chose the 'atheism' of the Egyptian father over the 'ancient customs' of his Jewish mother (*Vit. Mos.* 2.193).[24]

In the course of his commentary on Solomon and women, Josephus reports that in an attempt to gratify his foreign wives and his passion for them Solomon discarded his customs and worshipped their gods. Josephus maintains that Moses prohibited intermarriage because he knew that it would lead to the observance of foreign customs and the worship of other gods (*Ant.* 7.192).[25]

Josephus further illustrates the folly of exogamy in his story of two Jewish brothers, Asineus and Anileus (*Ant.* 18.310-379). According to Josephus, this pair of brothers had gained control over the whole of Mesopotamia. At the peak of their power, however, things began to deteriorate when Anileus decided to marry a foreign woman. Shortly after they were married, she began to worship openly her household gods. Despite warnings from friends and family, Anileus continued to associate with this woman. In Josephus's view, she was ultimately responsible for the ensuing political downfall and death of Anileus. For Josephus, exogamous relations are a transgression of Jewish law, and intermarriage can debilitate, and even destroy, the strongest of Diaspora Jews.[26] In Philo's view, as we will now see, the quest of some Alexandrian Jews for wealth had equally ruinous consequences.[27]

---

24. Siegal ('Defensive Structuring', p. 11) suggests that intentional socialization of children in the way of a given tradition is a common characteristic among minority groups seeking to 'preserve a cultural identity in the face of what they feel are external threats to that identity'. On the importance of socializing children within the Jewish tradition, see Barclay (*Jews in the Mediterranean Diaspora*, pp. 412-13) and the supporting texts from Philo and Josephus that he cites. On the socialization process, see pp. 101-102 above.

25. See similarly Josephus's comments on the Midianite apostasy, *Ant.* 4.126-155, esp. 4.139-140.

26. Siegel ('Defensive Structuring', p. 11) describes endogamy as a type of 'defensive structuring' on the part of minority groups wishing to preserve their (distinct) cultural identity. Barclay (*Jews in the Mediterranean Diaspora*, p. 411) notes that modern sociological studies 'have shown time and again [exogamy's] debilitating effect on Jewish affiliation in the immediate or the following generation, and Philo and Josephus understood this well enough'.

27. In his commentary on Israel after Joshua's death, Josephus also comments

e. *Seeking Financial Prosperity*

Philo maintains that even though Moses was seated in the lap of Egyptian luxury, he regarded riches as 'spurious' and 'was zealous for the discipline and culture of his kin and ancestors' (τὴν συγγενικὴν καὶ προγονικὴν ἐζήλωσε παιδείαν, *Vit. Mos.* 1.32). Contrariwise, Philo speaks of some Jews in Alexandria who had experienced a degree of financial success and had grown insolent as a result. Philo reports that these people

> look down on their relations and friends and transgress the laws [νόμους δὲ παραβαίνουσι] under which they were born and bred and subvert the ancestral customs, to which no blame can be justly attached, by changing their mode of life, and in their contentment with the present, lose all memory of the past [κινοῦσιν ἐκδεδιητημένοι καὶ διὰ τὴν τῶν παρόντων ἀποδοχὴν οὐδενὸς ἔτι τῶν ἀρχαίων μνήμην λαμβάνουσιν, 1.31].

For Philo, these fortune seekers had passed out of Judaism. As Harry A. Wolfson remarks, 'To adopt different modes of life and to lose all memory of the past naturally means to become completely severed from the body Israel.'[28]

Before considering one other reason for which Diaspora Jews were thought of as deserters of Judaism, I should note the close correlation of the items treated above. Reverence for and adherence to the ancient customs was part and parcel of being Jewish.[29] Rejecting 'idolatry', observing Mosaic dietary laws and marrying fellow Jews were three Jewish practices in particular that served to distinguish and to establish the Jews among other peoples and cultures. The Hellenistic-Jewish authors being read suggest, albeit in distinct ways and with differing degrees of intensity, that Jews should resist joining non-Jews in worship, meals and marriage. These writers think it wise to hold fast to their customs and to exercise due caution in fraternizing with Gentiles so that they might remain loyal to and holy before the one true God.[30]

upon the potentially negative effects that material prosperity can have on spiritual fidelity (*Ant.* 5.132).

28. Wolfson, *Philo*, I, p. 78. Contrast Feldman, *Jew and Gentile*, p. 81.

29. On the importance of group norms, see pp. 100-101 above.

30. E.P. Sanders ('Jewish Association with Gentiles and Galatians 2:11-14', in Robert T. Fortna and Beverly R. Gaventa [eds.], *The Conversation Continues: Studies in Paul and John in Honor of J. Louis Martyn* [Nashville: Abingdon Press, 1990], pp. 170-88 [180]) remarks, 'Monotheism is what led to [Jewish] separatism.'

Conflict at Thessalonica

The Alexandrian Jew who wrote *The Letter of Aristeas* (c. 150–100 BCE) explicitly indicates such:

> In his wisdom the legislator [i.e. Moses]...surrounded us with unbreakable palisades and iron walls to prevent our mixing with any of the other peoples in any matter, being thus kept pure in body and soul, preserved from false beliefs, and worshipping the only God omnipotent over all creation (139-140).

A survey of our sources thus far, then, suggests that those Jews who spurned the greatness and glory of Yahweh by failing to observe the God-given, time-honored customs (particularly those instructions concerning worship, diet and marriage) were frequently considered outsiders.[31] There is one other category of Jewish 'detractor' yet to consider: the critics of the Jewish Scriptures.

f. *Criticizing the Scriptures*

In his writings Philo will on occasion strike out against those whom he depicts as 'malicious critics' (κακοτεχνοῦντες) of the law (*Agr.* 157). Philo seemingly has these 'Scripture-critics' in view when he speaks of 'wretches' who 'ridicule' the story of God making garments of skin for Adam and the woman (*Quaest. in Gen.* 1.53; cf. Gen. 3); those 'not belonging to the divine chorus' who 'mock' at the story of God's changing the name of Abram to Abraham (*Quaest. in Gen.* 3.43; cf. Gen. 17); 'impious scoffers' who seek to devalue the story of Abraham's offering of Isaac (*Abr.* 178-193; cf. Gen. 22) and the story of Babel (*Conf. Ling.* 2-13; cf. Gen. 11) by comparing them to Greek

So similarly Gabriele Boccaccini, *Middle Judaism: Jewish Thought 300 BCE to 200 CE* (Minneapolis: Fortress Press, 1991), p. 252.

Social control theory (see pp. 93-94 above) contends that conformity to a given community's norms is achieved through social bonding and that bonding is accomplished through attachment to conventional people, commitment to agreed-upon conventions, involvement in norm-conforming activities and belief in conventional ways. Differential association theory (see pp. 90-93 above) suggests that all behavior, conventional and otherwise, is learned through socialization. Though, of course, in other words, our sources emphasize the importance of bonding and being socialized in the Jewish way. In fact, Philo, Josephus and the authors of *3* and *4 Maccabees* depict those people who have disregarded their ancestral customs as having departed from Judaism.

31. Labeling theory (see pp. 94-98 above) propounds that those who fail to comply with a community's customs run the risk of being viewed as a threat and treated as a deviant.

myths; and 'uncultivated', 'uneducated', 'stupid' and 'perverse' people who deride the story of the pottage sold by Jacob to Esau (*Quaest. in Gen.* 4.168; cf. Gen. 25).

In the course of his invective against these people, Philo fails to disclose their identity or arguments. It is likely, however, that these critics were 'well-educated Jews whose attitude to their Scriptures was less adulatory than that of Philo'.[32] From all indications, Philo had little affinity with or tolerance for these innovative antagonists who 'reject[ed] the sacred writings and talk[ed] nonsense about them' (*Quaest. in Gen.* 2.2). In fact, Philo would have viewed those 'who cherish[ed] a dislike of the ancestral constitution and ma[d]e it their constant study to denounce and decry the laws' (*Conf. Ling.* 2) as outside of Judaism.[33]

Having considered a range of actions and attitudes among Diaspora Jews which Philo, Josephus and the authors of *3, 4 Maccabees* regarded as (leading to) apostasy, I will now examine Paul's persecution of Christians. By considering Paul's persecutory activity, we stand to gain additional insight into why some Jews opposed Paul subsequent to his conversion/call.

3. *Paul's Pre-Christian Persecution of the Church*

Prior to his experience on the Damascus road, Paul 'persecuted (ἐδίωξα) the church of God' (1 Cor. 15.9; cf. Gal. 1.13-14, 23; Phil. 3.6; 1 Tim. 1.13; Acts 8.3; 9.1, 21; 22.4, 19; 26.10-11).[34] And based upon what Paul says in Gal. 1.22-23, the story of his conversion from a persecutor of the church to a proclaimer of faith in Christ circulated among early believers, at least among the Christian churches in Judea. Although the locale and nature of Paul's persecutory activity has generated considerable interest and debate among New Testament inter-

---

32. Barclay, 'Who Was Considered an Apostate?', p. 86.

33. Wolfson, *Philo*, I, pp. 83-84.

34. Scholars frequently suggest that Acts bungles and exaggerates some of the particulars of Paul's persecuting activity. Even if one is loath to accept some of the specifics of Acts' record of Paul's persecutions (e.g. the location of Paul's persecutions, Paul's association with the stoning of Stephen and the way Acts depicts Paul opposing Christians), at the very least Acts reinforces Paul's claim that he opposed Christians prior to his conversion.

preters,[35] these intriguing issues need not detain us here.[36] Rather, my aim in this section is to discover why Paul 'tried to destroy' (πορθεῖν)[37] the church prior to his revelatory encounter with Jesus Christ. This is in keeping with the purpose of this chapter.

Although Paul does not specifically indicate in his extant letters what prompted him to oppose Christians, on two separate occasions he links his persecution of the church with his zeal for things Jewish (Gal. 1.14; Phil. 3.6; cf. Acts 22.3-4). This positive correlation between zeal and persecution strongly suggests that it was Paul's fervor for Jewish ancestral customs, particularly the Torah and its interpretation in Pharisaic oral tradition, that propelled him to oppose believers in Jesus prior to his conversion.[38] As discussed above, faithful observance of time-

35. See, e.g., Hultgren, 'Paul's Pre-Christian Persecutions'; Hengel, *Pre-Christian Paul*, pp. 63-86; Simon Légasse, 'Paul's Pre-Christian Career According to Acts', in Richard Bauckham (ed.), *The Book of Acts in its Palestinian Setting* (BAFCS, 4; Grand Rapids: Eerdmans; Carlisle: Paternoster Press, 1995), pp. 365-90 [379-89]; and Lloyd Walter Rodgers, III, 'An Examination of Paul as Persecutor' (PhD dissertation, Southern Baptist Theological Seminary, 1989).

36. In passing I would note that Paul probably carried out the majority of his persecutions in Judea, particularly in and around Jerusalem and that for the most part employed the means of punishment which were at his disposal through the synagogue, namely the 39 stripes and ostracism. I would not dismiss out of hand, however, that Paul also participated in the incarceration of Christians and in mob action against Christians. As we will see below, zealots like Paul were willing to take extreme measures in an effort to preserve their ancestral customs. Cf. Légasse, 'Paul's Pre-Christian Career', pp. 385-86. See also the useful remarks by J. Louis Martyn, *Galatians* (AB, 33A; New York: Doubleday, 1997), pp. 161-63.

37. I take ἐπόρθουν as a conative imperfect in both Gal. 1.13 and 1.23. So also, e.g., Martyn, *Galatians*, p. 154 n. 185. On the translation and meaning of this term, see P.H. Menoud, 'Le sens du verbe πορθεῖν (Gal. 1.13, 23; Acts 9.21)', in *Apophoreta: Festschrift Ernst Haenchen* (BNZW, 30; Berlin: Alfred Töpelmann, 1964), pp. 178-86. In this article, Menoud argues that Paul attacked the church, not Christians. So similarly Hultgren, 'Paul's Pre-Christian Persecutions', pp. 108-10. To my mind, this is a false distinction. So similarly Hengel, *Pre-Christian Paul*, pp. 71-72, and Légasse, 'Paul's Pre-Christian Career', pp. 381-85.

38. So similarly, Jacques Dupont, 'The Conversion of Paul, and its Influence on his Understanding of Salvation by Faith', in W. Ward Gasque and Ralph P. Martin (eds.), *Apostolic History and the Gospel: Biblical and Historical Essays Presented to F.F. Bruce* (Exeter: Paternoster Press, 1970), pp. 176-94 (183-87); Légasse, 'Paul's Pre-Christian Career', pp. 383-84; Seyoon Kim, *The Origin of Paul's Gospel* (WUNT, 2.4; Tübingen: J.C.B. Mohr [Paul Siebeck], 1984), pp. 41-46; Dieter Lührmann, *Galatians* (trans. O.C. Dean, Jr; CCS; Minneapolis: Fortress

honored traditions was part and parcel of being Jewish, and those who failed to follow these revered conventions were frequently thought of and treated as deviants. Paul maintains that in his 'former life in Judaism' he was 'extremely zealous' (περισσοτέρως ζηλωτὴς) in keeping 'the traditions of [his] ancestors' (τῶν πατρικῶν μου παραδόσεων, Gal. 1.13-14).[39] At least in retrospect, Paul perceived his persecution of the church as an example of this zeal.[40]

By claiming to be a 'zealot', Paul was not, of course, identifying himself with the anti-Roman revolutionary group known as the Zealots.[41] Rather, the proper background against which to view Paul's statements concerning zeal is the long line of zealotism in Jewish tradition.[42] For the love of Yahweh and Torah, Jewish zealots violently

Press, 1992), p. 28; and Setzer, *Jewish Responses*, pp. 10, 13. Robert Jewett ('The Basic Human Dilemma: Weakness or Zealous Violence? Romans 7:7-25 and 10:1-18', *ExAud* 13 [1997], pp. 96-109) remarks, '[Paul's] persecution of the Church was in direct proportion to the passion with which he maintained his own conformity to the law. In this view, Paul was a kind of first century Ayatollah Khomeini.'

39. N.T. Wright (*What Saint Paul Really Said: Was Paul of Tarsus the Real Founder of Christianity?* [Grand Rapids: Eerdmans; Cincinnati, OH: Forward Movement Publications, 1997], p. 26) pictures the pre-Christian Paul as a 'Shammaite, a hard-line Pharisee—what we today would call a militant right-winger'. Cf. Donaldson, *Paul and the Gentiles*, p. 278. Paul reports in Phil. 3.6 that he was blameless regarding righteousness under the law (cf. Acts 23.1; 24.16).

40. Cf. Martyn (*Galatians*, p. 154): '[I]n Galatians Paul's extremely zealous persecution of the church is the initial item to come to his mind when he thinks of his former life as an intensely observant Jew (cf. 1 Cor 15:9; Phil 3:6).' Subsequent to his conversion and call, Paul would have regarded such zeal as unenlightened (1 Cor. 15.9; cf. Rom. 10.2). Jewett ('The Basic Human Dilemma') has forwarded the hypothesis that Rom. 7.7-25 'describes the dilemma of a [former] zealot [i.e. Paul] looking back on his career after discovering the destructive error of his ways'.

41. So rightly David Rhoads, 'Zealots', *ABD*, IV, pp. 1043-54 (1045); Donaldson, *Paul and the Gentiles*, p. 286; and Martyn, *Galatians*, p. 155. In fact, it is doubtful that such a group even existed in Paul's lifetime. Although many scholars have linked the so-called 'fourth philosophy' started by Judas of Galilee in 6 CE with the zealots (Josephus, *Ant.* 18.9; cf. *War* 2.118; see esp. Martin Hengel, *The Zealots: Investigations into the Jewish Freedom Movement in the Period from Herod I to 70 A.D.* [trans. David Smith; Edinburgh: T. & T. Clark, 1989]), the present scholarly consensus suggests that the Zealots were only one of several anti-Roman revolutionary factions which arose in Jerusalem during the Roman–Judean War in 66–70 CE (see, e.g., Terence L. Donaldson, 'Rural Bandits, City Mobs and the Zealots', *JSJ* 21 [1990], pp. 19-40).

42. So rightly Donaldson, 'Zealot and Convert', p. 672; Jewett, 'The Basic

opposed people (frequently fellow Jews!) whom they perceived to threaten the boundaries of the community lest the purity and identity of Israel be undermined.[43] Although only certain Jews are highlighted in extant literature as zealots for Yahweh,[44] there is good reason to believe that the ideal of zeal was pervasive throughout ancient Judaism.[45]

In addition to the texts already cited, one can support this claim by noting Acts 21.20 where James informs Paul that there are thousands of Christian Jews who are 'zealous for the law' (ζηλωταὶ τοῦ νόμου). Acts also records Paul saying to a group of Jews gathered at the Temple that he was once zealous for God even as they themselves still were (ζηλωτὴς ὑπάρχων τοῦ θεοῦ καθὼς πάντες ὑμεῖς ἐστε σήμερον, 22.3). Elsewhere, Philo contends that those Jews who speak falsely in God's name would and should be swiftly and severely punished 'for there are thousands who are watchful, full of zeal for the laws [ζηλωταὶ νόμων], strictest guardians of the ancestral institutions [φύλακες τῶν πατρίων ἀκριβέστατοι], merciless to those who do anything to subvert them'

Human Dilemma', p. 104; and Wright, *What Saint Paul Really Said*, p. 28.

43. Rhoads ('Zealots', p. 1044) defines zeal as 'behavior motivated by the jealous desire to protect one's self, group, space, or time against violations'. He adds, 'In the biblical tradition, human acts of zeal punished idolatrous violations of God's right to exclusive allegiance from Israel.' Cf. the apposite remarks by Donaldson, *Paul and the Gentiles*, p. 286. Communities that have clearly defined boundaries can react rather forcefully against those who deviate from the accepted norms. See further Coser, *Functions of Social Conflict*, pp. 67-73, 95-104.

44. Phinehas (the Old Testament character who slew Zimri, the Israelite, and Cozbi, his Midianite woman companion) is usually considered to be the prototype of zeal for Yahweh (Num. 25; cf. Ps. 106.31; Sir. 45.23-24; 1 Macc. 2.26, 54; *4 Macc.* 18.12; Philo, *Vit. Mos.* 1.301-305; *Spec. Leg.* 1.56-58; Josephus, *Ant.* 4.153-155). Other zealots who are celebrated in Jewish literature include: Simeon and Levi, who slew the men of Shechem for raping their sister Dinah (Gen. 34.1-31; on Simeon: cf. Jdt. 9.2-4; on Levi: cf. *Jub.* 30.19; *T. Levi* 6.3; *T. Ash.* 4.2-5); Moses, who disposed of the immoral Israelites at Baal-peor (Num. 25.1-5); Elijah, who killed the prophets of Baal at the brook Kishon (1 Kgs 18.40; cf. Sir. 48.1-2); Jehu, who slaughtered Baal worshippers in Israel (2 Kgs 10.16-27); and Josiah, who turned Israel back to God (2 Kgs 22.1-23.30; *2 Bar.* 66.5). Zeal for the law was especially pronounced during the Maccabean period. The author of 1 Macc. presents the revolutionary activity of Mattathias and his cohorts against the Syrians as something which was prompted by zeal for the law and the covenant (2.27, 50).

45. On the pervasiveness of zealotism in ancient Judaism, see esp. Dobschütz, *Paulus*, and Seland, *Establishment Violence*. One Jewish writer is concerned that zeal not be used as an excuse for needless plunder (*Pss. Sol.* 2.27).

(*Spec. Leg.* 2.253; cf. 1QS 9.23; *m. Sanh.* 9.6). Prior to his conversion, Paul was among these zealous custodians of the Jewish customs.

If Paul's persecutory activity was spurred on by his zeal for Jewish ancestral traditions, then it stands to reason that those people whom he persecuted were behaving and/or believing in some manner which Paul perceived to be incompatible with his understanding of the law.[46] To be sure, scholars have sought to pinpoint who[47] and what[48] incited Paul's

46. So also Donaldson, 'Zealot and Convert', and Jewett, 'The Basic Human Dilemma', p. 104. Note again my definitions of deviance and intergroup conflict in Chapters 4.5 and 5.4 above.

47. Interpreters frequently suggest that Paul persecuted Hellenistic-Jewish Christians because of their supposed liberalism toward the Temple and Torah. See, e. g., Kim, *Origin of Paul's Gospel*, pp. 44-50; Hengel, *Pre-Christian Paul*, pp. 79-84; and Heikki Räisänen, 'Paul's Conversion and the Development of His View of the Law', *NTS* 22 (1987), pp. 404-19. This line of interpretation has been called into question by the work of Hill, *Hellenists and Hebrews*. Hill demonstrates that Greek-speaking and Hebrew-speaking Jews in Jerusalem shared more in common, both ideologically and sociologically, than has usually been imagined.

48. Proposed reasons for why Paul persecuted the church are legion. They include: (1) The church's proclamation of a Messiah who was a condemned criminal and was crucified with the approval of an authoritative Jewish court. So, e.g., Kim, *Origin of Paul's Gospel*, pp. 44-50; Hengel, *Pre-Christian Paul*, 79-84; and Martyn, *Galatians*, p. 162. In arguing for this view, scholars often refer to 1 Cor. 1.23; Gal. 3.13 (= Deut. 21.3; cf. *Did.* 16.5); 5.11; 6.12. This interpretation has been challenged by, among others, Christopher Tuckett, 'Deuteronomy 21,23 and Paul's Conversion', in A. Vanhoye (ed.), *L'apôtre Paul, personnalité, style et conception du ministère* (BETL, 73; Leuven: Leuven University Press, 1986), pp. 345-50, and Paula Fredriksen, 'Paul and Augustine: Conversion Narratives, Orthodox Traditions, and the Retrospective Self', *JTS* NS 37 (1986), pp. 3-34 (11-13). (2) The Hellenistic-Jewish Christians' 'liberal' stance vis-à-vis the Temple and Torah (for representative bibliography, see n. 47 above). On the centrality of the Temple in the early controversies between Jews and Christian Jews, see Richard Bauckham, 'The Parting of the Ways: What Happened and Why', *ST* 47 (1993), pp. 135-51. For the view that the proclamation of Jesus as Messiah led some Christian Jews to reject parts of the law, see Setzer, *Jewish Responses*, p. 12, and Jewett, 'The Basic Human Dilemma', p. 104. (3) The veneration given to Jesus by believers with the related issue of monotheism. So Larry W. Hurtado, *One God, One Lord: Early Christian Devotion and Ancient Jewish Monotheism* (London: SCM Press, 1988), pp. 2, 122-23, 130 n. 4. (4) The claims that the Christians made about themselves as Jesus' disciples, i.e. that the Messiah had appeared to them. So Donaldson, 'Zealot and Convert', pp. 678-79. (5) The use of the Hebrew Scriptures by the followers of Jesus to support their beliefs and behavior. Thus A.E. Harvey, 'Did the Ways Have to Part?', *WFE* 2 (1992), pp. 51-54 (54). (6) Paul's belief that aggressive

zeal, but the paucity of evidence disallows definitive conclusions.[49]

Whoever the precise people and whatever the exact reason(s), it is clear enough that the pre-Christian Paul (violently) resisted Jewish believers in Jesus whom he viewed to be out of conformity with Torah.[50] He would have regarded those 'Christian' Jews, who in his estimation failed to uphold the ancestral traditions, as dangerously deviant and as a threat to the Jewish way (cf. the judgments of Philo, Josephus and the authors of *3, 4 Macc.* on pp. 154-58 above).[51] Prior to his conversion/call, Paul seemingly considered (many?) Jewish believers to be apostate; subsequent to his Damascus road experience, (some?) Jewish unbelievers (not to mention Jewish Christians) would have thought of him likewise. In an attempt to determine why Paul was perceived and responded to as an apostate, we will now examine some germane Pauline texts. By doing so, we will be able to identify more precisely the sorts of things which Paul did and said that caused controversy between him and other Jews.

4. *Paul's Conflict with his Own People*

According to Paul, he endured almost every hardship imaginable in his effort to disseminate the gospel (see esp. 2 Cor. 11.23-29), including opposition from his own people. In 2 Cor. 11.26d, Paul claims to have been endangered by his fellow Jews (κινδύνοις ἐκ γένους).[52] This

proclamation of the kingdom of God would be offensive to the Romans. See Paula Fredriksen, *From Jesus to Christ: The Origins of the New Testament Images of Jesus* (New Haven: Yale University Press, 1988), pp. 155-56.

49. It comes as no great surprise that Paul did not elaborate on his pre-Christian persecution of the church. In fact, based upon 1 Cor. 15.9 (cf. 1 Tim. 1.13) we may infer that Paul deeply regretted his persecutory activity. See similarly, Becker, *Paul*, p. 67.

50. Prior to his conversion/call, Paul enthusiastically attempted to protect and preserve what he (and other zealous Jews) perceived to be the proper Jewish way. Sociologically speaking, the pre-Christian Paul was an agent of censure, a guardian of Jewish boundaries, who opposed by means of formal and informal negative sanctions those Jews who deviated from the time-honored conventions.

51. Erikson (*Wayward Puritans*, p. 6) contends that the only way an outside observer can determine what type of behaviors (and beliefs) a group considers unacceptable (i.e. deviant) is to learn something about the standards of the group and how it responds to those group members who fail to uphold these standards. This is what I am seeking to do in this chapter.

52. In Rom. 15.31 Paul asks the Roman Christians to pray that he might 'be

cryptic comment implies that Paul felt harassed by his Jewish compatriots in the course of carrying out his apostolic call.[53] In the previous chapter I demonstrated that Thessalonica was one place where some Jews opposed Paul. But why did Paul experience such resistance from his own people as he sought to share the gospel with the Gentiles?

a. *Paul and the Synagogal Discipline*
I will begin my attempt to answer this complex question, by treating a passage where Paul offers some specific details about his conflict with other Jews.[54] In 2 Cor. 11.24 Paul writes, 'Five times I have received

delivered from unbelievers in Judea, and that [his] service for Jerusalem may be acceptable to the saints' (cf. 2 Thess. 3.2). It is likely that the Judean unbelievers to whom Paul refers were Jerusalem Jews. So James D.G. Dunn, *Romans 9–16* (WBC, 38B; Dallas, TX: Word Books, 1988), p. 883. Acts' record of Paul's arrest and trials in Jerusalem suggests that Paul's fears about his collection visit to the city were well founded (21.17–23.22).

53. C.K. Barrett (*A Commentary on the Second Epistle to the Corinthians* [BNTC; London: A. & C. Black, 1973], p. 299) thinks that Paul is alluding in 2 Cor. 11.26d to incidents where he considered his life to be at risk.

54. In 2 Cor. 11.25b Paul indicates that on one occasion he was stoned. Although he does not indicate who it was that stoned him or where this incident took place, most commentators connect this comment with Acts 14.19, a text which indicates that Jews and Gentiles in Lystra stoned Paul, dragged him out of the city and left him for dead (cf. 2 Tim. 3.11). So, e.g., Victor P. Furnish, *II Corinthians* (AB, 32A; Garden City, NY: Doubleday, 1984), p. 516; Barrett, *Second Corinthians*, p. 298; F.F. Bruce, *The Book of Acts* (NICNT; Grand Rapids: Eerdmans, rev. edn, 1988), p. 279; and Lüdemann, *Traditions in Acts*, p. 165.

Becker (*Paul*, pp. 174-76) makes much out of Paul's statement in 2 Cor. 11.25b and its supposed parallel in Acts 14.19. Appealing to Lev. 24.10-14 and Deut. 17.2-7 as the proper biblical backdrop against which to view this incident and referring to Acts 7.58-59 and to Jn 8.5 as New Testament parallels, Becker suggests that Paul's statement and Luke's narrative refer to the Jewish synagogal practice of capital punishment by stoning. Such a reading clearly goes beyond the evidence. Even if Paul were referring to the Lystra episode recorded by Luke, there is no good reason to assume with Becker that it was only the Jews who participated in the stoning of Paul. In fact, the Acts account suggests otherwise (14.19). Becker also ignores the fact that Luke reports Paul being stoned inside the city, not outside. Furthermore, if this were a 'legal' Jewish punishment, they would have made sure that Paul was dead. The incident in Lystra, then, should not be seen as an official Jewish punishment as provided for in *m. Sanh.* 6.1-6, but as a mob action of Jews and Gentiles against Paul (cf. Acts 14.5-6). *1 Clem.* 5.6 also indicates that Paul was stoned, but the text gives no further details. On this verse see further, Jerome D.

from the Jews thirty-nine lashes'. Paul is referring here to the Jewish synagogal discipline of flogging. Josephus remarks that the forty stripes save one was a 'most disgraceful penalty' (τιμωρίαν αἰσχίστην, *Ant.* 4.238), and descriptions of this punishment elsewhere lead us to accept Josephus's judgment.

Deuteronomy 25.1-3 records that if an individual was found guilty and deserved to be flogged, then the judge was to decide how many strokes the person would receive contingent upon the nature of the offense. The maximum number of strokes allowed was 40 in order that the one beaten would not be degraded! Later sources indicate that over time this number was reduced to 39 (so 2 Cor. 11.24; *Ant.* 4. 238, 248; *m. Mak.* 3.10),[55] probably to avoid exceeding the prescribed limit due to miscounting.[56] Although Paul's own experiences of the synagogal discipline may not mirror precisely the pattern set forth in the later Mishnah tractate *Makkot*, it is probable that there were distinct similarities.[57] To consider the procedure for scourging as described in *Makkot*, then, may give us a clearer image of what Paul endured on at least five different occasions.

According to *m. Mak.* 3.12-14, the guilty party's hands would be bound to pillars. Then the synagogue attendant would disrobe the individual and proceed to administer the punishment. One-third of the strokes were given in front and two-thirds were applied from the rear. The attendant was to strike the person as hard as possible with a three-thonged scourge made from calf-hide. While the stripes were being doled out, Deut. 28.58-59 was read repeatedly.[58] The force of the blows must have been great, for instructions are given in *Makkot* regarding

Quinn, '"Seven Time He Wore Chains" (1 Clem 5:6)', *JBL* 97 (1978), pp. 574-76.

55. Barrett (*Second Corinthians*, p. 296) asserts that 'there can be no doubt that [39 strokes] represents common practice in the first century'.

56. So Furnish, *II Corinthians*, pp. 515-16, and Pobee, *Persecution and Martyrdom*, p. 10. Pobee also suggests that the maximum number of strokes became 39 due to the introduction of the three-thonged scourge. To be struck with this instrument 13 times would equal 39 stripes. In *m. Mak.* 3.11 it is required that the number of stripes estimated be divisible by three.

57. So Sven Gallas, '"Fünfmal vierzig weniger einen...": Die an Paulus vollzogenen Synagogalstrafen nach 2 Kor 11,24', *ZNW* 81 (1990), pp. 178-90.

58. The text reads as follows: 'If you do not diligently observe all the words of this law that are written in this book, fearing this glorious and awesome name, the Lord your God, then the Lord will overwhelm both you and your offspring with severe and lasting afflictions and grievous and lasting maladies.'

what should be done in the event that recipients befouled themselves during the discipline or, worse yet, were killed as a result of the strokes.

According to *m. Mak.* 3.15, scourging frequently served as a substitute for extirpation and resulted in the reconciliation of the transgressor to the community.[59] Synagogal stripes were a high price to pay for renewed relations with the synagogue, and it is likely that some felt this excruciating punishment was too high a price and opted to leave the Jewish community altogether.[60] Apparently, Paul reckoned that the stripes were worth it.[61] At the time he wrote 2 Cor 11.24, Paul had yielded to this discipline on five occasions.[62]

59. On extirpation in Second Temple Judaism, see William Horbury, 'Extirpation and Excommunication', *VT* 35 (1985), pp. 13-38.

60. See the perceptive comments of A.E. Harvey, 'Forty Stokes Save One: Social Aspects of Judaizing and Apostasy', in A.E. Harvey (ed.), *Alternative Approaches to New Testament Study* (London: SPCK, 1985), pp. 79-96 (80-82).

61. We do not know where and when Paul received the 39 stripes. There is no good reason, however, to assume that these floggings occurred either prior to Paul's conversion or early on in his ministry in Judea. Contra Sanders, *Schismatics, Sectarians, Dissidents, Deviants*, pp. 6-10, 203-204, 263 n. 26. Prior to his conversion, it appears that Paul was meting out punishment, not receiving it (Gal. 1.13, 23). Furthermore, why would a zealous Pharisee who diligently observed the law be punished? Those who are committed to and observant of agreed-upon community norms tend to be supported, not opposed. Additionally, according to Paul, he experienced conflict with his fellow Jews throughout his ministry (note Gal. 5.11; Rom. 15.31).

62. Hultgren ('Paul's Pre-Christian Persecutions', p. 101 n. 8) asserts that Paul did not submit to the synagogal discipline. But it is clear that he did. If Paul had wanted to avoid the beatings, he could have stayed away from the synagogue. As Sanders ('Paul on the Law', p. 89) maintains, 'The only way to receive the thirty-nine stripes would be to show up voluntarily in a Jewish community and to submit to community discipline. *Punishment implies inclusion*' (emphasis his).

Why did Paul submit to these scourgings? Paul does not indicate why, but the following two reasons seem likely. First of all, despite the fact that Paul's deepest devotion lay with the 'Israel of God' (Gal. 6.16; cf. 3.7, 29), i.e. the church, Paul had a deep love for and loyalty to his people (see esp. Rom. 9.2-3). Furthermore, he stood convinced that Jews needed to confess Jesus as Lord in order to be saved (e.g. Rom. 10.1-13). Apparently, Paul felt it necessary to receive the stripes so that he could maintain access to the synagogue and thereby have the opportunity to share the gospel with 'Israel according to the flesh' (1 Cor. 10.18; cf. Rom. 9.3; 11.14; 16.7, 11). Secondly, it is likely that Paul yielded to the synagogal discipline so that he might have continued contact with Gentile God-fearers, who appear to have been particularly responsive to Paul's message.

Why was Paul persecuted/punished in this way?[63] According to *Mak.*
3.1-9, a person was liable to the lashes for a variety of reasons, including: engaging in 'improper' sexual or marital relations (3.1); eating
food deemed unclean (3.2-3); taking a mother bird and her young (3.4);
cutting one's hair in a way that transgressed the law or cutting the hair
of a dead person (3.5); writing or pricking one's skin in a permanent
fashion (3.6); and breaking various Nazarite rules (3.7-9). How applicable these later Mishnaic laws (ultimately compiled around the close
of the second century CE) were in Diaspora Jewish circles in Paul's day
is impossible to know. This uncertainty notwithstanding, Sven Gallas
has appealed to *m. Mak.* 3.2 in arguing that Paul received the 39 stripes
for eating unclean food.[64]

In arriving at this conclusion, Gallas notes other scholarly suggestions as to why Paul was scourged. He enumerates the following: Paul's
becoming a Christian and preaching Jesus as Messiah; his depreciation
of the law and his denial of salvation through Torah; his offering of
Messianic salvation to Gentiles; his social interaction with Gentiles,
including eating unclean food and encouraging others to do likewise;
his bringing of ill-repute on Judaism; his blasphemy of Yahweh; his
encouragement of people in the synagogues and in the cities to apostatize; his heresy or defection from Judaism; and his missionary success
among proselytes.[65]

The diversity of scholarly opinion indicates the complexity of the
issue at hand. Since neither Paul nor Acts indicates why he was flogged,
one must seek to surmise as much. In an effort to curb needless speculation, it will be most fruitful at this point to broaden the question from

63. Sanders ('Paul on the Law', p. 86) notes that while Paul would have perceived the stripes as persecution, the Jews who administered the 39 lashes would
have considered them as appropriate punishment. Once again we discover the difference one's perspective makes. The synagogal discipline can be described as a
negative formal sanction (an external aspect of social control). As noted on p. 102
above, groups will sometimes impose negative sanctions on wayward members in
an attempt to affect conformity and to discourage additional deviance.

64. Gallas, 'Synagogalstrafen', p. 184. Gallas cross-references Rom. 14.14 and
1 Cor. 8.8. Although what Paul ate and drank could well have been an offense for
which he was disciplined, it is methodologically suspect to argue such from the
tractate *m. Mak.* In fact, Sanders ('Paul on the Law', p. 86) suggests, 'It is fruit-
less...to search the list of things in Mishnah Makkot for which the rabbis decreed
corporal punishment.'

65. Gallas, 'Synagogalstrafen', pp. 183-84.

why Paul received the 39 strokes on five occasions to what prompted Jews to oppose Paul (the central concern of this chapter) and to turn straightway to Paul's Epistles to gather an answer.

b. *Circumcision as a Source of Contention*

To begin, I will examine Paul's letter to the Galatian churches. References to persecution are plentiful in this epistle.[66] As noted above, Paul mentions in Gal. 1.13, 23 his pre-Christian persecution of the church. Furthermore, in the course of the letter he alludes to the opposition of his Galatian converts (3.4 [?]; 4.29; cf. 1.7; 5.12) and of himself (4.12-20[?], 29). Because of the veiled nature of these remarks it is not possible to determine the specifics of the conflicts to which Paul alludes, although it seems clear enough that in 4.29 Paul is referring to Jewish oppression of at least Pauline Christians.[67] In Gal. 5.11 and 6.12, however, Paul expresses his opinion as to why he is and his Jewish Christian opponents are not being persecuted. These remarks merit careful consideration.

In 5.11a Paul poses the following rhetorical question: 'If I myself, brothers, am still preaching circumcision, why am I still being persecuted?'[68] Paul's query raises at least the following questions for the interpreter: (1) Was there a time that Paul actually preached circumcision, and if so, when? (2) By whom was it that Paul considered himself persecuted? Paul's statement about 'still preaching circumcision' (εἰ

---

66. Noted by, e.g., Ernst Baasland, 'Persecution: A Neglected Feature in the Letter to the Galatians', *ST* 38 (1984), pp. 135-50, and Goddard and Cummins, 'Ill or Ill-Treated'.

67. Paul's allegory of Sarah and Hagar in 4.21–5.1 has been the topic of much discussion. Here, it will suffice to say that I take Sarah/Jerusalem above/Isaac/children of promise to refer to Christian believers who are free from the law, and I understand Hagar/present Jerusalem/Ishmael/those of the flesh to represent Jews, and perhaps Jewish Christians, who are under the law. In any event, when Paul suggests in 4.29 that even as Ishmael persecuted Isaac so also those of the flesh persecute those of the Spirit today, he seemingly had in mind at least some non-Christian Jews. See James D.G. Dunn, *The Epistle to the Galatians* (BNTC; London: A. & C. Black, 1993), pp. 256-57. For the argument that the children of Hagar are the 'agitators', see Frank J. Matera, *Galatians* (SP, 9; Collegeville, MN: Liturgical Press, 1992), p. 178. Cf. Martyn, *Galatians*, p. 445.

68. The adverb ἔτι appears twice in 5.11a. A few ancient manuscripts, including D* F G 0278. 6. 1739. 1881 *pc* a b vg^mss; Ambst, omit (probably in error) the first of the two.

περιτομὴν ἔτι κηρύσσω) continues to befuddle exegetes.[69] Scholars are in basic agreement that this is a charge made against Paul by the 'agitators' who had come to the Galatian congregations after Paul. But this is where the agreement ends.[70] Were Paul's Jewish Christian opponents suggesting that Paul preached circumcision before he was converted?[71] Were they maintaining that he preached the gospel of circumcision before he embarked on his Gentile mission?[72] Were they contending that he continued to preach circumcision from time to time?[73] Did they understand Paul to be advocating spiritual circumcision?[74] Or, did Paul's rival missionaries accuse Paul of preaching circumcision to the Jews and not to the Gentiles?[75]

Although I am inclined to follow Terence L. Donaldson in thinking that Paul is referring in 5.11a 'to preconversion involvement in Jewish proselytizing activity',[76] I have nothing vested in this interpretation. Here, I would simply note that Paul denies he is presently preaching circumcision and claims this is why he continues to be persecuted.[77] In 5.11b Paul seeks to defend on theological grounds his position that Gentile believers should not be circumcised (or obligated to keep Torah) in order to be Abraham's children (cf. 3.7, 29; 4.28-31). He states that if he were still preaching circumcision (like his adversaries) then 'the scandal of the cross' (τὸ σκάνδαλον τοῦ σταυροῦ) would be removed. Paul's opponents in Galatia would have likely concurred with

69. Hans Dieter Betz (*Galatians* [Hermeneia; Philadelphia: Fortress Press, 1979], p. 270) states, 'What the Apostle has precisely in mind will in all likelihood always be hidden from our knowledge.'

70. Noted by Dunn, *Galatians*, p. 278.

71. See, e.g., Ernest De Witt Burton, *The Epistle to the Galatians* (ICC; Edinburgh: T. & T. Clark, 1921), p. 286. Cf. Donaldson, *Paul and the Gentiles*, pp. 275-84.

72. Watson, *Paul, Judaism and the Gentiles*, pp. 28-31.

73. Martyn (*Galatians*, p. 477) entertains this option.

74. So Peder Borgen, 'Observations on the Theme "Paul and Philo": Paul's Preaching of Circumcision in Galatia (Gal. 5:11) and Debates on Circumcision in Philo', in Sigfred Pedersen (ed.), *Die paulinische Literatur und Theologie* (Århus: Forlaget Aros; Göttingen: Vandenhoeck & Ruprecht, 1980), pp. 85-102.

75. Dunn, *Galatians*, pp. 279-80.

76. Donaldson, *Paul and the Gentiles*, p. 282. See further Donaldson's discussion on Jewish proselytism on pp. 52-60. Cf. Baasland, 'Persecution', p. 138.

77. John Zeisler, *The Epistle to the Galatians* (EC; London: Epworth Press, 1992), pp. 73, 79.

the author of *The Preachings of Peter* (written late second century CE in Syria [?]) who described Paul as 'the enemy man' who promulgated a 'lawless and absurd doctrine' (2.3).[78]

But who was persecuting Paul for not requiring Gentiles to enter the covenant community through circumcision? Some exegetes suggest that Paul considered himself to be persecuted by the rival missionaries in Galatia.[79] This interpretation, however, is problematic. At no time did Paul have direct contact with his Jewish Christian adversaries, and it does not appear that Paul is speaking in 5.11 of being verbally or psychologically harassed by them.[80]

Galatians 6.12 may be of some help in determining who 'persecuted' Paul. Having no more than picked up the pen Paul asserts to his Galatian converts: 'It is those who desire to make a good showing in the flesh that would compel you to be circumcised [ἀναγκάζουσιν ὑμᾶς περιτέμνεσθαι], only in order that they may not be persecuted [μὴ διώκωνται] for the cross of Christ.' Paul seems to be claiming that the 'agitators' required circumcision of Gentile converts, who would have included Galatian Christians (4.8), in order to avoid persecution, presumably from their fellow Jews.[81] While it is doubtful that Paul has captured fully his opponents' motivation for requiring circumcision of

78. On anti-Paulinism in the Pseudo-Clementine literature, see further Gerd Lüdemann, *Opposition to Paul in Jewish Christianity* (trans. M. Eugene Boring; Minneapolis: Fortress Press, 1989), pp. 171-94.

79. E.g. Matera, *Galatians*, p. 184, and Martyn, *Galatians*, p. 477.

80. In 5.11 Paul employs the verb διώκειν, the same term he uses in 1.13 and 1.23 to speak of his own persecution of the church (see also 4.29; 6.12). Baasland ('Persecution', p. 136) remarks, 'There is hardly any doubt that διώκω functions [in Galatians] more or less as a technical term for persecution of Christians...' On the other hand, Martyn (*Galatians*, p. 562 n. 54) maintains that when Paul speaks of persecution in 4.29, 5.11 and 6.12 he has 'inner-church developments' in view (contrast 1.13, 23). Despite Martyn's contention, it seems likely that Paul is speaking primarily of external, (non-Christian) Jewish opposition in 4.29, 5.11 and 6.12, even as he did in 1.13 and 1.23. So rightly, Sanders, *Paul, the Law, and the Jewish People*, p. 191, and Barclay, 'Paul among Diaspora Jews', p. 115. On reading the διώκειν texts together, see Baasland, 'Persecution', esp. pp. 136-40.

81. So also Richard N. Longenecker, *Galatians* (WBC, 41; Dallas, TX: Word Books, 1990), p. 291; Peder Borgen, 'The Early Church and the Hellenistic Synagogue', *ST* 37(1983), pp. 55-78 (71-72); Jack T. Sanders, 'Circumcision of Gentile Converts: The Root of Hostility', *BR* 7 (1991), pp. 20-25, 44 (24-25); and Sanders, *Paul, the Law, and the Jewish People*, p. 191.

Gentile converts,[82] he is almost certainly correct in claiming that their willingness to adhere to this (and presumably other) Jewish custom(s) protected them from the persecution/punishment which Paul received from the Jews, probably in the form of the 39 lashes.[83]

It may be that some Jewish Christians who were zealous for their traditions participated in the persecution/punishment of other Jewish Christians who were neglectful of the law, but this is far from clear.[84] It is fascinating to note that in Gal. 4.17 Paul remarks that the 'agitators' 'are zealous [ζηλοῦσιν] toward [his converts], but for no good purpose'.[85] Were they also zealous enough to punish fellow Jewish Christians who set aside time-honored Jewish customs such as circumcision? Elsewhere Paul indicates that he himself faced 'danger from false

---

82. A(nother) reason these missionaries and other Jewish Christians zealously observed Torah was because of their convictions (cf. the pre-Damascus Paul). See Borgen, 'The Early Church', p. 72, and Sanders, *Paul, the Law, and the Jewish People*, p. 192. Jewett ('Agitators') has argued that the rival missionaries came from Judea on a nomistic campaign which was spawned by rising Zealotic pressures. He maintains that the goal of the 'agitators' was 'to avert the suspicion that they were in communion with lawless Gentiles' (p. 205). Jewett suggests that these Judean Christians had 'convinced themselves that circumcision of Gentile Christians would thwart Zealot reprisals' (p. 205).

A number of commentators have embraced Jewett's thesis. See, e.g., Longenecker, *Galatians*, p. 291, and Timothy George, *Galatians* (NAC, 30; Nashville: Broadman & Holman Press, 1994), pp. 434-35. Jewett may be correct in suggesting that there was a rising tide of nationalism in the 40s and 50s in Judea. I am prepared to follow him that far. Nevertheless, as indicated above, I believe that it is historically inaccurate to speak of a formal Zealot party during these decades. Furthermore, Jewett fails to take into account the fact that zeal for the ancestral customs was widespread among the Jews of that period.

83. Cf. Burton (*Galatians*, pp. 349-50) who contends that if Paul's opponents are able to persuade Galatian believers to adhere to the physical requirements of the Jewish law, then 'they [i.e. the 'agitators'] will escape the persecution which the apostle himself had suffered (5[11]), and to which they would be subject at the hands of their fellow-Jews as members of the Christian sect of the Jewish community, if they favoured or did not successfully oppose its anti-legalistic tendency'. See also Sanders, 'Circumcision', p. 24. Social control theory (see pp. 93-94 above) contends that those who conform to group conventions escape the threat of negative sanctions. See also the insights of labeling theorists (pp. 94-98 above).

84. Sanders, *Paul, the Law, and the Jewish People*, p. 191.

85. On this verse see the insightful comments of Goddard and Cummins, 'Ill or Ill-Treated?', pp. 114-15.

brothers' (κινδύνοις ἐν ψευδαδέλφοις, 2 Cor. 11.26). Even if some law-observant Jewish Christians opposed some law-neglectful Jewish Christians, it is likely that they would have done so in reaction to and cooperation with other Jews.

It remains to be said that Paul's remark in 6.12 is more or less an inverted form of his statement in 5.11. Surely it is more than a fortuitous occurrence that circumcision and persecution appear in both verses. It should also be noted that in 5.11 and 6.12 Paul asserts his persecution results from his proclamation of the cross of Christ. In Paul's mind, then, both circumcision and 'Christ crucified' were factors in his conflict with his fellow Jews. Although Paul maintains that his preaching of the crucified Christ was a source of contention between him and other Jews (cf. 1 Cor. 1.23), it is difficult to decipher from Paul's polemical remarks in 5.11 and 6.12 how large a role his preaching of a crucified Messiah played in his conflict with other Jews.[86] While Paul suggests that his preaching of the cross was the cause of his persecution, Paul's Jewish Christian opponents would probably have retorted that it was his refusal to encourage Gentile converts to be obedient to Torah that incited the ire of other Jews.

It does appear that some Johannine Christians were later expelled from Jewish synagogues because of their belief in Jesus as the Messiah (9.22, 34; cf. 12.42; 16.2).[87] Furthermore, Christology was undoubtedly a source of significant controversy between Jews and Christians in the second century CE (as evidenced, e.g., in Justin's *1st Apol.* and *Dial. Try.*).[88] But as is frequently suggested, other Christian Jews contemporary with Paul (e.g. the Jerusalem apostles and Paul's opponents in Galatia) who *both* accepted and proclaimed Jesus as Messiah *and* observed the law seemed to have had far fewer conflicts with their compatriots.[89] It may be, then, that it was the social implications that

---

86. On the subject of the Messiah in Judaism, see, among others, Jacob Neusner, 'Varieties of Judaism in the Formative Age', in A. Green (ed.), *Jewish Spirituality from the Bible through the Middle Ages* (New York: Crossroad; London: SCM Press, 1989), pp. 171-97.

87. So, e.g., Setzer, *Jewish Responses*, p. 179.

88. On Justin's Christological assertions, see, e.g., Claudia J. Setzer, ' "You Invent a Christ!": Christological Claims as Points of Jewish–Christian Dispute', *USQR* 44 (1991), pp. 315-28, and Graham N. Stanton, 'Aspects of Early Jewish–Christian Polemic', *NTS* 31 (1985), pp. 377-92.

89. E.g. Sanders, *Paul, the Law, and the Jewish People*, pp. 192, 204-205 n. 77.

Paul drew (and taught others to draw) from his proclamation of Christ crucified that caused some Jews to stumble over Paul's gospel and to oppose him.[90] Precisely how offensive the Jewish hearers of Paul's preaching would have found his belief in Jesus as Messiah is unclear. Nonetheless, of this we can be certain: the fact that Paul did not require circumcision of his Gentile converts was a primary source of contention between Paul and other Jews, Christian and non-Christian alike.

Even though Paul never objects in his letters to the circumcision of Jews or Christian Jews and, according to Acts 16.3, circumcised Timothy,[91] it is clear from his letters that Paul no longer attached religious significance to this practice.[92] Of course Paul passionately insists in Galatians that Gentile converts must not be circumcised or forced to live under the law (2.3; 5.2-12; 6.12-16), but rumors abounded that Paul instructed Jews and Christian Jews in the Diaspora along similar lines (cf. Gal. 3.28; 1 Cor. 12.13; Col. 3.11). Upon his arrival in Jerusalem, Acts reports that James and other elders said to Paul that Jewish Christians who were 'zealous for the law' (ζηλωταὶ τοῦ νόμου) had been informed that he taught 'all the Jews who are among the Gentiles to abandon [ἀποστασίαν] Moses, telling them not to circumcise their children or observe the customs' (λέγων μὴ περιτέμνειν αὐτοὺς τὰ τέκνα μηδέ τοῖς ἔθεσιν περιπατεῖν, 21.20-21).[93] Whether or not this

90. Barclay ('Paul among Diaspora Jews', p. 112 n. 41) remarks: 'Perhaps Paul's social practices made explicit the potential of this message to question the validity of the law (Gal. 2.19; 3.13; 5.11).'

91. On the vexed issue of Paul circumcising Timothy, see, among others, Trebilco, *Jewish Communities in Asia Minor*, pp. 23-24, and Shaye Cohen, 'Was Timothy Jewish (Acts 16:1-3)?: Patristic Exegesis, Rabbinic Law, and Matrilineal Descent', *JBL* 105 (1986), pp. 251-86.

92. Gordon D. Fee (*The First Epistle to the Corinthians* [NICNT; Grand Rapids: Eerdmans, 1987], p. 312) writes: '[E]ven though [circumcision] was a matter to which [Paul] could acquiesce for pragmatic reasons (Acts 16:3), he was absolutely unyielding when anyone tried to give it religious significance.' Cf. similarly Daniel Boyarin, *A Radical Jew: Paul and the Politics of Identity* (Berkeley: University of California Press, 1994), p. 112.

93. On Acts 21.20-21, see the comments in George Foot Moore (*Judaism in the First Three Centuries of the Christian Era: The Age of the Tannaim* [3 vols.; Cambridge, MA: Harvard University Press, 1927], II, p. 21), and Alan F. Segal (*Paul the Convert: The Apostolate and Apostasy of Saul the Pharisee* [New Haven: Yale University Press, 1990], p. 145). See also Acts 21.28 where Luke reports Asian Jews saying that Paul is 'the man who is teaching everyone everywhere against the

accusation is historically accurate (Acts contends that it is not), some statements regarding circumcision which Paul makes in his letters could certainly give rise and substance to such reports. For example, in Gal. 5.6 Paul asserts that 'in Christ Jesus neither circumcision nor uncircumcision is any avail, but faith working in love'. He makes a similar statement in 6.15: 'neither circumcision counts for anything, nor uncircumcision, but a new creation'. Additionally, in 1 Cor. 7.19 Paul remarks, 'For neither circumcision counts for anything nor uncircumcision, but keeping the commandments of God', as if to suggest that circumcision was no longer a binding commandment! Furthermore, in Rom. 2.29 Paul spiritualizes circumcision altogether by maintaining that 'real circumcision is a matter of the heart' (cf. *Bar.* 9.4).[94]

Philo, Paul's erudite contemporary, could also speak of circumcision in a spiritual sense (*Migr. Abr.* 92; *Spec. Leg.* 1.9, 305; *Quaest. in Gen.* 3.47-52; *Quaest. in Exod.* 2.2), as could writers in the Hebrew Scriptures (Lev. 26.41; Deut. 10.16; 30.6; Jer. 4.4; 9.25; Ezek. 44.7, 9) and in Qumran (1QpHab 11.13; 1QS 5.5-6). Nonetheless, even though Philo (and others) could speak of circumcision symbolically, he expected both Jews and Jewish proselytes to be physically circumcised.[95] In *Migr. Abr.* 92 Philo remarks: 'It is true that receiving circumcision does indeed portray the excision of pleasure and all passions, and the putting away of impious conceit...but let us not on this account repeal the law laid down for circumcising.'

---

people and the law and this place'. Note also Acts 24.5 where Tertullus is recorded as calling Paul 'an agitator among all the Jews throughout the world'.

94. On Paul's devaluation of physical circumcision, see further Boyarin, *Radical Jew*, pp. 106-35. Cf. John M.G. Barclay, 'Paul and Philo on Circumcision: Romans 2.25-9 in Social and Cultural Context', *NTS* 44 (1998), pp. 536-56.

95. Whether or not Philo thought that converts to Judaism should be circumcised is a debated issue in Philonic studies. The dialogue centers upon the meaning of Philo's statement in *Quaest. in Exod.* 2.2: 'a sojourner [proselyte] is one who circumcises not his uncircumcision, but his desires and sensual pleasures and the other passions of the soul'. Some scholars (e.g. Neil J. McEleney, 'Conversion, Circumcision and the Law', *NTS* 20 [1974], pp. 328-33) take this text to mean that Philo did not insist on circumcision of proselytes. Nonetheless, John Nolland ('Uncircumcised Proselytes?' *JSJ* 12 [1981], pp. 173-94) and Peder Borgen ('The Early Church', p. 67) have convincingly demonstrated that Philo held spiritual and physical circumcision together. In Judaism, a male was not considered to be a full proselyte until he received circumcision. See, e.g., Cohen, 'Crossing the Boundary Line', pp. 26-30, and Donaldson, *Paul and the Gentiles*, pp. 58-60.

There were Diasporan Jews other than Paul who devalued physical circumcision. Philo's comments in *Migr. Abr.* 92-95 indicate that he knew of Jews who had completely spiritualized circumcision. And, of course, there is the famous story which Josephus relates about the conversion of King Izates to Judaism and the counsel that Ananias gave him not to be circumcised (*Ant.* 20.34-48). Nonetheless, circumcision of Jewish males and of male proselytes to Judaism was 'quintessentially Jewish'.[96] It is quite likely, therefore, that those Jews who neglected or encouraged the neglect of physical circumcision would have been contested by other Jews. In fact, Philo admonishes his Alexandrian Jewish readers to be faithful to the feasts and to circumcision on a physical level lest they 'incur the censure of the many and the charges they are sure to bring' (πρὸς τῷ καὶ τὰς ἀπὸ τῶν πολλῶν μέμψεις καὶ κατηγορίας ἀποδιδράσκειν, *Migr. Abr.* 93). The observance of physical circumcision, then, was a source of contention among Jews in Philo's and Paul's day.[97] Tension was created by those Jews who were indifferent to and/or neglectful of this ancestral tradition. And as Philo suggests, those Jews who did not faithfully execute this established rite were objects of their compatriots' censure. Paul was one such object.

c. *Controversy over Dietary Issues*
Thus far I have argued that circumcision was a primary source of conflict between Paul and his Jewish compatriots. Did other factors come into play as well? Based on Paul's account of the Antioch incident in Gal. 2.11-14 and other statements which he makes about food in his Epistles (e.g. 1 Cor. 8–10; Rom. 14.1-4, 13-23), one can surmise that Paul's lack of scruples about table fellowship with Gentiles also agitated his fellow Jews.

In an effort to buttress his apostolic authority and the validity of his gospel, Paul tells his Galatian converts a story of how he rebuked Peter at Antioch (2.11, 14). According to Paul, Peter and other Jewish Christians were eating with Gentile believers prior to the time that certain men from James arrived. Paul reports that these men, who he refers to as 'those of the circumcision' (τοὺς ἐκ περιτομῆς), caused Peter, Barnabas and the rest of the Jewish Christians in the church to separate

---

96. Cohen, 'Crossing the Boundary Line', p. 27.
97. Social conflict occurs when one party acts or thinks in a way is incompatible with and unacceptable to another party (see pp. 114-16).

themselves from Gentile Christians at meal times. In 2.13, Paul charges Peter with hypocrisy because of his tactical readjustment at the table upon the arrival of the Jerusalem delegation. Furthermore, he maintains that Peter's capitulating behavior distorted the truth of the gospel (2.14). At this point, we need not enter into what has become a very convoluted discussion about Jewish table fellowship with Gentiles.[98] For our purposes, I need only to make two observations from this passage.

First, Paul more or less calls Peter a 'coward' in 2.12. If Peter did indeed draw away from table fellowship with Gentile Christians because of fear, as Paul suggests, of whom or what might Peter have been fearful? Peter may have been informed by James's men that if reports were circulated about him associating freely with Gentiles, then it could undermine his mission to the Jews (2.8-9). Additionally, Peter could have been told by the Jerusalem delegation, perhaps at James's request, that if his behavior among Gentiles became known by Jerusalem Jews, then there might be negative repercussions for the Christians in that city.[99] In fact, it is conceivable that Peter himself could have faced a charge in a Jerusalem synagogal court for unscrupulous fraternization with Gentiles. And if in his defense Peter failed to convince the court of the validity and purity of his behavior, then he too might have been subjected to the dreadful strokes.[100]

It is also important to notice from Paul's account of his dispute with Peter at Antioch that his view on eating with Gentiles was the minority position among Jewish Christians. Paul reports that even Barnabas withdrew from table fellowship with Gentile believers once the men from James had arrived (2.13). If Paul's 'soft' stance on eating with Gentiles was anomalous among Jewish Christians at Antioch, one can but imagine the controversy that Paul's dining habits would have created among 'strict' non-Christian Jews.[101] While it is clear that some Jews dined (and experienced other types of social intercourse) with Gentiles, it appears that the majority of Jews did so on their own terms, that is, they ate their own food and drank their own wine (e.g. Dan. 1.3-17; Jdt. 10.5; 12.17-19; *Ep. Arist.* 181-294).[102]

---

98. See esp. Sanders, 'Jewish Association with Gentiles'. See also James D.G. Dunn, 'The Incident at Antioch (Gal. 2.11-18)', *JSNT* 18 (1983), pp. 3-57.

99. Sanders, 'Jewish Association with Gentiles', pp. 185-86.

100. Harvey, 'Forty Strokes Save One', p. 85.

101. Cf. Barclay, 'Paul among Diaspora Jews', p. 115.

102. Sanders ('Jewish Association with Gentiles', p. 178) remarks that in spite of

As observed (on pp. 158-61 above), Jews were for the most part wary of idolatry, and many, if not most, Jews were convinced that intimate association with Gentiles at the table (and elsewhere) could lead to idolatrous practices.[103] Against a backdrop of cautious social interaction of Jews with Gentiles, such Pauline statements as 'Eat whatever is sold in the meat market without raising any question on the ground of conscience' (1 Cor. 10.25), and 'I know and am persuaded in the Lord Jesus that nothing is unclean in itself' (Rom. 14.14a) would certainly have sounded like dangerously radical counsel to law-observant Jews and Christians.

We know that Paul himself, unlike Tiberius Julius Alexander and the three hundred men mentioned by the author of *3 Maccabees*, would not have participated in idolatrous worship.[104] Furthermore, he would likely have been uncomfortable with wittingly eating meat offered to idols (1 Cor. 10.14-22; cf. *Did.* 6.3). But his fellow Jews would likely have been set on edge by the fact that Paul casually dismissed Jewish dietary laws when interacting with and instructing those he considered to be children of Abraham.[105] Many Jews would have viewed Paul's interac-

---

some possible exceptions (e.g. *Jub.* 22.16; *Jos. Asen.* 7.1) most of the Jewish evidence suggests 'There was no barrier to social to intercourse with Gentiles, as long as one did not eat their meat or drink their wine'.

103. See Barclay, *Jews in the Mediterranean Diaspora*, p. 435. Esler (*Community and Gospel in Luke–Acts*, pp. 85-86) maintains that Jews avoided table-fellowship with Gentiles because the former regarded the latter as ritually unclean.

104. Cf. Barclay, *Jews in the Mediterranean Diaspora*, p. 385.

105. On the social implications of Paul's instruction on the law in general and on food and sabbath laws in particular, see John M.G. Barclay, ' "Do We Undermine the Law?": A Study of Romans 14.1–15.6', in James D.G. Dunn (ed.), *Paul and the Mosaic Law* (WUNT, 89; Tübingen: J.C.B. Mohr [Paul Siebeck], 1996), pp. 287-308.

The fact that Paul used the Jewish Scriptures in his letters to support his radical thinking and acting could have further engendered hostility between him and his fellow Jews (if indeed non-Christian Jews knew his writings). Additionally, when Paul was afforded the opportunity to speak in a Jewish synagogue, his (mis)use of the Scriptures in his message might have elicited a negative response from those who were not convinced. Furthermore, it is also likely that Paul defended himself with Scripture in his various synagogue trials. On at least five occasions (2 Cor. 11.24), we know that his hermeneutics were not favorably received by the synagogal authorities. Philo viewed those who criticized the Scriptures as deserters of Judaism. It is possible that some Jews could have formed a similar opinion of Paul for his 'innovative' interpretation and application of the Hebrew Bible.

tion with and instruction to his converts as irresponsible[106] and even as immoral.[107]

Paul and (many of) his compatriots would have agreed that God wanted them to *love* the nations,[108] but on the whole they would have had drastically different views on how God required Jews to *live* among the nations. It may be deduced, then, that Paul was among a small minority of Jewish Christians in his day who believed that ancestral rituals such as circumcision and dietary laws should be, if necessary, completely abrogated for the sake of the gospel.[109] Such an extreme— or, from the perspective of Paul's Jewish opponents, 'deviant'—stance frequently incited an unfavorable response.

5. *Conclusion*

To conclude, I would like to stress that Paul's conflict with his compatriots goes beyond the external acts of clipping a male's foreskin and dining with Gentiles. In order to understand the controversy between Paul and his people aright, one must give adequate attention to the all-important issue of community boundaries, which, of course, are based

106. Paul's instruction to the Corinthian widows to marry 'in the Lord' (1 Cor. 7.39) serves as an example. It appears that there were some Jewish people in the Corinthian congregation (7.18). If so, we know from the parallels adduced above that many Jews would not have approved of Paul advising Jewish widows in this manner. Such an exhortation could be viewed as an invitation to exogamy. Additionally, Paul frequently encourages congregations to whom he writes to exchange 'a holy kiss' (1 Thess. 5.26; 1 Cor. 16.20; 2 Cor. 13.12; Rom. 16.16) with no ethnic qualifications. We will see on p. 244 below that the 'sacred kiss' could lead to promiscuity.

107. In Rom. 3.8 Paul claims that he is slanderously charged by some people (probably Christian Jews) to promote evil so that good may come. Some of Paul's Gentile converts did not hold what Jews would have considered to be high moral standards (e.g. 1 Cor. 5.1-2; 6.12-20). Paul's gospel could have been perceived as an invitation to such behavior. Cf. Kruse, 'Paul's Persecution', p. 271.

108. For a survey of the range of attitudes of Jews toward Gentiles in the Jewish world in which Paul was socialized, see Donaldson, *Paul and the Gentiles*, pp. 51-78.

109. In reference to Paul's instruction in Rom. 14.1–15.6, Barclay ('"Do We Undermine the Law?"', p. 308) comments that Paul 'regards key aspects of the law as wholly dispensable for Christian believers and, more subtly, his theology introduces into the Roman Christian community a Trojan horse which threatens to undermine the integrity of those who sought to live according to the law'.

upon group norms. For Paul, incorporation into the people of God entailed co-crucifixion with Christ through baptism (e.g. Rom. 6.1-11; Gal. 2.20-21; 3.27; 5.24). And while Paul believed that the law of God is good (Rom 7.7, 12), he thought that Torah had reached its τέλος in Christ (Rom. 10.4). As a result, Paul taught that he and his converts no longer needed to live under the law (1 Cor. 9.20). Paul's vision was for a new community which was not defined along ethnic, power or gender lines (Gal. 3.28).[110] But Paul's ideal was slow in taking shape and was met with much Jewish resistance.[111] Perhaps this is part of the reason why Paul had so much difficulty in defining precisely what the church was and in articulating his own position in relation to Judaism.[112] Although Paul could refer to the church as a third entity (1 Cor. 10.32) and speak of his 'former life' in Judaism (Gal. 1.13) as 'refuse' (σκύβαλον, Phil. 3.6), *he* appears to have seen himself and his converts in some way as part of Judaism, albeit Paul's unique mutation thereof (Gal. 3.29; 6.16; Rom. 9–11).[113] It also seems that some of his fellow Jews, at least at the outset of Paul's association with a given synagogue, would have agreed that he fell within Judaism. Otherwise, it is difficult to explain why some Jews would have punished Paul or why Paul would have yielded to negative formal sanctions (i.e. the 39 lashes) on at least five occasions.[114]

What Paul and his people do not appear to have agreed upon is who constituted the people of God and what the entry requirements into this

110. Cf. Stephen Barton ' "All Things to All People": Paul and the Law in Light of 1 Corinthians 9.19-23', in Dunn (ed.), *Paul and the Mosaic Law*, pp. 271-85 (283-84).

111. Barclay, 'Paul among Diaspora Jews', p. 116: 'Paul's attempt to redefine a "Judaism" without ethnicity and without preserving the national way of life enshrined in the "ancestral customs" was hugely influential for later Christianity, but was clearly, and understandably, judged a contradiction in terms by his contemporaries.' As noted on pp. 117-18 above, divergent and competing ideologies can lead to (intense) conflict.

112. Hostility can result in boundary ambiguity, as Erikson (*Wayward Puritans*) and Ben-Yehuda (*Deviance and Moral Boundaries*) have demonstrated.

113. See Sanders, 'Paul on the Law', pp. 89-90, and Barclay, 'Paul among Diaspora Jews', pp. 116-17.

114. Sanders (*Paul, the Law, and the Jewish People*, p. 192) states: '*Punishment implies inclusion.* If Paul had considered that he had withdrawn from Judaism, he would not have attended synagogue. If the members of the synagogue had considered him an outsider, they would not have punished him' (emphasis his).

new community were. This is where their conflict reached the boiling point. While Paul could turn a blind eye to what he came to consider to be merely peripheral aspects of the law (e.g. circumcision, diet and calendar) and could boldly assert that his Gentile converts were part of the 'Israel of God' (Gal. 6.16; cf. 1 Thess. 4.5; 1 Cor. 5.1; 6.11; 12.3), it appears that a significant majority of his fellow Jews, even those who were 'Christian', thought that careful and faithful observance of Torah was part of the proselytizing package. And these Jews perceived Paul's compromising of divinely sanctioned norms entrusted to the Jewish people by Yahweh to pose a serious threat to the integrity and identity of the Jewish community.[115] Therefore, especially zealous Jews, like the pre-Damascus Paul, would have sought to make him toe the Torah-line in instructing his Gentile converts.

Jewish suspicion of Paul and his mission would have been heightened by the fact that Paul was by his own admission a 'chameleon' toward the ancestral customs.[116] He treated as disposable that which was most valuable to his people, that is, living under the law of God. To paraphrase Paul, he could take or leave the law contingent upon the circumstances at hand (1 Cor. 9.20-21).[117] Paul's pattern of occasional conformity in order 'to win the more' would have been viewed by many Jews as hypocrisy and would have understandably engendered hostility.[118] Whereas the pre-Christian Paul was known as a boundary-

115. Esler (*Community and Gospel in Luke–Acts*, pp. 88-89) observes that Paul's clash with the Jerusalem church was created by the former's revolutionary belief that 'the old boundaries which preserved the Jewish *ethnos* from outside contamination have, in Christ, ceased to have any significance...' and by the latter's conviction that the Jewish *ethnos* was elected by God and that the gospel should be distinctively and exclusively Jewish. Cf. Segal, *Paul the Convert*, pp. 125-26, and Barclay, 'Paul among Diaspora Jews', p. 117.

116. Contrast Mark D. Nanos (*The Mystery of Romans: The Jewish Context of Paul's Letter* [Minneapolis: Fortress Press, 1996]) who has argued that Paul was a thoroughly law-observant Jew.

117. On Paul's ethic of accommodation, see, e.g., Henry Chadwick, '"All Things to All Men" (I Cor. IX.22)', *NTS* 1 (1954–55), pp. 261-75; Peter Richardson, 'Pauline Inconsistency: I Corinthians 9:19-23 and Galatians 2:11-14', *NTS* 26 (1980–81), pp. 327-62; and Barton '"All Things to All People"'. In terms of deviance theory, Paul sought to avoid being labeled and/or treated as a deviant Jew by manipulating his physical environment, i.e., by strategically altering his behavior.

118. Smith, 'Persecution of Paul', p. 263.

maintainer, a preserver of Israel's customs; Paul, the apostle to the Gentiles, was perceived as a boundary-breaker, a perverter of his people's traditions. Those viewed as traitors are seldom treated with tender loving care![119] His compatriots might have wondered how Paul thought that he could be all things to all people when he blatantly disregarded the standards which his own people required! One could rightly say that what Paul did and failed to do and what he encouraged others to do and not to do was what brought Paul and his compatriots into continual conflict and was what prompted some, if not many, of his fellow Jews to view him as an apostate.[120] While it is likely that Paul's proclamation of 'Christ crucified' was offensive to some Jews, we can be relatively certain that Paul's Jewish contemporaries resented and resisted his law-free pedagogy and praxis.[121]

Over time in a given location, after Paul's message and methods had become known to a Jewish community and disciplinary action(s) taken against him had failed, it is likely that Paul was excommunicated from the synagogue. Luke records that some Jews saw Paul as one who was leading Israel astray (Acts 18.13; 21.21).[122] If this were indeed the case, then it seems rather unlikely that the relevant Jewish communities would have allowed Paul to remain perpetually in their fold. As Philip F. Esler writes, 'One must assume that those Jews [like Paul] who did fudge the boundaries between Jew and Gentile were rightly regarded as

119. C.K. Barrett (*Paul: An Introduction to his Thought* [London: Geoffrey Chapman, 1994], p. 1) remarks: '[Paul] was one of the most hated men in the ancient world; and not without reason. It was natural for Jews to think him a traitor. He had betrayed their law and therewith their national identity; he seemed to have renounced the natural responsibility that he owed to his fellow-countrymen by constituting himself an "apostle for the Gentiles".'

120. Barclay, 'Deviance and Apostasy', p. 123: 'Inasmuch as [Paul] *was viewed* by his contemporary Jews as an apostate, he *was* (historically speaking) an apostate, and no amount of pleading about the Jewish elements in his theology or the diversity within first-century Judaism can mask or alter that reality' (emphasis his). See also Barclay's ' "Do We Undermine the Law?" ', p. 308.

121. Cf. Segal, *Paul the Convert*, p. 133. Paul's preaching and praxis are perhaps best viewed together. Davies ('Paul and the People of Israel', p. 4) suggests, 'The immediate cause of the Jewish opposition to Paul centred in the law. But his understanding of the law was inextricably bound up with the significance which he ascribed to Jesus of Nazareth as the Messiah and with the challenge that this issued to all the fundamental symbols of the Jewish life.'

122. On Paul leading other Jews astray, see, e.g., Segal, *Paul the Convert*, p. 145, and Barclay, 'Paul among Diaspora Jews', pp. 116-17.

endangering the ethnic identity of the Jewish people and came under heavy pressure to conform or to abandon Judaism altogether.'[123] Paul's pattern of occasional conformity was probably judged by (many) Jews in Thessalonica (and elsewhere) as blatant non-conformity (i.e. 'apostasy'), and it may well be that Thessalonian Jewry ostracized Paul from their synagogue before they banished him from their city.[124]

The social-scientific study of deviance and conflict clarifies and enhances the picture I am painting here. In social-scientific terms, Paul failed to adhere to the time-honored conventions of Judaism and to fulfill the prescribed roles (or 'role set') of a law-observant Jew. Paul's neglect of Jewish norms, when coupled with his newfangled behaviors and beliefs, would have frequently created controversy between him and his compatriots, particularly those functioning in the capacity of moral entrepreneurs or agents of censure (e.g. synagogue leaders), who would have considered Paul as dangerously deviant and would have denounced him as an apostate. Apparently, not a few Diaspora Jewish communities viewed the praxis and proclamation of this Jewish itinerant preacher to the Gentiles as a threat to their boundaries (i.e. their cultural space, *ethos* or way). And as a result, they sought to control and to censure Paul by means of formal (e.g. the synagogal discipline) and informal (e.g. verbal harassment) sanctions. In most instances, it is likely that Paul did not possess sufficient social power to counter or to neutralize the judgments and/or actions of his non-Christian Jewish opponents.[125] Therefore, more often than not, Paul was likely labeled and treated as a 'sinner' by Diaspora Jews, at least by some of the more

123. Esler, *Community and Gospel in Luke–Acts*, p. 86.
124. The seemingly irreconcilable differences between Paul and Thessalonian Jewry resulted in a breach between the two parties. This was apparently a common experience for Paul with his Jewish compatriots as he traveled throughout the Western Mediterranean seeking to share his gospel with the Gentiles (cf. Rom. 15.18-21). Barclay ('Paul among Diaspora Jews', p. 118) suggests, 'Striving to maintain his position in the Jewish community, Paul found himself continually losing his association there. At least as far as he was concerned, a "parting of the ways" took place every time he was ostracized by a Diasporan synagogue.'
125. Barclay ('Deviance and Apostasy', p. 123) observes, 'Paul's social position in the Diaspora [Jewish] communities was generally weak: he was a newcomer, of low social status, with no economic or political power base on which to build his defence, and power struggles in the synagogue almost inevitably turned to his disadvantage.'

powerful and influential people in a given synagogue (i.e. those engaged in creating and legitimating the status quo).

Modern-day interpreters have described Paul as a 'sinner', 'renegade', 'heretic', 'libertine', 'traitor' and 'apostate' vis-à-vis Judaism. My foregoing comparison of Paul with other Diaspora Jews who were rejected as deviant and my examination of relevant Pauline texts suggests that Paul's Jewish contemporaries would have depicted him similarly. It is indeed ironic that the apostle who preached a gospel of grace to the Gentiles was perceived by many of his own people to have repeatedly transgressed God's covenant mercy. Indeed, the very στίγ-ματα ('marks') which Paul bore on his body were perpetual and painful reminders of the fact that his compatriots judged him (on numerous occasions) to be a transgressor of Torah (Gal. 6.17).

Based upon this investigation, then, I would conclude that it was a combination of Paul's own laxity in association with Gentiles (e.g. at the table)[126] and his law-free instruction of Gentile converts who he claimed to be children of Abraham (e.g. regarding circumcision) that engendered zealous resistance from his fellow Jews. Although I am unable to say definitively that these were the reasons that Paul came into conflict with Thessalonian Jewry, this study points favorably to such an explanation.[127] Whether one now regards Paul's interpretation of Judaism and his vision for one body in Christ as a creative innovation or an insidious distortion depends upon one's own context and commitments. The context and commitments of many of Paul's Jewish contemporaries clearly prompted them to repudiate him and his message.

126. Barclay ('"Do We Undermine the Law?"', p. 301) writes, 'In principle, it appears, [Paul] could see no objection to eating shellfish, hare or pork. Do we have reason to doubt that his diet was sometimes as scandalously "free" as his principles?'

127. So also Trebilco, *Jewish Communities in Asia Minor*, p. 21. Since social conflict is a complex phenomenon and is often traceable to multiple causes, it is likely that Paul's conflict with his fellow Jews would have involved other issues than those which are discernible in our extant sources.

Chapter 8

APOCALYPTIC AND POLEMIC: PAUL'S RESPONSE TO NON-CHRISTIAN OPPOSITION IN 1 (AND 2) THESSALONIANS

1. *Introduction*

In the previous chapter, I explored why Paul experienced conflict with other Jews. It is my intention here to consider how Paul responded to the non-Christian opposition which he and his Thessalonian converts encountered. Since Paul does not explicitly indicate how he was affected by this conflict, one must try to infer this from the Thessalonian correspondence.

In what follows I will argue that the conspicuous presence of apocalyptic[1] and polemical language in 1 (and 2) Thessalonians may be

---

1.   Throughout this work I employ the term 'apocalyptic' as both an adjective (as it usually is in English works) and a noun (cf. the German *Apocalyptik*) to speak of a particular theological worldview. So also, e.g., Luke Timothy Johnson, *The Writings of the New Testament: An Interpretation* (Philadelphia: Fortress Press, 1986), p. 48; N.T. Wright, *Christian Origins and the Question of God. I. The New Testament and the People of God* (London: SPCK, 1992), pp. 280-338; and Barclay, 'Paul among Diaspora Jews', p. 109. Since Paul's apocalyptic perspective is not limited to matters of eschatology, I will not use the terms 'apocalyptic' and 'eschatology' interchangeably (cf. George Ladd, 'New Testament Apocalyptic' *RevExp* 78 [1981], pp. 205-209). Nor will I describe Paul's thought-world as 'apocalyptic eschatology' (so David N. Scholer, ' "The God of Peace Will Shortly Crush Satan under Your Feet" (Romans 16:20a): The Function of Apocalyptic Eschatology in Paul', *ExAud* 5 [1989], pp. 53-61). Cf. Menken, *2 Thessalonians*, pp. 44-66, and Paul D. Hanson, *The Dawn of Apocalyptic* (Philadelphia: Fortress Press, 2nd edn, 1979).

There has been no small amount of debate among scholars about how the term 'apocalyptic' is best defined and about the importance of apocalyptic for Paul. It is not necessary here to enter into the fray of this discussion. For a useful introduction to the scholarly controversy over the word 'apocalyptic', see Richard E. Strum, 'Defining the Word "Apocalyptic": A Problem in Biblical Criticism', in J. Marcus

usefully explained as Paul's theological and rhetorical response to the *thlipsis* in Thessalonica. Although other interpreters have commented upon the apocalyptic letters and polemical contents, they typically fail to correlate these theological and epistolary features with the particular socio-historical circumstances of Paul and the Thessalonian congregation.[2] I will attempt to demonstrate below how the contingency of the intergroup conflict in Thessalonica helps to account for the concentration of apocalyptic motifs and the intensity of Pauline polemic in 1 (and 2) Thessalonians. In the course of this discussion I will draw upon New Testament parallels that indicate a positive correlation between intergroup conflict relations on the one hand and apocalyptic and /or polemical language on the other.

2. *Apocalyptic and Conflict*

Studies on apocalyptic in general[3] and Pauline apocalyptic in particular[4] have proliferated in recent years. As a result of increased scholarly

and M.L. Soards (eds.), *Apocalyptic and the New Testament* (JSNTSup, 24; Sheffield: JSOT Press, 1989), pp. 17-48. On the significance of apocalyptic for Paul, see Martinus C. de Boer, 'Paul and Jewish Apocalyptic Eschatology', in J. Marcus and M.L. Soards (eds.), *Apocalyptic and the New Testament* (JSNTSup, 24; Sheffield: JSOT Press, 1989), pp. 169-90. In the initial section below, I will note three apocalyptic motifs in 1 (and 2) Thess. that are widely recognized by the scholarly community as core components of apocalyptic thought.

    2.   E.g., in her monograph *Filling up the Measure*, Schlueter rightly detects the 'eschatological' and polemical language in 1 Thess. 2.14-16. In an attempt to emphasize the hyperbolic character of this passage, however, she pays inadequate attention to the influence of the historical conflict in Thessalonica on Paul's language. Additionally, Charles A. Wanamaker ('Apocalypticism at Thessalonica', *Neot* 21 [1987], pp. 1-10) roundly criticizes Pauline scholars for focusing on the theological aspects of Paul's apocalyptic thought while neglecting the social dimensions thereof. Yet in his discussion of the apocalyptic character of the Thessalonian Epistles, he himself fails to note explicitly the relationship between Paul's apocalyptic language and the Christians' social conflict.

    3.   See, e.g., Klaus Koch, *The Rediscovery of Apocalyptic* (SBT, 2.22; London: SCM Press, 1972); Paul S. Minear, *New Testament Apocalyptic* (Nashville: Abingdon Press, 1981); Christopher Rowland, *The Open Heaven: A Study of Apocalyptic in Judaism and Early Christianity* (New York: Crossroad, 1982); David Hellholm (ed.), *Apocalypticism in the Mediterranean World and the Near East* (Tübingen: J.C.B. Mohr [Paul Siebeck], 1983); Hanson, *The Dawn of Apocalyptic*; and Cook, *Prophecy and Apocalypticism.*

    4.   See, e.g., J. Christiaan Beker, *Paul's Apocalyptic Gospel: The Coming Tri-*

interest, a more precise understanding of the traits of apocalyptic thinking and writing has been achieved.[5] Furthermore, it is now widely recognized among Pauline interpreters that an apocalyptic perspective permeates Paul's Epistles, even the Corinthian correspondence and Romans where the apostle's apocalyptic worldview has often gone undetected or unacknowledged.[6] The publications of J. Christiaan Beker, J. Louis Martyn and Wayne A. Meeks have been particularly influential in shaping the contemporary academic understanding of Pauline apocalypticism as was the work of Ernst Käsemann in a previous generation.[7]

The apocalyptic one encounters in Paul is, of course, not identical to what one finds in Jewish apocalyptic.[8] Nor is the way in which Paul

---

umph of God (Philadelphia: Fortress Press, 1982) and *Paul the Apostle*; Jörg Baumgarten, *Paulus und die Apokalyptik: Die Auslegung apokalyptischer Überlieferungen in den echten Paulusbriefen* (WMANT, 44; Neukirchen–Vluyn: Neukirchener Verlag, 1975); Meeks, *First Urban Christians*, esp. pp. 171-80; Leander Keck, 'Paul and Apocalyptic Theology', *Int* 28 (1984), pp. 229-41; Vincent P. Branick, 'Apocalyptic Paul?', *CBQ* 47 (1985), pp. 664-75; J. Louis Martyn, 'Epistemology at the Turn of the Ages', in Farmer, Moule and Niebuhr (eds.), *Christian History and Interpretation*, pp. 269-87 and 'Apocalyptic Antinomies in Paul's Letter to the Galatians', *NTS* 31 (1985), pp. 410-24; and E. Earle Ellis, *Pauline Theology: Ministry and Society* (Grand Rapids: Eerdmans; Exeter: Paternoster Press, 1989), pp. 1-25.

5.   Wayne A. Meeks ('Social Functions of Apocalyptic Language in Pauline Christianity' in Hellholm [ed.], *Apocalypticism*, pp. 687-705 [689]) detects the following characteristics in apocalyptic literature: revealed secrets to the author, sudden and certain cosmic transformation, divine judgment and dualistic thinking. Cf. the more detailed lists of apocalyptic characteristics upon which there is some scholarly agreement in Branick, 'Apocalyptic Paul?', p. 665 n. 3, and David Aune, 'Apocalypticism', *DPL*, pp. 25-35.

6.   See Scholer, 'Apocalyptic Eschatology'.

7.   For select bibliography of the writings of Beker, Martyn and Meeks pertaining to apocalyptic in Paul, see nn. 4-5 above. For Käsemann, see, e.g., 'Die Anfänge christlicher Theologie', *ZTK* 57 (1960), pp. 162-85, and 'Zum Thema der urchristlichen Apokalyptic', *ZTK* 59 (1962), pp. 267-84. Interestingly, Martyn has dedicated his important commentary on Galatians to Käsemann.

8.   Robert H. Gundry ('The Hellenization of Dominical Tradition and the Christianization of Jewish Tradition in the Eschatology of 1–2 Thessalonians', *NTS* 33 [1987], pp. 161-87) notes this in reference to the Thessalonian letters. Perhaps the most obvious difference in Paul's apocalyptic orientation is the prominence he gives to Jesus' crucifixion and resurrection. See Keck, 'Paul and Apocalyptic Theology', p. 241. Segal (*Paul the Convert*, p. 159), who depicts Paul as an apocalyptic

seeks to employ apocalyptic necessarily the same as his Jewish predecessors. Apocalyptic is a relatively fluid ideology which may be variously applied.[9] Nevertheless, at least three themes in Jewish apocalyptic writings are detectable in Paul's Epistles, namely vindication, imminence and dualism.[10] My present interest is to highlight these particular apocalyptic traits in 1 (and 2) Thessalonians. By doing so I will lend credence to the common scholarly claim that 1 (and 2) Thessalonians is (are) among Paul's most apocalyptically-oriented Epistles.[11]

Vindication. In 1 Thessalonians Paul speaks of God's wrath (ὀργὴ θεοῦ) as both a present (2.16) and a future (1.10; 5.9) reality. In 2.16 Paul declares that divine judgment has come upon those Jews who hinder the servants and work of God (ἔφθασεν δὲ ἐπ᾽ αὐτοὺς ἡ ὀργὴ εἰς τέλος). Paul also informs his Thessalonian converts that God did not destine them for future wrath, but for salvation through the Lord Jesus (5.9).[12] He assures his afflicted converts (1.6; 2.14; 3.3-4)[13] that

Jew, suggests that Paul's belief that the final days had begun and his abrogation of special Jewish laws in the service of converting Gentiles makes his apocalyptic view of community unique. On Jewish apocalyptic literature, see, among others, John J. Collins, *The Apocalyptic Imagination: An Introduction to the Jewish Matrix of Christianity* (New York: Crossroad, 1984).

9. So George W.E. Nickelsburg, 'Social Aspects of Palestinian Jewish Apocalypticism', in Hellholm (ed.), *Apocalypticism*, pp. 641-54 (648), and Cook, *Prophecy and Apocalypticism*, esp. pp. 1-18.

10. These characteristics are drawn from Beker, *Paul's Apocalyptic Gospel*, p. 30.

11. E.g. Hurd ('Paul ahead of his Time', p. 33) contends, 'The most obvious observation that can be made about 1 Thess. is that it is a highly apocalyptic document.' Wanamaker ('Apocalypticism at Thessalonica', p. 2) maintains that 1 and 2 Thess. 'have the strongest apocalyptic orientation of any of the Pauline letters'. John M. Court ('Paul and the Apocalyptic Pattern', in Morna D. Hooker and Stephen G. Wilson [eds.], *Paul and Paulinism: Essays in Honour of C.K. Barrett* [London: SPCK, 1982], pp. 57-66) notes the presence of apocalyptic terms in 1 Thess., in particular ὠδίν, θλῖψις and τέλος.

12. Furthermore, Paul instructs the Thessalonians about sexual purity by informing them that the Lord will judge 'pagans' who live in the passion of their lusts (4.5-6).

13. On the Thessalonians' affliction, see Chapter 9. Paul offers much instruction on suffering in 1 Thess. Paul informs his converts that their affliction: links them with the apostles, the Lord and other Christian congregations (1.6; 2.14); was met with joy inspired by the Holy Spirit (1.6; 5.16); made them a model Christian assembly (1.7); was to be expected because of their election by God and their

they are loved, chosen and instructed (1.1; 1.4; 2.12; 4.7, 9; 5.24)[14] by the living, true and faithful God (1.9; 5.24). Paul propounds that this God of power and peace (1.5; 5.23) will rescue Christians from the coming destruction through his Son, the Lord Jesus Christ (1.10; 5.9). Paul contends, then, that God does and will vindicate himself (and by extension Paul and his converts) by judging unbelievers and by saving believers.[15] One may also note that Paul instructs beleaguered believers in Thessalonica not to retaliate against their opponents, but to love and to do good to all people (3.12; 5.15; cf. Rom. 12.14-21). Because Paul was convinced that God would ultimately 'settle the score' with those who resisted him and his people, he can admonish these harassed Christians not take recourse into their own hands.[16]

Imminence. This is another characteristic of apocalyptic which is readily detectable in 1 Thessalonians. Paul appears persuaded in this epistle that the parousia of Jesus (or, the Day of the Lord) would soon and suddenly transpire.[17] Despite the fact that a few of the Thessalonian

---

affiliation with Christ (3.3-4); involved the cunning schemes of Satan (3.5). If one accepts 2 Thess. as authentically Pauline, then three additional aspects of Paul's theology of suffering may be noted: (1) Present afflictions serve as a sign of God's righteous judgment in the future (1.5); (2) Suffering refines faith and prepares one for God's kingdom (1.5); (3) Those who suffer now will be comforted at the parousia (1.6-10).

14. Calvin J. Roetzel ('The Grammar of Election in Four Pauline Letters', in David M. Hay [ed.], *Pauline Theology*. II. *1 & 2 Corinthians* [Minneapolis: Fortress Press, 1993], pp. 211-33 [215-19]) notes the concentration of election language in 1 Thess. Cf. Riesner, *Paul's Early Period*, pp. 401-402. On the New Testament *hapax legomenon* θεοδίδακτος (4.9), see Calvin J. Roetzel, '*Theodidaktoi* and Handwork in Philo and 1 Thessalonians', in Vanhoye (ed.), *L'apôtre Paul*, pp. 324-31.

15. Jacob W. Elias (' "Jesus Who Delivers Us from the Wrath to Come" (1 Thess 1:10): Apocalyptic and Peace in the Thessalonian Correspondence', in Eugene H. Lovering, Jr [ed.], *SBL 1992 Seminar Papers* [SBLSP, 31; Atlanta: Scholars Press, 1992], pp. 121-32) rightly recognizes the present and future aspects of salvation and judgment in 1 Thess.

16. I noted on p. 123 above that avoidance or withdrawal is one tactic for dealing with conflict.

17. A.M. Hunter (*Paul and his Predecessors* [Philadelphia: Westminster Press, rev. edn, 1961], p. 105) suggests that Paul inherited the belief of the imminent parousia of Christ from pre-Pauline Christian tradition and that 'Paul probably believed to the end of his days in a speedy return of Christ.' So similarly, Sanders, 'Paul', p. 113 n. 3. Cf. Ellis, *Pauline Theology*, p. 16.

believers had already died (4.13-14),[18] Paul seems to think that he and
(many of) his converts will still be alive when the Lord descends from
heaven (4.15-17; cf. 5.10). Therefore, Paul encourages the Thessalonian
believers to stay morally alert and sober and to don the spiritual armor
of faith, love and hope as they await the imminent Day of the Lord
which will come like a thief in the night (5.1-11). Paul is not only
convinced that the coming of the Lord will be soon, but he also believes
the parousia will be a sudden and certain phenomenon, like the labor
pangs which come upon a pregnant woman (5.3). Paul maintains that at
the Lord's advent unbelievers who think they are at peace and secure
will experience inescapable destruction, whereas believers will inherit a
glorious salvation (5.3, 9). In 1 Thessalonians, then, Paul avers that God
will soon vindicate himself and his own through the cataclysmic and
climactic coming of his Son, Jesus Christ.

Dualism. In addition to and in keeping with the traits of vindication
and imminence, one finds frequently in 1 Thessalonians the apocalyptic
motif of dualism. The following dualities are present in the epistle: (1) a
cosmic (or spatial) duality (heaven /earth [1.10]); (2) a temporal duality
(this age/the coming age [1.10]); and, most commonly, (3) a social (or
ethical) duality (those who know/do not know God [4.5], insiders/
outsiders [4.12], the elect/the rest [4.13; 5.6] and children of light/
children of darkness [5.4-5]).[19] In Paul's apocalyptic perspective,
believers are pitted against the world and its inhabitants; they are called
by God to be different than unbelievers (4.5), who are subject to divine
destruction (5.3). Although outsiders (4.12) can 'turn' and become insiders (1.9), Paul instructs those inside to remember that they are no
longer children of darkness without hope (4.13; 5.5). Christians, according to Paul, though hindered and tempted by Satan (2.18; 3.5) and
subject to non-Christian opposition (3.4), will (soon) inherit salvation
when Jesus descends from heaven to gather believers to himself (1.10;
2.19; 4.16-17). As the elect wait for the imminent parousia, they are to
honor the Lord in all that they do and say (4.1-12; 5.12-21) so that they
might be found holy and blameless before God when the Lord comes

18. For whatever reason(s), Paul had not fully instructed his converts regarding
the future of the Christian dead during his stay in Thessalonica. Note 4.13a: 'But
we would not have you ignorant concerning those who are asleep...' On 4.13, see
the useful remarks by Riesner, *Paul's Early Period*, pp. 384-86.

19. For these categories, see Meeks, 'Social Functions of Apocalyptic Language', p. 689.

with all the saints (3.13; 5.23). In this epistle Paul looks through apocalyptic spectacles as he places all people into one of two categories and consigns them to one of two destinies.

One also discovers the apocalyptic traits being discussed in the disputed 2 Thessalonians. Compared to 1 Thessalonians, the motif of vindication is emphasized more, and the idea of imminence is stressed less. But these differences in emphasis may be explained by events affecting the congregation, namely the continuation and seeming escalation of external conflict (1.4) and the erroneous assumption of some Thessalonian believers that the Day of the Lord had come (2.2). In any event, in the second letter Paul, if it is he, instructs the afflicted and persecuted church (1.4-5) that God will repay those who oppose them when the Lord Jesus is revealed (1.6-7). Although the parousia of Jesus has yet to occur (2.1-12), the faithful Lord (3.3) will come in due course (2.6). At his coming, the harassed elect (1.11; 2.13) will receive rest (1.7), and the Lord will pour out vengeance on those who neither know God nor obey the gospel (1.8). Furthermore, Paul contends that unbelievers 'will suffer eternal destruction and exclusion from the presence of the Lord' (1.9).

That apocalyptic language suffuses the Thessalonian correspondence is beyond question. But why the concentration of apocalyptic in these Epistles? While not denying the merit of other possible explanations, I would suggest that the apocalyptic motifs of 1 (and 2) Thessalonians may be viewed as Paul's theological response to the hostile social relations that he and his converts had experienced/were experiencing with non-Christians.[20] The sociological study of deviance indicates that people who face social opposition may appeal to their belief system in an attempt to explain and to cope with their circumstances.[21] I would suggest that Paul uses apocalyptic theology for such a purpose in 1 (and 2) Thessalonians. Paul's dualistic mind-set assists him and his converts in making sense of the rejection, opposition and separation they had

20. So similarly Donfried, 'Theology of 1 Thessalonians', p. 244.

21. See p. 104 above. Siegel ('Defensive Structuring', p. 11) has observed that one way in which groups who are in conflict with their surrounding environment respond to external stress is by cultivating cultural identity symbols. One function of Paul's theological and ethical instruction in 1 (and 2) Thess. was to help his converts comprehend and respond to external stress. For the application of Siegel's article to 1 Peter, see Scot McKnight, *1 Peter* (NIVAC; Grand Rapids: Zondervan, 1996), pp. 131-35.

encountered/were encountering from Jewish and Gentile outsiders. Furthermore, Paul uses dualistic language to reinforce the boundaries between insiders and outsiders and to effect group loyalty and solidarity, thereby preparing the church for continued hostility.[22] In keeping with his apocalyptic *Weltanschauung*, Paul maintains that God will save Christians and punish their oppressors at the imminent parousia of Jesus.

Apocalyptic need not arise out of a social setting of opposition and alienation.[23] Nevertheless, some apocalyptically oriented documents did actually originate in a social context of conflict. The most notable New Testament example is Revelation. In this writing, John violently denounces Rome (= the throne of Satan [2.12-13; 12.9; 13.2]) for, among other reasons, its anti-God orientation and oppression of (some) Christians.[24] Most likely John himself (1.9) and Antipas of Pergamum (2.13) were objects of Roman opposition (cf. 6.9-11; 7.13-14; 20.4-6). Furthermore, John anticipates the continuation and escalation of conflict; he regards a portentous clash between the Roman imperial

22. Cf. similarly Meeks, 'Social Functions of Apocalyptic Language', p. 692; Segal, *Paul the Convert*, pp. 161-66; and Barclay, 'Conflict in Thessalonica', p. 518. I noted on p. 121 above that intergroup conflict can result in ingroup solidarity, enhanced awareness of ingroup identity and tightening of group boundaries. Paul's apocalyptic rhetoric would have encouraged and facilitated ingroup awareness and cohesiveness. Given the opposition that his converts were facing from outsiders, it is not surprising that Paul stresses the importance of ethical excellence and internal discipline in 1 (and 2) Thess. (e.g. 1 Thess. 4.1-8; 5.12-22; 2 Thess. 3.6-15). I also observed on p. 122 that external conflict can cause a group to stress internal norms and to 'crack down' on members who deviate from such.

23. So John J. Collins, 'The Genre Apocalypse in Hellenistic Judaism', in Hellholm (ed.), *Apocalypticism*, pp. 531-47 (546-47); Charles H. Talbert, *The Apocalypse: A Reading of the Revelation of John* (Louisville, KY: Westminster/John Knox Press, 1994), p. 5; and Richard Bauckham, *The Theology of the Book of Revelation* (NTT; Cambridge: Cambridge University Press, 1993), p. 15.

24. It is also likely that John (and his followers?) are in conflict with Jews (2.9; 3.9) and other believers in Jesus (2.2, 6, 14, 15, 20). Some scholars (e.g. Heikki Räisänen, 'The Clash between Christian Styles of Life in the Book of Revelation', *ST* 49 [1995], pp. 151-66 [163-64]) suggest that John is inventing, or at least exaggerating, the social opposition to Christians. Cf. Thomas B. Slater ('On the Social Setting of the Revelation to John', *NTS* 44 [1998], pp. 232-56 [232]) who persuasively argues 'that Revelation was a Christian response to religio-political pressures by indigenous Asian pagans upon Christians to conform to traditional social practices in Asia'.

establishment and the Christian movement as inevitable.[25] Through the medium of an apocalypse, John expresses his intense antipathy toward the Roman religo-political system.[26]

There is also a connection between apocalyptic idiom and social dislocation in 1 Peter.[27] This epistle is addressed to believers in Asia Minor who are experiencing conflict with outsiders (1.1, 6; 4.3-5, 13; 5.10). These Petrine Christians, who are characterized as Gentiles (2.12; 4.3), are being verbally abused by their former associates. They are being ridiculed for having altered their social networks and patterns of interaction (3.16; 4.4, 14). The writer encourages 'God's people' (2.10) to stand fast (5.12) and rejoice (1.6; 4.13) in the face of their sufferings and to fix their 'hope fully upon the grace that is coming to [them] at the revelation of Jesus Christ' (1.13; cf. 1.5, 7; 4.13; 5.1). Even though they are presently being harassed by unbelievers, the author assures them that their detractors 'will give an account to him who is ready to judge the living and the dead' (4.5). Furthermore, he instructs his readers that 'the end of all things is at hand' (4.7; cf. 1.20). 'And after [they] have suffered a little while, the God of grace, who called [them] to glory in Christ, will himself restore, establish, and strengthen [them]' (5.10). Those who do not obey the gospel of God (i.e. the word of the Lord [1.25]), however, will be damned (4.17-18) when the 'chief Shepherd is manifested' (5.4). As in 1 (and 2) Thessalonians, there is a positive correlation in 1 Peter between apocalyptic language and social conflict.

25. Talbert, *Apocalypse*, p. 11, and Slater, 'Social Setting of the Revelation', p. 254.

26. On Revelation as a response to a social crisis, see esp. A. Yarbro Collins, *Crisis and Catharsis: The Power of the Apocalypse* (Philadelphia: Westminster Press, 1984).

27. So rightly, e.g., Miroslav Volf, 'Soft Difference: Theological Reflections on the Relation between Church and Culture in 1 Peter', *ExAud* 10 (1994), pp. 15-30 (17-19). This correlation is lost on John Holdsworth ('The Sufferings of 1 Peter and "Missionary Apocalyptic"', in E.A. Livingstone [ed.], *Studia Biblica*. III. *1978 Papers on Paul and Other New Testament Authors* [JSNTSup, 3; Sheffield: JSOT Press, 1980], pp. 225-32 [230]) who thinks that the apocalyptic terminology in 1 Pet. bears no relation to the specific social circumstances of the Petrine congregations. He offers the unconvincing explanation that apocalyptic language in 1 Pet. is part of 'a missionary theology which sees a constant, ongoing and necessary disjunction [sic] and struggle between powers antipathetic to the Gospel...'

I could consider additional examples both inside[28] and outside[29] the New Testament which demonstrate the link between apocalyptic language and social dislocation. However, I need not belabor the point. I have already demonstrated from 1 (and 2) Thessalonians, Revelation and 1 Peter that apocalyptic rhetoric and social conflict are compatible partners. To attribute the pervasiveness of apocalyptic in the Thessalonian correspondence solely to the discordant social relations that Paul and his converts had experienced/were experiencing with outsiders would be too simplistic. To be sure, apocalyptic is a vital part of Paul's thought-world and 'is nowhere far from the surface of [his] mind'.[30] But in his occasional correspondence with Christian congregations Paul could emphasize or de-emphasize apocalyptic themes according to the circumstances at hand. I am suggesting that the prominence of apocalyptic in 1 (and 2) Thessalonians may be usefully explained by taking into account the existence of intergroup conflict.[31] An apocalyptic symbolic universe aids Paul and his Thessalonian converts[32] in explaining and in enduring non-Christian hostility.

3. *Polemic and Conflict*

In Chapter 1 above, I concluded that 1 Thess. 2.13-16 is authentically Pauline. Here I will reflect further on Paul's polemic against particular

28. E.g. Graham N. Stanton ('The Gospel of Matthew and Judaism', in *idem*, *A Gospel for a New People: Studies in Matthew* [Edinburgh: T. & T. Clark, 1992], pp. 146-68) has suggested that the prominence of apocalyptic in Matthew's Gospel may be attributed to the conflict relations that Matthean Christians were experiencing with Jewish and Gentile outsiders.

29. E.g. some writings of the Qumran community (esp. CD, 1QM and 1QS), *4 Ezra, 2 Bar.* and the *Apoc. Abr.* For a useful study on Qumranite apocalyptic, see Florentino García Martínez, *Qumran and Apocalyptic: Studies on the Aramaic Texts from Qumran* (STDJ, 9; Leiden: E.J. Brill, 1992). On *4 Ezra, 2 Bar.* and the *Apoc. Abr.* as apocalyptic responses to the fall of Jerusalem in 70 CE, see Philip F. Esler, 'God's Honour and Rome's Triumph: Responses to the Fall of Jerusalem in 70 CE in Three Jewish Apocalypses', in Esler (ed.), *Modelling Early Christianity*, pp. 239-58.

30. Barclay, 'Paul among Diaspora Jews', pp. 109-10.

31. Cf. the concentration of apocalyptic in Gal. and Paul's conflict with Christian Jews.

32. I will show on pp. 233-37 below that Paul's initial proclamation to the Thessalonian church was thoroughly apocalyptic. As a result, the apocalyptic character of his correspondence would have been intelligible to his converts.

Jews in 2.15-16. By doing so, I will adduce additional support for my view that Paul wrote the whole of 2.13-16. In this section I will seek to show that Paul's harsh denunciation of his Jewish opponents can be reasonably and persuasively explained as his response to recent negative experiences with fellow Jews. Furthermore, I will observe how Paul uses polemic not only as a tool to gain linguistic leverage in his struggle with fellow Jews but also as a rhetorical device to justify his mission to the Gentiles and to encourage his afflicted converts in Thessalonica.

In 2.15-16 Paul depicts 'the Jews' as those

> who killed the Lord Jesus and the prophets, and drove us out; they displease God and oppose all people by hindering us from speaking to the Gentiles so that they may be saved—so as always to fill up the measure of their sins; but [God's] wrath has come upon them at last.

In a text which understandably unnerves post-Holocaust readers, Paul makes the startling statement that the wrath of God has fallen upon those Jews who have set themselves against God's messengers (i.e. Jesus, the prophets and Paul and his helper[s]). But what prompts Paul to say in this particular epistle that his Jewish opponents displease God, oppose humanity, stockpile sins and incur wrath?

Scholarly strategies for answering this query abound. Some exegetes explain the polemic in 2.15-16 by denying the passage's authenticity (see Chapter 1). Other scholars seek to soften the intensity of the rhetoric by appealing to pre-synoptic tradition and/or to Paul's later remarks concerning Israel in Romans 9–11.[33] Additionally, interpreters have suggested the sardonic statements about 'the Jews' in 2.15-16 can be explained as a product of Paul's prejudicial attitudes,[34] as an example of Pauline hyperbole[35] or as an expression of apocalyptic theology.[36]

However, even if one recognizes that Paul is speaking apocalyptically, hyperbolically and even prejudicially in 2.15-16 and

---

33. E.g. Donfried, 'Paul and Judaism'. Cf. Johannes Munck, *Christ and Israel: An Interpretation of Romans 9–11* (trans. I. Nixon; Philadelphia: Fortress Press, 1967), p. 64. Contrast Mason ('Paul', pp. 199, 223) who considers Paul's negative comments in 1 Thess. 2.15-16 as his normal stance vis-à-vis Judaism and understands Paul's more positive statements about the Jewish people in Rom. as an exercise in diplomacy.

34. Wortham, 'The Problem of Anti-Judaism in 1 Thess 2:14-16'.

35. Schlueter, *Filling up the Measure*.

36. Okeke, 'I Thessalonians 2.13-16' and Hurd, 'Paul ahead of his Time'.

acknowledges the influence of traditional material upon this passage, one is still left to wonder why Paul so forcefully denounces his Jewish opponents in this particular letter. Nowhere else in his extant letters do we encounter Paul indulging in such invective against his non-Christian Jewish adversaries.[37] How may we account for this polemical anomaly?[38] I am persuaded that the vituperation is best explained as Paul's specific reaction to the Jewish opposition that he had experienced in Thessalonica (and perhaps at Berea [Acts 17.13] and Corinth [18.6, 12] as well).[39] Paul was seemingly rather angry about the Thessalonian Jewish hostility which had cut short his ministry to the Gentiles in that city. He was sufficiently incensed to take up the type of slanderous language used by Gentiles against Jews[40] and employ it against his (Thessalonian) Jewish opponents.[41]

This line of interpretation is, of course, not novel.[42] Other commentators have concluded similarly.[43] For example, George Milligan

---

37. Milligan (*Thessalonians*, p. 30) suggests 'that this is the only passage in the Pauline writings in which the designation "the Jews" is used in direct contrast to Christian believers in the sense which St John afterwards made so familiar in his Gospel'.

38. It is also intriguing to note the polemic in 2 Thess. 1.6, 8, 9; 2.10-12 against those who afflict the Thessalonian Christians. Drawing upon Old Testament texts (e.g. Isa. 2.10, 19, 21; 66.6-9; Jer. 10.25; Ps. 79.6; Mal. 1.11; Zech. 14.5), Paul roundly condemns those who trouble his converts by asserting that God will inflict vengeance upon them.

39. While Schlueter (*Filling up the Measure*, p. 53) acknowledges that Paul pens 2.14-16 in response to present or recent Jewish opposition, she stresses the hyperbolic and parenetic character of the passage. I am giving greater emphasis to the socio-historical circumstances which apparently prompted the polemic.

40. Paul remarks that those Jews who hinder him from speaking to the Gentiles so that they might be saved 'displease God' and 'oppose all people'. Cf. Tacitus, *Hist.* 5.5; and Josephus, *Apion* 2.121.

41. Johnson ('Anti-Jewish Slander') notes that even though such polemical language may well offend modern sensibilities such caustic comments were common in antiquity. He concludes his useful article by suggesting that 'there were not many [ancient] Jews or Gentiles who did not have at least one curse to deal with' (p. 441).

42. The fact that Paul's outburst against 'the Jews' is linked to his conflict with Thessalonian Jewry, however, is usually overlooked by commentators. E.g. Best (*Thessalonians*, p. 115) surmises that the vitriolic language of 2.15-16 is prompted by 'an unknown persecution in Paul's situation as he writes from Corinth'.

43. In addition to Milligan and Lünemann, who I refer to by name in the text, see, e.g., Donfried, 'Paul and Judaism', p. 248; Kruse, 'Paul's Persecution' p. 261;

suggests that Paul's attack on his Jewish adversaries in 2.15-16 was provoked by 'what he himself had suffered at the hands of his fellow-countrymen...'[44] Likewise, Gottlieb Lünemann maintains that Paul's recent conflict with his compatriots adequately accounts for this polemical outburst.[45]

That 2.15-16 is best understood in this vane becomes even more compelling when viewed alongside other New Testament examples of polemic against non-Christian Jews and the conflict situations which incited such remarks.[46] We turn to the Gospels of Matthew and John to illustrate.[47] Many Matthean scholars maintain that the writer of the First Gospel and those (primarily) Jewish Christians to whom he wrote had a strained relationship with unbelieving Jews, particularly the scribes and Pharisees.[48] Some interpreters of Matthew also suggest that the intense polemic in this Gospel arises from such conflict (note, e.g., 'hypocrites': 6.2, 5, 16; 7.5; 15.7; 23.13, 15, 23, 25, 27, 29; 'brood of vipers': 3.7; 12.24; 23.33; 'son(s) of hell': 23.15; 'blind': 23.17, 19, 26; 'blind

and Peter Stuhlmacher, *Paul: Rabbi and Apostle* (with P. Lapide; trans. L.W. Denef; Minneapolis: Fortress Press, 1984), p. 16.

44. Milligan, *Thessalonians*, 29. So similarly, Frame, *Thessalonians*, pp. 110-11, and Neil, *Thessalonians*, pp. 50-51.

45. Lünemann, *Thessalonians*, p. 67.

46. There are, of course, examples of Jews polemicizing against Jews outside of the New Testament. Perhaps the most notable example is the fierce polemic of the Qumran community against those teachers and authorities of the Jewish establishment with whom they disagreed. On Qumranite polemic, see Craig A. Evans, 'Faith and Polemic: The New Testament and First-Century Judaism', in Evans and Hagner (eds.), *Anti-Semitism and Early Christianity*, pp. 1-17.

47. Note also Rev. 2.9, 3.9 and the study by A. Yarbro Collins, 'Vilification and Self-Definition in the Book of Revelation', *HTR* 79 (1986), pp. 308-20.

48. See, e.g., Douglas R.A. Hare, *The Theme of Jewish Persecution of Christians in the Gospel According to St Matthew* (SNTSMS, 6; Cambridge: Cambridge University Press, 1967); Sjef van Tilborg, *The Jewish Leaders in Matthew* (Leiden: E.J. Brill, 1972); David E. Garland, *The Intention of Matthew 23* (NovTSup, 52; Leiden: E.J. Brill, 1979); George Smiga, *Pain and Polemic: Anti-Judaism in the Gospels* (New York: Paulist Press, 1992), pp. 52-96; Sean Freyne, 'Vilifying the Other and Defining the Self: Matthew's and John's Anti-Jewish Polemic in Focus', in Neusner and Frerichs (eds.), *'To See Ourselves as Others See Us'*, pp. 117-43; Scot McKnight, 'A Loyal Critic: Matthew's Polemic with Judaism in Theological Perspective', in Evans and Hagner (eds.), *Anti-Semitism and Early Christianity*, pp. 55-79; Meeks, 'Breaking Away', pp. 108-14; Saldarini, 'Jewish-Christian Conflict', esp. pp. 39-41; and Stanton, 'Matthew and Judaism', esp. pp. 156-57.

guides': 15.14; 23.16, 24; 'whitewashed tombs': 23.27; 'his blood be on us and our children': 27.25; cf. 23.35). Graham Stanton, for instance, understands this welter of Matthean polemic as a real response born out of anger and frustration which 'should be seen as part of the self-definition of the Christian minority which is acutely aware of the rejection and hostility of its "mother", Judaism'.[49] Like Paul, then, Matthew employs polemic to castigate his Jewish opponents, to confirm his own position and to comfort harried believers.

Since the seminal contributions of J. Louis Martyn[50] and Raymond E. Brown,[51] it has become virtually axiomatic for students of the Fourth Gospel to view the bitter polemic therein as the author's response to the recent expulsion of Johannine Christians from the synagogue (9.22; 12.42; 16.2).[52] Regardless of why (Was the rift over christological concerns?) and how (How, if at all, did the 'Twelfth Benediction', the *birkat ha-minim*, factor into the expulsions?) this rupture occurred, Johannine scholars suggest that the scathing rhetoric of the Gospel signals that these expelled Christian Jews were deeply scarred and resentful. In a position of dislocation from Judaism, the Gospel writer strikes out against his Jewish antagonists by: defining the 'Johannine community' over against 'the Jews' and Judaism (e.g. 2.6, 13; 3.25; 5.1; 6.4; 7.2; 11.55); informing his readers that 'the Jews' are to be feared (e.g. 7.13; 9.22; 19.38; 20.19); frequently portraying 'the Jews', and particularly Jewish leaders, as enemies of Jesus and his disciples and in concert with the 'world' (e.g. 1.10; 2.18, 20; 4.1; 6.41; 7.32; 8.13, 48; 12.42; 16.33; 17.14; 18.3, 12, 19); judging 'the Jews' to be untrue to their faith and tradition (e.g. 5.39-40; 7.19; 8.39-44; 10.31-39; 19.15); and declaring that 'the Jews' are fathered by the devil and that they wish to carry out his sinister desires (8.44).[53] John's attack against 'the Jews' appears to be connected to and exacerbated by the painful

49. Stanton, 'Matthew and Judaism', p. 157.

50. J. Louis Martyn, *History and Theology in the Fourth Gospel* (Nashville: Abingdon Press, 2nd edn, 1979).

51. Raymond E. Brown, *The Gospel According to John* (AB, 29-29A; 2 vols.; Garden City, NY: Doubleday, 1966).

52. See, among others, Robert Kysar, 'Anti-Semitism and the Gospel of John', in Evans and Hagner (eds.), *Anti-Semitism and Early Christianity*, pp. 113-27.

53. On polemic in the Fourth Gospel, see further Wayne A. Meeks, 'The Man from Heaven in Johannine Sectarianism', *JBL* 91 (1972), pp. 44-74; Rodney A. Whitacre, *Johannine Polemic: The Role of Tradition and Theology* (SBLDS, 67; Chico, CA: Scholars Press, 1982); and Smiga, *Pain and Polemic*, pp. 134-73.

parting of the Johannine community from Judaism.

Paul's polemic against 'the Jews' in 1 Thess. 2.15-16 has confounded would-be interpreters. I have suggested that this passage (and analogous texts in Matthew and John) is best understood as a (over-)reaction of the leader of an ostracized minority to opposition from a dominant majority. Paul and his converts in Thessalonica were facing hostile treatment from outsiders, as were the Matthean and Johannine communities. In an effort to help their readers (and themselves!) cope with the conflict and to compensate for their respective groups' impotence,[54] Paul, Matthew and John paint their opponents in dark hues and cast them in a less than flattering light. On p. 104 above I noted that condemnation of one's condemners is a way that people who are marginalized seek to neutralize their alienation. Furthermore, we observed in our overview of the social-scientific study of intergroup conflict that discordant relations between groups can result in ingroup glorification and outgroup denigration (p. 122). Additionally, there may be some validity to Bruce J. Malina's suggestion that first-century Mediterranean people (like Paul) were typically dyadic (i.e. group oriented) and were bent upon defending the honor of their group against other groups in ways which modern Westerners might deem excessive and offensive (e.g. Paul's polemic in 2.15-16).[55] Paul's virulent response to Jewish opposition becomes understandable, though not necessarily commendable, when viewed through such lens.

---

54. Johnson ('Anti-Jewish Slander', p. 424) points out, 'Abuse tends to gain in volume when it lacks power.' Katz ('Conflict Resolution', pp. 373-74) suggests that intergroup conflicts frequently revolve around the issue of power. See further pp. 117-18.

55. Malina, *New Testament World*, pp. 51-70. I noted on pp. 116-17 above that a degree of collective identity is a characteristic of intergroup conflict. While Malina may be accurate in claiming that intense ingroup loyalty marked (or marks) Mediterranean culture, it is over simplistic to state that in the New Testament world 'the individual was symptomatic and representative of some group' (p. 58). Paul, for example, demonstrates a degree of distinct individuality which is not merely determined by group loyalties (see, e.g., Gal. 1–2; 2 Cor. 10–13; and Phil. 3). deSilva ('"Worthy of his Kingdom"', p. 55 n. 12) offers additional examples of individuality in antiquity by citing Seneca (*Constant.* 16.3) and Epictetus (*Diss.* 1.29.50-54). Furthermore, deSilva notes (pp. 51-52 n. 8) that classicists have called into question whether ancient Mediterranean peoples were as other-oriented as Malina imagines.

4. *Conclusion*

In this chapter I have argued that Paul responded to the conflict that he and his Thessalonian converts faced by accentuating the apocalyptic motifs of vindication, imminence and dualism and by utilizing polemical rhetoric. While realizing that apocalyptic is part and parcel of Pauline thought and that polemic (or *vituperatio*) was an ancient rhetorical convention, I have argued that the prominence of apocalyptic and the presence of polemic in 1 (and 2) Thessalonians is usefully explained as Paul's reaction to the hostility that he and his fledgling congregation had encountered and were encountering. It is commonly suggested that apocalyptic and polemic are responses of an oppressed minority group to a dominant majority group with which it is at odds.[56] In the Thessalonian correspondence Paul combines apocalyptic with polemic to offer a powerful, if hostile, retort to his and his converts' plight.

56. E.g. Stanton, 'Matthew and Judaism', p. 165.

Part IV

THE THESSALONIAN'S ΘΛΙΨΙΣ

Chapter 9

THE NATURE AND SOURCE OF THE THESSALONIAN
CHRISTIANS' CONFLICT

1. *Introduction*

Having examined Paul's trouble in Thessalonica in Part III of this
study, we now turn in Part IV to explore the conflict relations of the
Thessalonian church with outsiders. In this chapter, I will focus upon
two aspects of this conflict. To begin, I will consider how the believers
were afflicted. I will then seek to determine the origin of their affliction.
The nature and source of the congregation's θλῖψις are important interpretive issues, for one's conclusions regarding these matters will color
how one construes the conflict in Thessalonica altogether.[1]

2. *The Thessalonians' ΘΛΙΨΙΣ*

In 1 Thessalonians Paul indicates that his converts experienced θλῖψις
both in conjunction with and subsequent to their conversion. Paul
recalls in 1.6 that they had received the word in much affliction (δεξάμενοι τὸν λόγον ἐν θλίψει πολλῇ). (He also speaks in 2.14 of their
having suffered at the hands of their own compatriots [τὰ αὐτὰ ἐπάθετε
καὶ ὑμεῖς ὑπὸ τῶν ἰδίων συμφυλετῶν]). Then in 3.3 Paul admonishes
the Thessalonians not to be shaken by their present afflictions (ἐν ταῖς
θλίψεσιν ταύταις). Furthermore, he reminds them that when he was
still with them he had instructed them to expect affliction (καὶ γὰρ ὅτε
πρὸς ὑμᾶς ἦμεν προελέγομεν ὑμῖν ὅτι μέλλομεν θλίβεσθαι, 3.4).

2 Thessalonians 1.4-7 also attests that the church in Thessalonica
experienced θλῖψις. There Paul(?) speaks of the 'persecutions' and
'afflictions' which the church was enduring with 'steadfastness and
faith' (ὑπὲρ τῆς ὑπομονῆς ὑμῶν καὶ πίστεως ἐν πᾶσιν τοῖς διωγμοῖς

1. Cf. Wanamaker, *Thessalonians*, p. 81.

ὑμῶν καὶ ταῖς θλίψεσιν αἷς ἀνέχεσθε, 1.4). He also assures his
assailed converts suffering for the kingdom of God that they would
receive rest at the revelation of the Lord Jesus (1.5-7). At a later time
when writing to the Corinthian church, Paul mentions that the assemblies in Macedonia (presumably congregations the apostle had founded
in Philippi, Thessalonica and Berea [?]) were (being) subject(ed) to a
'severe test of affliction' (ἐν πολλῇ δοκιμῇ θλίψεως, 2 Cor. 8.2).[2]

But what does Paul mean by saying that the Thessalonians experienced θλῖψις? In order to answer this question, we must first ascertain
the meaning of this term. Although θλῖψις seldom appears in extra-bib-
lical Greek, when it does it denotes 'pressure'.[3] In time, θλῖψις, along
with its corresponding verb θλίβειν, came to mean 'affliction' or
'oppression'.[4] θλῖψις occurs with some frequency and with various
nuances throughout the Septuagint. There it is most frequently used in
reference 'to the ills that befall the people of God'.[5] In the New Testament, θλῖψις occurs 45 times. New Testament writers in general and
Paul in particular tend to employ the word to speak of external tribulation. On occasion, however, Paul can use the word to refer to mental
distress (see, e.g., 2 Cor. 2.4; Phil. 1.17).

How does Paul utilize the word in 1 (and 2) Thessalonians (cf. 2 Cor.
8.2)? F.F. Bruce suggests that when Paul speaks of the missionaries'
'distress and affliction' (ἀνάγκη καὶ θλίψει) in 1 Thess. 3.7 that he
may have been speaking of psychological duress.[6] Although I am

2. Furnish (*II Corinthians*, p. 401) thinks Paul is referring in 2 Cor. 8.2 to the
'afflictions experienced by the Macedonian Christians' and cites 1 Thess. 1.6; 2.14;
and 3.3-4 as well as Phil. 1.29-30 in support. Barrett (*Second Corinthians*, p. 219)
concludes similarly and also cites 2 Thess. 1.4-10. Additionally, Barrett suggests
that the extreme poverty of the Macedonian churches of which Paul speaks in
2 Cor. 8.2 'was probably to a great extent a Christian phenomenon and the result of
persecution, for Macedonia seems on the whole to have been a prosperous province,
with flourishing agriculture and mining and lumbering industries'.

3. See, e.g., Galen's reference to the pressure of the pulse in *Diff. Feb.* 1.9. My
treatment of the term θλῖψις is informed by Heinrich Schlier, 'θλίβω, θλῖψις',
TDNT, III, pp. 139-48, and *BAGD*, 'θλῖψις', p. 362.

4. Milligan (*Thessalonians*, p. 10) maintians θλῖψις 'like the Lat[in] *tribulatio*,
is a good ex[ample] of a word transformed to meet a special want in religious
vocabulary'.

5. Best, *Thessalonians*, p. 79.

6. So Bruce, *Thessalonians*, p. 67. Cf. likewise Barclay, 'Conflict in Thessalonica', p. 514.

210   *Conflict at Thessalonica*

inclined with Charles A. Wanamaker to regard Bruce's suggestion as 'a modern interpretation of the word-pair [ἀνάγκη καὶ θλίψει] since in Paul they can be shown to denote almost always external or physical deprivation and /or oppression',[7] I readily acknowledge that the lack of concrete evidence we have regarding the apostles' situation (in Corinth) requires interpretive caution (cf. 2 Thess. 3.2; Acts 18.5-6, 12-17). Leaving 3.7 to one side, then, what does Paul mean when he refers to the Thessalonians' θλῖψις? To rephrase the question, was the church's affliction of which Paul speaks merely internal or psychological? Abraham J. Malherbe seems to think so. He remarks, 'it is reasonable to understand *thlipsis* in 1:6 [and 3:3-4] as the distress and anguish of heart experienced by persons who broke with their past as they received the gospel'.[8]

While Malherbe may be correct in contending that Paul's converts, like other converts in antiquity, experienced mental discomfort as a result of their conversion,[9] the following considerations make it clear that Paul had more than psychological turmoil in mind when speaking of his converts' θλῖψις.[10] First of all, in 1 Thess. 1.6 Paul claims that

7.   Wanamaker, *Thessalonians*, p. 135. So similarly Milligan, *Thessalonians*, p. 41; Best, *Thessalonians*, p. 141; and Marshall, *Thessalonians*, p. 41.

8.   Malherbe, *Paul and the Thessalonians*, p. 48. Despite this statement, Malherbe's view of the Thessalonians' *thlipsis* may be more nuanced. Earlier in the same work (p. 45), Malherbe refers to the 'social dislocation' and 'public criticism' that converts in antiquity experienced (cf. Malherbe, 'Conversion to Paul's Gospel', p. 235). This type of conflict certainly extends beyond the private, psychological sphere! Furthermore, it is likely that Paul and his converts would have regarded 'social dislocation' and 'public criticism' as θλῖψις. In fact, I will argue below that when Paul speaks of the Thessalonians' affliction he has at least verbal abuse and social ostracism in mind.

9.   It may be, however, that Malherbe's proposal of psychological affliction for Paul's Thessalonian converts is more attuned to the Western individualistic interpretive tradition than to a Mediterranean cultural milieu. See, among others, Malina (*New Testament World*, esp. pp. 53-60) who contends that Mediterranean culture both past and present is characterized by a dyadic personality.

In interpreting the Thessalonians' *thlipsis*, Malherbe draws upon the earlier work of Elpidius Pax, 'Beobachtungen zur Konvertitensprache im ersten Thessalonicherbrief', *SBFLA* 21 (1971), pp. 220-61, and 'Konvertitenprobleme im ersten Thessalonicherbrief', *BibLeb* 13 (1972), pp. 24-37.

10.   So rightly, e.g., Best, *Thessalonians*, p. 79; Frame, *Thessalonians*, p. 83; Martin, *Thessalonians*, p. 62; Morris, *Thessalonians*, p. 48 n. 37; Wanamaker, *Thessalonians*, p. 81; Barclay, 'Conflict in Thessalonica', pp. 514-15; deSilva,

the Thessalonians became imitators of the apostles and of the Lord through their experience of θλῖψις. Certainly the missionaries and the Lord (2.15; cf. 4.13) suffered far more than mental distress.[11] Secondly, Paul remarks in 1.7 that as a result of their (positive response to) affliction the assembly 'became an example to all the believers in Macedonia and Achaia' (cf. 2 Thess. 1.4). 'This [statement] implies very strongly that in v. 6 Paul was speaking about more than mere "distress and anguish of heart." After all, every convert to the faith could be said to undergo "distress and anguish of heart" in the sense suggested by Malherbe.'[12] Thirdly, in 2.14 Paul maintains that the Thessalonians suffered the same things as the Judean churches did. This comparison suggests that the Judean and Thessalonians Christians shared some type of external, verifiable afflictions. Otherwise, how would Paul have been able to measure the similarity of their suffering? Fourthly, Paul indicates that he sent Timothy to the Thessalonians to encourage them lest they be shaken by their unrelenting afflictions and thereby render the apostles' labor 'vain' (3.2-3, 5). Paul also tells his converts that he had tried time and again to return to them (2.17) and reminds them that he had told them while he was still in Thessalonica to expect to suffer affliction as Christians (3.3-4). Paul's considerable and continued concern for the spiritual steadfastness of the Thessalonians strongly suggests that they were facing something far more serious than psychological *Angst*.

Paul provides a solid clue as to the nature of his converts' affliction in 2.14. There he states that the Thessalonian believers, like the Judean Christians, were subject to suffering as a result of their having received

' "Worthy of his Kingdom" ', pp. 60-63; and Wayne A. Meeks, *The Origins of Christian Morality: The First Two Centuries* (New Haven: Yale University Press, 1993), p. 224 n. 32. Riesner (*Paul's Early Period*, p. 373) thinks, 'The θλίψεις doubtless refer not only to genuine persecutory measures as such, but also to every internal and external tribulation encountered by the young believers.'

One might also note that Malherbe fails to indicate other converts in antiquity could suffer much more than mental anguish. See, e.g., Epictetus, *Diss.* 3.22.53-55 in reference to opposition experienced by Cynic converts, and Philo, *Spec. Leg.* 4.178; *Virt.* 102-103 on the plight of Jewish proselytes.

11. So Weatherly, *Thessalonians*, p. 47, and Barclay, 'Conflict in Thessalonica', p. 514.

12. Wanamaker, *Thessalonians*, p. 81. The quote within the quote is from Malherbe, *Paul and the Thessalonians*, p. 48. See also Martin, *Thessalonians*, p. 62 n. 18.

the gospel. Although one can interpret 1.6 and 3.3-4 apart from 2.14, there is no good reason for doing so. In fact, it seems best to view the affliction mentioned in 1.6 and 3.3-4 in light of the suffering spoken of in 2.14. Against Malherbe, then, I would contend that the Thessalonians' θλῖψις is best understood as external, non-Christian opposition.[13]

If one considers 2 Thessalonians to be relevant,[14] then the nature of the Thessalonians' affliction becomes clearer still. In 1.4 Paul praises his converts for their 'steadfastness and faith in all [their] persecutions [διωγμοῖς] and in the afflictions [θλίψεσιν] which [they] are enduring'. Here, as in Rom. 8.35 (cf. Mt. 13.21; Mk 4.17), θλῖψις is virtually synonymous with διωγμός,[15] a term connoting external strife.[16] Furthermore, 1.5-8 maintains that God will afflict those who oppose the Thessalonians at the parousia of Jesus. Texts in 1 (and 2) Thessalonians clearly indicate that Paul's converts clashed with unbelievers.

Moreover, the church in Thessalonica was not the only Pauline congregation to experience external, non-Christian opposition. Paul's converts in Philippi also encountered conflict with outsiders, as Phil. 1.27-30 indicates (cf. 2 Cor. 8.2).[17] In this pericope Paul exhorts his converts

13. Pearson ('1 Thessalonians 2:13-16', p. 87) thinks that the θλῖψις terminology in 1 Thess. is a 'theological *topos*, revealing [Paul's] eschatologically oriented theology...' Although Paul can use θλῖψις to speak of Christian suffering in general (e.g. Rom. 5.3; cf. similarly ἀνάγκη in 1 Cor. 7.27), I have shown above that when Paul employs the term in 1 Thess. he has converts' external troubles in view. So also, e.g., Ernst Bammel, 'Preparation for the Perils of the Last Days', in William Horbury and Brian McNeil (eds.), *Suffering and Martyrdom in the New Testament* (Cambridge: Cambridge University Press, 1981), pp. 91-100 (99-100); Barclay, 'Conflict in Thessalonica', p. 514; and de Vos, *Church and Community Conflicts*, p. 155.

14. Professor Malherbe has indicated to me in personal conversation that he is inclined to think that 2 Thess. is authentic.

15. So also Best, *Thessalonians*, p. 253; Marshall, *Thessalonians*, p. 172; and Wanamaker, *Thessalonians*, p. 219.

16. Milligan (*Thessalonians*, p. 87) remarks that διωγμός refers to 'external persecutions inflicted by enemies of the Gospel'. Note Paul's use of the related verb διώκειν in Gal. 1.13, 23; 4.29; 5.11; 6.12; and Phil. 3.6.

17. On the Philippian's conflict, see, e.g., Mikael Tellbe, 'The Sociological Factors behind Philippians 3.1-11 and the Conflict at Philippi', *JSNT* 55 (1994), pp. 97-121, and de Vos, *Church and Community Conflicts*, pp. 262-65. See also the apposite remarks of Gordon D. Fee, *Paul's Letter to the Philippians* (NICNT; Grand Rapids: Eerdmans, 1995), pp. 30-32, and Frank Thielman, *Philippians* (NIVAC; Grand Rapids: Zondervan, 1995), pp. 91-95.

to live worthily of the gospel and not to be intimidated by their opponents. Then in language strikingly similar to 2 Thess. 1.5-8,[18] he informs
the Philippians that their steadfastness in the face of conflict signals
their opponents' destruction and the church's salvation. Furthermore,
Paul reminds his converts that the suffering which they are experiencing for Christ is a privilege (cf. 1 Thess. 3.3). Although not all Pauline congregations clashed with non-Christians (e.g. the Corinthian
assembly),[19] Paul claims that the Thessalonians and their sister congregation in Philippi suffered at the hands of unbelievers. And there is
every reason to trust his report.

Unfortunately, Paul does not indicate how outsiders sought to hinder
his converts in Thessalonica. This forces one to conjecture about the
precise nature of their hardships. One option which may be eliminated
at the outset, however, is some type of systematically organized and
officially supervised effort to eradicate the church.[20] Nothing in either
letter would suggest such a scenario. In fact, commentators on the
Thessalonian letters might consider abandoning the term 'persecution'
in reference to the church's conflict lest they give readers an erroneous
impression.[21] At the very least, interpreters should clearly indicate what
they mean by this loaded and often misleading word which only represents the perspective of those opposed and conjures up images of protracted, sanctioned violence.

To speculate further about the nature of the conflict, in my estimation
it is probable that the Thessalonians, like their founder, were objects of
verbal abuse.[22] One can in fact infer from Paul's injunction 'to aspire to
live quietly' and so 'command the respect of outsiders' (4.11-12) that

18. Rightly noted by L. Gregory Bloomquist, *The Function of Suffering in
Philippians* (JSNTSup, 78; Sheffield: JSOT Press, 1993), pp. 158-59. Cf. Jouette
M. Bassler, 'The Enigmatic Sign: 2 Thessalonians 1:5', *CBQ* 46 (1984), pp. 496-
510.

19. On the seemingly cordial relations of the Corinthian church with outsiders,
see Barclay, 'Thessalonica and Corinth', and de Vos, *Church and Community
Conflicts*, pp. 205-14.

20. So rightly, e.g., Collins, *Birth of the New Testament*, p. 112, and Hare, *Jewish Persecution of Christians*, p. 64.

21. Donfried ('Theology of 1 Thessalonians', p. 255 n. 53) recognizes the term
'persecution' may be misleading but persists in using it nevertheless.

22. So also, e.g., deSilva, '"Worthy of his Kingdom"', pp. 62-63.

his converts were all too prone to respond to the non-Christian criticism to which they were subject (cf. 5.15).[23]

According to 1 Peter, believers in Asia Minor were verbally abused by unbelievers. The author of this epistle repeatedly tells his recipients to anticipate verbal attacks and advises them how to respond to hostile accusations (e.g. 2.12, 15; 3.9, 16; 4.4, 14). Furthermore, the writer admonishes these assailed 'aliens' to emulate Christ who uttered no deceitful word and refused to retaliate when his enemies hurled insults at him (2.21-23).[24] Additionally, some of the Christians addressed by the letter to the Hebrews appear to have borne the brunt of verbal abuse.[25] Hebrews 10.33 indicates that the letter's recipients were previously exposed to public abuse and affliction (ὀνειδισμοῖς τε καὶ θλίψεσιν θεατριζόμενοι). It may also be that some Matthean Christians were pelted by verbal stones hurled by outsiders. In Mt. 5.11 one reads: 'Blessed are you when people insult you, persecute you, and falsely say all kinds of evil against you because of me' (cf. 5.44). Although one would like to know much more about the contexts and contents of such insults, the presence of verbal harassment signals tense social relations between these various Christian groups and the non-Christians with whom they interacted.[26]

The Thessalonian Christians also experienced strained social relations with unbelievers. In fact, the Thessalonians' turning to God from idols (1.9) appears to have altered, or even ruptured, (a number of) their former relational networks (2.14). One can imagine that Paul's converts were criticized, marginalized and perhaps ostracized by non-Christian family, friends and associates for joining an upstart religious movement whose leader encouraged a fair degree of social dislocation from the 'rest' (4.5, 13; cf., e.g., 1 Cor. 5.9-13; 2 Cor. 6.14–7.1).[27]

23. Barclay, 'Conflict in Thessalonica', p. 522, and de Vos, *Church and Community Conflicts*, pp. 160-61.

24. On 1 Pet. as a response to slander, see David L. Balch, *Let Wives Be Submissive: The Domestic Code in 1 Peter* (SBLMS, 26; Chico, CA: Scholars Press, 1981). See also Elliott, *Home for the Homeless*, esp. pp. 78-84.

25. See David A. deSilva, *Despising Shame: Honor Discourse and Community Maintenance in Hebrews* (SBLDS, 152; Atlanta: Scholars Press, 1995).

26. Elliott (*Home for the Homeless*, p. 81) suggests, 'Such harassment of Christians by local opponents seems to have been the rule rather than the exception.'

27. So similarly, e.g., Holmes, *Thessalonians*, p. 50; Richard, *Thessalonians*, p. 149; Barclay, 'Conflict in Thessalonica', pp. 516-20; and de Vos, *Church and Community Conflicts*, p. 159.

Although Paul taught his converts to view non-Christians as outsiders subject to wrath (1.10; 4.5, 12; 5.1-11; cf. 2 Thess. 1.5-12; 2.11-12), socially speaking, the Thessalonian believers would have been regarded and responded to as a dangerously deviant minority (see further Chapter 10).

While it is now impossible to know the precise actions taken against these 'deviants', political measures may have been employed. According to Acts 17, Jason and some of the other believers in Thessalonica were hauled before the politarchs and subjected to political sanctions (i.e. posting bond) for their association with Paul and Silas and for defying Caesar's decrees by proclaiming Jesus as king (see further pp. 71-81 above). Even though the politarchs purportedly exercised restraint in their initial dealings with the Christians, it seems likely that subsequent popular and political responses to the believers would not have always been as moderate.[28]

In fact, some exegetes have suggested that a few of the Thessalonian Christians were martyred for the faith.[29] Interpreters tend to arrive at such a conclusion by combining Paul's statements about the Thessalonians' affliction in 1.6, 2.14 and 3.3-4 with his instruction concerning those believers who had died in 4.13-18. For example, John Pobee suggests the

> phrase οἱ [sic] κοιμηθέντες διὰ τοῦ Ἰησοῦ [4.14] refers to the Christians who died in their zeal for Jesus as was demonstrated by their patient endurance of persecution, before the Parousia of Christ. The attendant circumstances of the death were the persecutions raging in the church of Thessalonica.[30]

---

28. Haenchen (*Acts*, p. 513) suggests that Gentile opposition against the assembly increased in severity after Paul's departure and likely 'cost the Christians of Thessalonica a good deal more than the price of bail'. So similarly, Bruce, *Thessalonians*, p. 16. On pp. 261-67 below I will argue that the Christians were viewed by some of their Gentile compatriots as politically subversive and that this was a source of conflict.

29. E.g. Pobee, *Persecution and Martyrdom*, pp. 113-14; Donfried, 'Cults of Thessalonica', pp. 349-50, and 'Theology of 1 Thessalonians', pp. 254-56; Juan Chapa, 'Is First Thessalonians a Letter of Consolation?', *NTS* 40 (1994), pp. 150-60 (156); Collins, *Birth of the New Testament*, p. 112; and Riesner, *Paul's Early Period*, pp. 386-87. One also finds the suggestion that some of the Thessalonian Christians were martyred among earlier interpreters. See, e.g., Kirsopp Lake, *The Earlier Epistles of St. Paul* (London: Rivingtons, 1914), p. 88.

30. Pobee, *Persecution and Martyrdom*, p. 114.

Pobee may be correct in taking διὰ τοῦ Ἰησοῦ with τοὺς κοιμη-
θέντες instead of with ἄξει and in suggesting that διά is best understood as expressing attendant circumstance; however, it is highly
unlikely that Paul is alluding in 4.14 to the martyrdom of some of his
converts. (Furthermore, Pobee's argument that the present participle
κοιμωμένων in 4.13 'is a reference to the continued and protracted persecution of Christians at Thessalonica which was taking the lives of
some Christians' is misdirected.[31] The participle refers to continued
sleep, not protracted 'persecution'.) Instead, Paul seems to be saying in
4.14 that God will bring with Jesus at the parousia those Thessalonian
believers who have died in Jesus (i.e. as Christians; cf. 1 Cor. 15.18).[32]

Although I would not positively identify the Christian dead of whom
Paul speaks in 4.13-18 as martyrs, I am nevertheless reluctant to dismiss out of hand the possibility that some of Paul's converts were victims of physical violence and that perhaps on the rarest of occasions
such opposition might have culminated in death.[33] It is true that Paul
does not explicitly indicate[34] or celebrate[35] martyrdom among the Thessalonians. He does state in 2.14, however, that the Thessalonian congregation suffered the same things (τὰ αὐτὰ ἐπάθετε) as the Judean
churches did. If this statement is to be taken literally,[36] then it is possible that one or two of the Thessalonian Christians could have been
martyred even as the Judean believers Stephen (Acts 7.54–8.1) and

31. Pobee, *Persecution and Martyrdom*, p. 113. Cf. Donfried, 'Cults of Thessalonica', p. 349. deSilva ('"Worthy of his Kingdom"', p. 62 n. 25) remarks that falling asleep 'is a rather passive image for such a violent departure from this life'.

32. So similarly Dobschütz, *Thessalonicherbriefe*, p. 191; Marshall, *Thessalonians*, p. 124; Bruce, *Thessalonians*, p. 98; and Wanamaker, *Thessalonians*, p. 169.

33. Cf. de Vos, *Church and Community Conflict*, p. 160.

34. Bruce (*Thessalonians*, p. 98) remarks 'the references in both 1 and 2 Thessalonians to the "afflictions" endured by the Christians of Thessalonica scarcely
give the impression that positive martyrdom was involved'. Contrast Bruce, *Acts of
the Apostles*, p. 372.

35. Barclay ('Conflict in Thessalonica', p. 514) contends that Paul would have
surely lauded those who died as martyrs and cites Phil. 2.25-30 and Rom. 16.4
where Paul applauds those who have risked their lives for the service of Christ to
support his position. Cf. deSilva, '"Worthy of his Kingdom"', p. 62 n. 25.

36. Schleuter (*Filling up the Measure*, p. 53) maintains that Paul is speaking
hyperbolically at this point. Cf. de Vos, *Church and Community Conflicts*, p. 160.
But see Donfried, 'Cults of Thessalonica', p. 349. Frame (*Thessalonians*, p. 110)
suggests that the comparison 'is intended to express not identity but similarity'.

James (12.1-3) were.[37] The fact that Paul speaks of the death of Jesus and the prophets in close connection with the Thessalonians' affliction may also lend credence to the view that a few of Paul's converts in Thessalonica died for their faith (2.15; cf. 1.6).[38]

Paul does not disclose precisely how the Thessalonians suffered. However, he does, as we have seen, indicate that his converts experienced considerable opposition. Carol J. Schlueter thinks that Paul exaggerates the severity of the Thessalonians' sufferings. But Schlueter, who has been unduly influenced by Birger A. Pearson, erroneously equates 'severe persecution' with martyrdom.[39] While not denying that Paul can speak hyperbolically, there is every reason to accept Paul's claim that his converts were sorely afflicted. As David A. deSilva notes, 'While it is indeed advisable to steer clear of images of rounding up Christians for the arena at this stage, there are no grounds for limiting the "affliction" to the mere subjective experience of feeling cut off from one's former social relations—those former social relations had a nasty way of letting the deviant know their feelings in this matter, too.'[40]

At this point I would also note that the social-scientific study of conflict suggests that intergroup conflict can be very intense, particularly in cases where the conflicting parties know one another, are in direct contact and/or competition with the other and are embroiled in ideological disputes.[41] I would contend, then, that it is best to regard the Thessalonians' affliction to which Paul repeatedly refers as external (i.e. observable, verifiable), non-Christian opposition which took the forms of verbal harassment, social ostracism, political sanctions and perhaps even some sort of physical abuse, which on the rarest of occasions may have resulted in martyrdom.[42]

37. James, the brother of Jesus (Josephus, *Ant.* 20.200-203), and Antipas (Rev. 2.13) also died martyrs' deaths in the first century CE. According to Sulpicius Severus (*Chron.* 2.29; cf. Eusebius, *Hist. Eccl.* 2.25.5), under Nero Paul was beheaded by a sword and Peter was crucified. On the execution of other Christians in Rome during Nero's reign, see Tacitus, *Ann.* 15.44; cf. Suetonius, *Ner.* 16.

38. Collins, *Birth of the New Testament*, p. 112.

39. Schlueter, *Filling up the Measure*, pp. 52-53, and Pearson, '1 Thessalonians 2:13-16', pp. 86-87. 'Persecution' simply suggests ill-treatment. It may or may not be physical; it may or may not result in death.

40. deSilva, ' "Worthy of his Kingdom" ', p. 63 n. 26.

41. See pp. 116-19 above. Cf., e.g., the ongoing conflicts in Northern Ireland and Israel.

42. Regardless of whether or not the Thessalonians were physically abused, one

3. *The Origin of the Thessalonians' Opposition*

Thus far in this chapter, I have discussed the nature of the Christians' affliction. We will now consider the source of their suffering. Paul gives a concrete clue regarding the origin of the church's opposition in 1 Thess. 2.14b. There he remarks: 'you [i.e. the Thessalonian congregation] suffered the same things from your own compatriots [τῶν ἰδίων συμφυλετῶν] as they [i. e. the Judean churches] suffered from the Jews [ὑπὸ τῶν Ἰουδαίων]'. But to whom is Paul referring when he speaks of his converts' συμφυλέται? Since one's answer to this question will in no small measure influence how one envisions the conflict on the whole, at this point we will proceed with much care and with due caution. I will begin this section by examining συμφυλέτης along lexical lines. Having done so, I will consider how Paul employs this particular term in 2.14. Finally, I will offer a few historical observations in an effort to strengthen my interpretation.

a. *Lexical Issues*

Although the word συμφυλέτης is a biblical Greek *hapax legomenon* and appears infrequently in other extant Greek literature,[43] it is clear enough that this Hellenistic Greek compound literally denotes those who belong to the same φυλή.[44] συμφυλέτης is seemingly synonymous with the more common Attic Greek term φυλέτης.[45] That Paul would choose to prefix σύν to φυλέτης is not surprising. This was a common

---

may still reasonably regard their suffering as severe. Verbal harassment, social ridicule and political sanctions constitute 'considerable affliction', at least from the perspective of those who are experiencing such treatment.

43. *BAGD* ('συμφυλέτης', p. 780) note that the word appears in *Inscriptiones Graecae* 7.2.505.18; *Doxographi Graeci* 655.8; *Rhetores Graeci* 7.49.22; Isocrates 12.145 (in the Blass edition); Herodianus; Philetaerus; and Hesychius.

44. So also Lünemann, *Thessalonians*, p. 67; Milligan, *Thessalonians*, p. 29; Collins, *Birth of the New Testament*, p. 111; Meeks, 'Social Functions of Apocalyptic Language', p. 691; and deSilva, ' "Worthy of his Kingdom" ', p. 75 n. 45.

45. Frame, *Thessalonians*, p. 110, and Bruce, *Thessalonians*, p. 46. Although φυλέτης is used frequently in Greek literature (e.g. Isocrates, *Panath.* 145.2; Plutarch, *Lyc.* 16.1; *Pericles* 10.1; *Pelopidas* 18.2; Dionysius of Halicarnassus, *Ant. Rom.* 9.41.3; Philo, *Migr. Abr.* 67.2; *Spec. Leg.* 2.82, 129; *Rer. Div. Her.* 9.6; Josephus, *Ant.* 4.14, 174, 175; 5.154, 299), it does not appear in the Greek New Testament.

practice in later Greek, and Paul was fond of forming compounds with σύν (e.g. 2 Cor. 6.18; Gal. 1.14; Phil. 2.2; 3.10, 17). Although prefixing a preposition to a word without altering its original meaning or force was frowned upon by Herodianus, a second-century CE grammarian (πολίτης δημότης φυλέτης ἄνευ τῆς σύν),[46] this sort of preference was lost on Paul.

With a basic definition of συμφυλέτης in place (i.e. of or from the same φυλή), we may now explore the semantical range of the term and its intended meaning in 2.14. Theoretically, the word could be used rather narrowly to refer to a particular citizenry division or voting tribe. The term φυλαί was used this way in Classical Greek (e.g. Herodotus, 6.111.1; Thucydides, 6.98.4). Furthermore, in Thessalonica 'four phylai are attested by inscriptions ranging in date from the Hellenistic period (?) to the third century A.D.'[47]

These facts notwithstanding, it is doubtful that Paul would have used συμφυλέτης in a strictly political sense. Although it is conceivable that a few of Paul's converts were citizens (some may have been artisans [4.11; cf. 2 Thess. 3.6-13]), I am not inclined to think that most of the congregation were citizens in a technical sense.[48] In fact, citizenship in Greek cities was not overly common,[49] and in at least some places was rather difficult to attain.[50] As A.J.M. Jones maintains, 'Though all citizens seem as a rule to have possessed equal rights, the citizenship might itself be limited to a relatively restricted number of the inhabitants. In all Greek cities citizenship was of course determined by birth and not

46. Found in Frame, *Thessalonians*, p. 110.

47. Nicholas F. Jones, *Public Organization in Ancient Greece: A Documentary Study* (Philadelphia: American Philosophical Society, 1987), p. 267.

48. Contrast de Vos (*Church and Community Conflicts*, p. 154) who goes beyond the evidence in suggesting that the Thessalonian church was comprised entirely of citizens who were artisans.

49. For example, in Athens during the fifth century BCE only the children of two freeborn Athenians qualified as citizens (Aristotle, *Ath. Pol.* 26). F.F. Bruce ('Citizenship', *ABD*, I, pp. 1048-49 [1048]) notes, 'The city (*polis*) was a political entity among the Greeks, and citizenship involved jealously guarded privileges.'

50. To illustrate, Athenodorus fixed a property qualification of five hundred drachmae for inclusion on the citizen's roll in Tarsus (Dio Chrysostom, *Or.* 34.23). This type of restriction, however, seems to have been an exception. See further, A.H.M. Jones, *The Greek City: From Alexander to Justinian* (Oxford: Clarendon Press, 1940), pp. 173-74.

by residence.'[51] It is not likely that the church was opposed solely by citizens of Thessalonica.

At the other end of the semantical spectrum are those scholars who suggest that Paul used συμφυλέτης to refer to local townspeople, so as to include Jews as well as Gentiles in the opposition of the Thessalonian church.[52] Interpreters who arrive at such a view, however, seem to be influenced more by their reading of Acts 17.1-10a than by lexicographical concerns.[53] According to Luke, Thessalonian Jews recruited a group from the *agora* who in turn assisted them in gathering a mob, setting the city in an uproar and attacking Jason's house where they anticipated finding Paul and Silas. While some Christians were caught up in the conflict for having harbored the missionaries, a careful reading of the narrative suggests that Paul and Silas were the focus of the Jewish-instigated riot.[54] If, however, one interprets Luke's account as indicating Jewish opposition to the Thessalonian Christians per se (as scholars who understand συμφυλέτης as 'local townspeople' tend to do), then there are compelling reasons for countering this conclusion.

To begin, I would point out that the term φυλή, which appears frequently in the Septuagint (410 times) and occasionally in the New Testament (31 times, 21 of which are in Revelation), carries the primary

51. *The Greek City*, p. 160; cf. p. 172. Cf. Lentz (*Luke's Portrait of Paul*, p. 33): 'Citizenship in Greek cities was not simply acquired by everyone upon birth in a given locale. Rather, citizenship throughout the Greek cities of the [Roman] empire was earned, bought, or inherited.'

52. E.g. George C. Findlay, *The Epistles to the Thessalonians* (Cambridge: Cambridge University Press, 1891), p. 75; Morris, *Thessalonians*, p. 82 n. 69; Milligan, *Thessalonians*, p. 29; Donfried, 'Paul and Judaism', p. 248; Sandnes, *Paul— One of the Prophets?*, p. 186 n. 4; Rigaux, *Thessaloniciens*, p. 443; Best, *Thessalonians*, p. 114; Marshall, *Thessalonians*, p. 79; Williams, *Thessalonians*, p. 79; Martin, *Thessalonians*, pp. 89-90; Holmes, *Thessalonians*, p. 82; and Weatherly, *Thessalonians*, p. 85.

53. E.g. Riesner (*Paul's Early Period*, p. 352), following Rigaux (*Thessaloniciens*, p. 443), maintains, 'In New Testament Greek, this word [i.e. συμφυλέτης] had apparently already lost its reference to ethnicity.' Tellingly, Riesner offers no support for this assertion. He does, however, seek to qualify this statement by suggesting 'even if [συμφυλέτης] refers to the Gentile compatriots of the Thessalonians, the Jews are not excluded as co-instigators'.

54. Cf. F.F. Bruce (*Thessalonians*, p. 16): 'Nothing is said in Acts 17:1-9 about persecution directed against the Thessalonian converts in general; it is against the missionaries and secondarily against their hosts...that the rabble is stirred up by disapproving Jews.'

meaning 'tribe' and by extension can mean 'people, race or nation'.[55] In Paul, φυλή appears twice, each time in reference to his belonging to the tribe of Benjamin (Rom. 11.1; Phil. 3.5). Although Paul does not employ φυλή in a more general way, throughout his Epistles he displays an acute awareness of his Jewishness (see, e.g., Rom. 9.3; 16.7, 11, 21 where Paul speaks of his Jewish kinspeople [συγγενής][56]). Furthermore, he is consistently careful to distinguish between Jews and Gentiles (see, e.g., Rom. 1.16; 2.9, 14, 28-29; 3.9, 29; 9.24, 30-31; 11.11, 13-14, 25-26; 15.7-13, 15-18, 26-27; 16.4; 1 Cor. 1.24; 5.1; 10.32; 12.13; 2 Cor. 11.26; Gal. 2.2-3, 7-9, 12-15; 3.28; Col. 3.11; Eph. 2.11-22).[57] Galatians 2.15 serves as a particularly illuminating example where Paul differentiates between those who are 'Jews by birth' (φύσει Ἰουδαῖοι) and 'Gentile sinners' (ἐξ ἐθνῶν ἁμαρτωλοί).[58]

In reference to 1 Thessalonians in particular, I would call attention to four texts where Paul distinguishes Jews from non-Jews. In 1.8 Paul identifies his converts as Gentiles, thereby differentiating them from Jews, by writing that the Christians' 'faith in God' (ἡ πίστις ὑμῶν ἡ πρὸς τὸν θεόν) had gone forth everywhere. On this verse Jon A. Weatherly remarks, 'The fact that Paul refers to their faith as "faith in

55. Christian Mauer, 'φυλή', *TDNT*, IX, pp. 245-50.
56. Suidas lists συγγενής as an alternative meaning of συμφυλέτης.
57. See esp. Terence L. Donaldson, '"The Gospel that I Proclaim among the Gentiles" (Gal. 2.2): Universalistic or Israel-Centred?', in L. Ann Jervis and Peter Richardson (eds.), *Gospel in Paul: Studies on the Corinthians, Galatians and Romans for Richard N. Longenecker* (JSNTSup, 108; Sheffield: Sheffield Academic Press, 1994), pp. 166-93, and *Paul and the Gentiles*, e.g. pp. 183-84. See also, Christopher D. Stanley, '"Neither Jew nor Greek": Ethnic Conflict in Graeco-Roman Society', *JSNT* 64 (1996), pp. 101-24, esp. 123-24. Hermann Strathmann ('λαός', *TDNT*, IV, pp. 29-57 [56]) rightly notes that Paul 'had no thought of surrendering his national consciousness as a Jew. Nor did he require a similar surrender of Greeks. The distinctions remain and are acknowledged in their own national and historical sphere.'

By distinguishing between Jews and non-Jews Paul stands in the long line of Jewish tradition. See, e.g., the use of ἀλλόφυλος to refer to peoples other than Jews in Exod. 34.15; Isa. 14.29; 1 Macc. 4.12; Acts 10.28; Philo, *Virt.* 160.3; 222.8; Josephus, *Ant.* 1.338; 4.183.

58. deSilva ('"Worthy of his Kingdom"', p. 74 n. 44) notes that the ethnic categories of Jew and Gentile are 'deeply etched in Paul's mind'. On Paul's ethnic dualism, see esp. Barclay, 'Paul among Diaspora Jews', pp. 107-11.

God" rather than "in Christ" is consistent with his stress on their conversion to the Christian faith from paganism. Had Paul intended to address Jewish Christians, faith in God would not have distinguished them from other Jews.'[59] Paul also characterizes his converts as Gentiles in 1.9 when he comments that they had 'turned to God from idols [ἐπεστρέψατε πρὸς τὸν θεὸν ἀπὸ τῶν εἰδώλων], to serve a living and true God' (cf. 1 Cor. 12.2; Gal. 4.8).[60] Like some other Jewish writers, Paul underscores here the difference between the living God of the Israelites and the 'dumb idols' from which his Gentile converts had turned (see, e.g., Bel 5; Sir. 18.1; *1 En.* 5; *Sib. Or.* 3.763; *Jos. Asen.* 8.5-6; cf. Pss. 114.4-8; 135.15-18; Isa. 40.18-20; 44.9-20; 46.6-7; Jer. 10.3-9; Hab. 2.18-19; Wis. 13.1-15, 17). Additionally, Paul differentiates between Jews and non-Jews in 2.16 when he remarks that Jews ('Ιουδαῖοι [2.14] is best understood ethnically) hinder his mission to 'the Gentiles' (τὰ ἔθνη). Finally, and rather ironically, one gains a

---

59. Weatherly, *Thessalonians*, p. 50. It is conceivable that there were some Jews in the Thessalonian church as Acts 17.4 suggests. Goulder ('Silas in Thessalonica', p. 96) thinks, 'It [i.e. the Thessalonian church] was probably a mixed body like the churches at Rome and Laodicea, which are addressed as if though they were Gentile (Rom. 11.13; Eph. 2.11-13; 3.1).' If there were Jews among the Thessalonian Christians when Paul wrote 1 Thess., their presence cannot be detected from the letter. (The fact that Paul does not refer directly to Old Testament texts or characters in 1 Thessalonians is sometimes used to support the idea that he was addressing Gentiles. See, e.g., Lightfoot, *Notes*, p. 16, and de Vos, *Church and Community Conflicts*, pp. 146-47. Cf. E. Springs Steele, 'The Use of Jewish Scriptures in 1 Thessalonians', *BTB* 14 [1984], pp. 12-17.) As E. Earle Ellis ('Paul and His Co-Workers', in *idem, Prophecy and Hermeneutic in Early Christianity: New Testament Essays* [Tübingen: J.C.B. Mohr (Paul Siebeck), 1978], pp. 3-22 [19 n. 73]) notes, '1 Thessalonians...presupposes a gentile congregation.' Johnson (*Writings of the New Testament*, p. 261) contends, 'The internal evidence [of 1 Thess.] strongly suggests a gentile majority in the community, with at best a Jewish minority. This issue is clouded by Acts' consistent concern for some success among the Jews in the Diaspora mission.' See also, e.g., deSilva, ' "Worthy of his Kingdom" ', p. 75 n. 45, and Malherbe, *Paul and the Thessalonians*, p. 15.

60. Best (*Thessalonians*, p. 82) observes, 'Obviously the Thessalonians were Gentiles before they became Christians for Jews would not have been described as turning from idolatry.' This observation holds even if 1 Thess. 1.9-10 is (part of) a pre-Pauline formula summarizing missionary preaching to the Gentiles as some scholars maintain (see, e.g., Best, *Thessalonians*, pp. 85-87). For, as Wanamaker (*Thessalonians*, p. 85) suggests, 'Paul presupposed that the Thessalonians would recognize their own experience in what he was writing'.

glimpse of Paul's Jewish consciousness in 4.5. Here he encourages his male, Gentile converts in Thessalonica to avoid living 'in the passion of lust like the Gentiles who do not know God' (τὰ ἔθνη τὰ μὴ εἰδότα τὸν θεόν).[61]

Given the fact that Paul is careful to distinguish between Jews and Gentiles both in 1 Thessalonians and his other Epistles, it seems most unlikely that he would have indiscriminately used συμφυλέτης to refer to the local townspeople of Thessalonica.[62] Instead, I would contend that Paul employed συμφυλέτης, which is best translated as 'compatriots' (so NRSV),[63] to speak of his converts' fellow Gentiles.[64] I hereby record my agreement with those commentators who understand συμφυλέτης to refer to non-Jewish, Thessalonian townsfolk.[65] This sig-

---

61. It may also be that by employing the *nomen gentilicium* Θεσσαλονικεύς in 1.1 (see 2 Thess. 1.1; cf. also Gal. 1.2; Ignatius, *Pol.*) Paul is acknowledging the Gentile composition of the church. Contrast 1 Cor. 1.2; 2 Cor. 1.1; Phil. 1.1; and Rom. 1.7. Richard (*Thessalonians*, p. 30) suggests that τῇ ἐκκλησίᾳ Θεσσαλονι-κέων is best translated 'to the community made up of Thessalonians [i.e. of Gentiles]'. Cf. de Vos, *Church and Community Conflicts*, pp. 144-47.

62. Barclay ('Conflict in Thessalonica', p. 514) comments, 'With his acute consciousness of the racial distinction between Jews and non-Jews, Paul could hardly refer to Jews as *symphyletai* (2:14) of his non-Jewish converts (1:9).'

63. Collins (*Birth of the New Testament*, p. 111) rightly observes, 'The most obvious meaning of "compatriots" (*symphyletoi*) [sic] is those who belong to the same race (*phyle*).' Karl Ludwig Schmidt ('ἔθνος', *TDNT*, II, pp. 364-72 [369]) suggests that φυλή denotes 'people as a national unity of common descent'.

64. One is left to wonder why Paul did not select a more common term to speak of his converts' fellow Gentiles. As already noted above, he could have used either φυλέτης or συγγενής to refer to the Thessalonian Christians' compatriots. Furthermore, he might have employed other terms of his time to denote relationship by race, including ὁμόφυλος (see, e.g., Isocrates, *Phil.* 108.4; 2 Macc. 4.10; *3 Macc.* 3.21; Philo, *Spec. Leg.* 2.80; 4.19; 4.159; *Virt.* 66.2; 82.3; Josephus, *Ant.* 3.13, 382; 4.204; Dio Chrysostom, *Or.* 32.36; *1 Clem.* 4:10) and ὁμοεθνής (see, e.g., Philo, *Spec. Leg.* 2.73, 122; *Virt.* 102.1; *Leg. Gai.* 212.6; Josephus, *Ant.* 10.203; 11.130, 233, 322; Diodorus 1.70.2; 5.24.3. 12.11.3; 12.29.3; 14.114.1; 17.100.4; 33.20.1; 37.2.6; and Dio Chrysostom, *Or.* 48.5). If Paul had wanted to indicate that his Gentile converts had suffered at the hands of both Jews and non-Jews, as some commentators contend, then the term συμπολίτης, i.e. fellow townsperson, would have been more appropriate (see, e.g., Eph. 2.19; Josephus, *Ant.* 19.175). So also deSilva, ' "Worthy of his Kingdom" ', p. 75 n. 45.

65. E.g. Dobschütz, *Thessalonicherbriefe*, pp. 109-10; Frame, *Thessalonians*, p. 110; Dibelius, *Thessalonicher*, p. 11; Bruce, *Thessalonians*, p. 46; Wanamaker, *Thessalonians*, p. 113; R.C.H. Lenski, *The Interpretation of St. Paul's Letters to the*

nals, then, Gentile opposition for Paul's Gentile converts. Contextual considerations make this interpretation even more persuasive.

b. *Contextual Factors*

The immediate context in which συμφυλέτης appears also suggests that Paul was referring to the Christians' fellow Gentiles when employing this term. Paul claims in 2.14 that his converts became imitators of the Judean churches by suffering at the hands of their compatriots the same things that they had suffered from the Jews.[66] Paul's description of the Thessalonians' opponents (τῶν ἰδίων συμφυλετῶν) in explicit and direct contrast to the Ἰουδαῖοι marks them off as Gentiles. As J.B. Lightfoot noted some time ago: 'That the Gentiles are here meant is clear from the marked opposition to ὑπὸ τῶν Ἰουδαῖοι, further enforced as it is by ἰδίων.'[67] The point of Paul's comparison in 2.14 between the church in Thessalonica and the churches of Judea, then, is not only they both suffered, but also that their sufferings came from their own compatriots (i.e. non-Jews and Jews respectively).[68] To but-

Colossians, to the Thessalonians, to Timothy, to Titus and to Philemon (Minneapolis: Fortress Press, 1961), p. 264; William Hendriksen, *I and II Thessalonians* (Grand Rapids: Baker Book House, 1964), pp. 70-71; D. Edmond Hiebert, *The Thessalonian Epistles: A Call to Readiness* (Chicago: Moody Press, 1971), pp. 113-14; Ronald A. Ward, *1 & 2 Thessalonians* (Waco, TX: Word Books, 1973), p. 73; Willi Marxsen, *Der erste Brief an die Thessalonicher* (ZB, 11.2; Zürich: Theologischer Verlag, 1979), p. 46; Foakes-Jackson, *Acts*, p. 161; Haenchen, *Acts*, p. 513; Malherbe, *Paul and the Thessalonians*, pp. 47, 95; Donaldson, *Paul and the Gentiles*, pp. 183, 227; Meeks, *Origins of Christian Morality*, p. 47; Sanders, *Schismatics, Sectarians, Dissidents, Deviants*, p. 8; Schlueter, *Filling up the Measure*, 197; Holtz, 'Judgment on the Jews', p. 283; Barclay, 'Conflict in Thessalonica', p. 514; deSilva, ' "Worthy of his Kingdom" ', p. 75 n. 45; and Collins, *Birth of the New Testament*, pp. 111-12.

66. In 2.14 Ἰουδαῖος could very well mean 'Judean' or 'Jew'. The broader meaning 'Jew' is required, however, in 2.15-16 where Ἰουδαῖος in the more general sense serves as the antecedent to the multiple participial phrases. So rightly, Bruce, *Thessalonians*, p. 46; and Walter Gutbrod, "Ἰσραήλ', *TDNT*, III, pp. 356-91 (380). It seems best, then, to take Ἰουδαῖος ethnically and in accord with my understanding of συμφυλέτης. If one were to interpret συμφυλέτης as fellow townsperson, then one would presumably need to translate Ἰουδαῖος as 'Judean', as Moule (*Birth of the New Testament*, p. 158) indicates.

67. Lightfoot, *Notes*, p. 32. Cf. Frame (*Thessalonians*, p. 110) who curtly comments: 'συμφυλέται are Gentiles as Ἰουδαίων shows.'

68. So also, e.g., Wanamaker, *Thessalonians*, p. 113; Meeks, *Origins of Chris-*

tress my position further still, I will now offer some historical observations.

c. *Historical Elements*

We have observed above that Paul addresses the Thessalonian congregation as Gentiles. If Paul's converts were indeed non-Jews, then it seems unlikely that Thessalonian Jews would have opposed them. The following thoughts lend support to this suggestion. To begin, the Jews in Thessalonica were a minority group as were Jews in (almost) every other Diasporan location.[69] While the civil authorities in Thessalonica may have been tolerant of Jewish religious practices and may have extended to the Jews religious privileges,[70] Thessalonian Jews likely would not have been powerful or daring enough to oppose Gentiles on their own.[71] To do so would have put in jeopardy their own religious liberty as well as their potentially precarious social standing in Gentile society. Indeed, it does appear that some Jews in some places cooperated with Gentiles in opposing Christians (see, e.g., Acts 14.5; 17.6; *Mart. Pol.* 7.2). Furthermore, there is evidence of Jews turning over Christian Jews to the relevant authorities in an effort to differentiate themselves (see, e.g., Acts 18.12; 24.9; 25.2; cf. Josephus, *War* 6.5; 7.10, 11). Nonetheless, there is no sidestepping the fact that 'Paul indicates only Gentile, not Jewish, opposition for his [Gentile] converts'.[72]

As we have seen above, Paul himself encountered Jewish opposition in Thessalonica. One might contend, therefore, that the Jewish community would have disciplined proselytes who had become Christians if they, like Paul, were thought to be negligent of Jewish customs, yet maintained contact with the synagogue. On the whole, however, it is

tian Morality, p. 47; Collins, *Birth of the New Testament*, p. 112; and Sanders, *Schismatics, Sectarians, Dissidents, Deviants*, p. 8.

69. Alexandria is a possible exception. Feldman (*Jew and Gentile*, p. 79) suggests, '[Alexandrian] Jews constituted the largest single religious and ethnic group in the city's cosmopolitan population...'

70. On the ability of Jews to practice freely their religion during this time period, see, e.g., Josephus, *Ant.* 14.202-210, 225-230, 241-264; 16.162-173.

71. See further Setzer, *Jewish Responses*, p. 82. Tellbe ('Conflict at Philippi', p. 115) notes in reference to Philippi that the Jews would not have dared to oppose Christians without the consent of the relevant authorities. This would likely have been the case in Thessalonica as well.

72. Barclay, 'Conflict at Thessalonica', p. 514. Cf. similarly, Bruce, *Thessalonians*, pp. 16, 46, 146.

doubtful that the Gentile Thessalonian congregation would have had (much) interaction with the Jewish community of that city before or after their conversion given its background in idolatry.[73] And as the social-scientific study of conflict indicates, conflict requires contact (see p. 116 above). Moreover, it is hard to imagine any compelling reason that the Thessalonian Jews would have afflicted Paul's Gentile converts.[74] Jews naturally only attacked Gentiles if they posed a real threat to their own community (e.g. the situation reported by 1 Macc.), and a small band of former 'idolaters' would hardly have impinged upon the integrity or security of the Jewish community in Thessalonica.

4. *Conclusion*

In this chapter I have considered the character and origin of the Thessalonian Christians' affliction. In regards to the nature of Thessalonians' conflict, I concluded that it is best understood as vigorous, non-Christian opposition which likely took the form of verbal harassment, social ostracism, political sanctions and perhaps (some kind of) physical abuse. As for the source of the church's suffering, based upon lexical, contextual and historical evidence, I determined that Paul's Gentile converts were troubled by unconverted Gentiles, precisely the people

73. So rightly Meeks, 'Breaking Away', p. 106. Cf. Frank Thielman (*Paul and the Law: A Contextual Approach* [Downers Grove, IL: InterVarsity Press, 1994], p. 70): 'If anything is clear about the nature of the Thessalonian church from Paul's two letters, it is that former pagans with no previous attachment to the synagogue and no apparent familiarity with Judaism made up the vast majority of the community.'

74. Collins (*Birth of the New Testament*, p. 112) suggests that it is not impossible to imagine that troublemaking Jews opposed Paul's Gentile converts for their having been informed by Paul that they were God's chosen and beloved and that they were no longer sinful Gentiles (1.4; 4.5). While it is possible that some Thessalonian Jews thought that Paul's Gentile mission fell within Judaism, it does not seem likely that such Jews would have opposed Paul's Gentile converts unless those converts were involved in the life of the Jewish community. Instead, the gaze of the Thessalonian Jews would have been fixed upon Paul. It was he who was Jewish; it was he who sought to stay in contact with the synagogue; it was he who some Jews viewed to be a perverter of their customs and an agitator of their people (see Acts 21.21; 24.5). It is true that Paul considered his Galatian converts to be objects of Jewish–Christian compulsion, but the situation in Galatia was distinctly different than the one in Thessalonica.

who persisted in worshipping the 'idols' from which the Thessalonian Christians had turned. I chose not to address why Paul's converts came into conflict with their compatriots so that I might pursue this important and intriguing question in the chapter which follows.

Chapter 10

WHAT PROMPTED THE THESSALONIAN CHRISTIANS'
COMPATRIOTS TO OPPOSE THEM?

1. *Introduction*

I argued in the previous chapter that the Thessalonian Christians met severe verbal, social and perhaps even physical opposition at the hands of their Gentile family, friends and neighbours. Here I wish to explore the causes of the church's clash with outsiders. Unfortunately, the Thessalonian correspondence does not satisfy our curiosity along these lines of inquiry. In fact, one searches 1 (and 2) Thessalonians in vain for any explicit explanation as to why the conflict between the Thessalonian congregation and non-Christians occurred.[1] It seems likely that Paul would have perceived at least some of the factors that generated and perpetuated the conflict, but for whatever reasons he does not express in his Epistle(s) to the Thessalonians why he thought that they had been and were being harassed.

If one hopes to explain what precipitated the conflict between believers and unbelievers in Thessalonica, then one must devise an interpretive strategy. In what follows, I will seek to determine why non-Christians responded negatively to Paul's converts by reading between the lines of the 1 (and 2) Thessalonians, by marshaling applicable literary parallels,[2] by drawing upon pertinent archaeological materials and by

---

1.   1 Thess. 1.6 associates the Thessalonians' affliction with their conversion. Additionally, Acts 17.7 suggests that the conflict at Thessalonica was political in orientation. I will explore these clues concerning the conflict in what follows.

2.   A word of methodological defense is in order here. I am aware that some of the parallels adduced in this chapter are geographically and chronologically removed from Thessalonica c. 50 CE. Furthermore, I recognize that the conflict in Thessalonica could be (and in some respects probably was) wholly unique. By drawing upon other texts, which are, of course, products of other social-historical contexts, I am not claiming that x = y (or this = that). I am suggesting that x and y

utilizing relevant social-scientific theories. At the outset of this chapter I will note the unsympathetic response of non-Christians to the Thessalonians' conversion. I will then discuss how the socio-religious exclusivity of Paul's converts seemingly fostered suspicion among outsiders and led to accusations against the Christians. In this second major division I will also explore the possible ill effects of the zealous evangelistic activity in which some of the Thessalonian assembly seem to have been engaged. Finally, I will consider how the church could have been perceived by their compatriots as subversive to the basic institutions (namely family, religion and politics) of Greco-Roman society in general and of Thessalonica in particular.

2. *Conversion to Pauline Christianity*

According to 1 Thess. 1.6 the Thessalonian Christians experienced affliction in conjunction with their conversion (δεξάμενοι τὸν λόγον ἐν θλίψει πολλῇ). Presumably, the believers' decision to abandon their former gods (viewed by Paul as 'idols') in order 'to serve a living and true God' (1.9) sparked an ongoing controversy with their Gentile compatriots.[3] While Paul is, of course, pleased with the 'turn' that his converts had made, his sentiments would not have been commonly shared. In fact, what delighted Paul would have disgusted the Christians' associates.[4] To abandon time-honored traditions for what Suetonius would

seem to be speaking of and reflecting *similar* types of situations and that y *might* therefore further illuminate x. I make every effort here to be sensitive to the particularities of the conflict in Thessalonica and to ancient life in that city.

I am seeking to counter in advance the potential charge of 'parallelomania'. In truth, most New Testament scholars appeal to literary parallels in carrying out their work. The question is not if we use parallels, the question is how we use them and if the parallels selected are appropriate. Ultimately, the readers of this work must judge whether the texts I have adduced actually are parallel. Nevertheless, even if one regards a particular text to be inapplicable, I have sought to construct my arguments so that my point will stand even if a given parallel falls.

3. Perkins ('1 Thessalonians and Hellenistic Religious Practices', p. 326) remarks, 'Conversion implied a break, a separation with one's past and social environment, which frequently led to hostility.'

4. Whittaker (*Jews and Christians*, p. 133) suggests that the friends and neighbors of Gentile Christian converts would have viewed 'their conversion from paganism with amazement and horror'. On conversion in the Greco-Roman world, see, e.g., A.D. Nock, *Conversion: The Old and the New in Religion from Alexander*

later call 'a new and mischievous superstition' (*superstitionis novae ac maleficae*, *Ner.* 16.2) would have been perceived by outsiders as sacrilege.

Celsus (fl. c. 178 CE) thought that it was 'impious to abandon the customs which [had] existed in each locality from the beginning' (*Contra Cels.* 5.25).[5] Additionally, Porphyry (232/3–305 CE) maintained that to honor the divinity according to one's ancestral custom was the hallmark of piety (*Marc.* 18). Eusebius, a church historian living and writing in the third and fourth centuries (c. 260–340 CE), was still sensitive to the novelty of Christianity (see, e.g., *Praep. Evang.* 4.1 and *Hist. Eccl.* 1.4).

However, it was not only the novelty of Pauline Christianity that would have raised the ire of the believers' compatriots. Their very act of converting to another religion and thereby abandoning their own religious customs would likely have provoked controversy, if not hostility, among the Christians' family and friends. We know that Gentile proselytes to Judaism, a religion whose antiquity was noted by Tacitus (*Hist.* 5.1; cf. Origen, *Contra Cels.* 5.25), were criticized, and even ostracized, by their associates for their willingness to convert.

The Hellenistic-Jewish writer of the romance *Joseph and Aseneth* (first century CE [?]) highlights the plight of the Jewish proselyte when he presents Aseneth as saying, 'All people have come to hate me, and on top of those my father and my mother, because I, too, have come to hate their gods and have destroyed them, and caused them to be trampled underfoot by men' (11.4; cf. 12.12; 13.11).[6] Additionally, Aseneth prays that the Lord, the 'father of orphans', 'protector of the persecuted' and 'helper of the afflicted' will have mercy on her (12.13), as one who is now 'an orphan, and desolate, and abandoned by all people' (12.7).

In his writings, Philo contends that proselytes, whom he mentions

---

the Great to Augustine of Hippo (Oxford: Clarendon Press, 1933); Michael Green, *Evangelism in the Early Church* (Grand Rapids: Eerdmans, 1970), pp. 144-65; and Segal, *Paul the Convert*, esp. pp. 72-114.

5.   Henry Chadwick (trans.), *Origen: Contra Celsum* (Cambridge: Cambridge University Press, 1953).

6.   On conversion in *Jos. Asen.*, see Randall D. Chesnutt, *From Death to Life: Conversion in Joseph and Aseneth* (JSPSup, 16; Sheffield: Sheffield Academic Press, 1995); Barclay, *Jews in the Mediterranean Diaspora*, pp. 204-16; and Boccaccini, *Middle Judaism*, pp. 254-56.

alongside widows and orphans (see, e.g., *Somn.* 2.273), should be treated by Jews with special sensitivity because of their having turned kinsfolk into mortal enemies by leaving the 'mythical fables and multiplicity of sovereigns, so highly honored by their parents and grandparents and blood relations' (*Spec. Leg.* 4.178; cf. *Virt.* 102-103). Elsewhere Philo encourages his Jewish readers to honor proselytes, not only by respecting them but also by extending to them extraordinary friendship and goodwill (*Spec. Leg.* 1.52).

Josephus's story of Izates's conversion to Judaism further illustrates the potentially precarious state of proselytes among their own people.[7] Helena, the mother of Izates, counsels her son against being circumcised. She regards circumcision as dangerous because 'if his subjects should discover that he was devoted to rites that were strange and foreign to themselves, it would produce much disaffection and they would not tolerate the rule of a Jew over them' (*Ant.* 20.38).

The comments of these three Hellenistic-Jewish writers indicate the unpopularity of proselytes in general and proselytes to Judaism in particular. Caustic comments from the Roman *literati* clarify why these three authors were concerned about the well-being of the Jewish proselyte. Tacitus remarks that those who renounce their ancestral traditions and convert to Judaism are taught at the outset to 'despise the gods, to disown their country, and to regard their parents, children, and brothers as of little account' ('Transgressi in morem eorum idem usurpant, nec quicquam prius imbuuntur quam contemnere deos, exuere patriam, parentes liberos fratres vilia habere', *Hist.* 5.5). Juvenal's commentary on proselytes to Judaism is no more positive. He states:

> Having been wont to flout the laws of Rome, they learn and practice and revere the Jewish law, and all that Moses handed down in his secret tome, forbidding to point out the way to any not worshipping the same rites, and conducting none but the circumcised to the desired fountain (*Sat.* 14.100-105).

Such slanderous statements indicate that much of the offense of conversion to another religion lay in abandoning one's own traditions.[8]

---

7. For a treatment of this account, see, among others, Gary Gilbert, 'The Making of a Jew: "God-Fearer" or Convert in the Story of Izates', *USQR* 44 (1991), pp. 299-313.

8. Barclay ('Conflict in Thessalonica', p. 514) remarks, 'From our cultural and historical distance we easily underestimate the social dislocation involved in turning, as Paul puts it, from "idols" to the "true and living God" (1:9); and we barely

Therefore, even if Paul's converts had been misperceived by their compatriots as Jewish proselytes, which as I will show below is unlikely, this would have in no way eliminated the potential for hostility. As it happens, the novelty of Pauline Christianity likely heightened non-Christian opposition to the church.

In light of the above observations, there is good reason to conclude that Paul is accurate in saying that the Thessalonian Christians experienced affliction in conjunction with their conversion. As noted in Chapter 4 (see p. 103), the sociology of deviance suggests that perceived violations of cultural conventions often prompt the majority (or those who wield power) to oppose the innovators. Although conversion appears to have been the initial cause of contention between believers and unbelievers in Thessalonica, this is only a partial explanation as to why the conflict occurred. The question remains: What was it that the Christians' compatriots found offensive enough to oppose? We now turn to address this question.

3. *The Thessalonian Christians as Exclusive*

Commenting on why the conflict in Thessalonica transpired, Wayne A. Meeks remarks: 'The reasons for this hostility are not too difficult to imagine. Unlike the many little clubs that were so much a part of the city life in the Roman empire, unlike even the multitude of cults into which one might be initiated, the Christians were exclusive.'[9]

Although the conflict situation in Thessalonica is more complex than Meeks suggests here, he has correctly noted a primary reason for the tension between Paul's converts and outsiders, namely the Christians' exclusiveness.[10] What caused the Thessalonian believers to embrace a separatist perspective? Their exclusivity may be positively linked to their reception and internalization of Paul's apocalyptically oriented instruction.[11]

---

appreciate the offense, even disgust, which such a change could evoke.'

9.   Meeks, 'Social Functions of Apocalyptic Language', p. 691.

10.   Cf. Alfred Ayer, 'Sources of Intolerance', in Susan Mendus and David Edwards (eds.), *On Toleration* (Oxford: Clarendon Press, 1987), pp. 83-100 (86), and Craig S. de Vos, 'Popular Graeco-Roman Responses to Christianity', in Philip F. Esler (ed.), *The Early Christian World* (London: Routledge, forthcoming).

11.   Differential association theory (see pp. 90-93 above) emphasizes that a person learns alternative patterns of belief and behavior through instruction.

a. *Paul's Apocalyptic Gospel and his Thessalonian Converts*

In Chapter 8 I noted that apocalyptic pervades 1 (and 2) Thessalonians. If Paul's letter(s) to the Thessalonians is (are) at all indicative, then one may conclude that his preaching in Thessalonica was also thoroughly apocalyptic. In fact, some scholars have suggested a portion of Paul's proclamation among the Thessalonians has been preserved in 1 Thess. 1.9b-10.[12] In these verses Paul recalls 'how [the Thessalonians] turned to God from idols, to serve a living and true God, and to wait for his Son from heaven, whom he raised from the dead, Jesus who delivers us from the wrath to come'. If these verses do in fact encapsulate a part of Paul's original preaching, then we have unequivocal evidence that the Thessalonian Christians embraced an apocalyptically laden gospel. But even if 1.9b-10 does not mirror precisely Paul's kerygma in Thessalonica, the concepts communicated in these verses were likely motifs in his gospel proclamation to the Thessalonians. Other kerygmatic statements in the Epistle(s) seem to suggest as much. Because Paul repeatedly refers in 1 Thessalonians to his founding visit (1.5; 2.1, 5, 10, 17; 3.4, 6), the content of his preaching and his converts' receptive response (1.5, 9; 2.1-2, 9-12; 3.3-4; 4.1-2, 11; 5.2; cf. 2 Thess. 2.15; 3.6), one can reconstruct with a degree of certainty the content of Paul's original instruction.[13]

Reading between the lines, then, Paul's original message to the Thessalonians may have approximated that which follows.[14] The Lord Jesus

12. On these verses as a pre-Pauline formula which Paul used in his mission among the Thessalonians, see Best, *Thessalonians*, pp. 85-87. For arguments against this position, see, e.g., Johannes Munck, '1 Thess i.9-10 and the Missionary Preaching of Paul: Textual Exegesis and Hermeneutic Reflections', *NTS* 9 (1962-63), pp. 95-110, and Wanamaker, *Thessalonians*, pp. 85-89. For the view that 1.9b-10 has similarities with Hellenistic Jewish missionary propaganda but is not a pre-Pauline formula as such, see Traugott Holtz, '"Euer Glaube an Gott": Zu Form und Inhalt von 1 Thess 1,9f', in Rudolf Schnackenburg, Joseph Ernst and Joachim Wanke (eds.), *Die Kirche des Anfangs: Festschrift für Heinz Schürmann* (Freiburg: Herder, 1978), pp. 459-88, and Richard, *Thessalonians*, p. 75.

13. Cf. Barclay, 'Conflict in Thessalonica', p. 516.

14. On the appropriateness of and controls for reading between the lines of a text, see A.J.M. Wedderburn, *The Reasons for Romans* (Minneapolis: Fortress Press, 1991), p. 67. He maintains that while such an enterprise is risky, it is necessary nonetheless. When reading between the lines, Wedderburn suggests the following safeguards: (1) 'what is read between the lines must not contradict what is pal-

Christ died and rose again (4.14) and is soon to return from heaven to earth (4.17) with the holy ones (3.13; cf. 2 Thess. 1.7). Upon his return, Christ will rescue the elect (1.4), that is, those who turn from idols and believe in the one true God and his Son, Jesus (1.9-10). Furthermore, at the parousia, which Paul apparently thought and taught was imminent (e.g. 4.15; cf. 1 Cor. 7.29; Rom. 13.11),[15] the wrath of God will fall on the children of darkness, that is, those who reject Jesus and oppose the gospel (2.16; 5.9; cf. 2 Thess. 1.8-9). Even though currently believers should expect to suffer for the(ir) faith (3.4), in heaven God will grant them rest from their affliction and give to them salvation (5.8; cf. 2 Thess. 1.7). Until the Day of the Lord, however, believers must live as children of light (5.5-8) by discerning and doing that which is good and pure (5.21-22). As those taught by God (4.9) and guided by the Spirit (5.19-20), they must: avoid sexual immorality (4.1-8), love and support one another in the Lord (4.9-10; 5.14), work diligently (4.11; cf. 2 Thess. 3.6-13), await eagerly the parousia (5.6; cf. 2 Thess. 2.1-12), respect spiritual authority (5.12-13) and resist the temptation to retaliate against those who oppose them (4.11-12; 5.15; cf. 2 Thess. 1.5-6).

From all indications, the Thessalonians eagerly embraced Paul's apocalyptic gospel.[16] In fact, some members of the congregation may have

pably set forth in the lines'; (2) what is read between the lines 'will become more plausible the better it helps to explain the connections between the ideas actually expressed in the text'.

15. Christopher L. Mearns ('Early Eschatological Development in Paul: The Evidence of I and II Thessalonians', *NTS* 27 [1980–81], pp. 137-57) contends that Paul did not think or teach that the eschaton was imminent while in Thessalonica. Mearns maintains that Paul adopted this perspective between leaving the city and writing 1 Thess. Mearns's novel proposal notwithstanding, Paul presumes in 1 Thess. that his readers hold to a futuristic eschatology (1.9-10; 5.1-2). For further refutation of Mearns's position, see pp. 280-81 n. 46 below.

16. We are left to infer what ideological and experiential factors prompted the Thessalonian Christians to respond positively to Paul's apocalyptic gospel. Meeks (*First Urban Christians*, p. 184) has suggested that Pauline Christians were in some sense dissatisfied with their lives prior to conversion (cf. Wanamaker, *Thessalonians*, p. 114). His 'status inconsistency' theory, however, has not convinced all. See, e.g., Barclay ('Conflict in Thessalonica', p. 520) who contends that 'it is doubtful that social or economic factors could ever provide a sufficient explanation [for conversion]'. Cf. de Vos, *Church and Community Conflicts*, p. 169. Jewett (*Thessalonian Correspondence*, pp. 131-32) surmises that Paul's gospel was readily received by the Thessalonians because it contained striking similarities to the Cabiric cult from which, according to Jewett, Paul's converts had come. Jewett's proposal,

become more apocalyptic than their teacher (5.14; cf. 2 Thess. 3.6-13)! As suggested in Chapter 2 (pp. 59-60), one of Paul's purposes for writing 2 Thessalonians was to quell the millenarian obsession of some of his converts. While it is probable that there were various degrees of enthusiasm among the Thessalonian Christians with regard to the parousia, it is clear that the gospel which they received from Paul was inextricably linked to an apocalyptic ideology.[17] We now turn to observe how the Thessalonians' reception of Pauline apocalyptic impacted both their interaction with non-Christians and their formation as a congregation.

In their important work, *The Social Construction of Reality*, Peter L. Berger and Thomas Luckmann posit that people inherit from their particular cultural context a symbolic universe or way of viewing reality.[18] Furthermore, Berger and Luckmann maintain that conflict may occur when the symbolic universe of the status quo is called into question.[19]

which as Barclay notes ('Conflict in Thessalonica', p. 519) presupposes far too much about the Cabiric cult and the economic plight of Paul's converts, also fails to convince.

Howard Clark Kee ('Pauline Eschatology: Relationships with Apocalyptic and Stoic Thought', in Erich Grässer and Otto Merk [eds.], *Glaube and Eschatologie: Festschrift für Werner Georg Kümmel zum 80. Geburtstag* [Tübingen: J.C.B. Mohr (Paul Siebeck), 1985] contends that there are elements of apocalyptic in Stoic thought that correlate remarkably well with Paul's apocalyptic message. Consequently, Kee is convinced that such thought-parallels made the Pauline Gospel intelligible and appealing to Gentiles.

Ramsey MacMullen ('Two Types of Conversion to Early Christianity', *VC* 37 [1983], pp. 174-92]) maintains that the vast majority of Gentile converts to Christianity were drawn to the faith not by words and logic, but by displays of divine power. (In support of his thesis, see Paul's statements in 1 Thess. 1.5; Gal. 3.5; 2 Cor. 12.12; and Rom. 15.19). On how educated Gentiles would have construed miraculous works, see Molly Whittaker, ' "Signs and Wonders": The Pagan Background', *SE* 5 (1968), pp. 155-58.

17. Meeks (*First Urban Christians*, p. 171) writes: 'It is remarkable that the former pagans who formed the Christian congregation in the Macedonian city [of Thessalonica] should have been persuaded that such apocalyptic images were an apt picture of their world and lives. Yet language of this sort is so frequent in Paul's letters that we must suppose that it was intelligible and important to his followers.'

18. See esp. pp. 92-104. Other New Testament interpreters have also employed in their work the sociology of knowledge as conceived by Berger and Luckmann. See, e.g., Esler, *Community and Gospel in Luke–Acts*, pp. 16-23.

19. Berger and Luckmann, *Social Construction of Reality*, p. 119. Coser

The authors suggest that cultures tends to discourage rival versions of reality which oppose the symbolic construct of the majority. They also contend that society seeks to perpetuate the dominant perspective by attaching a deviant label to those who adopt alternative ideologies.[20] Despite societal pressures to conform, however, people still choose to undergo alternation—a radical resocialization process which significantly alters one's symbolic universe.[21]

In the case of the Thessalonian Christians, their conversion to Pauline Christianity involved an ideological shift.[22] The apocalyptic perspective that they inherited from Paul encouraged them to adopt a new view of reality, which involved, among other things, the drawing of boundary lines between themselves and the rest of society. They had become children of light, while others remained in darkness (5.4-8); they were 'beloved and chosen by God' (1.4) as opposed to 'pagans who [did] not know God' (4.6); they were insiders, others were outsiders (4.12); and they were going to be saved (5.9), whereas others were going to be destroyed (5.3). As observed in Chapter 8 (pp. 196-97), Paul's propensity is to think dualistically and to view people in binary categories.[23] It stands to reason that he instructed and encouraged his Thessalonian converts to organize their thought-worlds likewise.

Interestingly, the opposition experienced by the Thessalonian Christians would have strengthened their apocalyptic perspective. Having been previously instructed by Paul that they would suffer affliction (3.3b-4),[24] they viewed conflicts with Satan (2.18; 3.5) and those

---

(*Functions of Social Conflict*, pp. 111-19) maintains that intergroup conflict on ideological issues is often intense.

20. Berger and Luckmann, *Social Construction of Reality*, p. 122. For a fuller discussion on the labeling perspective of deviance, see pp. 94-95 above.

21. Berger and Luckmann, *Social Construction of Reality*, pp. 157-59.

22. For an insightful study of conversion among Paul's Gentile congregations, see Segal, *Paul the Convert*, pp. 150-83. On the Thessalonian congregation in particular, see pp. 161-66. See also, Meeks, *First Urban Christians*, pp. 174-75.

23. To illustrate further, 1 Thess. 1.9 indicates that in Paul's thinking a person is either an idolater or a worshipper of God (cf. Rom 1.18-32). Cf. 2 Thess. 3.15 where one is either an enemy or a brother.

24. Meeks ('Social Functions of Apocalyptic Language', p. 692) suggests that instruction on suffering was part of the 'catechism' in Pauline mission areas. David Hill ('On Baptism and Suffering in 1 Peter', *NovT* 18 [1976], pp. 181-89 [183]) maintains that instruction on the inevitability of suffering 'formed part of the parenetic tradition of the primitive Church'.

ensnared by him as inevitable. When the inevitable occurred, therefore, it served to confirm their inherited ideology and to reinforce the boundaries between the Christians and the rest of society.[25]

b. *The Offensiveness of Social Exclusiveness*
The Thessalonian Christians' new view of reality did not occur in an ideological vacuum. Their symbolic (re)constructions had practical implications in everyday life. Conversion to Pauline Christianity appears to have significantly altered the Thessalonian believers' social interaction with non-Christians. In support of this statement, it is important to observe that Paul applauds his converts' ethical behavior among the 'pagans' who do not know God (4.1, 5).[26] The forceful, Jewish-oriented ethical language that Paul employs in his instruction regarding ἁγιασμός ('holiness') is meant to remind his converts of the perils of πορνεία ('immorality') and to reiterate that ἀκαθαρσία ('uncleanness') is not acceptable among those to whom God has given his Holy Spirit. That is to say, Paul's purpose in this pericope (i.e. 4.1-8) appears to be preventative, not corrective.[27] In fact, the affirmative tone of the letter suggests that Paul is guardedly optimistic that his converts will continue to live in the light and not revert to a nocturnal lifestyle (3.6-13; 5.4-11; cf. Rom. 13.11-14; Eph. 5.6-14). He is pleased that the assembly is loving, encouraging and building up one another and admonishes them 'to do so more and more' (περισσεύειν μᾶλλον, 4.10; cf. 5.11). Paul's affirmation of his converts and their care for one another suggests that

25. On the dialectical pattern of the Thessalonian Christians' conflict, see esp. Barclay, 'Conflict in Thessalonica', pp. 516-20, and Meeks, 'Social Functions of Apocalyptic Language', p. 692.

26. So rightly, e.g., O. Larry Yarbrough, *Not Like the Gentiles: Marriage Rules in the Letters of Paul* (SBLDS, 80; Atlanta: Scholars Press, 1985), p. 66, and de Vos, *Church and Community Conflicts*, p. 168. Contra Jewett (*Thessalonian Correspondence*, pp. 105-106) who maintains that the Pauline sexual ethic is being challenged by the ἄτακτοι.

27. Neil (*Thessalonians*, p. 77) rightly notes that 'the advice given here is prophylactic'. On this passage, see further George P. Carras, 'Jewish Ethics and Gentile Converts: Remarks on 1 Thes 4,3-8', in Collins (ed.), *The Thessalonian Correspondence*, pp. 306-15. The suggestion that Paul is seeking in this passage to address the problem of sexual misconduct within the church is not necessary. *Pace*, e.g., Best, *Thessalonians*, p. 166; Marshall, *Thessalonians*, p. 111; and Wanamaker, *Thessalonians*, p. 191.

the Christians were spurning their previous social networks. Furthermore, his commands for the church 'to aspire to live quietly' and 'to mind [its] own affairs' (4.11) would have encouraged additional distance between believers and outsiders, thereby reinforcing the boundaries between the two groups.[28]

It seems plausible, therefore, to aver that the Thessalonian Christians had withdrawn from participating in most all socio-religious activities as a result of their conversion and subsequent internalization of Paul's apocalyptic instruction. Although Paul would have certainly approved of his converts' guarded social interaction with non-Christians (cf., e.g., 1 Cor. 5.9-13; 6.1-6; 2 Cor. 6.14–7.1), the believers' fellow Gentiles would (understandably) have felt snubbed by such seemingly snobbish behavior. 1 Peter 4.4 reports that Petrine Christians had stopped participating in routine social activities (referred to by the writer as 'excesses of reckless living' [τῆς ἀσωτίας ἀνάχυσιν]), and unbelievers responded to their social withdrawal with astonishment and slander (ἐν ᾧ ξενίζονται μὴ συντρεχόντων ὑμῶν...βλασφημοῦντες). In an effort to be holy (see, e.g., 1 Thess. 4.3-4, 7; 5.23; 1 Pet. 1.14-16; 2.9; 3.5), Pauline and Petrine believers altered their socio-religious activities and networks. Outsiders would not have comprehended or appreciated the Christians' sectarian stance.[29] In fact, one classical historian contends that the early Christians' social exclusiveness was 'the chief cause of ["pagan"] suspicion, dislike, and readiness to persecute'.[30]

28. So similarly, deSilva, ' "Worthy of his Kingdom" ', pp. 64-73, and de Vos, *Church and Community Conflicts*, pp. 173-75.

29. Ramsey MacMullen, *Paganism in the Roman Empire* (New Haven: Yale University Press, 1981), p. 19. Stephen Benko (*Pagan Rome and the Early Christians* [London: Batsford, 1984], p. 47) remarks, 'The Christians' withdrawal from many daily activities of pagan life...[was] held against them as it alienated them from society.' Benko further notes that Celsus suggested 'if everybody acted the way the Christians did, the empire would fall apart' (Origen, *Contra Cels.* 8.48).

30. Ramsey MacMullen, *Christianizing the Roman Empire (A.D. 100–400)* (New Haven: Yale University Press, 1984), p. 19. J.N.D. Kelly (*The Epistles of Peter and of Jude* [BNTC; Peabody, MA: Hendrickson, 1969], p. 171) suggests that it was the Christians' reluctance 'to participate in the routine contemporary life, particularly conventionally accepted amusements, civic ceremonies, and any function involving contact with idolatry or what they considered immorality, that caused them to be hated, despised and themselves suspected of illicit practices'. Cf. de Vos, 'Graeco-Roman Responses', and Barclay, 'Conflict in Thessalonica', p. 515.

In Chapter 7 (see pp. 153-64) we observed that ancient Jews also tended toward social exclusiveness. In fact, in some regards (e.g. dietary restrictions and circumcision) the vast majority of Jews were less socially integrated than Paul (and Pauline Christians).[31] The refusal of most Jews to assimilate culturally often resulted in the charge of misanthropy. For example, Diodorus (mid first century BCE) remarks that the Jews 'made the hatred of humanity [τὸ μῖσος τὸ πρὸς τοὺς ἀνθρώπους] into a tradition' (34.1.2). Similarly, Tacitus comments that the Jews 'are extremely loyal toward one another, and always ready to show compassion, but toward every other people they feel only hate and enmity' ('apud ipsos fides obstinata, misericordia in promptu, sed adversus omnis alios hostile odium', *Hist.* 5.5). The sources suggest that Jewish and Christian exclusivity was derided and disdained by many Greeks and Romans.[32]

Although the Thessalonian believers had less than cordial relations with outsiders, it would be wrong to conclude that all of Paul's churches experienced conflict with non-Christians. It would be equally erroneous to surmise that all of Paul's congregations were exclusive in their social affiliations. Based upon Paul's extant Epistles to the Corinthians, believers in Corinth seemingly had harmonious relations with unbelievers. In contrast to the believers in Thessalonica, some of the (more well-to-do) Corinthian Christians appear to have been fully integrated and actively involved in society. The willingness of some within the church to take their personal grievances to civil law courts (1 Cor. 6.1-6), to engage in extra-marital sexual relations (6.12-20; cf. 5.1-5) and to participate in temple meals (10.14-22) indicates as much. Furthermore, non-Christians in the community were seemingly welcomed at the church's worship gatherings (14.24-25). Although Paul maintains that some within the Corinthian church had been afflicted (11.30-32), this affliction was not caused by non-Christians.[33]

31. On the anomalous character of Paul's rather high assimilation, but comparatively low acculturation and accommodation vis-à-vis Diaspora Judaism, see Barclay, 'Paul among Diaspora Jews'.

32. On Jewish relations with Greeks and Romans, see, among others, de Vos, *Church and Community Conflicts*, pp. 62-84.

33. On the different relational dynamics between Christians and non-Christians in Thessalonica and Corinth respectively, see Barclay, 'Thessalonica and Corinth'. Cf. de Vos, *Church and Community Conflicts*, pp. 206-14.

c. *Non-Christian Suspicion of Christians*

Not all Pauline congregations experienced strained social relations, however, this was clearly the case in Thessalonica. As a result of the church's exclusivity, outsiders may have perceived the assembly as a secretive group trying to conceal illicit or immoral practices. Non-Christians could have gained such an impression from the believers assembling in private quarters for worship, whether a *villa* or an *insula* (5.27; cf. Acts 17.5-6).[34] Furthermore, if unbelievers were aware that the church consistently, if not daily, shared meals together, then this might have heightened their suspicion of the Christians.[35] Additionally, if Paul's female and male converts exchanged the 'holy kiss' publicly (5.26), as William Klassen has argued,[36] then outsiders could have construed this intimate exchange as some kind of coded, if not perverted, sign.

Caecilius, a critic of Christianity of whom we know through Minucius Felix (fl. 200–240), made much of Christian secrecy. He depicts Christians as 'a secret tribe that shuns the light, silent in public, but talkative in private...' (*Oct.* 8.4). In his invective against Christians he also remarks, 'They recognize one another by secret signs and marks...' (9.2). Caecilius's perception of Christians as a secretive tribe led him to be suspicious of them. He contends, '[S]uspicions naturally attach to their secret and nocturnal rites' (9.4). He deduces, therefore, that the charges leveled against the Christians must be true due to 'the secrecy of this depraved religion' ('pravae religionis obscuritas', 10.1). Caecilius wonders, 'Why do [Christians] make such efforts to obscure and conceal whatever is the object of their worship, when things honor-

---

34. Acts 17.5 implies that at least some of the church met in Jason's home. Robert Jewett ('Tenement Churches and Communal Meals in the Early Church: The Implications of a Form-Critical Analysis of 2 Thessalonians 3:10' *BR* 38 [1993], pp. 24-32) has argued that the Thessalonian church met in *insula*-shops like some of the early Christian communities in Rome seemingly did.

35. Jewett ('Tenement Churches') contends that the Thessalonian church shared communal meals together daily. We know that the Corinthian assembly ate together (see 1 Cor. 11.17-34), although it is not possible to discern how frequently. (On 1 Cor. 11.17-34, see esp. the work of Gerd Theissen, *The Social Setting of Pauline Christianity: Essays on Corinth* [ed. and trans. John H. Schütz; Edinburgh: T. & T. Clark, 1982], pp. 145-74). Pliny (*Ep.* 10.96) reports that Bithynian Christians were in the habit of sharing a weekly meal.

36. William Klassen, 'The Sacred Kiss in the New Testament: An Example of Social Boundary Lines', *NTS* 39 (1993), pp. 122-35.

able always rejoice in publicity, while guilt loves secrecy?' (10.1).[37]

d. *Roman Distrust of Foreign Religions*
On the whole, Romans were suspicious of foreign cults. And when they were given reason to think that outside groups threatened the stability of Roman society by engaging in anti-social acts, they would move swiftly and forcefully against them.[38] For example, Livy (59 BCE–12 CE) recounts how for purposes of state security the Roman senate suppressed a feared Bacchanalian conspiracy (39.8-19). Additionally, Valerius Maximus reports that in 139 BCE Chaldeans (astrologers) and Jews were expelled from Rome by Cornelius Hispalus for infecting the Romans with foreign customs (1.3.3). In a later period, the Julio-Claudians took a strong stand against the Druids due to reportedly degrading rites (Pliny, *HN* 29.54; 30.13; Suetonius, *Claud.* 25.5), and Tiberius demolished the Temple of Isis in Rome because of a case of gross sexual immorality in 19 CE (Josephus, *Ant.* 18.65-80).

Even when there was little 'hard' evidence against foreign cults, the Roman suspicion of these groups was great. Therefore, when those in positions of political authority came to believe that these outsiders were undermining Roman customs, they took swift action against these suspect strangers.[39] The Romans' prevalent distrust of foreign religions appears to be one of the primary reasons that Nero's charge against the Roman Christians stuck. Although Tacitus apparently did not think that Roman Christians started the fire,[40] he clearly believed that they were deserving of the 'exemplary punishment' which they received at Nero's behest (*Ann.* 15.44). Tacitus and his contemporaries Pliny and Suetonius regarded Christianity as a deplorable 'superstition' (Tacitus, *Ann.*

37. De Vos ('Graeco-Roman Responses') notes: '[A]ccusations of magic and conspiracy were traditionally linked in Graeco-Roman thought with secret nocturnal rites. Since the Christians practiced the latter it would simply have been assumed that they practiced the former.'

38. See MacMullen, *Enemies of the Roman Order*.

39. E.A. Judge ('Judaism and the Rise of Christianity: A Roman Perspective', *TynBul* 45 [1994], pp. 355-68 [360]) suggests that since most Romans did not know what the Christians did at their meetings they would have concluded the Christians were engaged in criminal behavior.

40. So A.N. Sherwin-White, 'The Early Persecutions and the Roman Law Again', *JTS* NS 3 (1952), pp. 201-13 (208), and W.H.C. Frend, 'Persecutions: Some Links between Judaism and the Early Church', *JEH* 9 (1958), pp. 141-58 (153 n. 6). Cf. Benko, *Pagan Rome and the Early Christians*, p. 16.

15.44; Pliny, *Ep.* 10.96; Suetonius, *Ner.* 16.2). If one could ask Tacitus why he thought Roman Christians deserved Nero's wrath, he would probably reply because they were haters of humanity ('odio humani generis', *Ann.* 15.44). Tacitus's charge of misanthropy against Christians was likely prompted by his knowledge of their exclusive, secretive ways.[41]

In his Harvard ThD dissertation 'Thessalonicans Honor Romans', Holland Lee Hendrix highlights ancient Thessalonica's ongoing concern for good relations with Rome. Given the sensitivity of the citizenry to this all-important relationship, is it possible that some Thessalonians construed the Christians as an anti-Roman association and opposed them based upon such a perception? I will take up this question later in this chapter when I explore the possibility that Paul and the Thessalonian assembly were judged by some outsiders as politically subversive.

e. *Common Accusations against the Christians*
'Pagan' suspicion of and disdain for the Christians' exclusive and secretive ways led some detractors of the faith to circulate rumors about and to lodge accusations against the Christians.[42] In addition to atheism, a charge which I will address later, early believers were accused of, among other things, cannibalism and sexual libertinism.[43] Caecilius gives a revolting description of what he claims to be a Christian initiation. He reports that an infant is beaten to death by a neophyte, then its blood is drunk and its body is eaten (*Oct.* 9.5). Octavius and other Christian apologists would dismiss such a charge as nonsense (*Oct.* 31.1-2; and, e.g., Athenagoras, *Leg. pro Christ.* 35-36).[44]

More relevant to this study is the common (later) perception among non-Christian critics of Christianity that believers engaged in sexually

41. Tacitus appears to have been relatively well informed about Christian origins. One may conclude that he knew something about their practices as well.
42. Benko (*Pagan Rome and the Early Christians*, p. 59) suggests, 'The Romans believed that when Christians claimed exclusive possession of divine knowledge, they were capable of anything. This attitude encouraged the Romans to give credence to the most outrageous rumors about Christians.'
43. On the charges of sexual immorality and cannibalism, see the discussion in Benko, *Pagan Rome and the Early Christians*, pp. 54-78. On cannibalism, consult McGowan, 'Eating People'.
44. Origen (*Contra Cels.* 6.40) remarks, 'These allegations [of cannibalism] are now condemned even by the multitude and by people entirely alien to our religion as being a false slander against the Christians' (trans. Chadwick).

immoral activity. For example, in *Metamorphoses* Apuleius depicts the baker's wife, who is most likely a Christian, as 'cruel and perverse, crazy for men and wine, headstrong and obstinate, grasping in her mean thefts and a spendthrift in her loathsome extravagances, an enemy of fidelity and a foe to chastity' (9.14).[45] Interestingly, Paul instructs his converts in 1 Thessalonians that it is the will of God that they 'abstain from immorality' (ἀπέχεσθαι ὑμᾶς ἀπὸ τῆς πορνείας, 4.3), for 'God has not called [believers] for uncleanness [ἀκαθαρσίᾳ], but in holiness [ἁγιασμῷ]' (4.7; cf. 2.3, where Paul maintains that his appeal was not made in error or uncleanness [ἀκαθαρσίας]).

Karl P. Donfried has suggested that Paul stresses the importance of sexual purity so as 'to distinguish the behaviour of the Thessalonian Christians from that of their former heathen and pagan life which is still alive in the various cults of the city'.[46] Furthermore, Donfried and others have maintained that the cults of Dionysus and Cabirus were particularly influential in Thessalonica during Paul's time and that these groups had strong phallic and sexual symbolism.[47] If the cults of Dionysus and Cabirus were as important and as sexually oriented as it appears, then these groups may have been subject to rumors and accusations from outsiders.[48] Paul did not want the church to be accused of, much less be guilty of, sexual immorality.

45. Caecilius contends that Christians 'fall in love almost before they are acquainted; everywhere they introduce a kind of religion of lust, a promiscuous "brotherhood" and "sisterhood" by which ordinary fornication, under cover of a hallowed name, is converted to incest' (*Oct.* 9.2).

46. Donfried, 'Cults of Thessalonica', p. 342.

47. Donfried, 'Cults of Thessalonica', p. 342. See also Charles Edson, 'Macedonia. II. State Cults in Thessalonica', *HSCP* 51 (1940), pp. 127-36, and 'Macedonia. III. Cults of Thessalonica', *HTR* 41 (1948), pp. 153-204; Rex E. Witt, 'The Egyptian Cults in Ancient Macedonia', in Basil Laourdas and Ch. Makaronas (eds.), *Ancient Macedonia* (Thessaloniki: Institute for Balkan Studies, 1970), pp. 324-33; Robert M. Evans, *Eschatology and Ethics: A Study of Thessalonica and Paul's Letters to the Thessalonians* (Princeton, NJ: McMahon Printing, 1968), pp. 63-86; and Jewett, *Thessalonian Correspondence*, pp. 113-32. But note Koester's ('Apocalyptic Schemata of 2 Thessalonians', pp. 442-45) strong words of warning to interpreters about going beyond the evidence in an attempt to comment more fully on the cultic life in ancient Thessalonica and his scathing critique of Jewett for doing so.

48. On the conflict between the cult of Dionysus and Greek society, see Euripides, *Bacc.* 200; 215; 233; 260; 352; 1325. See also the Roman ban on this mystery cult as recorded by Livy 39.8-19.

Ironically, the church's practice of greeting one another with a holy kiss' (1 Thess. 5.26) might have led outsiders to infer that the Christians were sexually involved with one another. If the kiss was a lip to lip encounter[49] and was exchanged publicly as well as liturgically,[50] then believers would have been particularly vulnerable to such charges. Klassen suggests that by exchanging the sacred kiss the Christians 'risked the slander of those who were outside looking in...'[51] Similarly, Lillian Portefaix thinks 'the Christian practice of greeting sisters and brothers with a holy kiss must have contributed greatly to the bad name of Christians and have affected particularly the wife of a "mixed marriage" '.[52] The early church writers found charges of sexual licentiousness much more difficult to deflect than other accusations. This is most likely due to the fact that some Christians did engage in such practices. Intriguingly, in some cases the sacred kiss may have encouraged and culminated in sexual activity (see, e.g., Clement of Alexandria, *Paedag.* 3.11-12).

Nevertheless, Christians would not necessarily have had to engage in illicit, immoral activities to have been accused of them. In a forthcoming article entitled 'Popular Graeco-Roman Responses to Christianity', Craig S. de Vos argues that because non-Christians considered believers to be anti-social atheists, they would have simply assumed that Christians were guilty of deviant activity. De Vos's understanding of Greco-Roman accusations against Christians as 'stereotypic charges levelled against those who were perceived to threaten society' makes good sense of the evidence to hand and usefully employs the interactionist perspective on deviance (see pp. 94-98 above).

It seems as though not a few early believers were regarded and responded to as dangerously deviant. Greek and Roman unbelievers who desired to affirm community norms and to protect group boundaries would have conceived of and characterized Christians as misfits.

49. See Benko, *Pagan Rome and the Early Christians*, p. 83.
50. Even if believers only exchanged the holy kiss in their private meetings, word of such a custom would have eventually spread to the non-Christian community. Additionally, it should be noted that privacy was not easily had in Greco-Roman cities. See, e.g., de Vos, *Church and Community Conflicts*, pp. 28-42.
51. Klassen, 'Sacred Kiss', p. 133.
52. Portefaix, *Sisters Rejoice*, pp. 189-90. Tertullian reports that a non-Christian husband would not allow a believing wife to exchange a kiss with a Christian brother (*Ad Uxor.* 2.4).

Once stigmatized as deviant, believers would have been particular susceptible to (groundless) accusations and in most instances would have been unable to alter popular, if incorrect, public perceptions. What the Christians actually did, however, was not as important to unbelieving outsiders as what they were thought to be capable of doing and were said to have done.

f. *Active Christian Proselytism?*

Even though the Thessalonian congregation tended toward separatism, was probably perceived as stand-offish and was presumably subject to non-Christian suspicion and accusations, 1 Thess. 4.11-12 indicates that neither Paul nor his converts were wholly exclusive in their perspective and praxis. In 4.11-12 Paul exhorts the church 'to aspire to live quietly, to mind your own affairs, and to work with your hands, as we charged you; so that you may behave properly toward outsiders, and be dependent on nobody'. This passage suggests that there was still some interaction between Christians and non-Christians, as do 3.13 and 5.15 where Paul encourages the congregation to love and to do good to all people. But why is it necessary for Paul to remind the assembly to live quietly, to mind their own affairs and to work with their hands? And how do these injunctions relate to Paul's concern that the Christians behave properly toward those outside and be dependent on no person?

Many interpreters have maintained that Paul is seeking in 4.11-12 to counter an eschatological extremism among his converts which had led them to abandon everyday activities.[53] Other commentators have contended that Paul is addressing those poorer church members who were depending on wealthier believers to provide for them.[54] Yet both of these interpretations fail to account adequately for Paul's instruction 'to

53. E.g. Frame, *Thessalonians*, p. 159; Bicknell, *Thessalonians*, p. 41; Neil, *Thessalonians*, p. 86; Rigaux, *Thessaloniciens*, pp. 519-21; Best, *Thessalonians*, pp. 175-77; and Bruce, *Thessalonians*, p. 91.

54. Wanamaker, *Thessalonians*, p. 163; Williams, *Thessalonians*, pp. 149-50; and Ronald Russell, 'The Idle in 2 Thess. 3:6-12: An Eschatological or a Social Problem?', *NTS* 34 (1988), pp. 105-19. Bruce W. Winter (*Seek the Welfare of the City: Christians as Benefactors and Citizens* [FCGRW; Grand Rapids: Eerdmans; Carlisle: Paternoster Press, 1994], pp. 42-60) thinks that Paul is prohibiting the Thessalonian Christians from living the life of a client in 1 Thess. 4.11-12 and 2 Thess. 3.6-13. If this were indeed the case, then one is left to wonder why Paul did offer more direct and explicit instruction to patrons and their clients.

live quietly' and 'to mind your own affairs'.[55] Furthermore, both explanations give insufficient attention to Paul's concern that his converts
'behave properly toward outsiders'. Although Ronald Hock's theory
that Paul is advocating political quietism in 4.11-12 avoids these particular pitfalls,[56] it is far from clear how involved Paul's converts would
have been in the political affairs of the city. If the Thessalonian church
was comprised primarily of the urban poor, as Hock himself seems to
think, then it does not seem likely that Paul's converts would have
spent 'their time in the market place talking politics'.[57] Furthermore,
given the presumed proximity of the parousia (4.15; cf., e.g., 1 Cor.
7.26-31) and the 'other-worldly' mentality of Paul and the church in
Thessalonica (cf. 1 Cor. 3.19; 6.2; 2 Cor. 6.14-7.1; 10.1-3; Rom. 13.1-7,
11-14; cf. also Jn 15.19; 18.36; 1 Jn 2.15; 5.4), it strikes me as unlikely
that the Thessalonian Christians, even the ones who were citizens and
thereby members of the city's *demos*, would have been overly active in
the political process.[58]

What, then, is the most compelling explanation for the Pauline
injunctions in 4.11 and the desired results of such commands in 4.12? I
am inclined to concur with those scholars who argue that Paul is
addressing in 4.11-12 (and perhaps in 5.14 and 2 Thess. 3.6-13) those
within the congregation who were neglecting their daily responsibilities
in order to propagate the gospel.[59] John M.G. Barclay contends that in
4.11-12 Paul is rebuking 'those who interfere all too readily in the busi-

55. Barclay, 'Conflict in Thessalonica', pp. 521-22.

56. Ronald F. Hock, *The Social Context of Paul's Ministry: Tentmaking and
Apostleship* (Philadelphia: Fortress Press, 1980), pp. 46-47. Cf. Dobschütz, *Thessalonicherbriefe*, p. 180, and de Vos, *Church and Community Conflicts*, pp. 160-70.

57. Marshall, *Thessalonians*, 116. Cf. Martin (*Thessalonians*, 137): 'Most
people in the church were not wealthy enough to involve themselves in public life
even if they had been so inclined.' So also, Best, *Thessalonians*, p. 175.

58. Contrast de Vos (*Church and Community Conflicts*, p. 175) who thinks that
the Thessalonian congregation was comprised exclusively of citizens from the arti-
san class and thereby understands 4.11-12 as Paul's instruction to his politically
provocative and disruptive converts 'to renounce their citizenship and become like
metics'.

On the separatist outlook which pervades Pauline and Johannine literature, see
the insightful discussion of H. Richard Niebuhr, *Christ and Culture* (New York:
Harper & Row, 1951), pp. 46-48, 159-67.

59. See esp. Barclay, 'Conflict in Thessalonica', pp. 520-25. Cf. Malherbe, *Paul
and the Thessalonians*, pp. 99-101.

ness of nonbelievers and behave disgracefully towards them'.[60] Furthermore, Barclay posits that Paul is encouraging those Christians who are actively promoting the gospel not to provoke outsiders needlessly (e.g. by publicly denouncing unbelievers' gods, warning non-Christians of their impending doom and perhaps even vandalizing their icons) and not to place undue economic pressure on the church to support their full-time evangelistic activity.[61] Drawing upon parallels from Lucian and Dio Chrysostom, Abraham J. Malherbe has argued that Paul is counseling his converts in 4.11-12 to be different than those Cynic converts who abandoned their occupations for meddlesome evangelism.[62] For the good of the gospel and the congregation, Paul did not want his converts to be meddlers in others' affairs (4.11b), mere busybodies (περιεργαζομένοι) as 2 Thess. 3.11 puts it. Similarly, Petrine Christians are encouraged not to interfere in others' business and thereby bring unnecessary hardship upon themselves (μὴ γὰρ τις ὑμῶν πασχέτω...ὡς ἀλλοτριεπίσκοπος, 1 Pet. 4.15).[63]

That at least some of the Thessalonian believers were engaged in active evangelism may be further implied by Paul's statement that 'the word of the Lord has sounded forth from you [ἀφ' ὑμῶν... ἐξήχηται] not only in Macedonia and Achaia but in every place your faith in God has become known'.[64] The verb ἐξήχειν is a New Testament *hapax legomenon* which means 'to ring out'.[65] Paul states in 1.8 that the word

60. Barclay, 'Conflict in Thessalonica', p. 522.

61. Barclay, 'Conflict in Thessalonica', pp. 522-23. Barclay notes that Paul may have emphasized his own ministry among the Thessalonians in 1 Thess. 2.1-12 to remind them of the need to follow 'his methods as well as his message' (523).

62. Malherbe, *Paul and the Thessalonians*, pp. 99-101.

63. The meaning of the term ἀλλοτριεπίσκοπος is not entirely clear, but it appears to mean 'mischief-maker' or 'busybody'. See Edward Gordon Selwyn (*The First Epistle of St. Peter* [Grand Rapids: Baker Book House, 2nd edn, 1947]) who suggests that the author is encouraging his readers not to be social nuisances and to avoid engaging in 'tactless attempts to convert neighbours' (225). Kelly (*Epistles of Peter and of Jude*, p. 189) conjectures that the writer may be countering the Christians' 'excessive zeal for making converts', their sowing seeds of 'discord in family or commercial life' and their 'over-eager denunciation of pagan habits'.

64. See James Ware, 'The Thessalonians as a Missionary Congregation: 1 Thessalonians 1,5-8' *ZNW* 83 (1992), pp. 126-31; Bruce, *Thessalonians*, p. 171; Neil, *Thessalonians*, p. 22; Marshall, *Thessalonians*, p. 56. Cf. otherwise, Paul Bowers ('Church and Mission in Paul' *JSNT* 44 [1991], pp. 89-111 [98-99]) who contends that the Thessalonians were not involved in propagating the gospel.

65. *BAGD*, 'ἐξηχέω', p. 276.

of the Lord had actually sounded forth from the congregation, not merely that there had been positive reports about the Thessalonians' reception of the gospel circulating among other Christian assemblies.[66] While Paul does portray the gospel as an active force ringing forth from the assembly, thereby stressing the power of the word of God (1.5; 2.13; cf. Rom. 1.16), it appears that it was the believers themselves who communicated the word of the Lord to others.[67] It takes human instruments to dispense the gospel (Rom. 10.14-16).

Active religious dissemination is not without parallel in ancient Thessalonica. A first-century CE inscription (*IT* 255) which was recovered in the excavations of Thessalonica's Sarapeion states that Sarapis instructed Zenainetos in a dream to return to his hometown (Opus) and to tell his political rival (Eurynomos) to establish the worship of Egyptian deities Sarapis and Isis. Hendrix suggests that this inscription may indicate 'the "metropolitan" character of Thessalonica's Egyptian cult establishment and presents an interesting parallel to the diffusion of early Christianity from the city to which Paul may refer in 1 Thess 1:8'.[68]

Like their founder who 'saw in the outsider a potential insider',[69] some of the church seemingly sought to convert unbelievers by propagating the apocalyptic gospel which they had recently and readily received (2.13). Their proclamation could have included: the declaration that the Lord Jesus Christ who died and rose again would soon return to rescue Christians and to judge non-Christians (1.10; 4.14; 5.9; cf. 2 Thess. 1.5-10; 2.10-12); the denunciation of their former gods as idols (1.9); and the condemnation of their former behavioral patterns (4.5; 5.7). Although the Thessalonians may have been persuaded some, the majority of outsiders likely regarded them to be a nuisance and their message to be nonsense (cf. 1 Cor. 1.23).[70] Aggressive evangelism was a good way to win converts, but it was also a good way to make ene-

---

66. Contra Wanamaker, *Thessalonians*, p. 83. It may be of significance that the prepositional phrase to be taken with ἐξήχειν is ἀφ' ὑμῶν not περὶ ὑμῶν.

67. So Ware, '1 Thessalonians 1,5-8', p. 128.

68. Holland Lee Hendrix, 'Thessalonica', *ABD*, VI, pp. 523-27 (525).

69. Meeks, *First Urban Christians*, p. 107.

70. Barclay ('Conflict in Thessalonica', p. 524) suggests, 'Christians who continually reminded their unconverted spouses or friends of the sudden destruction about to fall on idolaters surely aroused extreme annoyance among those they did not intimidate.'

mies, as Paul knew full well (2.2). The Christians' evangelistic zeal could well have intensified the hostility and antipathy of unbelievers toward the Pauline community.

Scholars disagree as to whether or not ancient Judaism was a missionary religion, or put differently, whether or not Jews engaged in active proselytism.[71] Although I am inclined to think that individual Jews in antiquity actively promoted their religious beliefs,[72] I need not enter into the fray of this complex conversation here.[73] However, it is worth noting that at least in Rome interest in and conversion to Judaism appears to have been rather common.[74] Actual conversion to Judaism would, of course, have required significant interaction between Jews and non-Jews. Whether such interaction is best described as proselytism is a debated issue, as are the reported expulsions of the Jews from Rome for proselytizing activity (see Dio Cassius 57.18.5 [cf. Suetonius, *Tib.* 36; Tacitus, *Ann.* 2.85] on the 19 CE expulsion and Suetonius [*Claud.* 25] on the expulsion in the 40s CE [cf. Dio Cassius 60.6.6]). As we saw earlier in this chapter, however, conversion to Judaism (and probably Jewish proselytism itself) was a subject of scorn by Roman *literati* (e.g. Tacitus, *Hist.* 5.5; Epictetus, *Diss.* 2.9.20; Juvenal, *Sat.* 5.14.96-106; cf. Horace, *Carm.* 1.4.143; Augustine, *De civ. D.* 6.11; Origen, *Contra Cels.* 5.41.4-6).

We know that in Thessalonica conversion to Pauline Christianity was

---

71. E.g. Louis Feldman (*Jew and Gentile*), Gabriele Boccaccini (*Middle Judaism*) and Dieter Georgi (*The Opponents of Paul in Second Corinthians* [Philadelphia: Fortress Press, 1986]) are convinced that Jews in antiquity were engaged in missionary activity, while Scot McKnight (*A Light among the Gentiles: Jewish Missionary Activity in the Second Temple Period* [Minneapolis: Fortress Press, 1991], Shaye Cohen ('Was Judaism in Antiquity a Missionary Religion?', in Menachem Mor [ed.], *Jewish Assimilation and Accommodation: Past Traditions, Current Issues and Future Prospects* [New York: University Press of America, 1992], pp. 14-23) and Martin Goodman (*Mission and Conversion: Proselytizing in the Religious History of the Roman Empire* [Oxford: Clarendon Press, 1994]) are not.

72. Cf. Donaldson, *Paul and the Gentiles*, pp. 54-60, and Talbert, *Reading Acts*, pp. 129-30. In addition to passages cited in the text below, see, e.g., Jon.; *Jos. Asen.*; Josephus, *Ant.* 20.24-42; and Mt. 23.15.

73. For an illuminating survey of Jewish attitudes toward Gentiles and the proselytism thereof in the time of Paul, see Donaldson, *Paul and the Gentiles*, pp. 51-78.

74. Steve Mason, 'Josephus's *Against Apion* as a *Logos Protreptikos*: An Invitation to Judean Philosophy', (unpublished paper).

a source of contention between believers and unbelievers. And I would argue, based on the preceding discussion, that it is possible that the Christians' active if not aggressive promotion of their novel religion created conflict with non-Christians. Aggressive proselytism would have been particularly offensive to those self-respecting Thessalonians who valued and guarded their established socio-religious customs.[75] In fact, some non-Christian Thessalonians may have viewed Paul's converts not only as exclusive and offensive, but also as disruptive and even subversive to the basic institutions of Thessalonian culture.[76]

75. Cf. Barclay ('Conflict in Thessalonica', p. 524): 'The countercultural thrust of the Christian message would hardly be welcomed by those who represented the values of Greco-Roman society.'

76. According to Broom, Bonjean and Broom (*Sociology*, p. 164) an institution is 'an established pattern of norms and values that organizes social life to fulfill social functions'. Like other sociologists, they suggest that there are five basic institutions in modern society: the family, religion, government, education and the economic system. In what follows I will consider the perceived adverse effect of the Thessalonian Christians on the familial, religious and political life of their day. I am aware that the labeling of these particular aspects of social life is a modern phenomenon. Nevertheless, these basic institutions were in existence in antiquity as well, even if they were not conceived in such clear-cut categories.

In the following discussion I will not treat the institutions of education or economics as potential sources of conflict between Christians and non-Christians, although one might do so with interesting results. Extant evidence concerning the negative impact that the Christian presence had on education and economics is sparse. It is interesting to note, however, that some 'pagans' perceived Christianity as an inferior philosophical school (e.g. Galen, *Puls. Diff.* 2.4; 3.3). Pertaining to economics, Luke reports that in Ephesus one Demetrius incited his fellow silversmiths and eventually the entire city to turn against Paul because of the negative impact of the Christian mission on his business, the making of silver shrines of Artemis (Acts 19.23-41). In addition, Pliny reports to Trajan that the spread of Christianity in Bithynia had led to the temples being almost entirely deserted (*Ep.* 10.96). This, too, would have had financial implications. Furthermore, as we will see, the Christians were often blamed for droughts and famine. Such accusations would naturally have been linked to the economy. Although financial demise can certainly lead to conflict, we do not have any evidence that the arrival of Christianity in Thessalonica had any economic impact one way or another. Although Jewett (*Thessalonian Correspondence*, pp. 118-23, 165-68) makes much of the Thessalonian Christians' economic woes, he does not consider the economic effect that Pauline Christianity might have had on the larger economic community in Thessalonica. As indicated above, evidence is simply lacking.

It is fair to say that educational and economic issues might enter into the ensuing

4. *The Thessalonian Christians as Subversive*

a. *To the Family*

In a Greco-Roman context, the family or household (οἶκος) would have been 'the primary social unit'.[77] The household served as 'a chief basis, paradigm and reference point for religious and moral as well as social, political, and economic organization, interaction, and ideology'.[78] Furthermore, for the Greeks and Romans, the home represented a place of harmony, security and identity. To be sure, such lofty ideals were not always realized; nevertheless, 'secular ethicists saw the stability of the city-state as dependent upon responsible management of the household'.[79]

According to Acts, the Christian mission experienced considerable success in converting entire households.[80] The most notable example in Acts is the conversion of the household of the Roman centurion Cornelius at Caesarea (10.1–11.18). Luke also indicates, however, that Paul

discussion. This simply indicates that there is often an overlap in the selected categories. These categories, while not arbitrary, are surely not air-tight compartments. This would have been especially true in antiquity. Family, religion, politics, education and economics all tend to merge at points. Despite an inevitable blurring of the lines, the categories I have chosen are useful for presentation purposes and are therefore retained. I have selected the categories (i.e. the institutions) I believe are most relevant to the conflict situation in Thessalonica.

77. Elliott, *Home for the Homeless*, p. 221. So also P.H. Towner ('Households and Household Codes', *DPL*, pp. 417-19 [417]) who asserts, 'The basic unit of the Greco-Roman society in which Paul lived and ministered was the household (oikos, oikia)'. On the use of οἶκος and οἰκία in ancient Greek literature, see further Craig S. de Vos, 'The Significance of the Change from ΟΙΚΟΣ to ΟΙΚΙΑ in Luke's Account of the Philippian Gaoler (Acts 16.30-4)', *NTS* 41 (1995), pp. 292-96.

78. Elliott, *Home for the Homeless*, p. 213.

79. Towner, 'Households', p. 417. Cicero (*Off.* 1.53-55) saw the household as a microcosm of the state. Wayne A. Meeks ('"Since Then You Would Need to Go out of the World": Group Boundaries in Pauline Christianity', in Thomas J. Ryan [ed.], *Critical History and Biblical Faith* [Villanova, PN: College Theology Society, 1979], pp. 1-23 [9]) suggests, 'One of the most powerful causes for the hostility of the Roman literary classes toward oriental cults, including Judaism and Christianity, was precisely the fear that they would disrupt households and, consequently, undermine the social order.'

80. On the conversion of households in (Luke–)Acts, see the full-length study by David Lertis Matson, *Household Conversion Narratives in Luke–Acts: Pattern and Interpretation* (JSNTSup, 123; Sheffield: Sheffield Academic Press, 1996).

converted Lydia and her household (16.15), the Philippian jailer and his household (16.32-34) and Crispus, a Corinthian synagogue official, and his household (18.8). Paul himself mentions in 1 Corinthians his having won and baptized the household of Stephanas (1.16; 16.15). It may have been a missionary strategy among some sectors of the early church to convert the head of the household thinking that the rest of the household would likely (feel obligated to or be required to) follow suit (cf. Acts 20.20). By converting entire households, Christian missionaries could preserve the unity of the family and add much-needed members to their nascent assemblies.

Although winning households to the faith *in toto* may have been a preferred strategy among early Christian missionaries, this was not always possible to achieve. It is clear that in some instances conversion to Christianity divided families. This occurred in Corinth. In 1 Cor. 7.12-16 Paul advises believing spouses not to divorce their unbelieving mates so that the non-Christian partner might be saved (cf. 1 Cor. 7.27). Christian wives in the congregations addressed by 1 Peter were dealing with a similar relational dilemma. The author of the letter exhorts Christian wives to 'be submissive to [their non-Christian] husbands, so that some [non-Christian husbands] may be won without a word by the behavior of their wives' (3.1). 1 Peter also exhorts Christian slaves to be submissive to their unbelieving masters (2.18-25).[81] Such texts suggest that conversion to Christianity of some household members and not of others could foster considerable tension in domestic relations.[82] Moreover, it is clear that at some times and in some places conversion to Christianity did create acute conflict among family members. The Lukan Jesus remarks:

---

81. For an insightful study on domestic relations in 1 Pet. see Balch, *Let Wives Be Submissive*. Balch explains the Christian suffering which is repeatedly mentioned in 1 Pet. (2.18-25; 3.13-17; 4.1-5, 12-19; 5.9-11) in the following way: '[C]ertain slaves and wives converted to Christianity; therefore, persons in Roman society reacted by accusing them of being immoral, perhaps seditious, and certainly insubordinate. The author of 1 Peter directed the Aristotelian household duty code to this tense situation' (p. 95). On the tensions between Christian wives and their non-Christian husbands, see further, Portefaix, *Sisters Rejoice*, pp. 192-99.

82. On the familial disruption created by conversion to the Christian faith as evidenced in the Gospels of Mk and Mt., see Stephen C. Barton, *Discipleship and Family Ties in Mark and Matthew* (SNTSMS, 80; Cambridge: Cambridge University Press, 1994). Note, e.g., Mk 3.31-35 and Mt. 10.34-39; 12.46-50. See also Lk. 8.19-21; 9.59-60; 12.49-53; 14.26-27; 18.28-30.

Do you think that I have come to give peace on earth? No, I tell you, but rather division; for henceforth in one house there will be five divided, three against two and two against three; they will be divided, father against son and son against father, mother against daughter and daughter against mother, mother-in-law against her daughter-in-law and daughter-in-law against her mother-in-law (12.49-51//Mt. 10.34-39; cf. Lk. 8.21).

Early critics of Christianity observed the divisive effect that the Christian movement had on some households, and they were critical of such. Celsus is convinced the Christianity divides families. He claims that illiterate yokels and stupid women (i.e. Christians) deceptively buttonhole impressionable children and teach them to disobey their fathers and tutors (Origen, *Contra Cel.* 3.55). Aelius Aristides (d. 181 CE) also seems to have thought that Christianity had a disruptive effect on the family. In the course of a speech in which he defends the heroes of the Golden Age of Greece, he berates the Cynics. In the midst of his scathing critique, he compares the behavior of the Cynics to 'those blasphemous people in Palestine' (ὑπὲρ τῶν τεττάρων, 2.394).[83] Aristides continues his speech by claiming that

They [i.e. the Cynics and by comparison the 'blasphemous people in Palestine'] are incapable as far as they are concerned of contributing any matter whatsoever toward any common good, but when it comes to undermining home life, bringing trouble and discord into families and claiming to be leaders of all things, they are the most skillful men (ὑπὲρ τῶν τεττάρων, 2.394-396).[84]

Stephen Benko has argued 'those blasphemous people in Palestine' of whom Aristides speaks are Christians.[85] Such a conclusion is plausible. However, even if Aristides is not referring to Christians in this passage, his comments highlight the fact that Greeks and Romans looked with much suspicion and disdain on movements that sowed familial discord. Christianity fell into such a category.

Malherbe has observed that there is a concentration of kinship language in 1 Thessalonians,[86] and he convincingly argues that one of the

83. Benko, *Pagan Rome and the Early Christians*, p. 46.
84. Benko, *Pagan Rome and the Early Christians*, p. 46.
85. Benko, *Pagan Rome and the Early Christians*, p. 46.
86. Malherbe, *Paul and the Thessalonians*, p. 48. Malherbe notes that God is referred to as 'father' on five occasions; that Paul refers to himself as the Thessalonians' 'father' and 'nurse'; and that the Thessalonian Christians are called 'children' and 'brothers'. The term 'brothers', Malherbe observes, is used 18 times

reasons for the frequency of familial terminology in the letter is that Paul was aware of the fact that the Thessalonian Christians' conversion had created domestic tensions.[87] Throughout 1 Thessalonians Paul seeks to reinforce the believers' affection for their sisters and brothers in the faith and to drive a wedge between the congregation and the members' former associations.[88] As we have seen, those Thessalonians who turned to Christ through Paul's ministry became a part of a new family, the ἐκκλησία.[89] Their incorporation into this new community via conversion and baptism prompted them to supplement, or even supplant, natural kinship ties with spiritual ones.[90]

The alteration of former relational networks is common in cases of religious conversion.[91] Although in most instances converts do not completely sever ties with family, friends and associates, these relationships often become secondary, and social interaction with fellow devotees is given priority.[92] Stephen C. Barton has demonstrated that adherents to other groups in antiquity, in particular converts to Judaism, Cynicism and Stoicism, also subordinated family ties for the sake of their

in 1 Thess. He notes that this number is exceeded only by 1 Cor., a letter which is approximately three times longer.

87. Malherbe, *Paul and the Thessalonians*, p. 50. See additionally Malherbe's 'God's New Family in Thessalonica', in L. Michael White and O. Larry Yarbrough (eds.), *The Social World of the First Christians: Essays in Honor of Wayne A. Meeks* (Minneapolis: Fortress Press, 1995), pp. 116-25. Cf. deSilva, '"Worthy of his Kingdom"', pp. 64-69, and de Vos, *Church and Community Conflicts*, p. 173.

88. So rightly, Smith, *Comfort One Another*, p. 99. deSilva ('"Worthy of his Kingdom"') has demonstrated that 1 Thess. may be usefully read as a type of honor discourse whereby Paul seeks to legitimate the Christians' new group loyalties and to negate their former social networks and the resistance arising therefrom.

89. Lucian considered familial talk among believers to be nonsense which was begun by 'their first lawgiver', whom Lucian depicts as a 'crucified sophist' (*Peregr.* 13). Caecilius also scorned the Christian use of familial language among themselves. He asserts that by calling one another 'brother' and 'sister' the Christians were merely turning fornication into incest (*Oct.* 9.2).

90. Meeks, *First Urban Christians*, p. 88.

91. On conversion as resocialization, see pp. 100-101 above.

92. In the case of Christianity, this community, of course, would be the church. Significant and frequent interaction between fellow believers in the church context is essential to reinforce one's faith commitment (note, e.g., Heb. 10.23-25). For, 'it is only within the religious community, the *ecclesia*, that the conversion can be effectively maintained as plausible' (Berger and Luckmann, *Social Construction of Reality*, p. 158).

religious or philosophical commitments and that they often encountered criticism and opposition for doing so.[93] Non-Christians would likely have viewed as subversive the sudden and decisive shift of commitment by Paul's converts from their 'real' family to a 'fictive' one. Furthermore, the Christians' conversion and the relational ramifications thereof probably created sharp disagreement and considerable discord between believing and unbelieving family members.[94] Meeks is right, then, in suggesting that 'concern about replacement of family loyalties by this new "family of God" may have been one reason for the "affliction" and suffering of the [Thessalonian] believers in this letter [i.e. 1 Thess.]'.[95]

b. *To Religion*

In all likelihood, the Thessalonian believers' religious exclusiveness was another cause of conflict with their compatriots.[96] To worship a deity to the exclusion of all other gods would not only have been viewed by outsiders as strange and snobbish, it would also have been perceived as disruptive or even subversive.[97] In Thessalonica, as in other Greek communities, there was a panoply of gods who were looked to for protection and provision. These gods were a significant part of Thessalonian life and culture, and it was assumed that the inhabitants would pay proper homage to at least some of the city's

93. Barton, *Discipleship and Family Ties*.

94. Wright (*Christian Origins*, I, p. 450) states, 'What we seem to be faced with [in early Christianity] is the existence of a community which was perceived to be subverting the normal social and cultural life of the empire precisely by its quasi-familial, quasi-ethnic life *as* a community' (emphasis his).

95. Wayne A. Meeks, *The Moral World of the First Christians* (London: SPCK, 1987), p. 129.

96. I am aware that 'In the cities of the ancient world, religion was inextricably intertwined with social and political life' (Robert L. Wilken, *The Christians as the Romans Saw Them* [New Haven: Yale University Press, 1984], p. 58). The purpose of this section is to highlight the Christians' exclusive religious devotion and the conflict spawned by such. Earlier I focused on the Christians' social exclusivity and the results thereof. Here I am considering the religious or theological exclusivity of the Christians. The categories certainly overlap; the difference is largely one of emphasis.

97. Peter Garnsey ('Religious Toleration in Classical Antiquity', in W.J. Sheils [ed.], *Persecution and Toleration* [Oxford: Basil Blackwell, 1984], pp. 1-27 [3]) notes, 'Religious deviance was dangerous in principle because it prejudiced that good relations between gods and men on which the safety of the state was held to depend.' So also de Vos, 'Graeco-Roman Responses'.

gods.[98] As Robert Wilken suggests, 'Piety toward the gods was thought to insure the well-being of the city, to promote a spirit of kinship and mutual responsibility, indeed, to bind together the citizenry.'[99] The Thessalonian Christians' refusal to worship any god but their own, coupled with their newfangled assumption that the very gods which they had previously venerated were 'dumb idols', would have branded them as 'dangerous atheists'.[100]

The charge of atheism against the Christians appears frequently in Christian apologetic literature from the middle of the second century CE onwards.[101] How significant the charge of atheism was in Christian and 'pagan' relations prior to this time, however, is a matter of debate. Joseph Walsh is convinced that the charge of atheism against the Christians did not take on major significance until the reign of Marcus Aurelius (161–180 CE).[102] By surveying the primary literature of the period, Walsh concludes that the accusation of atheism was only one of many sources of 'pagan' disgust with Christianity before 150 CE.[103] He maintains that the charge of atheism came to the fore only after: (1) 'pagans' learned more about Christianity; (2) the more sensational and fear-inspiring charges against the Christians had lost their credibility; (3) the natural catastrophes of 160–61 CE had drawn attention to Christian atheism.[104] Although Walsh helpfully highlights a vast array of reasons

98. Garnsey ('Religious Toleration', p. 24) remarks that in antiquity each community 'was proud and protective of its indigenous cults and in normal circumstances was not disposed to supplement them or permit them to be undermined or subverted from within'. On cultic life in Thessalonica, see, among others, Donfried, 'Cults of Thessalonica'; de Vos, *Church and Community Conflict*, pp. 140-43; Hill, *Establishing the Church in Thessalonica*, pp. 61-66; and Jewett, *Thessalonian Correspondence*, pp. 126-32.

99. Wilken, *Christians as the Romans Saw Them*, p. 58.

100. Frend ('Persecutions', p. 155) suggests that it would have been a serious source of contention between Christians and 'pagans' that 'while living as members of a community, [the Christians] deliberately rejected the gods on whom the prosperity of that community rested'.

101. See, e.g., Justin Martyr, *1st Apol.* 4-6; 13; 46; *2nd Apol.* 3; *Diog.* 2.6; *Mart. Pol.* 3.2; 9.2; 12.2; Tertullian, *Ad Nat.* 1.1-3; and Athenagoras, *Leg. pro Christ.* 3. Note also Lucian, *Alex.* 25, 38; and Julian, *c. Gal.* 43B.

102. Joseph Walsh, 'On Christian Atheism' *VC* 45 (1991), pp. 255-77. Frend ('Persecutions', p. 156) argues that the charge of atheism against the Christians had gained prominence by c. 130 CE.

103. Walsh, 'Atheism', pp. 255-56.

104. Walsh, 'Atheism', pp. 264-67.

that the non-Christian Greeks and Romans found Christianity repulsive, he fails to give sufficient weight to the fact that 'pagans' would have been offended by the Christians' religious exclusivity from the outset. The fact that the charge of atheism does not feature prominently in the literature until after 160 CE does not necessarily suggest that atheism was not a source of contention prior to that time. A similar charge can be expressed in a variety of ways. As we have seen, social exclusiveness (misanthropy) and religious exclusiveness (atheism) would have been closely linked in Greco-Roman culture. To refuse to participate in civic cultic events would have been viewed as denial, or at least blatant neglect, of the gods. The Christians' refusal to honor the gods, then, would have been a source of conflict from the first.[105]

But why would religious exclusiveness on the part of Christians have been so resented by and repulsive to the 'pagan'? The answer to this query, which I have hinted at above, may now be addressed more fully. G.E.M. de Ste Croix gives a plausible answer to this question. He maintains, 'The monotheistic exclusiveness of the Christians was believed to alienate the goodwill of the gods, to endanger what the Romans called the *pax deorum* (the right harmonious relationship between gods and men), and to be responsible for disasters which overtook the community.'[106]

It was a common belief among Greeks and Romans that neglect of the gods could instigate their wrath. Horace, a first-century CE poet, eloquently states his respect for and fear of the gods.

> For the sins of your forefathers, Romans, not for your own deserts,
> shall you pay retribution, until you have restored the temples and the
> ruinous shrines of the gods and images befouled with black smoke.

105. G.E.M. de Ste Croix ('Why Were the Early Christians Persecuted?', *Past and Present* 26 [1963], pp. 6-38 [26]) rightly contends that even though the earliest surviving apologies concerning the charge of Christian atheism are mid second century CE, 'there is no reason to think that the situation was different earlier'. De Vos ('Graeco-Roman Responses') avers: 'Indeed, this complaint [i.e. 'atheism'] was probably the primary problem [between Greco-Roman unbelievers and Christians], as everything else stemmed from it.'

106. De Ste Croix, 'Why Were the Early Christians Persecuted?', p. 24. Robin Lane Fox (*Pagans and Christians* [San Francisco: HarperCollins, 1986], p. 425) is similarly convinced that Christian atheism would have been the 'basic cause of [Christian] maltreatment'. He adds, 'Some intellectual pagans decried the forms of contemporary cult, but almost all concurred with them when necessary; the Christians refused to concur, and their lack of respect was intolerable.'

> You hold empire, because you walk humbly before the gods: from this everything should start, to this refer every outcome. The gods because they were neglected have imposed much suffering on the sorrowing West (*Carm.* 3.6.1-8).[107]

Fear of the gods' retribution was apparently a common anxiety among 'pagans'. And in many communities, and most likely in Thessalonica from the time Pauline Christianity was introduced, it would have been apparent to family and friends that the Christians rejected, or at least neglected, the gods.[108] Therefore, if the gods' wrath was manifested (e.g. if crops failed or natural disasters struck), the Christians could have become the scapegoats. The familiar quip of Tertullian (c. 160–200 CE) illustrates as much: 'If the Tiber reaches the walls, if the Nile does not rise to the fields, if the sky doesn't move or the earth does, if there is famine, if there is plague, the cry is at once: "The Christians to the lion!"' (*Apol.* 40.2).[109] 'Pagans' would have viewed with suspicion the Thessalonian Christians' refusal to worship any deity but their own, which would have left Paul's converts open to accusations if anything 'abnormal' were to happen. Fascinatingly, Tacitus (*Ann.* 12.43) reports that 51 CE was a particularly ominous year fraught with earthquakes and famine.[110] If such natural disasters impacted Thessalonica as well as Rome, then the populace could have held Paul's converts responsible for bringing such tragedies upon the city.

It is true that Greeks and Romans also viewed the Jews as 'atheists' and reviled them for worshipping a single, invisible deity.[111] Neverthe-

---

107. Whittaker (trans.), *Jews and Christians*, p. 206.

108. The Thessalonian congregation would not have been very large, at least at first. As a result, the Christians' abstention from worshipping the gods could have gone unnoticed by the larger community. If, however, some of the Christians were involved in active proselytism and had been subject to political sanctions, then observant outsiders could have detected their withdrawal from the local cults. Furthermore, in ancient city life privacy was not easily had. People tended to live close together and to interact frequently with one another. See, e.g., John E. Stambaugh and David L. Balch, *The New Testament in its Social Environment* (LEC, 2; Philadelphia: Westminster Press, 1986), pp. 107-10.

109. Cf. Tertullian, *Ad Nat.* 1.9; Cyprian, *Ep.* 75; Arnobius, *Ad. Gent.* 1.1, 1.13; and Augustine, *De civ. D.* 2.3.

110. Barclay ('Conflict in Thessalonica', pp. 527-28) and Winter (*Seek the Welfare of the City*, pp. 53-54) also note this text from Tacitus but for different reasons than I.

111. See, e.g., the comments of Pliny, *HN* 13.46; Dio Cassius 37.17.2; Josephus,

less, 'atheism' does not seem to have created the same degree of conflict for the Jews as it did for the early Christians. How can one explain their divergent experiences? In all probability, it was the antiquity of the Jews which spared them such acute conflict with Gentiles over the issue of exclusive monotheism.[112] Even Tacitus, who was by no means a friend of the Jews, could bring himself to acknowledge that at least some of the religious practices of the Jews were 'commended by their antiquity' ('antiquitate defenduntur', *Hist.* 5.5). In a society where the ancient was valued, the Jews were excused for their extravagant superstition. According to de Ste Croix, 'The gods would forgive the inexplicable monotheism of the Jews, who were, so to speak, licensed atheists.'[113]

In some Diasporan locations, 'pagans' may have connected Christianity with Judaism.[114] It is doubtful, however, that this connection would have been made in Thessalonica. I argued in Chapters 3 and 6 above that the Jews of Thessalonica repudiated Paul and his message. If this was indeed the case, then the parting of the ways between Thessalonian Jews and Christians was much nearer to 50 CE than to 70 CE.[115] In Thessalonica, observant outsiders could have differentiated between Jews and Christians. Therefore, Paul's converts in Thessalonica would have been unable to deter Gentile criticism and opposition by gathering under the umbrella of Judaism.[116] Because of the conflict between Paul

Apion 2.65-67, 79, 148; and Juvenal, *Sat.* 14.97-98.

112. So rightly de Ste Croix, 'Why Were the Early Christians Persecuted?', p. 25. See also Fox (*Pagans and Christians*, pp. 428-29) who supports such a conclusion and offers additional reasons why for the most part the Jews had more amiable relations with the Romans.

113. De Ste Croix, 'Why Were the Early Christians Persecuted?', p. 25.

114. Cf. Judge ('Judaism and the Rise of Christianity') who argues that the Romans never saw Christianity as a part of Judaism.

115. Judith Lieu (' "The Parting of the Ways": Theological Construct or Historical Reality', *JSNT* 56 [1994], pp. 101-19) is right to stress that relations between Jews and Christians differed from place to place and that any attempt to discover in a general sense when and how the parting of the ways between the two groups occurred is misguided. Cf. Barclay, 'Paul among Diaspora Jews', p. 118.

116. Tellbe ('Conflict at Philippi') argues that Paul seeks to persuade his Philippian converts who were encountering conflict with Roman authorities not to seek Jewish shelter. Winter (*Seek the Welfare of the City*, pp. 124-43) suggests that Paul's Gentile converts in Galatia were moving toward Judaism so that they would not have to participate in the imperial cult. The Thessalonian Christians seemingly had no such option.

and Thessalonian Jewry, non-Christians in the city could have perceived Pauline Christianity as neither Jew nor Greek, but as a third entity (cf. 1 Cor. 10.32).

Historians and theologians sometimes characterize Greco-Roman religiosity as passionless and perfunctory. While it does in fact appear that 'paganism' was contractual and communal, this should not lead one to infer that Gentiles were disinterested in religion.[117] In truth, many Gentiles were extremely pious and held strong religious convictions.[118] Even though 'pagans' tended to be tolerant of others' beliefs, one should not equate tolerance with indifference. In fact, the opposition of Christians in Thessalonica (and elsewhere) indicates that in some instances 'pagans' were neither tolerant of nor indifferent to other religious convictions.[119] It would be less than precise to aver that the Thessalonian Christians' monotheistic exclusiveness was the only reason that they encountered conflict with their compatriots. Nevertheless, it makes good sense to think that it was a factor in their clash with outsiders.

c. *To Government*

Acts 17.7 portrays a Jewish-instigated crowd coming before the Thessalonian politarchs accusing Paul, Silas and their converts of 'acting against the decrees of Caesar, saying that there is another king, Jesus'. This alleged accusation against Paul *et al.* provides a suitable springboard for our present discussion. Because the charge recorded by Luke indicates that the conflict in Thessalonica was political in orientation, the potential role that politics played in the conflict merits further investigation. In this section I will attempt to discover how

117. On the vitality of Greco-Roman religious life, see esp. Nock, *Conversion*; Fox, *Pagans and Christians*; and MacMullen, *Paganism in the Roman Empire*.

118. E.g. Saturninus, the proconsul of Scillium, while trying Christians remarks, 'We too are a religious people...' (*Pass. Sanct. Scillitan.* 3). For text and translation, see Hebert Musurillo (ed.), *The Acts of the Christian Martyrs* (Oxford: Clarendon Press, 1972), pp. 86-87. Wilken (*Christians as the Romans Saw Them*, p. 63) notes, '[T]he Roman belief in divine providence, in the necessity of religious observance for the well-being of society, and in the efficacy of traditional rites and practices, was no less sincere than the beliefs of the Christians.'

119. Garnsey ('Religious Toleration', p. 24) contends, 'The usual picture of civic cults as supple and receptive to foreign influences is a distortion of the truth'. Fox (*Pagans and Christians*, p. 425) asserts, 'The persecutions [post 250 CE] are good evidence that the essential continuity of pagan religiousness was still significant.'

charges of political subversion could have arisen by considering statements in 1 (and 2) Thessalonians which outsiders could (mis)construe as politically subversive and by examining epigraphic, numismatic and artistic evidence which enables a better understanding of the political atmosphere in Thessalonica in the middle of the first century CE.[120]

Earlier in this chapter I noted that in 1 Thessalonians Paul repeatedly refers to his initial visit to Thessalonica and to the contents of his instruction on that occasion. Because of Paul's reiteration of his previous instruction, I was able to reconstruct with some degree of confidence the basic content of Paul's preaching in Thessalonica. I will now consider statements in 1 Thessalonians that have political overtones. My working presupposition will be once again that there is a positive correlation between Paul's original proclamation and his epistolary communication.

In 1 Thessalonians Paul frequently refers to the coming of the Lord (παρουσία) (2.19; 3.13; 4.15; 5.23; cf. 2 Thess. 1.10; 2.1, 2, 3).[121] Additionally, he speaks of waiting for the Son of God (1.9) who is soon to be revealed from heaven (5.2; cf. 2 Thess. 1.10; 2.2). On the Day of the Lord the wrath of God will be poured out upon 'those who do not know God' (1.10; 5.9; cf. 2 Thess. 1.5-10; 2.10-12). Paul also reminds the Thessalonian Christians that they are citizens of another kingdom, the Kingdom of God (2.12; cf. 2 Thess. 1.5; Phil. 3.20). All of these statements could have political overtones and could have been understood by outsiders as politically subversive. As Pheme Perkins points out, 'Taken out of context...there is quite enough in the language of Christian belief to arouse suspicion and even hostility without presuming that the Christians engaged in any direct polemic against the civic cult.'[122]

On one occasion in 1 Thessalonians, however, Paul does appear to criticize overtly the Roman political system of his day. And as we will

---

120. Donfried ('Cults of Thessalonica', pp. 344-46) employs a similar strategy in attempting to understand the interplay between Paul's proclamation and the political situation in Thessalonica.

121. Koester ('Apocalyptic Schemata of 2 Thessalonians', p. 446) suggests that the term παρουσία 'has been introduced by Paul in this letter [i.e. 1 Thess.]' and 'that it is a political term which is closely related to the status of the community'. See also Gundry, 'Eschatology of 1-2 Thessalonians', p. 162.

122. Perkins, '1 Thessalonians and Hellenistic Religious Practices', p. 326.

see, the close ties between Thessalonica and Rome would have rendered his criticism all the more controversial. In 1 Thess. 5.3 Paul declares, 'When they say, "Peace and security" [εἰρήνη καὶ ἀσφάλεια], then sudden destruction will come upon them as travail comes upon a woman with child, and there will be no escape.' Here, in an apocalyptic *tour de force*, Paul declares that those who presume that they are safe (i.e. non-Christians, the so-called children of darkness) will encounter sudden destruction on the day of the Lord's visitation.

The phrase εἰρήνη καὶ ἀσφάλεια is of particular interest. The context indicates that this phrase reflects the perspective of outsiders. In a 1960 article, Ernst Bammel proposed that εἰρήνη καὶ ἀσφάλεια was a Roman imperial slogan.[123] For the most part, exegetes have either ignored or rejected Bammel's proposal. However, in the 1980s both Karl Donfried[124] and Klaus Wengst[125] argued that εἰρήνη καὶ ἀσφάλεια is best understood as a Roman imperial slogan which was in circulation when Paul penned 1 Thessalonians. Helmut Koester also advocated this interpretation in a 1990 article[126] as did Holland Lee Hendrix one year later in an essay published in a Festschrift for Koester.[127]

My purpose here is not to note all the exegetes who have espoused or entertained this interpretation of εἰρήνη καὶ ἀσφάλεια. Furthermore, it is not my intent to suggest that the Old Testament antecedents of this phrase (see, e.g., Jer. 6.14; 8.11; Ezek. 13.10-16; Mic. 3.5) commonly adduced by commentators are irrelevant.[128] Rather, I am interested in demonstrating that the most likely context of εἰρήνη καὶ ἀσφάλεια is a political one, 'inasmuch as *pax et securitas* was a popular slogan of the imperial Roman propaganda machine'.[129]

---

123. 'Ein Beitrag zur paulinischen Staatsanschauung', *TLZ* 85 (1960), pp. 837-40.

124. Donfried ('Cults of Thessalonica', p. 344) maintains that 1 Thess. 5.3 is a 'frontal attack on the *Pax et Securitas* programme of the early Principate'.

125. Wengst, *Pax Romana*, p. 77.

126. Koester, 'Apocalyptic Schemata of 2 Thessalonians'.

127. Holland Lee Hendrix, 'Archaeology and Eschatology at Thessalonica', in Birger A. Pearson (ed.), *The Future of Christianity: Essays in Honor of Helmut Koester* (Minneapolis: Fortress Press, 1991), pp. 107-18.

128. See, e.g., Richard, *Thessalonians*, p. 260, and Wanamaker, *Thessalonians*, p. 180. Cf. Malherbe (*Paul and the Thessalonians*, p. 81) who suggests that Paul may be countering an Epicurean outlook in 5.3.

129. Holmes, *Thessalonians*, p. 167.

In his monograph *Pax Romana*, Wengst remarks on the meaning of this slogan. He writes,

> the combination of these terms [i.e. εἰρήνη καὶ ἀσφάλεια] expresses an important claim of the Pax Romana: Roman power brings peace as a permanent state free of wars; it guarantees security from hostile attacks from beyond the bounds of the empire and by preventing armed quarrels within its frontiers; and finally, too, 'inner security', the maintaining of order and the preservation of the security of law is part of that. So 'peace and security' is a conservative slogan which affirms the existing order and wants to see it preserved. Paul takes it up in 1 Thess. 5:3. However, he regards it as a foolish slogan, which Christians will not repeat.[130]

But why does Paul's critique of the *Pax Romana* arise in 1 Thessalonians (cf. Rom. 13.1-7)?[131] And why would such a perspective elicit a hostile response in Thessalonica? The judicious work of Hendrix is helpful at this point. In his article 'Eschatology and Archaeology at Thessalonica', Hendrix discusses various archaeological materials in an effort to demonstrate 'a distinctive sensitivity to propaganda about Roman rule in the Julio-Claudian period on the part of the Thessalonians'.[132] I will summarize the evidence he presents below.

Epigraphic materials from the first centuries BCE and CE indicate the following: (1) Some of the decrees of the city's assembly were issued in conjunction with an official Roman group (*IT* 32-33). (2) 'Roma and Roman Benefactors' became a part of the city cult of 'the gods' (*IT* 4). (3) The priesthood of 'the gods' became less significant as a civic religion (*IT* 4, 31-32, 132-133, 226), while the 'priest and agonothete of the Imperator Caesar Augustus' became more prominent (*IT* 31-32, 132-133). (4) A temple was built, probably between 27 BCE and 14 CE, in honor of Augustus (*IT* 31). Based on the Thessalonian epigraphic record from this period, Hendrix concludes, 'Thessalonica's [political

---

130. Wengst, *Pax Romana*, pp. 78-79. Cf. Holmes (*Thessalonians*, p. 167): 'The promise of peace and security was what Rome offered to those peoples who submitted (willingly or unwillingly) to Roman rule and military power; it was seen as Rome's gift to those it conquered, virtually equivalent to an offer of deliverance or "salvation" from turmoil or danger. But from Paul's perspective, any such claims are illusory and deceptive and therefore dangerous.'

131. For a fascinating study of the Christian apologists' critique of the Roman State, see Elaine Pagels, 'Christian Apologists and "The Fall of the Angels": An Attack on Roman Imperial Power?', *HTR* 78 (1985), pp. 301-25.

132. Hendrix, 'Archaeology and Eschatology', p. 114.

and civic religious] interests increasingly were influenced by Romans and by regard for the Roman emperor.'[133]

Turning to numismatic evidence, 'one encounters [in the Julio-Claudian period] a significant number of issues of a coin type that was novel in Thessalonica's minting history'.[134] This coin type featured 'the laureate head of Julius on the obverse with the legend θεός and a bareheaded Octavian on the reverse with the legend "of the Thessalonicans" '.[135] What is of particular interest about this Thessalonian issue is

133. Hendrix, 'Archaeology and Eschatology', p. 115. Elsewhere, Hendrix ('Beyond "Imperial Cult" and "Cults of the Magistrates"', in Kent H. Richards [ed.], *SBL 1986 Seminar Papers* [SBLSP, 25; Atlanta: Scholars Press, 1986], pp. 301-308 [308]) contends, 'In Macedonia, thresholds for offering divine honors to humans were generally high.' He is convinced that 'Relative to other quarters of the Roman Empire, Macedonia manifests a rather low imperial theology and a comparatively restrained religious response to Roman benefactors, magistrates, and emperors' ('Archaeology and Eschatology', p. 112 n. 15). Hendrix is inclined to think, therefore, that the term 'imperial cult' is misleading and that it should not be used in reference to the Thessalonians' benefaction of the emperor (see 'Archaeology and Eschatology', p. 112 n. 15; 'Thessalonicans Honor Romans', p. 253; and 'Beyond "Imperial Cult"'). It does appear, however, that in Thessalonica there was an acute sensitivity to Rome and her representatives. And there is good reason to think that those who criticized or failed to recognize the authority of Rome and her rulers would have invited opposition.

S.R.F. Price (*Rituals and Power: The Roman Imperial Cult in Asia Minor* [Cambridge: Cambridge University Press, 1984]) has shown that the imperial cult had made significant inroads into Asia Minor around the middle of the first century CE. Winter (*Seek the Welfare of the City*, pp. 125-26) indicates the presence of the imperial cult in Corinth around this time. Tellbe ('Conflict in Philippi', pp. 108-109) suggests that in Philippi, a city located only some one hundred miles northwest of Thessalonica on the Via Egnatia, 'the Imperial cult played a conspicuous and important role in the city life as a means of demonstrating loyalty to Rome'. Certainly one should allow for local diversity and not assume facilely that distinct socio-historical contexts are equivalent. Nevertheless, it is striking how close Macedonia, Achaia and Asia Minor are geographically. I am inclined, therefore, to think that the imperial cult may also have played a larger role in Thessalonian religious life than Hendrix has suggested. Benefaction may have led to veneration, at least for some, even if there is presently no extant evidence to support such a claim. Cf. deSilva, ' "Worthy of his Kingdom" ', pp. 60-62.

134. Hendrix, 'Archaeology and Eschatology', p. 115.

135. Hendrix, 'Archaeology and Eschatology', p. 115. As Hendrix notes, this coin type may be found in B.V. Head, *A Catologue of Greek Coins in the British Museum*. V. *Macedonia, etc.* (London: Longmans, 1879), p. 115 nos. 58-59, 61.

that it is a direct, 'unoriginal imitation of an *as* issued by Octavian in 38 BCE in honor of Julius's deification'.[136] According to Hendrix, such a rigid imitation of Roman numismatic propaganda is striking and significant.[137]

In his valuable article, Hendrix also notes that archaeologists have found in Thessalonica fragments of a statue of Augustus which many experts date to Claudius's reign.[138] It is not clear, according to Hendrix, whether the statue was made in Thessalonica or imported to Thessalonica, although Hendrix favors the latter option. Regardless, this statue 'represents a Claudian adaptation of an Augustan prototype' and further demonstrates the Thessalonians' interest in imperial media.[139]

Based upon his careful investigation of the archaeological material, Hendrix maintains that there was 'a distinctive sensitivity to propaganda about Roman rule on the part of the Thessalonians' and that Paul's citation of the slogan εἰρήνη καὶ ἀσφάλεια 'was intended to resonate with a feature of the Thessalonian political environment...'[140] Furthermore, Hendrix suggests that 'if the Thessalonians' θλίψις had been a result of political opposition involving Roman or Roman-related interests, Paul's apocalyptic critique of Roman "peace and security" might seem more comprehensible'.[141] Unfortunately, the purview of his

136. Hendrix, 'Archaeology and Eschatology', p. 116. As Hendrix indicates, this issue appears in S. Weinstock, *Divus Julius* (Oxford: Clarendon Press, 1971), pl. 30 no. 3.

137. Hendrix, 'Archaeology and Eschatology', p. 116.

138. Hendrix, 'Archaeology and Eschatology', pp. 116-17.

139. Hendrix, 'Archaeology and Eschatology', p. 117. Tacitus observes that Jews do not set up statues in their cities, and especially not in their Temples, in honor of their kings or of the Caesars ('Igitur nulla simulacra urbibus suis, nedum templis sistunt; non regibus haec adulatio, non Caesaribus honor', *Hist.* 5.5). It is likely that Paul, given his disdain of 'idolatry' (1.9), would have instructed his 'pagan' converts to pay no heed to such 'idols/icons'.

Barclay ('Conflict in Thessalonica', p. 584) notes that 'when passions were high and opportunity provided, Jews engaged in acts of vandalism against religious objects they scorned'. I am not suggesting that Paul vandalized the statue of Augustus or that he encouraged his Gentile converts to do so. (Interestingly, Caecilius [*Oct.* 8.5] remarks that Christians 'spit upon the gods'). I am contending, however, that Paul and his converts would not have attached the same significance to such statues as other Thessalonians did.

140. Hendrix, 'Archaeology and Eschatology', pp. 117-18.

141. Hendrix, 'Archaeology and Eschatology', p. 118 n. 43.

article does not allow Hendrix to discuss the implications of Paul's indictment of the Roman government.

It is at this point, then, that I might be able to supplement Hendrix's fine work. Based on the political overtones of Paul's original proclamation as evidenced in 1 Thessalonians (see pp. 261-62 above) and the significant archaeological materials indicating the city's sensitivity to Roman interests, I would suggest: (1) Paul's apocalyptic message was sufficiently disturbing to some Thessalonians to lead to political accusations against him and his converts during his stay in the city. (2) Political accusations factored into Paul's forced departure from the city. (3) Some of the church may have been brought again before the politarchs on charges of political subversion and, if so, were probably subjected to more severe sanctions than previously (i.e. beyond the posting of bond).[142]

Donfried is convinced that the Thessalonian Christians' affliction was caused by political opposition.[143] As we have seen, the conflict situation in Thessalonica defies a single explanation. Nevertheless, I would concur with Donfried that political issues played an important role in the conflict with their compatriots which Paul's Thessalonian converts experienced.

5. *Conclusion*

In this chapter I have explored some possible explanations as to why the Thessalonian congregation experienced conflict with non-Christians. In short, I suggested that the believers' conversion marked the

142. It appears that Christians and Jews elsewhere were also thought to be politically subversive. It may be that the author of 1 Pet. is seeking to dissuade his auditors from being (perceived as) politically subversive when he writes, 'For the Lord's sake accept the authority of every human institution, whether of the emperor as supreme, or of governors, as sent by [God] to punish those who do wrong and praise those who do right' (2.13-14). Pliny informs Trajan that some former Christians had recanted their faith and demonstrated as much by worshipping his statue and the images of the gods and cursing Christ ('Omnes et imaginem tuam deorumque simulacra venerati sunt: et Christo maledixerunt', *Ep.* 10.96). Presumably, those Christians whom Pliny had executed would not worship the emperor and the gods. Pliny may well have viewed such 'inflexible obstinacy' as political subversion. *3 Macc.* 3.7 indicates that some Jews living in and around Alexandria were accused of being disloyal to the king (Ptolemy IV) and hostile to his government.

143. Donfried, 'Cults of Thessalonica', p. 347.

start of their strained relations with outsiders. Furthermore, I contended that because Paul's Thessalonian converts tended toward separatism, both ideologically and socially, unbelievers would have looked upon them with great suspicion and would have circulated rumors about and made accusations against them. Additionally, active proselytism on the part of some Thessalonian Christians seemingly exacerbated the already tense relations. I also maintained that the conflict arose because non-Christians viewed the church to be subversive to the foundational institutions of Greco-Roman society, namely family, religion and government. In my treatment of the Thessalonians' *thlipsis* I have sought to be sensitive to the textual, socio-historical and archaeological evidence and would contend that my conclusions are entirely plausible, especially considering the paucity of materials at our disposal.

In concluding this chapter I would like to note that the reason I have not offered a single explanation for the church's conflict is because no one explanation will suffice. It is almost a certainty that different factors would have prompted different people to oppose Paul's converts. Social scientists who study conflict observe that any given conflict can be traced to a variety of causes (see p. 119 above). Despite the fact that the precise reasons for the clash between Christians and non-Christians in Thessalonica are all too elusive, it may be positively concluded that the conflict occurred because unbelievers wanted to control and to censure a novel religious movement which they viewed as ideologically and socially deviant. It seems likely that outsiders sought to hinder the believers in order to: demonstrate their disapproval, affirm their own social mores and persuade Paul's converts to jettison their new-found faith and return to their former lives.[144] Despite profound pressure from unbelievers to apostatize, the believers refused to revert to their previous beliefs and practices (see p. 272 below). And when one couples the Christians' dogged commitment to the faith with the fact that some of them may have been willing to retaliate for the faith (1 Thess. 5.15; cf. Rom 12.17-21), the relational dynamic which emerges is one of considerable intergroup conflict.

---

144. So similarly, deSilva, ' "Worthy of his Kingdom" ', p. 63.

Chapter 11

THE IMPACT OF INTERGROUP CONFLICT
ON THE THESSALONIAN CONGREGATION

1. *Introduction*

What were the consequences of the discordant relations between Christians and non-Christians in Thessalonica on the fledgling Pauline fellowship in that city? I will seek to answer this question in the concluding chapter of this project. In doing so, I will once again employ 1 Thessalonians as my primary source. I will scour the epistle for evidence which might shed light on the stated query. The social sciences will also inform this investigation. In particular, I will draw upon conflict theory in assessing how external opposition affected the Thessalonian church. In what follows I will also take note of apparently relevant data from 2 Thessalonians. However, given the widespread scholarly skepticism concerning the letter's authenticity, I will regard the letter as a secondary source and will not build arguments or base conclusions on its contents.

I will argue in this chapter that intergroup conflict had three principal effects on the Thessalonian congregation. First, I will contend that the affliction experienced by these Pauline believers reinforced their new-found faith. I will then suggest that the conflict served to strengthen congregational relations. Finally, I will argue that the suffering to which these Christians were subject heightened their eschatological hope.

2. *Affliction and Faith*

Paul's unplanned, premature departure from Thessalonica left his converts in a precarious position. Not only was the Thessalonian assembly relatively immature spiritually,[1] but it also faced the formidable chal-

---

1.   In 3.10 Paul indicates that he prays continuously to see his converts 'face to

lenge of coping with external hostility.[2] 1 Thessalonians 2.17–3.13 indicates that Paul was gravely concerned about the spiritual survival of the church (note esp. 3.1, 5, 7). Specifically, he was anxious that his converts might be shaken (σαίνεσθαι)[3] by their afflictions and as a result abandon the faith (3.3).[4]

Although early Christian writings tend to conceal them, there were some people who actually defected from the faith.[5] The writer of Hebrews suggests as much by repeatedly urging his readers to persevere and not to emulate those who have fallen away (παραπεσόντας, 6.6).[6]

---

face' in order to 'supply what is lacking in [their] faith'. Donfried ('Theology of 1 and 2 Thessalonians', pp. 20-21) suggests that hope was the particular aspect missing from the Thessalonians' faith. Such a theory is not necessary. Furthermore, as we will see below, the majority of the assembly was not flagging in hope. Paul's statement in 3.10 simply indicates that the Thessalonian congregation 'is a young community whose formation and development are not yet sufficiently advanced...' (Richard, *Thessalonians*, p. 171). So similarly, Marshall, *Thessalonians*, p. 98, and Bammel, 'Preparation for the Perils', p. 92.

2. Paul states in 1.6 and 2.14 that his converts had suffered for their faith in the past. Paul's remark in 3.3 (θλίψεσιν ταύταις) indicates the continuation of external opposition in the present (cf. 2 Thess. 1.4-5 and 2 Cor. 8.1-2). So rightly, Donfried, 'The Theology of 1 Thessalonians', p. 251; Johanson, *To All the Brethren*, p. 57; and Barclay, 'Conflict in Thessalonica', p. 514 n. 5. *Pace* Wanamaker (*Thessalonians*, pp. 42, 130) who argues that the church was no longer experiencing affliction when Paul wrote 1 Thess.

3. On the meaning of this New Testament *hapax legomenon*, see, e.g., Henry Chadwick, '1 Thess. 3:3: σαίνεσθαι', *JTS* NS 1 (1950), pp. 156-58.

4. Roetzel ('The Grammar of Election', p. 217) suggests that Paul's repeated use of election and sanctification language in 1 Thess. may be explained in part by the fact that 'The danger of [the Thessalonians'] defection was real...and the need for [their] encouragement was urgent.'

5. See the illuminating work of Wilson, 'Apostate Minority'. In this article, Wilson suggests that 'apostasy' was more common than scholars of early Christianity usually suppose. For studies on 'apostasy' from a sociological perspective, see David G. Bromley (ed.), *Falling from the Faith: Causes and Consequences of Religious Apostasy* (Newbury Park, CA: Sage, 1988), and *idem* (ed.), *The Politics of Religious Apostasy: The Role of Apostates in the Transformation of Religious Movements* (Westport, CT: Praeger, 1998) I intend to pursue in a future study the topic of deviation and defection among the earliest Christians making full use of the social sciences.

6. On the topic of 'apostasy' in Hebrews, see David deSilva, 'Exchanging Favor for Wrath: Apostasy in Hebrews and Patron–Client Relationships', *JBL* 115

The 'apostasy' of which the author speaks may have been prompted in part by external opposition from non-Christians, including public harassment, confiscation of property and imprisonment (10.32-34).[7]

Paul seems to think that the temptation to apostatize was particularly acute for those in the throes of suffering (3.3-5). Consequently, he was anxious to see the Thessalonians become more established in their received faith lest they succumb to the temptation to return to their former patterns of belief and behavior (3.2). It was Paul's continued concern for the Thessalonians' steadfastness in the face of affliction that prompted his unsuccessful attempts (καὶ ἅπαξ καὶ δίς) to return to Thessalonica (2.18) and that ultimately led him to send Timothy from Athens in his stead (3.1-2). Paul remarks in 3.5, '[W]hen I could bear it no longer, I sent that I might know your faith, for fear that somehow the tempter had tempted you and that our labor would be in vain' (cf. 2 Thess. 3.3).

Timothy's return to Paul in Corinth allayed, at least temporarily,[8] Paul's intense anxiety about his converts' continuation in the faith. For, when Timothy came to Paul from Thessalonica, he brought with him the good news of the church's faith (3.6). This positive report comforted Paul in the midst of his 'distress and affliction' (ἀνάγκη καὶ θλίψει, 3.7; cf. 2 Thess. 3.2) and prompted him to write his converts to comfort and encourage them in the Lord.[9]

Some interpreters have taken Paul's exhortation to 'help the weak' (ἀντέχεσθε τῶν ἀσθενῶν, 5.14c) as evidence that at least a few of the Thessalonians were flagging in their new-found faith.[10] It may be that

(1996), pp. 91-116. See also, I.H. Marshall, 'The Problem of Apostasy in New Testament Theology', *PRS* 14 (1987), pp. 65-80 (74).

7.   Wilson, 'Apostate Minority', p. 205. See also William L. Lane, *Hebrews 9–13* (WBC, 47B; Dallas, TX: Word Books, 1991), pp. 296-301.

8.   1 Thess. 3.8, 10 indicate that Paul continued to be concerned about his converts' steadfastness in the faith even after Timothy's positive report. Rightly recognized by, e.g., Patte, *Paul's Faith*, p. 131; Palmer, '1 Thessalonians 1–3', p. 29; and Johanson, *To All the Brethren*, p. 58.

9.   So also Best, *Thessalonians*, p. 15, and Patte, *Paul's Faith*, p. 126. On 1 Thess. as a letter of consolation (λόγος παραμυθητικός), see Donfried ('Theology of 1 Thessalonians') and Smith (*Comfort One Another*). Although Juan Chapa ('Is First Thessalonians a Letter of Consolation?', pp. 150-60) notes multiple features that 1 Thess. shares in common with letters of consolation in antiquity, he stops short of identifying 1 Thess. as such.

10.   See, e.g., David Alan Black, 'The Weak in Thessalonica: A Study in Pauline

the protracted experience of external opposition, the death of a few fellow Christians and /or some other unspecified hardship had unsettled the faith of some.[11] But even if this were this case, based upon Paul's explicitly positive comments about the church's faith (3.6-7; cf. 2 Thess. 1.3), one may reasonably conclude that the majority of the assembly was persevering in the faith and was weathering the storm of suffering. Although intergroup conflict can result in group defection, conflict theorists point out that conflict relations can also reduce disaffiliation (see p. 122 above). This appears to have been the case in Thessalonica, for there is not a shred of evidence in 1 (or 2) Thessalonians to suggest that Paul's converts had 'apostatized'.[12] It is conceivable that Paul was uninformed or sought to conceal congregational disidentification. However, this is unlikely in light of Timothy's recent visit to the assembly and Paul's repeated praise of his converts in 1 Thessalonians.[13]

How could it be that the believers' conflict with unbelievers buttressed the Christians' commitment? While in Thessalonica, Paul had instructed his converts to anticipate affliction (καὶ γὰρ ὅτε πρὸς ὑμᾶς ἦμεν, προελέγομεν ὑμῖν ὅτι μέλλομεν θλίβεσθαι, 3.4), for such was their lot (3.3).[14] Paul also taught the church to view itself as distinct from the rest of society.[15] Therefore, when the Thessalonians actually

---

Lexicography', *JETS* 25 (1982), pp. 307-21; Bruce, *Thessalonians*, p. 123; Richard, *Thessalonians*, p. 277; Hill, *Establishing the Church in Thessalonica*, pp. 233-41; and Hemphill, *Spiritual Gifts*, p. 31. Frame (*Thessalonians*, p. 198) and Bicknell (*Thessalonians*, p. 59) offer the unconvincing suggestion that Paul is referring in 5.14c to those who are morally weak (see 1 Thess. 4.1).

11. If so, then these people would have found timely Paul's commands to 'rejoice always, pray constantly [and] give thanks in all circumstances' (5.16-18a).

12. So also Bammel, 'Preparation for the Perils', p. 100, and de Vos, *Church and Community Conflicts*, pp. 168. The apostasy spoken of in 2 Thess. 2.3 is to take place in the future.

13. Cf. Paul's correspondence with the Corinthians, Galatians and Philippians. The apostle does not tend to cover over what he perceives to be congregational problems. Even at those points where Paul is most diplomatic, e.g. in parts of Rom. and Phile., he can also be quite frank.

14. Jewett (*Thessalonian Correspondence*, pp. 94, 171) suggests that the congregation was surprised at the presence of 'persecution'. This seems unlikely in light of the facts that they 'received the word in much affliction' (1.6) and that Paul had instructed them to expect continued affliction (3.4).

15. On the social (ethical) dualisms in 1 (and 2) Thess., see further pp. 196-97 above.

encountered opposition from outsiders, it served to confirm and to reinforce Paul's apocalyptic instruction all the more. The apostle's apocalyptic teaching prepared his converts for external opposition and provided them with a ready explanation of non-Christian hostility.

As other scholars have noted,[16] there seems to have been a complex
correlation between the Thessalonians' social dislocation and ideological orientation. On the one hand, the Christians' conflict with unbelievers would have severely strained or even severed former relational
networks, thereby making it undesirable or untenable for the believers
to return to their pre-conversion associations and activities. On the
other hand, the converts' conflict with their compatriots would have
confirmed their new worldview and convinced them that there was no
pressing reason to revert to their old patterns of life, even if they
could.[17] Conflict with their fellow Gentiles, therefore, fortified the
Thessalonians' faith and urged them to curtail, or even to cut off, intimate social contact with outsiders. In writing 1 Thessalonians, Paul
seeks to strengthen further his converts' faith by reiterating that suffering as a Christian is inevitable and profitable (3.3-4; cf. 2 Thess. 1.5)
and by reinforcing the community's boundaries through the use of dualistic apocalyptic categories and fictive kinship language.

3. *Conflict and Community*

Not only did the believers' clash with outsiders seemingly bolster the
church's faith, but the affliction that the assembly experienced also
appears to have engendered especially good relations between Paul and
the Thessalonians and among the Thessalonian Christians themselves.
Paul's admiration for and approval of the church in Thessalonica is
apparent throughout 1 Thessalonians.[18] For example, in 1.7 Paul refers

16. In particular, Meeks, 'Social Functions of Apocalyptic Language', pp. 689-
95, and Barclay, 'Conflict in Thessalonica', pp. 516-20.

17. For insightful treatments of the conversion process and its social effects, see
Berger and Luckman, *Social Construction of Reality*, pp. 157-63, and Segal, *Paul
the Convert*, pp. 72-114.

18. Most commentators agree that in 1 Thess. Paul displays his fondness of and
pleasure with the Thessalonians. E.g. Lünemann, *Thessalonians*, p. 4; Milligan,
Thessalonians, pp. xxx-xxxi; Neil, *Thessalonians*, pp. xxvii-xxviii; Best, *Thessalonians*, p. 15; Marshall, *Thessalonians*, p. 10; and Martin, *Thessalonians*, p. 47. Jewett (*Thessalonian Correspondence*, p. 177) thinks that Paul is responding to 'the
crisis of a radicalized and hence vulnerable millenarianism by writing 1 Thessa-

to the congregation as an exemplary assembly (a τύπος)[19] for all those believers living in Macedonia and Achaia.[20] That the Thessalonian Christians were special to Paul is also suggested by Paul's frequent use of familial language throughout 1 Thessalonians.[21] In this epistle Paul refers to his converts as ἀδελφοί 18 times. Additionally, he speaks of himself as a father and as a nurse to his converts and likens them to children (2.7, 11). Furthermore, in 2.8 Paul records his deep care for the church and his commitment to share himself and not merely his message with the assembly. Paul's eager desire to see his spiritual children 'face to face' also shows his fond affection for the congregation (2.17-18; 3.6, 10) as does his referring to them as 'beloved by God' (1.4), 'taught by God' (4.9) and his 'glory and joy' (2.20).

1 Thessalonians teems with Pauline accolades of his converts, and I am persuaded that Paul's profuse praise of the church is more than a rhetorical ploy.[22] Such a sustained outpouring of praise from Paul toward his converts is in fact uncommon in his other extant letters.[23] How may we explain the elevated status of the Thessalonian congrega-

lonians'. Paradoxically, earlier in his work on p. 72 Jewett concurs with those scholars who stress the primarily affirmative tone of the letter.

19. Patte (*Paul's Faith*, p. 134) takes τύπος to mean 'typical of what happens to those who receive the word'. This interpretation may be partially correct. However, such a reading cloaks the fact that Paul is holding up the Thessalonian church as an example for other believers to follow.

20. Paul remarks in 1.8-9a that the Thessalonians' faith was so widespread that in his contact with other Macedonian and Achaian Christians he did not have to say anything about his fruitful Thessalonian mission because these believers had already heard of it and were speaking about it to him. Although Paul did not need to boast about the Thessalonians to other believers, it is likely that he did! So also Best, *Thessalonians*, p. 81. Cf. 2 Thess. 1.4 and 2 Cor. 8.1-5.

21. Malherbe ('God's New Family') helpfully highlights the concentrated use of fictive kinship language in 1 Thessalonians.

22. Scholars have identified the epistolary genre of 1 Thess. as parenetic (so Malherbe, *Paul and the Thessalonians*, pp. 68-78) and the rhetorical genre of the epistle as epideictic (e.g. Jewett, *Thessalonian Correspondence*, pp. 71-72). Praise is a central feature of both classifications. I am not aware of an interpreter who has called into question Paul's basic sincerity in writing to his Thessalonian converts in such a way. Neil (*Thessalonians*, pp. xxvii-xxviii) notes that 'the praise which [Paul] lavishes upon these ordinary working-folk of Thessalonica might be dubbed flattery or insincerity. But he is so obviously in deadly earnest.'

23. So also Bammel, 'Preparation for the Perils', p. 91.

tion in Paul's eyes? While not denying other possible explanations,[24] I would suggest that it was the Thessalonians' conversion to and continuation in the faith despite extreme suffering that so endeared them to him.[25]

Did the Thessalonians also view Paul positively? Some scholars think not. As noted in Chapter 6 (p. 144 above), interpreters such as Lütgert, Jewett and Donfried contend with reference to 2.1-12 that some of Paul's converts (identified by Lütgert and Jewett as the ἄτακτοι) were openly critical of their apostle.[26] Even if Paul is engaged in impression management in 1 Thessalonians, views that posit problems between Paul and the Thessalonians do not commend themselves. There is, in fact, no unequivocal textual evidence to support arguments for poor relations between Paul and his converts. Contrariwise, upon his return from Thessalonica, Timothy tells Paul that the church has fond memories of its missionaries and longs to see them (3.6). It seems doubtful to me that Paul would have intentionally distorted Timothy's report in order to smooth over troubled relations with the church. To have wittingly falsified the situation would have been an 'ironical

24. E.g. the Thessalonians' eager reception and internalization of Paul's apocalyptic message and the congregation's fond affection of the apostle.

25. Wanamaker (*Thessalonians*, p. 83) concurs that it was the Thessalonians' experience of and response to external hostility that 'accounts for the unique esteem in which the community in Thessalonica was held by Paul and his mission congregations'. Cf. Helmut Koester, 'Apostel und Gemeinde in den Briefen an die Thessalonicher', in Dieter Lührmann and Georg Strecker (eds.), *Kirche: Festschrift für Günther Bornkamm zum 75. Geburtstag* (Tübingen: J.C.B. Mohr [Paul Siebeck], 1980), pp. 287-98.

26. Cf. Goulder ('Silas in Thessalonica') who argues that Paul's converts, many of whom Goulder thinks were formerly God-fearers, opposed Paul and his teaching and that Silas, a 'Jerusalem man', was the person responsible for sowing seeds of congregational and theological discord. When Paul addresses in 1 Thess. the need to keep working, the proximity of the parousia, matters pertaining to sexual purity and issues concerning his own integrity, Goulder is convinced that he is countering problems created by Silas's teaching of a realized eschatology. Goulder also thinks that 2 Thess. is meant to oppose realized eschatology. It should be noted that Goulder draws the vast majority of his parallels from 1 Cor. I will indicate in the text below why I do not follow the type of proposal which Goulder offers. Goulder spells out this 'two missionaries, two missions' argument, which is in essence a restatement of Baur's well-known thesis (as Goulder himself acknowledges), more fully in *St. Paul Versus St. Peter: A Tale of Two Missions* (Louisville, KY: Westminster/John Knox Press, 1994).

insult' and would likely have undermined the good will which existed between Paul and the Thessalonians.[27] From all indications, the Thessalonian Christians were as fond of Paul as he was of them.

Interestingly, conflict theorists have noted that intergroup conflict can strengthen the relational bonds between a group's leader(s) and followers provided that the leader(s) respond(s) to the conflict with skill and sensitivity.[28] Indeed, portions of 1 Thessalonians may be read as Paul's attempt to help his converts (and himself!) cope with continued conflict (1.6-10; 2.13-16; 2.17–3.13; 4.11-12; 5.1-11, 15; cf. 2 Thess. 1.5-12). One can imagine that this personal and well-crafted epistle buoyed the congregation when it was read (5.27) and further strengthened the bonds of friendship which existed between the church and Paul. In short, I would suggest that Paul and the Thessalonians shared a reciprocal affection and admiration which was forged on the anvil of affliction.

We turn now to investigate the impact of the conflict on the believers' relations with one another. Under some circumstances, intergroup conflict can adversely affect a group by undermining its sense of unity. For instance, the external opposition experienced by the Philippian congregation seemingly exacerbated that assembly's disunity.[29] In other contexts, however, external adversity can draw a community closer together thereby enhancing its sense of solidarity, identity and boundaries.[30] This appears to have been what happened in Thessalonica.

Paul does, in fact, command his converts to respect and esteem their leaders and 'to be at peace with one another' (5.12-13). And building upon the work of Schmithals and Lütgert,[31] Jewett construes these commands, along with 2.1-12 and 5.19-22, as Paul's attempt to counter criticism from the ἄτακτοι (5.14).[32] For Jewett, the ἄτακτοι (or 'millenarian

27. So Johanson, *To All the Brethren*, p. 52.

28. E.g. Rex, *Social Conflict*, pp. 40, 43, and Deutsch, *Resolution of Conflict*, pp. 77-80.

29. So Davorin Peterlin, *Paul's Letter to the Philippians in the Light of Disunity in the Church* (NovTSup, 79; Leiden: E.J. Brill, 1995), p. 55; Fee, *Philippians*, p. 366; and de Vos, *Church and Community Conflicts*, pp. 265-75.

30. So Keith A. Roberts (*Religion in a Sociological Perspective* [Belmont, CA: Wadsworth, 1995], p. 71) On other possible outcomes of intergroup conflict, see further pp. 120-23 below.

31. Schmithals, *Paul and the Gnostics*, and Lütgert, 'Enthusiasten in Thessalonich'.

32. Jewett, *Thessalonian Correspondence*, pp. 102-105. Cf. similarly Jeffrey A.D. Weima, *Neglected Endings: The Significance of Pauline Letter Closings*

radicals')[33] were those rebellious, lower-class Thessalonian congregants who resisted on principle the structures of everyday life including the work ethic, the sexual ethic, and the authority of congregational leadership. They also refused to prepare for the future παρουσία of Christ because they felt they were already experiencing and embodying his presence completely in their ecstatic activities.[34]

Although I would agree with Jewett that the Thessalonian assembly had a millenarian mindset,[35] there is insufficient evidence to support his particular understanding of the ἄτακτοι. It does in fact appear that some

(JSNTSup, 101; Sheffield: JSOT Press, 1994), pp. 184-86; Frame, *Thessalonians*, p. 195; and Hemphill, *Spiritual Gifts*, pp. 28-29. Contrast Best (*Thessalonians*, p. 228) who rightly notes, 'There is insufficient evidence to indicate any division between the [leaders and members].'

33. There is a significant amount of scholarly debate regarding how best to translate ἄτακτος. Originally, the term was used to speak of 'people who failed to keep their proper position, whether in the army or in civil life' (Marshall, *Thessalonians*, p. 150). Over time the word came to mean 'undisciplined, unruly, or disorderly' (Hill, *Establishing the Church in Thessalonica*, p. 224). The term is often rendered as 'idle' (RSV, NRSV and NIV). This interpretation is in keeping with the apparent meaning of the verbal and adverbial cognates of ἄτακτος in 2 Thess. 3.7, 11 and in P.Oxy. 275, 725 (so Milligan, *Thessalonians*, pp. 153-54). Other translators (KJV, NASB) render the word more literally as 'disorderly'. Can these seemingly divergent translations be correlated? Many commentators believe so. See, e.g., Frame, *Thessalonians*, p. 197; Morris, *Thessalonians*, p. 168; Bruce, *Thessalonians*, p. 122; Wanamaker, *Thessalonians*, p. 197; Weatherly, *Thessalonians*, p. 182; Malherbe, *Paul and the Thessalonians*, p. 92; Russell, 'The Idle in 2 Thess. 3:6-12', p. 108; and Black, 'The Weak in Thessalonica', p. 315 n. 20. See otherwise, Collins (*Birth of the New Testament*, p. 94), Richard (*Thessalonians*, p. 276) and Holmes (*Thessalonians*, p. 180) who contend that the term means 'disorderly'. Cf. de Vos (*Church and Community Conflicts*, pp. 164-66) who maintains that Paul employs ἄτακτος to refer the Thessalonian Christians' civil disobedience. I am inclined to concur with Marshall (*Thessalonians*, p. 151) who thinks that 'the general context in the letter [i.e. 1 Thess.] indicates that the specific type of disorderliness in mind here lay in a refusal to work and conform to the normal way of life of employees' (cf. 2 Thess. 3.6-15). I will show below that Jewett's understanding of the ἄτακτοι as insubordinate to the church's leaders (including Paul) lacks textual support.

34. Jewett, *Thessalonian Correspondence*, p. 176.

35. I would disagree, however, with Jewett's contention that the Thessalonians eagerly embraced a radically realized eschatology because of 'an unwillingness to live with the uncertainty of a future eschatology' (p. 97). See further pp. 282-85 below.

of Paul's converts were more interested in meddling than in working (4.11-12; cf. 2 Thess. 3.11). Furthermore, it is probable that Jewett and many other commentators are correct in correlating 1 Thess. 4.11-12 with 5.14a and with 2 Thess. 3.6-13, thereby identifying the ἄτακτοι as those who would not work.[36] However, Jewett's contention that the ἄτακτοι called into question the eschatological and sexual instructions of the apostle and overtly challenged the authority of congregational leaders is not convincing. I will now turn to counter Jewett's proposal that the ἄτακτοι were creating congregational upheaval.

To begin I note that the commands given in 5.12-22 are directed to the entire congregation, not simply the ἄτακτοι (see esp. the presence of ἀδελφοί in 5.12, 14 and ὁρᾶτε μή τις ['See that none of you...'] in 5.15). This fact renders unlikely Jewett's suggestion that 5.12-13 and 5.19-22 were written specifically to counter the ἄτακτοι, which in turn calls into question the idea that the ἄτακτοι were intentionally flouting Pauline authority and disrupting the assembly. Additionally, it does not appear that the activity of ἄτακτοι was opposed by the church or that their behavior had undermined congregational relations.[37] In fact, it appears to be Paul, not the Thessalonians, who was concerned about the potentially adverse effect of the ἄτακτοι on the assembly (5.14; cf. 2 Thess. 3.6-15).[38]

---

36. Jewett, *Thessalonian Correspondence*, pp. 104-105. See also, e.g., Best, *Thessalonians*, p. 230; Marshall, *Thessalonians*, pp. 150-51; Bruce, *Thessalonians*, pp. 122-23; Wanamaker, *Thessalonians*, p. 163; Hill, *Establishing the Church in Thessalonica*, pp. 225-26; Goulder, 'Silas in Thessalonica', pp. 88-89; and cautiously, Barclay, 'Conflict in Thessalonica', p. 525 n. 46. It may be that some of the ἄτακτοι thought that the παρουσία was imminent (or even present [see 2 Thess. 2.2]) and that this conviction reinforced their decision not to work. So, e.g., Neil, *Thessalonians*, p. 124, and Maarten J.J. Menken, 'Paradise Regained or Still Lost?: Eschatology and Disorderly Behaviour in 2 Thessalonians', *NTS* 38 (1992), pp. 271-89. For the argument that there is no correlation between the eschatological and 'vocational' issues, see Russell, 'The Idle in 2 Thess. 3:6-12'.

37. Jewett (*Thessalonian Correspondence*, p. 178) correctly observes that the ἄτακτοι remained a part of the assembly and that they were supported financially by the church. However, this leads him to offer the implausible suggestion that 'their behavior and theology were approved by a sizable and influential segment of the membership'.

38. As to why Paul, if it is indeed he, is so authoritarian in tone when dealing with the ἄτακτοι in 2 Thess. 3.6-15, one might note that intergroup conflict can prompt a group's leader(s) to tighten group boundaries by 'cracking down' on those who would seek to deviate from group norms. Paul set forth his (and thereby the

It is also worth noting here that while 5.12-22 is intended for 'all the brethren',[39] it is neither necessary nor advisable to read the pericope as an attempt on Paul's part to redress community deficiencies. In fact, the overall affirmative tone of 1 Thessalonians[40] and the lack of space Paul devotes to addressing these congregational concerns suggests that no significant problems stand behind the terse injunctions.[41] In contradistinction to Jewett and other commentators who read 5.12-22 to indicate internal divisions among the Thessalonians, then, I understand this passage as preventative, not corrective. Paul was sufficiently skilled as a pastor to recognize that 'an ounce of pastoral prevention was worth a pound of congregational cure'!

The fact that Paul does not explicitly mention actual congregational divisions at any point in 1 (or 2) Thessalonians reinforces further my position. The conspicuous absence of such evidence stands in marked contrast to Paul's correspondence with the Corinthians (e.g. 1 Cor. 1.10; 11.18-19), the Galatians (5.15, 26), the Romans (12.16; 14.1–15.6) and even the Philippians (2.1-4; 4.2). Paul's silence on the issue of infighting should not, of course, lead one to conclude naïvely that there was no internal tension whatsoever within the Thessalonian congregation. It is doubtful that such a church ever has or ever will exist![42]

church's position) concerning work through instruction (3.6, 10) and by example (3.7-9; cf. 1 Thess. 2.9-12). Even still, Paul recommends ostracism (at meal times?), not excommunication, for these 'deviant' congregants (3.6, 14-15; cf. 1 Cor. 5.2). On Paul's instruction in 2 Thess. 3.6-15, see, e.g., Göran Forkman, *The Limits of Religious Community: Expulsion from the Religious Community within the Qumran Sect, within Rabbinic Judaism, and within Primitive Christianity* (ConBNT, 5; Lund: C.W.K. Gleerup, 1972), pp. 132-39; James T. South, *Disciplinary Practices in Pauline Texts* (Lewiston, NY: Edwin Mellen Press, 1992); and John Kurichialnil, '"If Any One Will Not Work, Let Him Not Eat"', *Biblebhashyam* 21 (1995), pp. 184-203.

39. Also noted by, e.g., Malherbe, *Paul and the Thessalonians*, p. 89, and Hemphill, *Spiritual Gifts*, p. 24.

40. For useful remarks on how to detect Paul's tone in a particular letter, see Barclay, 'Mirror-Reading', p. 84.

41. Marshall (*Thessalonians*, p. 146) states, 'In view of Paul's general commendation of the Thessalonians elsewhere in the letter it would be wrong to find serious deficiencies in the life of the church reflected in this section [i.e. 5.12-24].' Cf. Barclay ('Thessalonica and Corinth', p. 51): 'The tone of 1 Thessalonians is that of positive reinforcement, not rebuke or correction.'

42. Hemphill (*Spiritual Gifts*, p. 31) remarks, 'When believers are working

Nevertheless, one may reasonably infer from a comparison with Paul's other congregational letters that his silence regarding internal divisions among the Thessalonians suggests that he was satisfied with the church's unity. It is likely that Timothy upon his return would have informed Paul of any significant tensions among the Thessalonians if they were indeed present. And based upon Paul's other extant Epistles to churches, one may justifiably conclude that he would have clearly and directly addressed disruptive church infighting if he had been informed thereof. 1 Thessalonians 4.13-18 and 5.1-11, as well 2 Thess. 2.1-15 and 3.6-15 (if Pauline), demonstrate Paul's tack in dealing with issues that he believes threaten a congregation. He states the particular problem (in the aforementioned pericopes, deep grief, questions and /or confusion about the parousia and idleness) and then proceeds to offer instruction and admonition. So, when Paul says that the Thessalonians have no need for anyone to write to them concerning love one for another (4.9; cf. 2 Thess. 1.3), it makes good sense to conclude that congregational relations are strong. His admonition to his converts to 'encourage one another and build one another up, *just as you are doing*' (5.11; cf. 4.9) suggests the same.

As indicated at the outset of this section, it appears that the believers' conflict with outsiders was a factor in forging the congregational cohesion and cooperation of which Paul so approvingly speaks. I have argued in Part IV of this study that the Thessalonians' conversion to Pauline Christianity was met with hostility by their Gentile compatriots and that for various reasons the congregation continued to experience conflict relations even after conversion. It is likely that the believers would have avoided, when possible, those people who perceived and responded to them as social deviants. Moreover, they would have turned to their faith community (or from an unbeliever's perspective, 'deviant subculture') for support. That the Christians' conflict with outsiders encouraged them to avoid and/or to neglect former reference groups and to strengthen their relations with one another[43] is a plausible, if but

together in a community setting there will almost invariably be disagreements and the resulting tension.'

43. It is a frequent observation among students of religion that conversion prompts people to alter their former relational networks and to commit themselves to the group to which they have converted. See, e.g., Roberts, *Religion in Sociological Perspective*, pp. 118-19. (Note 1 Thess. 1.9-10 in this context). This is particular true in cases where former associates actively oppose a person's conversion.

a partial, explanation for the unity which seems to have typified the Thessalonian assembly.[44]

4. *Opposition and the Parousia*

Even a casual reader is likely to detect the eschatological tenor of the Thessalonian letters, as eschatology suffuses 1 and 2 Thessalonians (1.10; 2.19-20; 3.13; 4.13–5:11; 5.23; 2 Thess. 1.5–2.12).[45] I suggested in Chapter 8 above (pp. 195-97) that the eschatology of both of these Epistles is of the not-too-distant future variety. Although many scholars perceive eschatological discrepancies between the two documents and maintain that these disparities render 2 Thessalonians inauthentic, I am inclined to think that the letters' eschatological variation is better explained by the contingencies of the Thessalonian context than by the presence of a pseudographer. Nevertheless, whether a scholar attributes one or both of the letters now known as 1 and 2 Thessalonians and the eschatological orientation(s) therein to Paul, there is virtual unanimity among New Testament interpreters that the 'real' Paul clearly believed that the parousia was imminent and that he instructed his converts in Thessalonica (and elsewhere) to think likewise.[46] Here I wish to explore

44. Cf. deSilva, ' "Worthy of his Kingdom" ', pp. 63-69.
45. I understand eschatology to be a specific aspect of apocalyptic theology.
46. Mearns ('Early Eschatological Development in Paul') thinks that Paul's eschatological outlook changed from a realized to a future eschatology between the time that he visited Thessalonica and wrote 1 Thess. because of the death of some Thessalonian believers. Then by the time that Paul wrote 2 Thess., Mearns maintains, he had shifted to a deferred apocalyptic. It seems quite unlikely that Paul would have made such an eschatological shift because a few of his converts had died. It stretches the imagination to think that Paul had not known other believers who had died in the 15 or so years which had elapsed between his conversion and his writing of 1 Thess. Furthermore, as Wanamaker (*Thessalonians*, p. 87) notes, futuristic eschatology was a part of the 'initial élan of early Christianity... Had the early followers of Jesus not believed that he would soon return from heaven as the messianic Lord, Christianity would almost certainly not have come into existence.' For further critique of Mearns's proposal, see L. Joseph Kreitzer, *Jesus and God in Paul's Eschatology* (JSNTSup, 19; Sheffield: JSOT Press, 1987), pp. 177-79.

It is more likely that Paul had not fully instructed his converts concerning the future of the Christian dead at the parousia and that he seeks to do so in 4.13-18. (So also, e.g., Bruce, *Thessalonians*, p. 95; Riesner, *Paul's Early Period*, p. 385; and Herbert Jurgensen, 'Awaiting the Return of Christ: A Re-Examination of 1 Thessalonians 4.13–5.11 from a Pentecostal Perspective', *JPT* 4 [1994], pp. 81-

how the opposition which the Thessalonians experienced from unbelievers shaped their inherited eschatological orientation.

In his important work *The Thessalonian Correspondence*, Jewett suggests that the Thessalonians had rejected Paul's future eschatological stance for a thoroughgoing realized eschatology.[47] In Jewett's perception, the congregation's eschatological perspective had been called into question by the church's experience of 'persecution'[48] and by the death of a few fellow believers.[49] He avers, 'In the case of the Thessalonians, the radicality of the realized eschatology rendered them vulnerable to collapse when death and persecution arose.'[50] Furthermore, Jewett holds that 5.1-11 is designed to counter the Thessalonians' 'unwillingness to live with the uncertainty of future eschatology'.[51]

It is clear that Paul thought the deaths of some church members had created consternation among the Thessalonians (4.13). However, it does not appear that unforeseen deaths, continued conflict or realized eschatology had caused those believers who remained to forfeit their eschatological hope. 1 Thessalonians 4.13-18 suggests that Paul's converts were grieved because they had not anticipated that death would precede the parousia not because they had grown weary in waiting for their Lord's coming. If some among the living were in danger of losing hope,[52] it was seemingly not for themselves, but for those who had died

113 [92]). As for 5.1-11, it is clear that Paul is *reminding* (see 5.1-2; cf. 1.9-10) his converts, some of whom were overly anxious for the parousia (cf. 2 Thess. 2.2), that the Day of the Lord, which had not yet come, would come surely and suddenly.

47. So also, Goulder ('Silas in Thessalonica') who, like Jewett, Lütgert and Schmithals, tends to read 1 and 2 Thess. while wearing 'Corinthian spectacles'.

48. Jewett (*Thessalonian Correspondence*, 94) remarks, '[T]he Thessalonians were for some reason surprised or perturbed that persecution would be a part of their life in the new age, and that its presence cast doubt on the vitality of their faith.'

49. Jewett (*Thessalonian Correspondence*, p. 96) writes, '[I]t appears that the Thessalonians believed that the presence of the new age should have eliminated the possibility of death for true believers, so that when deaths occurred, they fell into despair about their eschatological faith, discounting the possibility of ever seeing their loved ones again.'

50. Jewett, *Thessalonian Correspondence*, p. 177.

51. Jewett, *Thessalonian Correspondence*, p. 97.

52. Some scholars understand Paul's admonitions to 'encourage the fainthearted' (παραμυθεῖσθε τοὺς ὀλιγοψύχους) and/or to 'help the weak' (ἀντέχεσθε τῶν ἀσθενῶν) to suggest as much (5.14). See, e.g., Black, 'The Weak in Thessalonica', p. 321; Hill, *Establishing the Church in Thessalonica*, pp. 230-41; Jewett,

prior to the parousia, an event which Paul had taught the Thessalonians to believe would soon come like a 'thief in the night' (5.2).[53] Paul's comments about 'the times and the seasons' (5.1-11), therefore, should not be understood as an attempt to counter his converts' waning enthusiasm for a future eschatology, but as a pastoral reminder to be patient and morally prepared for the imminent coming of Christ.[54]

If one considers 2 Thessalonians to be authentically Pauline, as both Jewett and I do, then Paul's plea for the Thessalonians 'not to be quickly shaken in mind [μὴ ταχέως σαλευθῆναι ἀπὸ τοῦ νοὸς] or excited [θροεῖσθαι], either by spirit or word or by letter purporting to be from us, to the effect that the Day of the Lord has come [ὡς ὅτι ἐνέστηκεν ἡ ἡμέρα τοῦ κυρίου]' (2.2) is applicable. Here, Paul urges his converts not to give credence to the claim that the Day of the Lord has arrived. How did such an assertion arise, and what did the Thessalonians understand it to mean?

As one might anticipate by now, Jewett thinks that the claim originated from those millenarian radicals who championed, in contradistinction to Paul, a realized eschatology.[55] Although Jewett is right to insist that ἐνέστηκεν means 'already arrived',[56] his contention that the congregation understood the Day of the Lord as having come in some

---

Thessalonian Correspondence, p. 97; and Hemphill, *Spiritual Gifts*, p. 31.

53. So also Barclay, 'Conflict in Thessalonica', p. 517, and 'Thessalonica and Corinth', p. 52. That Paul had instructed his converts when he was with them to expect the parousia to be both soon and sudden is evidenced in 4.15, 17 and 5.1-3. It may be that Paul so stressed the imminence of the Lord's coming that he failed to prepare the church properly for the possibility that death might come before Jesus did. Paul's remark that 'we would not have you ignorant' (4.13) signals additional, if not novel, instruction.

54. So rightly Barclay, 'Conflict in Thessalonica', p. 517.

55. Jewett, *Thessalonian Correspondence*, p. 176. Cf. Lütgert, 'Enthusiasten in Thessalonich', pp. 82-87; Schmithals, *Paul and the Gnostics*, pp. 202-12; Donfried, 'Theology of 1 and 2 Thessalonians', p. 88; and Goulder, 'Silas in Thessalonica', pp. 98-100.

56. Jewett, *Thessalonian Correspondence*, pp. 97-98. So also, e.g., Bicknell, *Thessalonians*, p. 74; Martin, *Thessalonians*, pp. 227-28; and Menken, 'Paradise Regained or Still Lost?', pp. 280-81. Dobschütz (*Thessalonicherbriefe*, pp. 267-68) and Dibelius (*Thessalonicher*, p. 29) unsuccessfully argued that ἐνέστηκεν means 'is imminent'.

internal and personal way is unconvincing.[57] As other interpreters have recognized, it is quite unlikely that Paul would have opposed a spiritualized interpretation of the Day of the Lord by spelling out the external signs which were meant to occur prior to Jesus' coming.[58] It is more likely that the Thessalonians' eager expectation of the parousia prompted some of the membership, sufficiently armed with Paul's verbal and written instruction, to interpret an unspecified and unusual external calamity (cf. 1 Thess. 2.16) as marking the arrival of the Day of the Lord and to conclude that the Lord himself would soon descend with all his saints to rescue them from their present plight and to punish their opponents.[59] Roger Aus correctly concludes,

> The addressees of Second Thessalonians do not maintain that the *parousia*, the visible coming of the Lord Jesus in his glory, has occurred. They do maintain, however, that his Day has *started* to come, therefore they can also express it as 'having come' (emphasis his).[60]

57. The idea that the Thessalonians thought that the Day of the Lord had come in some spiritualized sense is rightly rejected by, among others, Marshall, *Thessalonians*, p. 186; Wanamaker, *Thessalonians*, p. 240; and Richard, *Thessalonians*, pp. 343-44.

58. So Dobschütz, *Thessalonicherbriefe*, p. 267; Best, *Thessalonians*, p. 276; Martin, *Thessalonians*, pp. 228-29; Menken, 'Paradise Regained or Still Lost?', pp. 274-75; and Barclay, 'Conflict in Thessalonica', p. 527. *Pace* Goulder ('Silas in Thessalonica', p. 99) who suggests that 'Paul' resorted to spelling out an eschatological program in 2 Thess. 2.3-12 because his attempt to alleviate grief in 1 Thess. 4.13-18 was unsuccessful.

59. So Barclay, 'Conflict in Thessalonica', pp. 527-28. Barclay notes that although Paul probably intended no temporal distinction between the parousia of Christ and the Day of the Lord, some of his converts seemingly did. Cf. Holland, *The Tradition that You Received from Us*, pp. 96-105. Menken ('Paradise Regained or Still Lost?', p. 285) imagines that the author of 2 Thess. is countering the claim that 'Christ had already returned on earth and was already performing his task or was on the point of doing so'. If this were indeed the situation, one is left to wonder why the writer, who Menken understands to be someone other than Paul, did not identify this so-called Christ as deceptively evil. If Paul wrote the letter, Menken's suggestion is even less plausible, for the Thessalonians were instructed in the initial epistle that they would be caught up in the clouds upon the Lord's return. This fact in and of itself would have nullified the claim which had shaken the congregation.

60. Roger D. Aus, 'The Relevance of Isaiah 66:7 to Revelation 12 and 2 Thessalonians 1', *ZNW* 7 (1976), pp. 252-68 (264). Note similarly Neil, *Thessalonians*, p. 159; Morris, *Thessalonians*, pp. 216-17; Richard, *Thessalonians*, pp. 343-44; and Marshall, *Thessalonians*, p. 186.

Furthermore, Aus (and others) has rightly noted the positive correlation between the Thessalonians' eschatological orientation and their afflictions.[61]

From all appearances, then, the Thessalonian Christians eagerly embraced Paul's instruction concerning the imminent parousia of Christ, and the afflictions which they were experiencing served to heighten their enthusiasm for and preoccupation with the Lord's coming. In 1 Thessalonians Paul seeks, among other things, to comfort his converts in their suffering and in the loss of their Christian loved ones and to encourage them to steadfastness as they await the coming of their heavenly Savior.[62] 2 Thessalonians may be plausibly read as Paul's attempt to support his converts in the throes of intensified intergroup conflict[63] and to correct what he considered to be potentially disastrous eschatological excesses[64] which were linked to, if not spawned by, the church's experience of external hostility. The desire to escape to another time and another place is a common reaction of those who are suffering oppression.[65] Paul's verbal and written instruction about the

61. Aus, 'Relevance of Isaiah 66:7', pp. 263-64, and 'Liturgical Background', p. 438; Barclay, 'Conflict in Thessalonica', pp. 519, 527-28; Wanamaker, *Thessalonians*, p. 240; Martin, *Thessalonians*, p. 229; and Bammel, 'Preparation for the Perils'.

62. Susan R. Garrett ('Paul's Thorn and Cultural Models of Affliction', in White and Yarbrough [eds.], *The Social World of the First Christians*, pp. 82-99 [90]) rightly notes that Paul is concerned in 1 Thess. 3.1-5 that his converts patiently endure their sufferings. Cf. 1.3; 2 Thess. 1.4; 3.15; Jas 5.11; and 1 Pet. 5.8-9.

63. Edgar Krentz ('Through a Lens: Theology and Fidelity in 2 Thessalonians', in Bassler [ed.], *Pauline Theology*, I, pp. 52-62) rightly suggests that 2 Thess. is a response to suffering. Krentz is not entirely accurate, however, in claiming that '2 Thessalonians is essentially a letter with one theme: faithful endurance under persecution' (p. 61).

64. Some of the assembly became even more eager for the parousia than their teacher. So also Henry Cadbury ('Overconversion in Paul's Churches', in Sherman E. Johnson [ed.], *The Joy of Study: Papers on New Testament and Other Related Subjects Presented to Honor Frederick Clifton Grant* [New York: Macmillan, 1951], pp. 43-50 [46-47]) who insightfully remarks, 'To judge from his letters Paul's mind was antithetic in structure just as his speech tends to elaborated antithesis...and such a preacher is sure to make some converts who are more radical than himself.'

65. See Roberts's (*Religion in Sociological Perspective*, pp. 265-76) useful discussion on this topic, which includes a fascinating section on the theme of future

imminent return of the Lord which would result in salvation for Christians and destruction for non-Christians appears to have led some of his beleaguered converts to cope with their plight on earth by looking eagerly, sometimes too eagerly, for their hope from heaven.

5. *Conclusion*

At the outset of 1 Thessalonians, Paul tells his converts that in his prayers he thanks God for their 'work of faith and labor of love and steadfastness of hope' (τοῦ ἔργου τῆς πίστεως καὶ τοῦ κόπου τῆς ἀγάπης καὶ τῆς ὑπομονῆς τῆς ἐλπίδος, 1.3; cf. 2 Thess. 1.3). Was the Thessalonian congregation truly characterized by faith, love and hope? In this chapter I have noted that some commentators are convinced that the church in Thessalonica was flagging in faith, lacking in love and /or waning in hope. My evaluation of the evidence in 1 (and 2) Thessalonians has led me to conclude otherwise. Although Paul does reiterate to his converts the importance of putting on the breastplate of faith and love as well as the helmet of hope (5.8), I have shown that there are good reasons to think that they had never actually taken off these vital pieces of the spiritual panoply. Unless Paul is less than honest with his converts (and consequently we belated readers) and/or I have misread Paul's correspondence to his converts, the church in Thessalonica appears to have been persevering in apocalyptic faith, excelling in congregational love and thriving (some too much so) in Christian hope. Although one may explain the presence of faith, love and hope among the Thessalonians in a variety of ways, I have posited here that conflict with outsiders played a pivotal role in reinforcing their received faith, deepening their shared love and heightening their Christian hope. Conflict theorists indicate that intergroup conflict can have both constructive and destructive effects on an ingroup. With the aid of Paul's apocalyptic theology and pastoral sensitivity, the Thessalonians were able to flourish in faith, love and hope in the midst of external opposition.

One is left to wonder how the Thessalonian congregation fared in subsequent years.[66] The church virtually disappears from apostolic[67]

---

eschatology in the hymnody of oppressed Christians.

66. Paul's later epistolary remarks about (2 Cor. 8.1-5; 11.9; Rom. 15.26) and personal contacts with (1 Cor. 16.5; cf. Acts 19.21; 20.1-6) the churches in Mace-

and ecclesiastical history[68] until the fourth century CE when Theodoret comments on the city of Thessalonica and the church therein (*Hist. Eccl.* 5.17).[69] In the tenth century Cameniata gives Thessalonica the title of 'the orthodox city'.[70] This is indeed an ironic turn of events, for as we have seen in this study Paul and his converts would have been regarded by their respective compatriots as anything but 'orthodox'.

donia imply that his relationship with the Thessalonian assembly remained 'outstandingly happy' (so Bruce, *Thessalonians*, p. xxvii).

67. The city is mentioned by name in Phil. 4.16; 2 Tim. 4.10; and Acts 17.11, 13; 20.4; 27.2. See also Acts 17.1-10a where Luke offers a stylized summary of Paul's sojourn in the city.

68. There are passing references to the Thessalonian church in Eusebius, *Hist. Eccl.* 4.26, and Tertullian, *De praescr. haeret.* 36.

69. The conspicuous absence of Thessalonica from the writings of the early church fathers leads Walter Bauer (*Orthodoxy and Heresy in Earliest Christianity* [trans. Philadelphia Seminar on Christian Origins; ed. Robert A. Kraft and Geherd Krodel; Mifflintown, PA: Sigler Press, 1996], pp. 74-75) to conjecture that c. 100 CE Christians in Thessalonica departed from the teaching of Paul. As Bauer admits, however, this suggestion is prompted by silence, not evidence.

70. Noted by Lightfoot, 'The Church of Thessalonica', p. 269 n. 1.

CONCLUSION

1. *Study Summary*

In this project I have addressed an important issue in Thessalonian research which has previously received inadequate scholarly attention, namely the discordant relations between Christians and non-Christians in Thessalonica. By engaging in detailed exegesis and by drawing upon the social sciences, I have been able to spell out in some detail the specifics and dynamics of Paul's and his converts' clash with outsiders. Paul, I have contended, was vigorously opposed by unbelievers while in Thessalonica and was ultimately driven from the city by some non-Christian Jews. Paul's controversy with his Jewish compatriots was seemingly over the apostle's law-free living and teaching. I also suggested that the apocalyptic and polemical nature of the Thessalonian letter(s) may be partially and usefully explained as Paul's response to non-Christian opposition. Paul's converts in Thessalonica, I have argued, were verbally, socially and perhaps physically harassed by their fellow Gentiles and were perceived by some of their former associates as exclusive, offensive and even subversive. The conflict which the Christians encountered with outsiders apparently reinforced the congregation's faith, love and hope.

2. *Contributions of this Volume and Suggestions for Further Research*

As to the contributions of this work, I have sought to demonstrate herein that the language of affliction in 1 (and 2) Thessalonians is best construed as external opposition which Paul and the Thessalonian Christians experienced at the hands of unbelievers. This interpretation has significant implications not only for how one understands such terminology in the Epistle(s) but also for how one construes the whole of 1 (and 2) Thessalonians. I have shown in this project that the Thessalonian correspondence is best read with the intergroup conflict between insiders and outsiders clearly in view.

I have also evinced that the conflict in Thessalonica had varied origins, multiple causes and mixed effects. While Paul ran into trouble
with Thessalonian Jews in particular for his radical message and
methodology, Paul's Gentile converts came into conflict with their own
compatriots over their conversion to Pauline Christianity and the resocialization process that this 'turning' entailed. Paul responded to the
conflict in Thessalonica with apocalyptically laced and polemically
charged rhetoric which may be described as pastoral toward insiders
and as less than charitable toward outsiders. To paraphrase 1 Thess.
5.21-22, the Thessalonian believers reacted to their affliction by holding
fast to that which was 'good' (i.e. Pauline Christianity) and by abstain-
ing from that which was 'evil' (i.e. their former lives in 'idolatry'). This
study has enabled, then, a more nuanced view of the conflict between
Christians and non-Christians in Thessalonica in particular and of the
conflict between believers and unbelievers in early Christianity (where
it existed) in general.

Additionally, my work has underscored the probability that 1 Thess.
2.13-16 is authentically Pauline and has highlighted the congruity
which exists between 1 and 2 Thessalonians. Although most contemporary scholars affirm the integrity of 1 Thess. 2.13-16, the majority of
modern-day exegetes deny the authenticity of 2 Thessalonians. Perhaps
this project will prompt some interpreters to re-evaluate their position
on the authorship of 2 Thessalonians. I have suggested here that both
Epistles were written by Paul to an immature, yet committed and close-
knit, congregation which was opposed by outsiders and preoccupied
with the parousia.

Furthermore, one may view my approach to utilizing the social sciences in this work as somewhat unqiue. While not devising a 'model'
per se, I thoroughly discuss the social-scientific theories which I
employ in this study and carefully apply these theoretical insights
where they legitimately fit. As a result, I preserve the integrity and
complexity of both the historical and social-scientific material.[1] I view

---

1.   In writing a fiery response to Philip F. Esler's highly critical review
('Community and Gospel in Early Christianity: A Response to Richard Bauckham's
Gospels for All Christians', *SJT* 51 [1998], pp. 235-48) of a volume which he
edited (*The Gospel for All Christians: Rethinking the Gospel Audiences* [Grand
Rapids: Eerdmans; Edinburgh: T. & T. Clark, 1998]), Richard Bauckham
('Response', [p. 251]) remarks: 'In the New Testament field the combination of
well trained and practised historical judgment and social scientific proficiency is

my use of deviance and conflict theory here in somewhat the same way that David G. Horrell views his use of Anthony Giddens's 'structuration theory' in his work—as an heuristic tool which 'offers resources for a theoretical framework, yet encourages the researcher also to remain open to the contextually and historically specific nature of the arena of investigation'.[2] By drawing upon the social-scientific study of deviance and conflict, I have been able to demonstrate how differences can arise between parties, how difference can be thought of as deviance and how deviance can lead to disagreement. Specifically, I have discovered that Paul and his Thessalonian converts were viewed as dangerously different by their respective compatriots and that Jewish and Gentile outsiders pressured Paul and the church to conform to the accepted conventions of the day. In 1 (and 2) Thessalonians we discover traces of Paul's perception of and response to this non-Christian opposition and oppression.

As for issues that have arisen from my research that merit further scholarly exploration, I would suggest that the conflict relations between Christians and non-Christians which are evidenced in, for example, Philippians, 1 Peter and Revelation, and the controversy between believers which is indicated in, for example, the Corinthian correspondence, Galatians, the Pastoral Epistles, the Johannine letters, 2 Peter and Jude, might be usefully explored by using insights from the social-scientific study of deviance and conflict. These theoretical constructs could sensitize interpreters to the social realities that stand behind the heated, and at times hostile, rhetoric in these documents.

Ideally, this study will not only contribute to the critical inquiry of 1 (and 2) Thessalonians and to the social-scientific interpretation of the New Testament, but will also spark further discussion and research in the following areas: Acts' depiction of the Pauline mission; the conversion of God-fearers to Christianity and their presence in Pauline assemblies; Jewish responses to Paul; early Jewish–Christian relations; evangelism in the early church; the phenomenon of 'apostasy' in Diaspora Judaism and early Christianity; apocalyptic elements in Pauline

---

unfortunately rare.' If Bauckham's assessment is accurate, which I fear it is, then I hope that this study proves to be an exception to the rule!

2.   David G. Horrell, 'The Development of Theological Ideology in Pauline Christianity: A Structuration Theory Perspective', in Esler (ed.), *Modelling Early Christianity*, pp. 224-36 (224). See more fully Horrell's monograph *Social Ethos of the Corinthian Correspondence*.

thought; the presence of polemic in apocalyptically oriented documents; and the response of Greeks and Romans to the early Christians.

This study has demonstrated that Paul's and the Thessalonians' conflict was, in part, a clash between 'deviant' Christians and particular power structures of that day. Indeed, 1 (and 2) Thessalonians may be instructively read as Paul's attempt to manage and to sort through his and his converts' conflict with non-Christian outsiders. People embroiled in conflict, both then and now, face the challenge of how to respond to it. Ultimately, those in the throes of conflict must discover for themselves how to use conflict creatively, to express dissent responsibly and to wield power equitably.

BIBLIOGRAPHY

Aarde, A. van, 'The Struggle against Heresy in the Thessalonian Correspondence and the Origin of the Apostolic Tradition', in Collins (ed.), *The Thessalonian Correspondence*, pp. 418-25.

Akers, Ronald L., *Deviant Behavior: A Social Learning Approach* (Belmont, CA: Wadsworth, 3rd edn, 1985).

Aune, David E., 'Apocalypticism', *DPL*, pp. 25-35.

—'Magic in Early Christianity', *ANRW* II.23.2, pp. 1507-77.

—*The New Testament in its Literary Environment* (LEC, 8; Philadelphia: Westminster Press, 1987).

Aus, Roger D., 'The Liturgical Background of the Necessity and Propriety of Giving Thanks According to 2 Thes 1:3', *JBL* 92 (1973), pp. 432-38.

—'The Relevance of Isaiah 66:7 to Revelation 12 and 2 Thessalonians 1', *ZNW* 7 (1976), pp. 252-68.

Ayer, Alfred, 'Sources of Intolerance', in Susan Mendus and David Edwards (eds.), *On Toleration* (Oxford: Clarendon Press, 1987), pp. 83-100.

Baarda, T.J., '1 Thess. 2:14-16: Rodrigues in "Nestle–Aland"', *NedTTs* 39 (1985), pp. 186-93.

Baasland, Ernst, 'Persecution: A Neglected Feature in the Letter to the Galatians', *ST* 38 (1984), pp. 135-50.

Bacon, B.W., 'Wrath "unto the Uttermost"', *The Expositor*, Eighth Series, 22 (1922), pp. 356-76.

Bailey, John A, 'Who Wrote II Thessalonians?', *NTS* 25 (1978–79), pp. 131-45.

Balch, David L., *Let Wives Be Submissive: The Domestic Code in 1 Peter* (SBLMS, 26; Chico, CA: Scholars Press, 1981).

Bammel, Ernst, 'Ein Beitrag zur paulinischen Staatsanschauung', *TLZ* 85 (1960), pp. 837-40.

—'Judenverfolgung und Naherwartung: Zur Eschatologie des ersten Thessalonicherbriefs', *ZTK* 56 (1959), pp. 294-315.

—'Preparation for the Perils of the Last Days', in William Horbury and Brian McNeil (eds.), *Suffering and Martyrdom in the New Testament* (Cambridge: Cambridge University Press, 1981), pp. 91-100.

Barclay, John M.G., 'Conflict in Thessalonica', *CBQ* 55 (1993), pp. 512-30.

—'Deviance and Apostasy: Some Applications of Deviance Theory to First-Century Judaism and Christianity', in Esler (ed.), *Modelling Early Christianity*, pp. 114-27.

—' "Do We Undermine the Law?": A Study of Romans 14.1–15.6', in Dunn (ed.), *Paul and the Mosaic Law*, pp. 287-308.

—*Jews in the Mediterranean Diaspora from Alexander to Trajan (323 BCE–117 CE)* (Edinburgh: T. & T. Clark, 1996).

—'Mirror-Reading a Polemical Letter: Galatians as a Test Case', *JSNT* 31 (1987), pp. 73-93.

—*Obeying the Truth: Paul's Ethics in Galatians* (Minneapolis: Fortress Press, 1988).

—'Paul among Diaspora Jews: Anomaly or Apostate?', *JSNT* 60 (1995), pp. 89-120.

—'Paul and Philo on Circumcision: Romans 2.25-29 in Social and Cultural Context', *NTS* 44 (1998), pp. 536-56.

—'Thessalonica and Corinth: Social Contrasts in Pauline Christianity', *JSNT* 47 (1992), pp. 49-72.

—'Who Was Considered an Apostate in the Jewish Diaspora?', in Graham N. Stanton and Guy Stroumsa (eds.), *Tolerence and Intolerance in Early Judaism and Christianity* (Cambridge: Cambridge University Press, 1998), pp. 80-98.

Baron, Robert A., and Donn Byrne, *Social Psychology: Understanding Human Interaction* (Boston: Allyn & Bacon, 5th edn, 1987).

Barrett, C. K., *The Acts of the Apostles.* II. *Introduction and Commentary on Acts XV–XXVIII* (ICC; 2 vols.; Edinburgh: T. & T. Clark, 1998).

—*A Commentary on the Second Epistle to the Corinthians* (BNTC; London: A. & C. Black, 1973).

—*Paul: An Introduction to his Thought* (London: Geoffrey Chapman, 1994).

Barton, Stephen C., '"All Things to All People": Paul and the Law in the Light of 1 Corinthians 9.19-23', in Dunn (ed.), *Paul and the Mosaic Law*, pp. 271-85.

—*Discipleship and Family Ties in Mark and Matthew* (SNTSMS, 80; Cambridge: Cambridge University Press, 1994).

Bassler, Jouette, 'The Enigmatic Sign: 2 Thessalonians 1:5', *CBQ* 46 (1984), pp. 496-510.

Bassler, Jouette (ed.), *Pauline Theology.* I. *Thessalonians, Philippians, Galatians, Philemon* (Minneapolis: Fortress Press, 1991).

Bauckham, Richard, 'The Parting of the Ways: What Happened and Why', *ST* 47 (1993), pp. 135-51.

—'Response to Philip Esler', *SJT* 51 (1998), pp. 249-53.

—*The Theology of the Book of Revelation* (NTT; Cambridge: Cambridge University Press, 1993).

Bauckham, Richard (ed.), *The Gospel for All Christians: Rethinking the Gospel Audiences* (Grand Rapids: Eerdmans; Edinburgh: T. & T. Clark, 1998).

Bauer, Walter, *Orthodoxy and Heresy in Earliest Christianity* (trans. Philadelphia Seminar on Christian Origins; ed. Robert A. Kraft and Geherd Krodel; Mifflintown, PA: Sigler Press, 1996).

Baumgarten, Jörg, *Paulus und die Apokalyptik: Die Auslegung apokalyptischer Überlieferungen in den echten Paulusbriefen* (WMANT, 44; Neukirchen–Vluyn: Neukirchener Verlag, 1975).

Baur, F.C., *Paul the Apostle of Jesus Christ: His Life and Work, his Epistles and his Doctrine* (trans. Allen Menzies; 2 vols.; London: Williams & Norgate, 2nd edn, 1875-76).

Beals, Alan R., and Bernard J. Siegel, *Divisiveness and Social Conflict: An Anthropological Approach* (Stanford, CA: Stanford University Press, 1966).

Beck, Norman A., *Mature Christianity: The Recognition and Repudiation of the Anti-Jewish Polemic of the New Testament* (Selingrove: Susquehanna University Press, 1985).

Becker, Howard S., *Outsiders: Studies in the Sociology of Deviance* (New York: Free Press, 1963).

Becker, Jürgen, *Paul: Apostle to the Gentiles* (trans. O.C. Dean, Jr; Louisville, KY: West-minster/John Knox Press, 1993).

Beker, J. Christiaan, *Heirs of Paul: Paul's Legacy in the New Testament and in the Church Today* (Edinburgh: T. & T. Clark, 1992).

—*Paul the Apostle: The Triumph of God in Life and Thought* (Philadelphia: Fortress Press, 1980).

—*Paul's Apocalyptic Gospel: The Coming Triumph of God* (Philadelphia: Fortress Press, 1982).

Benko, Stephen, *Pagan Rome and the Early Christians* (London: Batsford, 1984).

Ben-Yehuda, Nachman, *Deviance and Moral Boundaries: Witchcraft, the Occult, Science Fiction, Deviant Sciences and Scientists* (Chicago: University of Chicago Press, 1985).

Bercovitz, J. Peter, 'Paul and Thessalonica', *Proceedings* 10 (1990), pp. 123-35.

Berger, Peter L., and Thomas Luckman, *The Social Construction of Reality: A Treatise in the Sociology of Knowledge* (New York: Doubleday, 1966).

Best, Ernest, *A Commentary on the First and Second Epistles to the Thessalonians* (HNTC; Peabody, MA: Hendrickson, 1972).

Betz, Hans Dieter, *Galatians* (Hermeneia; Philadelphia: Fortress Press, 1979).

Bicknell, E.J., *The First and Second Epistles to the Thessalonians* (WC; London: Methuen, 1932).

Bisno, Herb, *Managing Conflict* (SHSG, 52; Newbury Park, CA: Sage, 1988).

Black, David Alan, 'The Weak in Thessalonica: A Study in Pauline Lexicography', *JETS* 25 (1982), pp. 307-21.

Bloomquist, L. Gregory, *The Function of Suffering in Philippians* (JSNTSup, 78; Sheffield: JSOT Press, 1993).

Boardman, Susan K., and Sandra V. Horowitz, 'Constructive Conflict Management and Social Problems: An Introduction', *JSI* 50 (1994), pp. 1-12.

Boccaccini, Gabriele, *Middle Judaism: Jewish Thought 300 BCE to 200 CE* (Minneapolis: Fortress Press, 1991).

Boer, Martinus C. de, 'Paul and Jewish Apocalyptic Eschatology', in Marcus and Soards (eds.), *Apocalyptic and the New Testament*, pp. 169-90.

Boer, Willis Peter de, *The Imitation of Paul: An Exegetical Study* (Kampen: Kok, 1962).

Boers, Hendrikus, 'The Form Critical Study of Paul's Letters: I Thessalonians as a Case Study', *NTS* 22 (1976), pp. 140-58.

Borgen, Peder, 'The Early Church and the Hellenistic Synagogue', *ST* 37 (1983), pp. 55-78.

—'Observations on the Theme "Paul and Philo": Paul's Preaching of Circumcision in Galatia (Gal. 5:11) and Debates on Circumcision in Philo', in Sigfred Pedersen (ed.), *Die paulinische Literatur und Theologie* (Århus: Forlaget Aros; Göttingen: Vandenhoeck & Ruprecht, 1980), pp. 85-102.

Bowers, Paul, 'Church and Mission in Paul', *JSNT* 44 (1991), pp. 89-111.

Boyarin, Daniel, *A Radical Jew: Paul and the Politics of Identity* (Berkeley: University of California Press, 1994).

Braithwaite, John, *Crime, Shame and Reintegration* (Cambridge: Cambridge University Press, 1989).

Branick, Vincent P., 'Apocalyptic Paul?', *CBQ* 47 (1985), pp. 664-75.

Brant, Jo-Ann A., 'The Place of *mimesis* in Paul's Thought', *SR* 22 (1993), pp. 285-300.

Brawley, Robert L., *Luke–Acts and the Jews: Conflict, Apology, and Conciliation* (SBLMS, 33; Atlanta: Scholars Press, 1987).

Broer, Ingo, '"Der ganze Zorn ist schon über sie gekommen": Bemerkungen zur Inter-
    polationshypothese und zur Interpretation von 1 Thess 2,14-16', in Collins (ed.), *The
    Thessalonian Correspondence*, pp. 137-59.
Bromley, David G. (ed.), *Falling from the Faith: Causes and Consequences of Religious
    Apostasy* (Newbury Park, CA: Sage, 1988).
—*The Politics of Religious Apostasy: The Role of Apostates in the Transformation of
    Religious Movements* (Westport, CT: Praeger, 1998).
Broom, Leonard, Charles M. Bonjean and Dorothy H. Broom, *Sociology* (Belmont, CA:
    Wadsworth, 1990).
Brown, Raymond E., *The Gospel According to John* (AB, 29-29A; 2 vols.; Garden City,
    NY: Doubleday, 1966).
—*An Introduction to the New Testmament* (ABRL; New York: Doubleday, 1997).
Bruce, F.F., *The Acts of the Apostles: The Greek Text with Introduction and Commentary*
    (Grand Rapids: Eerdmans; Leicester: Apollos, 3rd edn rev. and enlarged, 1990).
—*The Book of Acts* (NICNT; Grand Rapids: Eerdmans, rev. edn, 1988).
—'Citizenship', *ABD*, I, pp. 1048-49.
—*1 & 2 Thessalonians* (WBC, 45; Waco, TX: Word Books, 1982).
Burton, Ernest De Witt, *Galatians* (ICC; Edinburgh: T. & T. Clark, 1921).
—'The Politarchs', *AJT* 2 (1898), pp. 598-632.
Cadbury, Henry J., 'Overconversion in Paul's Churches', in Sherman E. Johnson (ed.), *The
    Joy of Study: Papers on New Testament and Related Subjects Presented to Honor
    Frederick Clifton Grant* (New York: Macmillan, 1951), pp. 43-50.
Carras, George P., 'Jewish Ethics and Gentile Converts: Remarks on 1 Thes 4,3-8', in
    Collins (ed.), *The Thessalonian Correspondence*, pp. 306-15.
Cartwright, Dorwin, 'The Nature of Group Cohesiveness', in Dorwin Cartwright and Alvin
    Zander (eds), *Group Dynamics: Research and Theory* (New York: Harper & Row,
    3rd edn, 1968), pp. 91-109.
Cassidy, Richard J., 'The Non-Roman Opponents of Paul', in Earl J. Richard (ed.), *New
    Views on Luke–Acts* (Collegeville, MN: Liturgical Press, 1990), pp. 150-62.
Chadwick, Henry, ' "All Things to All Men" (I Cor. IX. 22)', *NTS* 1 (1954–55), pp. 261-75.
—'1 Thess. 3:3: σαίνεσθαι', *JTS* NS 1 (1950), pp. 156-58.
Chadwick, Henry (trans.), *Origen: Contra Celsum* (Cambridge: Cambridge University
    Press, 1953).
Chapa, Juan, 'Is First Thessalonians a Letter of Consolation?', *NTS* 40 (1994), pp. 150-60.
Chesnutt, Randall D., *From Death to Life: Conversion in Joseph and Aseneth* (JSPSup, 16;
    Sheffield: Sheffield Academic Press, 1995).
Clinard, Marshall B., and Robert F. Meier, *Sociology of Deviant Behavior* (New York:
    Holt, Rinehart & Winston, 6th edn, 1985).
Cohen, Albert, *Delinquent Boys* (New York: Free Press, 1955).
Cohen, Albert, and James Short, 'Research on Delinquent Subcultures', *JSI* 14 (1958),
    pp. 20-35.
Cohen, Shaye, 'Crossing the Boundary Line and Becoming a Jew', *HTR* 82 (1989), pp. 13-
    33.
—'Was Judaism in Antiquity a Missionary Religion?', in Menachem Mor (ed.), *Jewish
    Assimilation and Accomodation: Past Traditions, Current Issues and Future Pros-
    pects* (New York: University Press of America, 1992), pp. 14-23.
—'Was Timothy Jewish (Acts 16:1-3)?: Patristic Exegesis, Rabbinic Law, and Matrilineal
    Descent', *JBL* 105 (1986), pp. 251-68.

Cohen, Yehudi A., 'Social Boundary Systems', *CA* 10 (1969), pp. 103-17.

Collins, A. Yarbro, *Crisis and Catharsis: The Power of the Apocalypse* (Philadelphia: Westminster Press, 1984).

—'Vilification and Self-Definition in the Book of Revelation', *HTR* 79 (1986), pp. 308-20.

Collins, John J., *The Apocalyptic Imagination: An Introduction to the Jewish Matrix of Christianity* (New York: Crossroad, 1984).

—*Between Athens and Jerusalem: Jewish Identity in the Hellenistic Diaspora* (New York: Crossroad, 1986).

—'The Genre Apocalypse in Hellenistic Judaism', in Hellholm (ed.), *Apocalypticism*, pp. 531-47.

Collins, Raymond F., *The Birth of the New Testament: The Origin and Development of the First Christian Generation* (New York: Crossroad, 1993).

—' "The Gospel of Our Lord Jesus" (2 Thes 1,8): A Symbolic Shift of Paradigm', in Collins (ed.), *The Thessalonian Correspondence*, pp. 426-40.

—*Letters that Paul Did not Write* (GNS, 28; Wilmington, DE: Michael Glazier, 1988).

—*Studies on the First Letter to the Thessalonians* (BETL, 66; Leuven: Leuven University Press, 1984).

Collins, Raymond F. (ed.), *The Thessalonian Correspondence* (BETL, 87; Leuven: Leuven University Press, 1990).

Cook, Stephen J., *Prophecy and Apocalypticism: The Postexilic Social Setting* (Minneapolis: Fortress Press, 1995).

Corley, Bruce (ed.), *Colloquy on New Testament Studies: A Time for Reappraisal and Fresh Approaches* (Macon, GA: Mercer University Press, 1983).

Coser, Lewis A., *The Functions of Social Conflict* (New York: Free Press, 1956).

—*Masters of Sociological Thought: Ideas in Historical and Social Context* (New York: Harcourt, Brace, Jovanovich, 1971).

—'Some Functions of Deviant Behavior and Normative Flexibility', *AJS* 68 (1962), pp. 172-81.

Court, John M., 'Paul and the Apocalyptic Pattern', in Morna D. Hooker and Stephen G. Wilson (eds.), *Paul and Paulinism: Essays in Honour of C.K. Barrett* (London: SPCK, 1982), pp. 57-66.

Cranfield, C.E.B., 'A Study of 1 Thessalonians 2', *IBS* 1 (1979), pp. 215-26.

Cunningham, Scott, *'Through Many Tribulations': The Theology of Persecution in Luke–Acts* (JSNTSup, 142; Sheffield: Sheffield Academic Press, 1997).

Davies, W.D. 'Paul and the People of Israel', *NTS* 24 (1977), pp. 4-39.

Denis, A.-M., 'L'apôtre Paul prophète, "messianique" des gentils. Etude thématique de 1 Thess II, 1-6', *ETL* 33 (1957), pp. 245-315.

Denney, James, *The Epistles to the Thessalonians* (EB; New York: Hodder & Stoughton, n.d.).

Dentler, Robert A., and Kai T. Erikson, 'The Functions of Deviance in Groups', *SocProb* 7 (1959), pp. 98-107.

deSilva, David A., *Despising Shame: Honor Discourse and Community Maintenance in Hebrews* (SBLDS, 152; Atlanta: Scholars Press, 1995).

—'Exchanging Favor for Wrath: Apostasy in Hebrews and Patron-Client Relationships', *JBL* 115 (1996), pp. 91-116.

—' "Worthy of his Kingdom": Honor Discourse and Social Engineering in 1 Thessalonians', *JSNT* 64 (1996), pp. 49-79.

Deutsch, Morton, 'Constructive Conflict Resolution: Principles, Training, and Research', *JSI* 50 (1994), pp. 13-32.

—*Resolution of Conflict: Constructive and Destructive Processes* (New Haven: Yale University Press, 1973).

Dibelius, Martin, *An die Thessalonicher I, II: An die Philipper* (HNT, 11; Tübingen: J.C.B. Mohr [Paul Siebeck], 1937).

Dobschütz, Detlef von, *Paulus und die jüdische Thorapolizei* (Inaugural dissertation, Friedrich Alexander Universität, Erlangen, 1968).

Dobschütz, Ernst von, *Die Thessalonicherbriefe* (MeyerK; Göttingen: Vandenhoeck & Ruprecht, 1909).

Donaldson, Terence L., ' "The Gospel that I Proclaim among the Gentiles" (Gal. 2.2): Universalistic or Israel-Centred?', in L. Ann Jervis and Peter Richardson (eds.), *Gospel in Paul: Studies on Corinthians, Galatians and Romans for Richard N. Longenecker* (JSNTSup, 108; Sheffield: Sheffield Academic Press, 1994), pp. 166-93.

—*Paul and the Gentiles: Remapping the Apostle's Convictional World* (Minneapolis: Fortress Press, 1997).

—'Proselytes or "Righteous Gentiles"?: The Status of Gentiles in Eschatological Pilgrimage Patterns of Thought', *JSP* 7 (1990), pp. 3-27.

—'Rural Bandits, City Mobs and the Zealots', *JSJ* 21 (1990), pp. 19-40.

—'Zealot and Convert: The Origin of Paul's Christ–Torah Antithesis', *CBQ* 51 (1989), pp. 655-82.

Donfried, Karl P., 'The Cults of Thessalonica and the Thessalonian Correspondence', *NTS* 31 (1985), pp. 336-56.

—'Paul and Judaism: 1 Thessalonians 2:13-16 as a Test Case', *Int* 38 (1984), pp. 242-53.

—'The Theology of 1 Thessalonians as a Reflection of its Purpose', in Horgan and Kobelski (eds.), *To Touch the Text*, pp. 243-60.

—'The Theology of 1 and 2 Thessalonians', in *The Theology of the Shorter Pauline Letters* (NTT; Cambridge: Cambridge University Press, 1993), pp. 1-113.

—'2 Thessalonians and the Church of Thessalonica', in Bradley H. McLean (ed.), *Origins and Method: Towards a New Understanding of Judaism and Christianity: Essays in Honour of John C. Hurd* (JSNTSup, 86; Sheffield: JSOT Press, 1993), pp. 128-44.

—'War Timotheus in Athen? Exegetische Überlegungen zu 1 Thess 3,1-3', in Johannes Joachim Degenhardt (ed.), *Die Freude an Gott-unsere Kraft: Festschrift für Otto Bernhard Knoch zum 65. Geburtstag* (Stuttgart: Katholisches Bibelwerk, 1991), pp. 189-96.

Douglas, Jack D., and Frances C. Waksler, *The Sociology of Deviance: An Introduction* (Boston: Little, Brown & Co., 1982).

Duke, James T., *Conflict and Power in Social Life* (Provo, UT: Brigham Young University Press, 1976).

Dunn, James D.G., *The Epistle to the Galatians* (BNTC; London: A. & C. Black, 1993).

—'The Incident at Antioch (Gal. 2:11-18)', *JSNT* 18 (1983), pp. 3-57.

—'The Question of Anti-Semitism in the New Testament Writings of the Period', in James D.G. Dunn (ed.), *Jews and Christians: The Parting of the Ways A.D. 70–135* (WUNT, 66; Tübingen: J.C.B. Mohr [Paul Siebeck], 1992), pp. 177-211.

—*Romans 9–16* (WBC, 38B; Dallas: Word Books, 1988).

Dunn, James D.G. (ed.), *Paul and the Mosaic Law* (WUNT, 89; Tübingen: J.C.B. Mohr [Paul Siebeck], 1996).

Dupont, Jacques, 'The Conversion of Paul, and its Influence on his Understanding of Salvation by Faith', in W. Ward Gasque and Ralph P. Martin (eds.), *Apostolic History and the Gospel: Biblical and Historical Essays Presented to F.F. Bruce* (Exeter: Paternoster Press, 1970), pp. 176-94.

Eckart, Karl-Gottfried, 'Der zweite echte Brief des Apostels Paulus an die Thessalonicher', *ZTK* 58 (1961), pp. 30-44.

Edson, Charles, 'Macedonia. II. State Cults in Thessalonica', *HSCP* 51 (1940), pp. 127-36.

—'Macedonia. III. Cults of Thessalonica', *HTR* 41 (1948), pp. 153-204.

Ehrenberg, V., and A.H.M. Jones, *Documents Illustrating the Reigns of Augustus and Tiberius* (Oxford: Clarendon Press, 1949).

Elias, Jacob W., ' "Jesus Who Delivers Us from the Wrath to Come" (1 Thess 1:10): Apocalyptic and Peace in the Thessalonian Correspondence', in Eugene H. Lovering (ed.), *SBL 1992 Seminar Papers* (SBLSP, 31; Atlanta: Scholars Press, 1992), pp. 121-32.

Ellingworth, Paul, and Eugene A. Nida, *A Translator's Handbook on Paul's Letters to the Thessalonians* (New York: United Bible Societies, 1976).

Elliott, Gregory C., Herbert L. Ziegler, Barbara M. Altman and Deborah Scott, 'Understanding Stigma: Dimensions of Deviance and Coping', *DB* 3 (1982), pp. 275-300.

Elliott, John H., *A Home for the Homeless: A Sociological Exegesis of 1 Peter, its Situation and Strategy* (Philadelphia: Fortress Press, 1981).

—*What Is Social-Scientific Criticism?* (GBSNTS; Philadelphia: Fortress Press, 1993).

Ellis, E. Earle, 'Coworkers, Paul and His', *DPL*, pp. 183-89.

—'Paul and his Co-Workers', in *idem, Prophecy and Hermeneutic in Early Christianity: New Testament Essays* (Tübingen: J.C.B. Mohr [Paul Siebeck], 1978), pp. 3-22.

—*Pauline Theology: Ministry and Society* (Grand Rapids: Eerdmans; Exeter: Paternoster Press, 1989).

Erikson, Kai, 'Notes on the Sociology of Deviance', *SocProb* 9 (1962), pp. 307-14.

—*Wayward Puritans: A Study in the Sociology of Deviance* (New York: John Wiley & Sons, 1966).

Eshleman, J. Ross, and Barbara G. Cashion, *Sociology: An Introduction* (Boston: Little, Brown & Co., 1983).

Esler, Philip F., 'Community and Gospel in Early Christianity: A Response to Richard Bauckham's *Gospels for all Christians*', *SJT* 51 (1998), pp. 235-48.

—*Community and Gospel in Luke–Acts: The Social and Political Motivations of Lucan Theology* (SNTSMS, 57; Cambridge: Cambridge University Press, 1987).

—'God's Honour and Rome's Triumph: Responses to the Fall of Jerusalem in 70 CE in Three Jewish Apocalypses', in Esler (ed.), *Modelling Early Christianity*, pp. 239-58.

—'Introduction', in Esler (ed.), *Modelling Early Christianity*, pp. 1-20.

Esler, Philip F. (ed.), *Modelling Early Christianity: Social-Scientific Studies of the New Testament in its Context* (London: Routledge, 1995).

Evans, Craig A., 'Faith and Polemic: The New Testament and First-Century Judaism', in Evans and Hagner (eds.), *Anti-Semitism and Early Christianity*, pp. 1-17.

Evans, Craig A., and Donald A. Hagner (eds.), *Anti-Semitism and Early Christianity: Issues of Polemic and Faith* (Minneapolis: Fortress Press, 1993).

Evans, Robert M., *Eschatology and Ethics: A Study of Thessalonica and Paul's Letters to the Thessalonians* (Princeton, NJ: McMahon Printing, 1968).

Farmer, William R., C.F.D. Moule and R. Richard Niehbuhr (eds.), *Christian History and Interpretation: Studies Presented to John Knox* (Cambridge: Cambridge University Press, 1967).

Fee, Gordon D., *The First Epistle to the Corinthians* (NICNT; Grand Rapids: Eerdmans, 1987).

—*God's Empowering Presence: The Holy Spirit in the Letters of Paul* (Peabody, MA: Hendrickson, 1994).

—*Paul's Letter to the Philippians* (NICNT; Grand Rapids: Eerdmans, 1995).

—'Pneuma and Eschatology in 2 Thessalonians 2.1-12: A Proposal about "Testing the Prophets" and the Purpose of 2 Thessalonians', in Thomas E. Schmidt and Moisés Silva (eds.), *To Tell the Mystery: Essays in New Testament Eschatology in Honor of Robert H. Gundry* (JSNTSup, 100; Sheffield: JSOT Press, 1994), pp. 196-215.

Feldman, Louis, *Jew and Gentile in the Ancient World: Attitudes and Interactions from Alexander to Justinian* (Princeton, NJ: Princeton University Press, 1993).

—'The Omnipresence of the God-Fearers', *BARev* 12 (1986), pp. 58-63.

Filley, Alan C., *Interpersonal Conflict Resolution* (Glenview, IL: Scott, Foresman & Co., 1975).

Findlay, George G., *The Epistles to the Thessalonians* (Cambridge: Cambridge University Press, 1891).

Fisher, Ronald J., *The Social Psychology of Intergroup and International Conflict* (New York: Springer, 1990).

Foakes-Jackson, F.J., *The Acts of the Apostles* (MNTC; London: Hodder & Stoughton, 1931).

Forkman, Göran, *The Limits of Religious Community: Expulsion from the Religious Community within the Qumran Sect, within Rabbinic Judaism, and within Primitive Christianity* (ConBNT, 5; Lund: C.W.K. Gleerup, 1972).

Forsyth, D.R., *Group Dynamics* (Pacific Grove, CA: Brooks/Cole Publishing, 2nd edn, 1990).

Fowl, Stephen, 'A Metaphor in Distress: A Reading of NHΠIOI in 1 Thessalonians 2.7', *NTS* 36 (1990), 469-73.

Fox, Robin Lane, *Pagans and Christians* (San Francisco: HarperCollins, 1986).

Frame, James E., *A Critical and Exegetical Commentary on the Epistles of St Paul to the Thessalonians* (ICC; Edinburgh: T. & T. Clark, 1912).

Fredriksen, Paula, *From Jesus to Christ: The Origins of the New Testament Images of Jesus* (New Haven: Yale University Press, 1988).

—'Paul and Augustine: Conversion Narratives, Orthodox Traditions, and the Retrospective Self', *JTS* NS 37 (1986), pp. 3-34.

Freilich, Morris, Douglas Raybeck and Joel Savishinsky (eds.), *Deviance: Anthropological Perspectives* (New York: Bergin & Garvey, 1991).

Frend, W.H.C., 'Persecutions: Some Links between Judaism and the Early Church', *JEH* 9 (1958), pp. 141-58.

Freyne, Sean, 'Vilifying the Other and Defining the Self: Matthew's and John's Anti-Jewish Polemic in Focus', in Neusner and Frerichs (eds.), *'To See Ourselves as Others See Us'*, pp. 117-43.

Friedrich, Gerhard, '1 Thessalonicher 5,1-11, der apologetische Einschuß eines Späteren', *ZTK* 70 (1973), pp. 288-315.

Funk, Robert W., 'The Apostolic *Parousia*: Form and Significance', in Farmer, Moule and Niebuhr (eds.), *Christian History and Interpretation*, pp. 249-68.

Furnish, Victor P., *Jesus According to Paul* (UJTS; Cambridge: Cambridge University Press, 1993).

—*II Corinthians* (AB, 32A; Garden City, NY: Doubleday, 1984).

Fusco, Vittorio, 'Luke–Acts and the Future of Israel', *NovT* 38 (1996), pp. 1-17.

Gager, John G., *Kingdom and Community: The Social World of Early Christianity* (Englewood Cliffs, NJ: Prentice–Hall, 1975).

—*The Origins of Anti-Semitism: Attitudes toward Judaism in Pagan and Christian Antiquity* (Oxford: Oxford University Press, 1983).

Gallas, Sven, '"Fünfmal vierzig weniger einen...": Die an Paulus vollzogenen Synagogalstrafen nach 2 Kor 11,24', *ZNW* 81 (1990), pp. 178-90.

Garland, David E., *The Intention of Matthew 23* (NovTSup, 52; Leiden: E.J. Brill, 1979).

Garnsey, Peter, 'Religious Toleration in Classical Antiquity', in W.J. Sheils (ed.), *Persecution and Toleration* (Oxford: Basil Blackwell, 1984), pp. 1-27.

Garrett, Susan R., 'Paul's Thorn and Cultural Models of Affliction', in White and Yarbrough (eds.), *The Social World of the First Christians*, pp. 82-99.

—'Sociology of Early Christianity', *ABD*, VI, pp. 88-99.

Gaston, Lloyd, *Paul and the Torah* (Vancouver: University of British Columbia Press, 1987).

Gaventa, Beverly Roberts, *First and Second Thessalonians* (Interpretation; Louisville, KY: Westminster/John Knox Press, 1998).

George, Timothy, *Galatians* (NAC, 30; Nashville: Broadman & Holman Press, 1994).

Georgi, Dieter, *The Opponents of Paul in Second Corinthians* (Philadelphia: Fortress Press, 1986).

Getty, Mary Ann, 'The Imitation of Paul in the Letters to the Thessalonians', in Collins (ed.), *The Thessalonian Correspondence*, pp. 277-83.

Gibbs, Jack P., 'Conceptions of Deviant Behavior: The Old and the New', *PSR* 9 (1966), pp. 9-14.

Gilbert, Gary, 'The Making of a Jew: "God-Fearer" or Convert in the Story of Izates', *USQR* 44 (1991), pp. 299-313.

Gilliard, Frank D., 'Paul and the Killing of the Prophets in 1 Thess. 2:15', *NovT* 36 (1994), pp. 259-70.

—'The Problem of the Antisemitic Comma between 1 Thessalonians 2.14 and 15', *NTS* 36 (1989), pp. 481-502.

Gillman, John, 'Paul's ΕΙΣΟΔΟΣ: The Proclaimed and the Proclaimer (1 Thess 2,8)', in Collins (ed.), *The Thessalonian Correspondence*, pp. 62-70.

Glaser, Daniel, 'Criminality Theories and Behavioral Images', *AJS* 61 (1956), pp. 433-44.

Goddard, A.J., and S.A. Cummins, 'Ill or Ill-Treated?: Conflict and Persecution as the Context of Paul's Original Ministry in Galatia (Galatians 4.12-20)', *JSNT* 52 (1993), pp. 93-126.

Goode, Erich, 'On Behalf of Labeling Theory', *SocProb* 22 (1975), pp. 570-83.

Goodman, Martin, *Mission and Conversion: Proselytizing in the Religious History of the Roman Empire* (Oxford: Clarendon Press, 1994).

Gordon, J. Dorcas, *Sister or Wife?: 1 Corinthians 7 and Cultural Anthropology* (JSNTSup, 149; Sheffield: Sheffield Academic Press, 1997).

Goulder, Michael D., *St. Paul Versus St. Peter: A Tale of Two Missions* (Louisville, KY: Westminster/John Knox Press, 1994).

—'Silas in Thessalonica', *JSNT* 48 (1992), pp. 87-106.

Green, Michael, *Evangelism in the Early Church* (Grand Rapids: Eerdmans, 1970).

Gundry, Robert H., 'The Hellenization of Dominical Tradition and the Christianization of Jewish Tradition in the Eschatology of 1–2 Thessalonians', *NTS* 33 (1987), pp. 161-78.

Gutbrod, Walter, 'Ισραήλ', *TDNT*, III, pp. 356-91.

Haenchen, Ernst, *The Acts of the Apostles: A Commentary* (trans. Bernard Noble and Gerald Shinn; rev. trans. R.M. Wilson; Oxford: Basil Blackwell, 1971).

Hagan, John, 'Labelling and Deviance: A Case Study in the "Sociology of the Interesting" ', *SocProb* 20 (1973), pp. 447-58.

Hagner, Donald A., 'Paul's Quarrel with Judaism', in Evans and Hagner (eds.), *Anti-Semitism and Early Christianity*, pp. 128-50.

Hanson, Paul D., *The Dawn of Apocalyptic* (Philadelphia: Fortress Press, 2nd edn, 1979).

Hare, Douglas R.A., *The Theme of Jewish Persecution of Christians in the Gospel According to St Matthew* (SNTSMS, 6; Cambridge: Cambridge University Press, 1967).

Harnisch, Wolfgang, *Eschatologische Existenz: Ein exegetischer Beitrag zum Sachanliegen von 1 Thessalonicher 4,13–5,11* (FRLANT, 110; Göttingen: Vandenhoeck & Ruprecht, 1973).

Harris, Gerald, 'The Beginnings of Church Discipline: 1 Corinthians 5', *NTS* 37 (1991), pp. 1-12.

Harvey, A.E., 'Did the Ways Have to Part?', *WFE* 2 (1992), pp. 51-54.

—'Forty Strokes Save One: Social Aspects of Judaizing and Apostasy', in A.E. Harvey (ed.), *Alternative Approaches to New Testament Study* (London: SPCK, 1985), pp. 79-96.

Head, B.V., *A Catalogue of the Greek Coins in the British Museum*. V. *Macedonia, etc.* (London: Longmans, 1879).

Hellholm, David (ed.), *Apocalypticism in the Mediterranean World* (Tübingen: J.C.B. Mohr [Paul Siebeck], 1983).

Hemer, Colin J., *The Book of Acts in the Setting of Hellenistic History* (ed. Conrad H. Gempf; WUNT, 49; Tübingen: J.C.B. Mohr [Paul Siebeck], 1989).

Hemphill, Kenneth S., *Spiritual Gifts Empowering the New Testament Church* (Nashville: Broadman Press, 1988).

Hendriksen, William, *I and II Thessalonians* (Grand Rapids: Baker Book House, 1964).

Hendrix, Holland Lee, 'Archaeology and Eschatology at Thessalonica', in Birger A. Pearson (ed.), *The Future of Christianity: Essays in Honor of Helmut Koester* (Minneapolis: Fortress Press, 1991), pp. 107-18.

—'Beyond "Imperial Cult" and "Cults of the Magistrates" ', in Kent H. Richards (ed.), *SBL 1986 Seminar Papers* (SBLSP, 25; Atlanta: Scholars Press, 1986), pp. 301-308.

—'Thessalonica', *ABD*, VI, pp. 523-27.

—'Thessalonica', in Helmut Koester and Holland Lee Hendrix (eds.), *Archaeological Resources for New Testament Study: A Collection of Slides on Culture and Religion in Antiquity*. I (Philadelphia: Fortress Press, 1986), pp. 1-49.

—'Thessalonicans Honor Romans' (ThD dissertation, Harvard University, 1984).

Hengel, Martin, *Acts and the History of Earliest Christianity* (trans. John Bowden; London: SCM Press, 1979).

—*The Pre-Christian Paul* (trans. John Bowden; London: SCM Press; Philadelphia: Trinity Press International, 1991).

—*The Zealots: Investigations into the Jewish Freedom Movement in the Period from Herod I until 70 A.D.* (trans. David Smith; Edinburgh: T. & T. Clark, 1989).

Hengel, Martin, and Anna Maria Schwemer, *Paul between Damascus and Antioch: The Unknown Years* (trans. John Bowden; Louisville, KY; Westminster/John Knox Press, 1997).

Henneken, Bartholomäus, *Verkündigung und Prophetie im ersten Thessalonicherbrief: Ein Beitrag zur Theologie des Wortes Gottes* (SBib, 29; Stuttgart: Katholisches Bibelwerk, 1969).

Herrmann, P., 'Inschriften aus dem Heraion von Samos', *MDAIAA* 77 (1962), pp. 306-27.

Hiebert, D. Edmond, *The Thessalonian Epistles: A Call to Readiness* (Chicago: Moody Press, 1971).

Hilgenfeld, Adolf H., 'Die beiden Briefe an die Thessalonicher, nach Inhalt und Ursprung', *ZWT* 5 (1862), pp. 225-64.

Hill, Craig C., *Hellenists and Hebrews: Reappraising Division within the Earliest Church* (Minneapolis: Fortress Press, 1992).

Hill, David, 'On Baptism and Suffering in 1 Peter', *NovT* 18 (1976), pp. 181-89.

Hill, Judith Lynn, *Establishing the Church in Thessalonica* (Ann Arbor, MI: University Microfilms, 1990).

Hirschi, Travis, *Causes of Delinquency* (Berkeley, CA: University of California Press, 1969).

Hirschi, Travis, and Michael R. Gottfredson, *A General Theory of Crime* (Stanford, CA: Stanford University Press, 1990).

Hock, Ronald F., *The Social Context of Paul's Ministry: Tentmaking and Apostleship* (Philadelphia: Fortress Press, 1980).

Holdsworth, John, 'The Sufferings in 1 Peter and "Missionary Apocalyptic" ', in E.A. Livingstone (ed.), *Studia Biblica 1978. III. Papers on Paul and Other New Testament Authors* (JSNTSup, 3; Sheffield: JSOT Press, 1980), pp. 225-32.

Holland, Glenn S., ' "Anti-Judaism" in Paul: The Case of Romans', *Proceedings* 10 (1990), pp. 190-203.

—' "A Letter Supposedly from Us": A Contribution to the Discussion about the Authorship of 2 Thessalonians', in Collins (ed.), *The Thessalonian Correspondence*, pp. 394-402.

—*The Tradition that You Received from Us: 2 Thessalonians in the Pauline Tradition* (HUT, 24; Tübingen: J.C.B. Mohr [Paul Siebeck], 1988).

Hollmann, Georg, 'Die Unechtheit des zweiten Thessalonicherbriefs', *ZNW* 5 (1904), pp. 28-38.

Holmberg, Bengt, *Sociology and the New Testament: An Appraisal* (Minneapolis: Fortress Press, 1990).

Holmes, John G., John H. Ellard and Helmut Lamm, 'Boundary Roles and Intergroup Conflict', in Worchel and Austin (eds.), *Psychology of Intergroup Relations*, pp. 343-63.

Holmes, Michael W., *1 & 2 Thessalonians* (NIVAC; Grand Rapids: Zondervan, 1998).

Holsten, C., 'Zur Unechtheit des ersten Briefes an die Thessalonicher und zur Abfassungszeit der Apokalypse', *JProtTheo* 36 (1877), pp. 731-32.

Holtz, Traugott, *Der erste Brief an die Thessalonicher* (EKKNT, 13; Zürich: Benzinger Verlag; Neukirchen–Vluyn: Neukirchener Verlag, 1986).

—' "Euer Glaube an Gott": Zu Form und Inhalt von 1 Thess 1,9f.', in Rudolf Schnackenburg, Joseph Ernst and Joachim Wanke (eds.), *Die Kirche des Anfangs: Festschrift für Heinz Schürmann* (Freiburg: Herder, 1978), pp. 459-88.

—'The Judgment on the Jews and the Salvation of All Israel: 1 Thes 2,15-16 and Rom 11,25-26', in Collins (ed.), *The Thessalonian Correspondence*, pp. 284-94.

Holtzmann, Heinrich J., 'Zum zweiten Thessalonicherbrief', *ZNW* 2 (1901), pp. 97-108.

Horbury, William, 'Extirpation and Excommunication',*VT* 35 (1985), pp. 13-38.

—'I Thessalonians ii.3 as Rebutting the Charge of False Prophecy', *JTS* NS 33 (1982), pp. 492-508.

Horgan, Maurya P., and Paul J. Kobelski (eds.), *To Touch the Text: Biblical and Related Studies in Honor of Joseph Fitzymer* (New York: Crossroad, 1989).

Horrell, David G., 'The Development of Theological Ideology in Pauline Christianity: A Structuration Theory Perspective', in Esler (ed.), *Modelling Early Christianity*, pp. 224-36.

—*The Social Ethos of the Corinthian Correspondence: Interests and Ideology from 1 Corinthians to 1 Clement* (SNTW; Edinburgh: T. & T. Clark, 1996).

—'Social-Scientific Interpretation of the New Testament: Retrospect and Prospect', in David G. Horrell (ed.), *Social-Scientific Approaches to New Testament Interpretation* (Edinburgh: T. & T. Clark, 1999), pp. 3-27.

Horsley, G.H.R., 'The Politarchs', in David Gill and Conrad Gempf (eds.), *The Book of Acts in its Graeco-Roman Setting* (BAFCS, 2; Grand Rapids: Eerdmans; Carlisle: Paternoster Press, 1994), pp. 419-43.

Hostetler, John A., *Amish Society* (Baltimore: The Johns Hopkins University Press, 3rd edn, 1980).

Hughes, Frank Witt, *Early Christian Rhetoric and 2 Thessalonians* (JSNTSup, 30; Sheffield: JSOT Press, 1989).

Hultgren, Arland J., *Paul's Gospel and Mission: The Outlook from his Letter to the Romans* (Philadelphia: Fortress Press, 1985).

—'Paul's Pre-Christian Persecutions of the Church: Their Purpose, Locale, and Nature', *JBL* 95 (1976), pp. 97-111.

—'The Self-Definition of Paul and his Communities', *SEÅ* 56 (1991), pp. 78-100.

Hunter, A.M., *Paul and his Predecessors* (Philadelphia: Westminster Press, rev. edn, 1961).

Hurd, John C., 'Paul ahead of his Time: 1 Thess. 2:13-16', in Richardson (ed.), *Anti-Judaism in Early Christianity*, pp. 21-36.

Hurtado, Larry W., *One God, One Lord: Early Christian Devotion and Ancient Jewish Monotheism* (London: SCM Press, 1988).

Jervell, Jacob, *The Unknown Paul: Essays on Luke–Acts and Early Christian History* (Minneapolis: Augsburg, 1984).

Jewett, Robert, 'The Agitators and the Galatian Congregation', *NTS* 17 (1970 –71), pp. 198-212.

—'The Basic Human Dilemma: Weakness or Zealous Violence?: Romans 7:7-25 and 10:1-18', *ExAud* 13 (1997), pp. 96-113.

—*Dating Paul's Life* (London: SCM Press, 1979).

—'A Matrix of Grace: The Theology of 2 Thessalonians as a Pauline Letter', in Bassler (ed.), *Pauline Theology*, I, pp. 63-70.

—'Tenement Churches and Communal Meals in the Early Church: The Implications of a Form-Critical Analysis of 2 Thessalonians 3:10', *BR* 38 (1993), pp. 24-32.

—*The Thessalonian Correspondence: Pauline Rhetoric and Millenarian Piety* (FFNT; Philadelphia: Fortress Press, 1986).

Johanson, Bruce C., *To All the Brethren: A Text-Linguistic and Rhetorical Approach to 1 Thessalonians* (ConBNT, 16; Stockholm: Almqvist & Wiksell, 1987).

Johnson, Luke Timothy, *The Acts of the Apostles* (SP, 5; Collegeville, MN: Liturgical Press, 1992).

—'The New Testament's Anti-Jewish Slander and Conventions of Ancient Polemic', *JBL* 108 (1989), pp. 419-41.

—*The Writings of the New Testament: An Interpretation* (Philadelphia: Fortress Press, 1986).

Johnson, Sherman E., 'Notes and Comments (I Thess. 2:16)', *ATR* 23 (1941), pp. 173-76.

Jones, A.H.M., *The Greek City from Alexander to Justinian* (Oxford: Clarendon Press, 1940).

Jones, Nicholas F., *Public Organization in Ancient Greece: A Documentary Study* (Philadelphia: American Philosophical Society, 1987).

Judge, E.A. 'The Decrees of Caesar at Thessalonica', *RTR* 30 (1971), pp. 1-7.

—'Judaism and the Rise of Christianity: A Roman Perspective', *TynBul* 45 (1994), pp. 355-68.

—'The Social Identity of the First Christians: A Question of Method in Religious History', *JRH* 11 (1980), pp. 201-17.

Jurgensen, Hubert, 'Awaiting the Return of Christ: A Re-Examination of 1 Thessalonians 4.13–5.11 from a Pentecostal Perspective', *JPT* 4 (1994), pp. 81-113.

Käsemann, Ernst, 'Die Anfänge christlicher Theologie', *ZTK* 57 (1960), pp. 162-85.

—'Zum Thema der urchristlichen Apokalyptik', *ZTK* 59 (1962), pp. 267-84.

Katz, Daniel, 'Nationalism and Strategies of International Conflict Resolution', in Herbert C. Kelman (ed.), *International Behavior: A Social-Psychological Analysis* (New York: Holt, Rinehart & Winston, 1965), pp. 356-90.

Keck, Leander E., 'Images of Paul in the New Testament', *Int* 43 (1989), pp. 341-51.

—'Paul and Apocalyptic Theology', *Int* 28 (1984), pp. 229-41.

Kee, Howard Clark, 'Pauline Eschatology: Relationships with Apocalyptic and Stoic Thought', in Erich Grässer and Otto Merk (eds.), *Glaube und Eschatologie: Festschrift für Werner Georg Kümmel zum 80. Geburtstag* (Tübingen: J.C.B. Mohr [Paul Siebeck], 1985), pp. 135-58.

Kelly, J.N.D., *The Epistles of Peter and of Jude* (BNTC; Peabody, MA: Hendrickson, 1969).

Kemmler, Dieter Werner, *Faith and Human Reason: A Study of Paul's Method of Preaching as Illustrated by 1–2 Thessalonians and Acts 17,2-4* (NovTSup, 50; Leiden: E.J. Brill, 1975).

Kidder, Louise H., and V. Mary Stewart, *The Psychology of Intergroup Relations: Conflict and Consciousness* (New York: McGraw–Hill, 1975).

Kim, Seyoon, *The Origin of Paul's Gospel* (WUNT, 2.4; Tübingen: J.C.B. Mohr [Paul Siebeck], 1984).

Kitsuse, John I., 'Societal Reaction to Deviant Behavior: Problems of Theory and Method', *SocProb* 9 (1962), pp. 247-56.

Klassen, William, 'The Sacred Kiss in the New Testament: An Example of Social Boundary Lines', *NTS* 39 (1993), pp. 122-35.

Knox, John, *Chapters in a Life of Paul* (ed. Douglas R.A. Hare; London: SCM Press, rev. edn, 1989).

—'A Note on II Thessalonians 2:2', *ATR* 18 (1936), pp. 72-73.

Koch, Klaus, *The Rediscovery of Apocalyptic* (SBT, 2.22; London: SCM Press, 1972).

Koester, Helmut, 'Apostel und Gemeinde in den Briefen an die Thessalonicher', in Dieter Lührmann and Georg Strecker (eds.), *Kirche: Festschrift für Günther Bornkamm zum 75. Geburtstag* (Tübingen: J.C.B. Mohr [Paul Siebeck], 1980), pp. 287-98.

—'Archäologie und Paulus in Thessalonike', in Lukas Bormann, Kelly Del Tredici and Angela Standhartinger (eds.), *Religious Propaganda and Missionary Competition in the New Testament World: Essays Honoring Dieter Georgi* (Leiden: E.J. Brill, 1994), pp. 393-404.

—*Introduction to the New Testament*. II. *History and Literature of Early Christianity* (Philadelphia: Fortress Press, 1982).

—'From Paul's Eschatology to the Apocalyptic Schemata of 2 Thessalonians', in Collins (ed.), *The Thessalonian Correspondence*, pp. 441-58.

—'The Text of 1 Thessalonians', in Dennis E. Groh and Robert Jewett (eds.), *The Living Text: Essays in Honor of Ernest W. Saunders* (Lanham, MD: University Press of America, 1985), pp. 219-27.

—'1 Thessalonians: Experiment in Christian Writing', in F.F. Church and Timothy George (eds.), *Continuity and Disconuity in Church History: Essays Presented to George Huntston Williams on the Occasion of his 65th Birthday* (SHCT, 19; Leiden: E.J. Brill, 1979), pp. 33-44.

Kornhauser, Ruth R., *Social Sources of Delinquency* (Chicago: University of Chicago Press, 1978).

Kraabel, A.T., 'The Disappearance of the "God-Fearers" ', *Numen* 28 (1981), pp. 113-26.

Kreitzer, L. Joseph, *Jesus and God in Paul's Eschatology* (JSNTSup, 19; Sheffield: JSOT Press, 1987).

Krentz, Edgar, 'Through a Lens: Theology and Fidelity in 2 Thessalonians', in Bassler (ed.), *Pauline Theology*, I, pp. 52-62.

Kriesberg, Louis, *The Sociology of Social Conflicts* (Englewood Cliffs, NJ: Prentice–Hall, 1973).

Kruse, Colin G., 'The Price Paid for a Ministry among Gentiles: Paul's Persecution at the Hands of the Jews', in Michael J. Wilkins and Terence Paige (eds.), *Worship, Theology and Ministry in the Early Church: Essays in Honor of Ralph P. Martin* (JSNTSup, 87; Sheffield: JSOT Press, 1992), pp. 260-72.

Kümmel, Werner Georg, 'Das literarische und geschichtliche Problem des ersten Thessalonicherbriefes', in W.C. van Unnik (ed.), *Neotestamentica et Patristica: Eine Freundesgabe Oscar Cullmann zum 60. Geburtstag* (NovTSup, 6; Leiden: E.J. Brill, 1962), pp. 213-22.

Kurichialnil, John, ' "If Any One Will Not Work, Let Him Not Eat" ', *Biblebhashyam* 21 (1995), pp. 184-203.

Kysar, Robert, 'Anti-Semitism and the Gospel of John', in Evans and Hagner (eds.), *Anti-Semitism and Early Christianity*, pp. 113-27.

Ladd, George, 'New Testament Apocalyptic', *RevExp* 78 (1981), pp. 205-209.

Lake, Kirsopp, *The Earlier Epistles of St. Paul* (London: Rivingtons, 1914).

Lake, Kirsopp, and Henry J. Cadbury, *The Beginnings of Christianity*. Part I: *The Acts of the Apostles*. IV. *English Translation and Commentary* (5 vols.; Grand Rapids: Baker Book House, 1965).

Lane, William L., *Hebrews 9–13* (WBC, 47B; Dallas: Word Books, 1991).

Laub, Franz, *Erster und zweiter Thessalonicherbrief* (Würzburg: Echter Verlag, 2nd edn, 1988).

—'Paulinische Autorität in nachpaulinischer Zeit (2 Thess)', in Collins (ed.), *The Thessalonian Correspondence*, pp. 403-17.

Lauderdale, Pat, Jerry Parker, Phil Smith-Cunnien and James Inverarity, 'External Threat and the Definition of Deviance', *JPP* 46 (1984), pp. 1058-68.

Légasse, Simon, 'Paul et les Juifs d'après 1 Thessaloniciens 2,13-16', *RB* 104 (1997), pp. 572-91.

—'Paul's Pre-Christian Career According to Acts', in Richard Bauckham (ed.), *The Book of Acts in its Palestinian Setting* (BAFCS, 4; Grand Rapids: Eerdmans; Carlisle: Paternoster Press, 1995), pp. 365-90.

Lemert, Edwin, 'Issues in the Study of Deviance', *SQ* 22 (1981), pp. 285-305.

—*Social Pathology* (New York: McGraw–Hill, 1951).

Lenski, R.C.H., *The Interpretation of St. Paul's Epistles to the Colossians, to the Thessalonians, to Timothy, to Titus and to Philemon* (Minneapolis: Fortress Press, 1961).

Lentz, John Clayton, Jr, *Luke's Portrait of Paul* (SNTMS, 77; Cambridge: Cambridge University Press, 1993).

LeVine, Robert A., and Donald Campbell, *Ethnocentrism: Theories of Conflict, Ethnic Attitudes and Group Behavior* (New York: John Wiley & Sons, 1972).

Levinskaya, Irina, *The Book of Acts in its Diaspora Setting* (BAFCS, 5; Grand Rapids: Eerdmans; Carlisle: Paternoster Press, 1996).

Levitin, Teresa E., 'Deviants as Active Participants in the Labeling Process: The Visibly Handicapped', *SocProb* 22 (1975), pp. 548-57.

Liazos, Alexander, 'The Poverty of the Sociology of Deviance: Nuts, Sluts, and Perverts', *SocProb* 20 (1972), pp. 103-20.

Lieu, Judith, '"The Parting of the Ways": Theological Construct or Historical Reality?', *JSNT* 56 (1994), pp. 101-19.

Lightfoot, J.B., 'The Church of Thessalonica', in *idem*, *Biblical Essays* (London: Macmillan, 1893), pp. 253-69.

—*Notes on the Epistles of St. Paul (1 and 2 Thessalonians, 1 Corinthians 1–7, Romans 1–7, Ephesians 1:1-14)* (Winona Lake, IN: Alpha Publications, n.d.).

Lindemann, Andreas, 'Zum Abfassungszweck des zweiten Thessalonicherbriefes', *ZNW* 68 (1977), pp. 34-47.

Longenecker, Richard N., *Galatians* (WBC, 41; Dallas, TX: Word Books, 1990).

Lowe, M., 'Who Were the ΙΟΥΔΑΙΟΙ?', *NovT* 18 (1976), pp. 101-30.

Lüdemann, Gerd, *Early Christianity According to the Traditions in Acts: A Commentary* (trans. John Bowden; London: SCM Press, 1989).

—*Opposition to Paul in Jewish Christianity* (trans. M. Eugene Boring; Minneapolis: Fortress Press, 1989).

—*Paul: Apostle to the Gentiles: Studies in Chronology* (trans. F. Stanley Jones; London: SCM Press, 1984).

Lührmann, Dieter, 'The Beginnings of the Church at Thessalonica', in David L. Balch, Everett Ferguson and Wayne A. Meeks (eds.), *Greeks, Romans, and Christians: Essays in Honor of Abraham J. Malherbe* (Minneapolis: Fortress Press, 1990), pp. 237-49.

—*Galatians* (trans. O.C. Dean, Jr; CCS; Minneapolis: Fortress Press, 1992).

Lünemann, Gottlieb, *The Epistles to the Thessalonians* (trans. Paton J. Gloag; Edinburgh: T. & T. Clark, 1880).

Lütgert, E. Wilhelm, 'Die Volkommenen im Philipperbrief und die Enthusiasten in Thessalonich', *BFCT* 13 (1909), pp. 547-654.

Lyons, George, *Pauline Autobiography: Toward a New Understanding* (SBLDS, 73; Atlanta: Scholars Press, 1985).

MacMullen, Ramsey, *Christianizing the Roman Empire (A.D. 100–400)* (New Haven: Yale University Press, 1984).

—*Enemies of the Roman Order: Treason, Unrest, and Alienation in the Empire* (Cambridge: Harvard University Press; London: Oxford University Press, 1966).

—*Paganism in the Roman Empire* (New Haven: Yale University Press, 1981).

—'Two Types of Conversion to Early Christianity', *VC* 37 (1983), pp. 174-92.

McEleney, Neil J., 'Conversion, Circumcision and the Law', *NTS* 20 (1974), pp. 328-33.

McGowan, Andrew J., 'Eating People: Accusations of Cannibalism against Christians in the Second Century', *JECS* 2 (1994), pp. 413-42.

McKnight, Scot, *A Light among the Gentiles: Jewish Missionary Activity in the Second Temple Period* (Minneapolis: Fortress Press, 1991).

—'A Loyal Critic: Matthew's Polemic with Judaism in Theological Perspective', in Evans and Hagner (eds.), *Anti-Semitism in Early Christianity*, pp. 55-79.

—*1 Peter* (NIVAC; Grand Rapids: Zondervan, 1996).

Mack, Raymond W., and Richard C. Snyder, 'The Analysis of Social Conflict: Toward an Overview and Synthesis', *JCR* 1 (1957), pp. 212-48.

Malherbe, Abraham J., 'Conversion to Paul's Gospel', in Abraham J. Malherbe, Frederick W. Norris and James W. Thompson (eds.), *The Early Church in its Context: Essays in Honor of Everett Ferguson* (Leiden: E.J. Brill, 1998), pp. 230-44.

—'Exhortation in First Thessalonians', *NovT* 25 (1983), pp. 238-56.

—' "Gentle as a Nurse": The Cynic Background to 1 Thessalonians 2', *NovT* 12 (1970), pp. 203-17.

—'God's New Family in Thessalonica', in White and Yarbrough (eds.), *The Social World of the First Christians* (Minneapolis: Fortress Press, 1995), pp. 116-25.

—*Paul and the Thessalonians: The Philosophic Tradition of Pastoral Care* (Philadelphia: Fortress Press, 1987).

—'Paul: Hellenistic Philosopher or Christian Pastor?', *ATR* 68 (1986), pp. 3-13.

Malina, Bruce J., *The New Testament World: Insights from Cultural Anthropology* (Atlanta: John Knox Press, 1981).

Malina, Bruce J., and Jerome H. Neyrey, *Calling Jesus Names: The Social Value of Labels in Matthew* (FFSF; Sonoma, CA: Polebridge Press, 1988).

—'Conflict in Luke–Acts: Labelling and Deviance Theory', in Neyrey (ed.), *The Social World of Luke–Acts*, pp. 97-122.

Manson, T.W., 'St Paul in Greece: The Letters to the Thessalonians', *BJRL* 35 (1952), pp. 428-47.

Manus, Chris U., 'Luke's Account of Paul in Thessalonica (Acts 17:1-9)', in Collins (ed.), *The Thessalonian Correspondence*, pp. 27-38.

Marcus, Joel, and Marion L. Soards (eds.), *Apocalyptic and the New Testament: Essays in Honor of J. Louis Martyn* (JSNTSup, 24; Sheffield: JSOT Press, 1989).

Marshall, I.H., 'The Problem of Apostasy in New Testament Theology', *PRS* 14 (1987), pp. 65-80.

—*1 and 2 Thessalonians* (NCB; Grand Rapids: Eerdmans; London: Marshall, Morgan & Scott, 1983).

Martin, D. Michael, *1, 2 Thessalonians* (NAC, 33; Nashville: Broadman & Holman Press, 1995).

Martínez, Florentino García, *Qumran and Apocalyptic: Studies on the Aramaic Texts from Qumran* (STDJ, 9; Leiden: E.J. Brill, 1992).

Martyn, J. Louis, 'Apocalyptic Antinomies in Paul's Letter to the Galatians', *NTS* 31 (1985), pp. 410-24.

—'Epistemology at the Turn of the Ages', in Farmer, Moule and Niebuhr (eds.), *Christian History and Interpretation*, pp. 269-87.

—*Galatians* (AB, 33A; New York: Doubleday, 1997).

—*History and Theology in the Fourth Gospel* (Nashville: Abingdon Press, 2nd edn, 1979).

Marx, Karl, *Capital* (New York: Vintage Books, 1977).

Marx, Karl, and Friedrich Engels, *The Manifesto of the Communist Party* (New York: Pantheon Books, 1967).

Marxsen, Willi, *Der erste Brief an die Thessalonicher* (ZB, 11.1; Zürich: Theologischer Verlag, 1979).

—*Der zweite Thessalonicherbrief* (ZB, 11.2; Zürich: Theologischer Verlag, 1982).

Mason, Steve, 'Josephus's *Against Apion* as a *Logos Protreptikos*: An Invitation to Judean Philosophy' (unpublished paper).

—'Paul, Classical Anti-Jewish Polemic, and the Letter to the Romans', in David J. Hawkin and Tom Robinson (eds.), *Self-Definition and Self-Discovery in Early Christianity: A Study in Changing Horizons* (SBEC, 26; Lewiston, NY: Edwin Mellen Press, 1990), pp. 181-223.

Masson, Charles, *Les deux Epitres de Saint Paul aux Thessaloniciens* (CNT, 11a; Paris: Delachaux & Niestlé, 1957).

Matera, Frank J., *Galatians* (SP, 9; Collegeville, MN: Liturgical Press, 1992).

Matson, David Lertis, *Household Conversion Narratives in Luke–Acts: Patterns and Interpretation* (JSNTSup, 123; Sheffield: Sheffield Academic Press, 1996).

Matsueda, Ross L., 'The Current State of the Differential Association Theory', *CD* 34 (1988), pp. 277-306.

Matza, David, *Delinquency and Drift* (New York: John Wiley & Sons, 1964).

Matza, David, and Graham Sykes, 'Techniques of Neutralization: A Theory of Delinquency', *ASR* 22 (1957), pp. 664-70.

Mauer, Christian, 'φυλή', *TDNT*, IX, pp. 245-50.

Mead, George, 'The Psychology of Punitive Justice', *AJS* 23 (1918), pp. 577-602.

Mearns, Christopher L., 'Early Eschatological Development in Paul: The Evidence of I and II Thessalonians', *NTS* 27 (1980–81), pp. 137-57.

Meeks, Wayne A., 'Breaking Away: Three New Testament Pictures of Christianity's Separation from the Jewish Communities', in Neusner and Frerichs (eds.), *'To See Ourselves as Others See Us'*, pp. 93-115.

—*The First Urban Christians: The Social World of the Apostle Paul* (New Haven: Yale University Press, 1983).

—'The Man from Heaven in Johannine Sectarianism', *JBL* 91 (1972), pp. 44-74.

—*The Moral World of the First Christians* (London: SPCK, 1987).

—*The Origins of Christian Morality: The First Two Centuries* (New Haven: Yale University Press, 1993).

—' "Since Then You Would Need to Go out of the World": Group Boundaries in Pauline Christianity', in Thomas J. Ryan (ed.), *Critical History and Biblical Faith* (Villanova, PN: College Theology Society, 1979), pp. 1-23.

—'Social Functions of Apocalyptic Language in Pauline Christianity', in Hellholm (ed.), *Apocalypticism,* pp. 687-705.

Meier, Robert F., 'Norms and the Study of Deviance: A Proposed Research Strategy', *DB* 3 (1981), pp. 1-25.

Menken, Maarten J.J., 'Paradise Regained or Still Lost?: Eschatology and Disorderly Behaviour in 2 Thessalonians', *NTS* 38 (1992), pp. 271-89.

—*2 Thessalonians* (NTR; London: Routledge, 1994).

Menoud, P.H., 'Le sens du verbe πορθεῖν (Gal. 1.13, 23; Acts 9.21)', in *Apophoreta: Festschrift für Ernst Haenchen* (BNZW, 30; Berlin: Alfred Töpelmann, 1964), pp. 178-86.

Merton, Robert K., *Social Theory and Social Structure* (New York: Free Press, rev. edn, 1957).

Metzger, Bruce, *A Textual Commentary on the Greek New Testament* (New York: United Bible Societies, 1971).

Meyers, Eric M., and A.T. Kraabel, 'Archaeology, Iconography, and Nonliterary Written Remains', in Robert A. Kraft and George W.E. Nickelsburg (eds.), *Early Judaism and its Modern Interpreters* (BMI; Philadelphia: Fortress Press; Atlanta: Scholars Press, 1986), pp. 175-210.

Milligan, George, *St Paul's Epistles to the Thessalonians* (London: Macmillan, 1908).

Minear, Paul S., *New Testament Apocalyptic* (Nashville: Abingdon Press, 1981).

Mitford, T.B., 'A Cypriot Oath of Allegiance to Tiberius', *JRS* 1 (1930), pp. 75-79.

Moffatt, James, *Introduction to the New Testament* (Edinburgh: T. & T. Clark, 3rd edn, 1927).

Moore, George Foot, *Judaism in the First Three Centuries of the Christian Era: The Age of the Tannaim* (3 vols.; Cambridge, MA: Harvard University Press, 1927).

Moore, R.I., *The Formation of a Persecuting Society: Power and Deviance in Western Europe, 950–1250* (Oxford: Basil Blackwell, 1987).

Morgan-Gillman, Florence, 'Jason of Thessalonica (Acts 17,5-9)', in Collins (ed.), *The Thessalonian Correspondence*, pp. 39-49.

—*Women who Knew Paul* (ZSNT; Collegeville, MN: Liturgical Press, 1992).

Morris, Leon, *The First and Second Epistle to the Thessalonians* (NICNT; Grand Rapids: Eerdmans, rev. edn, 1991).

—'ΚΑΙ ΑΠΑΞ ΚΑΙ ΔΙΣ', *NovT* 1 (1956), pp. 205-208.

Morton, A.Q., and J. McLeman, *Christianity and the Computer* (London: Hodder & Stoughton, 1964).

Moule, C.F.D., *The Birth of the New Testament* (London: A. & C. Black, 3rd rev. edn, 1982).

Munck, Johannes, *Christ and Israel: An Interpretation of Romans 9–11* (trans. I. Nixon; Philadelphia: Fortress Press, 1967).

—'1 Thess i.9-10 and the Missionary Preaching of Paul: Textual Exegesis and Hermeneutic Reflections', *NTS* 9 (1962–63), pp. 95-110.

Murphy-O'Connor, Jerome, *Paul: A Critical Life* (Oxford: Clarendon Press, 1996).

Musurillo, Herbert (ed.), *The Acts of the Christian Martyrs* (Oxford: Clarendon Press, 1972).

Nanos, Mark D., *The Mystery of Romans: The Jewish Context of Paul's Letter* (Minneapolis: Fortress Press, 1996).

Neil, William, *The Epistle [sic] of Paul to the Thessalonians* (MNTC; New York: Harper & Brothers, 1950).

Neusner, Jacob, 'Varieties of Judaism in the Formative Age', in A. Green (ed.), *Jewish Spirituality from the Bible through the Middle Ages* (New York: Crossroad; London: SCM Press, 1989), pp. 171-97.

Neusner, Jacob, and Ernest S. Frerichs (eds.), *'To See Ourselves as Others See Us': Christians, Jews, 'Others' in Late Antiquity* (Chico, CA: Scholars Press, 1985).

Neyrey, Jerome H. (ed.), *The Social World of Luke–Acts: Models for Interpretation* (Peabody, MA: Hendrickson, 1991).

Nickelsburg, George W.E., 'Social Aspects of Palestinian Jewish Apocalypticism', in Hellholm (ed.), *Apocalypticism*, pp. 641-54.

Niebuhr, H. Richard, *Christ and Culture* (New York: Harper & Row, 1951).

Nigdelis, P.M., 'Synagoge(n) und Gemeinde der Juden in Thessaloniki: Fragen auf grund einer neuen jüdischen Grabinschrift der Kaiserzeit', *ZPE* 102 (1994), pp. 297-306.

Nock, A.D., *Conversion: The Old and the New in Religion from Alexander the Great to Augustine of Hippo* (Oxford: Clarendon Press, 1933).

Nolland, John, 'Uncircumcised Proselytes?', *JSJ* 12 (1981), pp. 173-94.

O'Brien, Peter T., *Colossians and Philemon* (WBC, 44; Waco, TX: Word Books, 1982).

Okeke, G.E., 'I Thessalonians 2.13-16: The Fate of the Unbelieving Jews', *NTS* 27 (1980–81), pp. 127-36.

Orchard, J. Bernard, 'Thessalonians and the Synoptic Gospels', *Bib* 19 (1938), pp. 19-42.

Pagels, Elaine, 'Christian Apologists and "The Fall of the Angels": An Attack on Roman Imperial Power?', *HTR* 78 (1985), pp. 301-25.

Palmer, Daryl W., 'Thanksgiving, Self-Defence, and Exhortation in 1 Thessalonians 1–3', *Colloqium* 14 (1981), pp. 23-31.

Pate, C. Marvin, *The End of the Age Has Come: The Theology of Paul* (Grand Rapids: Zondervan, 1995).

Patte, Daniel, *Paul's Faith and the Power of the Gospel: A Structural Introduction to the Pauline Letters* (Philadelphia: Fortress Press, 1983).

Pax, Elpidius, 'Beobachtungen zur Konvertitensprache im ersten Thessalonicherbrief', *SBFLA* 21 (1971), pp. 220-61.

—'Konvertitenprobleme im ersten Thessalonicherbrief', *BibLeb* 13 (1972), pp. 24-37.

Payne, William D., 'Negative Labels: Passageways and Prisons', *CD* 19 (1973), pp. 33-40.

Pearson, Birger A., *The Emergence of the Christian Religion: Essays on Early Christianity* (Harrisburg, PN: Trinity Press International, 1997).

—'1 Thessalonians 2:13-16: A Deutero-Pauline Interpolation', *HTR* 64 (1971), pp. 79-94.

Peerbolte, Lambertus J. Lietaert, 'The KATEXON/KATEXΩN of 2 Thess. 2:6-7', *NovT* 39 (1997), pp. 138-50.

Perkins, Pheme, '1 Thessalonians and Hellenistic Religious Practices', in Horgan and Kobelski (eds.), *To Touch the Text*, pp. 325-34.

Pesch, Rudolf, *Die Apostelgeschichte* (EKKNT, 5.2; Zürich: Benzinger Verlag; Neukirchen–Vluyn: Neukirchener Verlag, 1986).

—*Die Entdeckung des ältesten Paulus-Briefes. Paulus-neu gesehen: Die Briefe an die Gemeinde der Thessalonicher* (Freiburg: Herder, 1984).

Peterlin, Davorin, *Paul's Letter to the Philippians in the Light of Disunity in the Church* (NovTSup, 79; Leiden: E.J. Brill, 1995).

Pfitzner, Victor C., *Paul and the Agon Motif: Traditional Athletic Imagery in the Pauline Literature* (NovTSup, 16; Leiden: E.J. Brill, 1967).

Pfohl, Stephen J., *Images of Deviance and Social Control: A Sociological History* (New York: McGraw–Hill, 2nd edn, 1994).

Pfuhl, Edwin H., Jr, *The Deviance Process* (New York: Van Nostrand, 1980).

Piven, Frances Fox, 'Deviant Behavior and the Remaking of the World', *SocProb* 28 (1981), pp. 489-508.

Plevnik, Joseph, '1 Thess. 5,1-11: Its Authenticity, Intention and Message', *Bib* 60 (1979), pp. 71-90.

Pobee, John S., *Persecution and Martyrdom in the Theology of Paul* (JSNTSup, 6; Sheffield: JSOT Press, 1985).

Pohill, John B., *Acts* (NAC, 26; Nashville: Broadman Press, 1992).

Portefaix, Lilian, *Sisters Rejoice: Paul's Letter to the Philippians and Luke–Acts as Seen by First-Century Philippian Women* (ConBNT, 20; Stockholm: Almqvist & Wiksell, 1988).

Porter, Jack Nusan, and Ruth Taplin, *Conflict and Conflict Resolution: A Sociological Introduction with Updated Bibliography and Theory Section* (Lanham, MD: University Press of America, 1987).

Price, S.R.F., *Rituals and Power: The Roman Imperial Cult in Asia Minor* (Cambridge: Cambridge University Press, 1984).

Pruitt, D.G., and J.Z. Rubin, *Social Conflict: Escalation, Stalemate, and Settlement* (New York: Random House, 1986).

Quinn, Jerome D., ' "Seven Times He Wore Chains" (1 Clem 5:6)', *JBL* 97 (1978), pp. 574-76.

Räisänen, Heikki, 'The Clash between Christian Styles of Life in the Book of Revelation', *ST* 49 (1995), pp. 151-66.

—'Paul's Conversion and the Development of his View of the Law', *NTS* 22 (1987), pp. 404-19.

Ramsay, W.M., *St. Paul the Traveller and Roman Citizen* (repr.; Grand Rapids: Baker Book House, 1960).

Reat, N. Ross, 'Insiders and Outsiders in the Study of Religious Traditions', *JAAR* 51 (1983), pp. 459-76.

Reese, James M., *1 and 2 Thessalonians* (NTM, 16; Wilmington, DE: Michael Glazier, 1979).

Reicke, Bo, 'Judaeo-Christianity and the Jewish Establishment, A.D. 33–66', in Ernst Bammel and C.F.D. Moule (eds.), *Jesus and the Politics of his Day* (Cambridge: Cambridge University Press, 1984), pp. 145-52.

Rex, John, *Social Conflict: A Conceptual and Theoretical Analysis* (London: Longmans, 1981).

Reynolds, Joyce M., and Robert F. Tannenbaum, *Jews and God-Fearers at Aphrodisias* (Cambridge: Cambridge Philological Society, 1987).

Rhoads, David, 'Zealots', *ABD*, VI, pp. 1043-54.

Richard, Earl J., 'Contemporary Research on 1 (& 2) Thessalonians', *BTB* 20 (1990), pp. 107-15.

—'Early Pauline Thought: An Analysis of 1 Thessalonians', in Bassler (ed.), *Pauline Theology*, I, pp. 39-51.

—*First and Second Thessalonians* (SP, 11; Collegeville, MN: Liturgical Press, 1995).

Richardson, Peter, 'Pauline Inconsistency: I Corinthians 9:19-23 and Galatians 2:11-14', *NTS* 26 (1980–81), pp. 347-62.

Richardson, Peter (ed.), *Anti-Judaism in Early Christianity*. I. *Paul and the Gospels* (Waterloo, ON: Wilfrid Laurier University Press, 1986).

Riesner, Rainer, *Paul's Early Period: Chronology, Mission Strategy, Theology* (trans. Doug Stott; Grand Rapids: Eerdmans, 1998).

Rigaux, Béda, *Saint Paul: Les Epitres aux Thessaloniciens* (EBib; Paris: J. Gabalda, 1956).

Roberts, Keith A., *Religion in Sociological Perspective* (Belmont, CA: Wadsworth, 1995).

Robertson, A.T., *Word Pictures in the New Testament* (6 vols.; Nashville: Broadman Press, 1931).

Rodd, Cyril S., 'On Applying a Sociological Theory to Biblical Studies', *JSOT* 19 (1981), pp. 95-106.

Rodgers, Lloyd Walter, III, 'An Examination of Paul as Persecutor' (PhD dissertation, Southern Baptist Theological Seminary, 1989).

Roetzel, Calvin J., 'The Grammar of Election in Four Pauline Letters', in David M. Hay (ed.), *Pauline Theology. II. 1 & 2 Corinthians* (Minneapolis: Fortress Press, 1993), pp. 211-33.

—'*Theodidaktoi* and Handwork in Philo and 1 Thessalonians', in Vanhoye (ed.), *L'apôtre Paul*, pp. 324-31.

Rogers, Joseph W., and M.D. Buffalo, 'Fighting Back: Nine Modes of Adaptation to a Deviant Label', *SocProb* 22 (1974), pp. 101-18.

Rosenblatt, Marie-Eloise, *Paul the Accused: His Portrait in the Acts of the Apostles* (ZSNT; Collegeville, MN: Liturgical Press, 1995).

Rosner, Brian S., ' "That Pattern of Teaching": Issues and Essays in Pauline Ethics', in Brian S. Rosner (ed.), *Understanding Paul's Ethics: Twentieth-Century Approaches* (Grand Rapids: Eerdmans; Carlisle: Paternoster Press, 1995).

Ross, Marc Howard, *The Culture of Conflict: Interpretations and Interests in Comparative Perspective* (New Haven: Yale University Press, 1993).

Rowland, Christopher, *The Open Heaven: A Study of Apocalyptic in Judaism and Early Christianity* (New York: Crossroad, 1982).

Russell, Ronald, 'The Idle in 2 Thess. 3:6-12: An Eschatological or a Social Problem?', *NTS* 34 (1988), pp. 105-19.

Sagarin, Edward, *Deviants and Deviance: An Introduction to the Study of Disvalued People and Behavior* (New York: Holt, Rinehart & Winston, 1975).

Ste Croix, G.E.M. de, 'Why Were the Early Christians Persecuted?', *Past and Present* 26 (1963), pp. 6-38.

Saldarini, Anthony J., 'The Gospel of Matthew and Jewish–Christian Conflict', in David L. Balch (ed.), *Social History of the Matthean Community* (Minneapolis: Fortress Press, 1991), pp. 38-61.

—*Matthew's Christian–Jewish Community* (CSHJ; Chicago: University of Chicago Press, 1994).

Sanders, E.P., 'Jewish Association with Gentiles and Galatians 2:11-14', in Robert T. Fortna and Beverly R. Gaventa (eds.), *The Conversation Continues: Studies in Paul and John in Honor of J. Louis Martyn* (Nashville: Abingdon Press, 1990), pp. 170-88.

—*Paul* (ed. Keith Thomas; Past Masters; Oxford: Oxford University Press, 1991).

—'Paul', in John Barclay and John Sweet (eds.), *Early Christian Thought in its Jewish Context* (Festschrift Morna D. Hooker; Cambridge: Cambridge University Press, 1996), pp. 112-29.

—'Paul on the Law, his Opponents, and the Jewish People in Philippians 3 and 2 Corinthians 11', in Richardson (ed.), *Anti-Judaism in Early Christianity*, pp. 75-90.

—'Paul's Attitude toward the Jewish People', *USQR* 33 (1978), pp. 175-87.

—*Paul, the Law, and the Jewish People* (Minneapolis: Fortress Press, 1983).

Sanders, Jack T., 'Christians and Jews in the Roman Empire: A Conversation with Rodney Stark', *SocAn* 53 (1992), pp. 433-45.

—'Circumcision of Gentile Converts: The Root of Hostility', *BR* 7 (1991), pp. 20-25, 44.

—*The Jews in Luke–Acts* (London: SCM Press, 1987).

—'Paul between Jews and Gentiles in Corinth', *JSNT* 65 (1997), pp. 67-83.

—*Schismatics, Sectarians, Dissidents, Deviants: The First One Hundred Years of Jewish– Christian Relations* (London: SCM Press, 1993).

Sandnes, Karl Olav, *Paul—One of the Prophets?: A Contribution to the Apostle's Self- Understanding* (WUNT, 43; Tübingen: J.C.B. Mohr [Paul Siebeck], 1991).

Schelling, T. C., *Strategy of Conflict* (Cambridge, MA: Harvard University Press, 1960).

Schervish, Paul G., 'The Labeling Perspective: Its Bias and Potential in the Study of Politi- cal Deviance', *ASoc* 8 (1973), pp. 47-57.

Schippers, R., 'The Pre-Synoptic Tradition in 1 Thessalonians II 13-16', *NovT* 8 (1966), pp. 223-34.

Schlier, Heinrich, 'θλίβω, θλῖψις', TDNT, III, , pp. 139-48.

Schlueter, Carol J., *Filling up the Measure: Polemical Hyperbole in 1 Thessalonians 2.14- 16* (JSNTSup, 98; Sheffield: JSOT Press, 1994).

Schmidt, Daryl D., 'The Syntactical Style of 2 Thessalonians: How Pauline Is It?', in Collins (ed.), *The Thessalonian Correspondence*, pp. 383-93.

—'1 Thess 2:13-16: Linguistic Evidence for an Interpolation', *JBL* 102 (1983), pp. 269-79.

Schmidt, Karl Ludwig, 'ἔθνος', TDNT, II, pp. 364-72.

Schmithals, Walter, *Paul and the Gnostics* (trans. John E. Steely; Nashville: Abingdon Press, 1972).

Scholer, David N., ' "The God of Peace Will Shortly Crush Satan under Your Feet" (Romans 16:20a): The Function of Apocalyptic Eschatology in Paul', *ExAud* 5 (1989), pp. 53-61.

Schur, Edwin, *Labeling Deviant Behavior: Its Sociological Implications* (New York: Harper & Row, 1971).

—*The Politics of Deviance: Stigma Contests and the Uses of Power* (Englewood Cliffs, NJ: Prentice–Hall, 1980).

Segal, Alan F., *Paul the Convert: The Apostolate and Apostasy of Saul the Pharisee* (New Haven: Yale University Press, 1990).

Seland, Torrey, *Establishment Violence in Philo and Luke: A Study of Non-Conformity to the Torah and Jewish Vigilante Reactions* (BIS, 15; Leiden: E.J. Brill, 1995).

Selwyn, Edward Gordon, *The First Epistle of St. Peter* (Grand Rapids: Baker Book House, 2nd edn, 1947).

Setzer, Claudia J., *Jewish Responses to Early Christians: History and Polemics, 30–150 CE* (Minneapolis: Fortress Press, 1994).

—' "You Invent a Christ!": Christological Claims as Points of Jewish–Christian Dispute', *USQR* 44 (1991), pp. 315-28.

Sherif, Muzafer, *In Common Predicament: Social Psychology of Intergroup Conflict and Cooperation* (ISBS; Boston: Houghton Mifflin, 1966).

Sherif, Muzafer, and Carolyn W. Sherif, *Groups in Harmony and Tension: An Integration of Studies on Intergroup Relations* (New York: Harper & Row, 1953).

Sherif, Muzafer, *et al.*, *Intergroup Conflict and Cooperation: The Robber's Cave Experi- ment* (Norman, OK: University of Oklahoma Press, 1961).

Sherwin-White, A.N., 'The Early Persecutions and the Roman Law Again', *JTS* NS 3 (1952), pp. 201-13.

—*Roman Society and Roman Law in the New Testament* (Oxford: Clarendon Press, 1963).

Siegel, Bernard, 'Defensive Structuring and Environmental Stress', *AJS* 76 (1970), pp. 11-32.

Siegel, Larry J., *Criminology* (St Paul, MN: West, 4th edn, 1992).

Silva, Moisés, *Philippians* (BECNT; Grand Rapids: Baker Book House, 1992).

Simmel, Georg, *Conflict and the Web of Group-Affiliation* (trans. Kurt H. Wolff; New York: Free Press, 1955).

Simpson, J.W., Jr, 'The Future of Non-Christian Jews: 1 Thessalonians 2:15-16 and Romans 9–11' (PhD dissertation, Fuller Theological Seminary, 1988).

—'The Problems Posed by 1 Thessalonians 2:15-16 and a Solution', *HBT* 12 (1990), pp. 42-72.

—'Thessalonians, Letters to the', *DPL*, pp. 932-39.

Slater, Thomas B., 'On the Social Setting of the Revelation of John', *NTS* 44 (1998), pp. 232-56.

Slingerland, Dixon, ' "The Jews" in the Pauline Portion of Acts', *JAAR* 54 (1986), pp. 305-21.

Smallwood, E. Mary, *The Jews under Roman Rule from Pompey to Diocletian: A Study in Political Relations* (Leiden: E.J. Brill, 2nd edn, 1981).

Smiga, George, *Pain and Polemic: Anti-Judaism in the Gospels* (New York: Paulist Press, 1992).

Smith, Abraham, *Comfort One Another: Reconstructing the Rhetoric and Audience of 1 Thessalonians* (LCBIS; Louisville, KY: Westminster/John Knox Press, 1995).

Smith, Morton, 'The Reason for the Persecution of Paul and the Obscurity of Acts', in E.E. Urbach, R.J. Werblowsky and C. Wirszubske (eds.), *Studies in Mysticism and Religion: Presented to Gershom G. Scholem* (Jerusalem: Magnes Press, 1967), pp. 261-68.

South, James T., *Disciplinary Practices in Pauline Texts* (Lewiston, NY: Edwin Mellen Press, 1992).

Stambaugh, John E., and David L. Balch, *The New Testament in its Social Evironment* (LEC, 2; Philadelphia: Westminster Press, 1986).

Stanley, Christopher D., ' "Neither Jew nor Greek": Ethnic Conflict in Graeco-Roman Society', *JSNT* 64 (1996), pp. 101-24.

Stanton, Graham N., 'Aspects of Early Jewish–Christian Polemic', *NTS* 31 (1985), pp. 377-92.

—'The Gospel of Matthew and Judaism', in *idem*, *A Gospel for a New People: Studies in Matthew* (Edinburgh: T & T Clark, 1992), pp. 146-68.

—'Matthew's Gospel and the Damascus Document in Sociological Perspective', in *A Gospel for a New People*, pp. 85-107.

Stanton, H.U. Weitbrecht, ' "Turned the World upside down" ', *ExpTim* 44 (1932–33), pp. 526-27.

Stark, Rodney, *Sociology* (Belmont, CA: Wadsworth, 5th edn, 1994).

Steele, E. Springs, 'The Use of Jewish Scriptures in 1 Thessalonians', *BTB* 14 (1984), pp. 12-17.

Stegemann, Wolfgang, *Zwischen Synagoge und Obrigkeit: Zur historischen Situation der lukanischen Christen* (FRLANT, 152; Göttingen: Vandenhoeck & Ruprecht, 1991).

314   *Conflict at Thessalonica*

Stendahl, Krister, *Paul among the Jews and Gentiles and Other Essays* (Philadelphia: Fortress Press, 1976).
Stowers, Stanley Kent, 'The Social Sciences and the Study of Early Christianity', in William Scott Green (ed.), *Approaches to Ancient Judaism. V. Studies in Judaism and its Greco-Roman Context* (BJS, 32; Atlanta: Scholars Press, 1985), pp. 149-81.
—'Social Status, Public Speaking and Private Teaching: The Circumstances of Paul's Preaching Activity', *NovT* 26 (1984), pp. 59-82.
Strathmann, Hermann, 'λαός', *TDNT*, IV, pp. 29-57.
Strum, Richard E., 'Defining the Word "Apocalyptic": A Problem in Biblical Criticism', in Marcus and Soards (eds.), *Apocalyptic and the New Testament*, pp. 17-48.
Stuhlmacher, Peter, *Paul: Rabbi and Apostle* (with P. Lapide; trans. L.W. Denef; Minneapolis: Fortress Press, 1984).
Sumner, William G., *Folkways* (Boston: Ginn, 1906).
Sutherland, Edwin H., *Principles of Criminology* (Philadelphia: Lippincott, 3rd edn, 1939).
Sutherland, Edwin H., and Donald R. Cressey, *Criminology* (Philadelphia: Lippincott, 8th edn, 1970).
Tajfel, Henri, *Human Groups and Social Categories: Studies in Social Psychology* (Cambridge: Cambridge University Press, 1981).
Tajra, Harry W., *The Trial of St. Paul: A Juridical Exegesis of the Second Half of the Acts of the Apostles* (WUNT, 35; Tübingen: J.C.B. Mohr [Paul Siebeck], 1989).
Talbert, Charles H., *The Apocalypse: A Reading of the Revelation of John* (Louisville, KY: Westminster/John Knox Press, 1994).
—*Reading Acts: A Literary and Theological Commentary on the Acts of the Apostles* (New York: Crossroad, 1997).
Tannenbaum, Frank, *Crime and Community* (Boston: Ginn, 1938).
Taylor, Donald M., and Fathali M. Moghaddam, *Theories of Intergroup Relations: International Social Psychological Perspectives* (New York: Praeger, 1987).
Tellbe, Mikael, 'The Sociological Factors behind Philippians 3.1-11 and the Conflict at Philippi', *JSNT* 55 (1994), pp. 97-121.
Theissen, Gerd, *The Social Setting of Pauline Christianity: Essays on Corinth* (ed. and trans. John H. Schütz; Edinburgh: T. & T. Clark, 1982).
Thielman, Frank, *Paul and the Law: A Contextual Approach* (Downers Grove, IL: InterVarsity Press, 1994).
—*Philippians* (NIVAC; Grand Rapids: Zondervan, 1995).
Thio, Alex, *Deviant Behavior* (New York: HarperCollins, 4th edn, 1995).
Thurston, Bonnie, *Reading Colossians, Ephesians, and 2 Thessalonians: A Literary and Theological Commentary* (New York: Crossroad, 1995).
Thurston, Robert W., 'The Relationship between the Thessalonian Epistles', *ExpTim* 85 (1973), pp. 52-56.
Tilborg, Sjef van, *The Jewish Leaders in Matthew* (Leiden: E.J. Brill, 1972).
Toch, Hans, *The Social Psychology of Social Movements* (New York: Bobbs-Merrill, 1965).
Touval, S., and I.W. Zartman, *International Mediation in Theory and Practice* (Boulder, CO: Westview, 1985).
Towner, P.H., 'Households and Household Codes', *DPL*, pp. 417-19.
Trebilco, Paul R., *Jewish Communities in Asia Minor* (SNTMS, 69; Cambridge: Cambridge University Press, 1991).

Trilling, Wolfgang, *Untersuchungen zum zweiten Thessalonicherbrief* (Leipzig: St Benno, 1972).

—*Der zweite Brief an die Thessalonicher* (EKKNT, 14; Zürich: Benzinger Verlag; Neukirchen–Vluyn: Neukirchener Verlag, 1980).

Troyer, Ronald J., and Gerald E. Markle, 'Creating Deviance Rules: A Macroscopic Model', *SQ* 23 (1982), pp. 157-69.

Tuckett, Christopher M., 'Deuteronomy 21,23 and Paul's Conversion', in Vanhoye (ed.), *L'apôtre Paul*, pp. 345-50.

Turner, E.G., 'Tiberius Julius Alexander', *JRS* 44 (1954), pp. 54-64.

Turner, John C., and Howard Giles (eds.), *Intergroup Behavior* (Chicago: University of Chicago Press, 1981).

Turner, Jonathan H., *The Structure of Sociological Theory* (Homewood, IL: Dorsey Press, rev. edn, 1978).

Turner, Ralph H., 'Deviance Avowal as Neutralization of Commitment', *SocProb* 19 (1972), pp. 308-21.

—'Value Conflict in Social Disorganization', *SSR* 38 (1954), 301-308.

Turner, Victor, *Schism and Community in an African Society* (New York: Humanities Press, 1957).

Vander Stichele, Caroline, 'The Concept of Tradition and 1 and 2 Thessalonians', in Collins (ed.), *The Thessalonian Correspondence*, pp. 499-504.

Vanhoye, A. (ed.), *L'apôtre Paul: Personnalité, style et conception du ministère* (BETL, 3; Leuven: Leuven University Press, 1986).

Verhoef, Eduard, 'Die Bedeutung des Artikels τῶν in 1 Thess 2,15', *BN* 80 (1995), pp. 41-46

Volf, Miroslav, 'Soft Difference: Theological Reflections on the Relation between Church and Culture in 1 Peter', *ExAud* 10 (1994), pp. 15-30.

Vos, Craig S. de, *Church and Community Conflicts: The Relationships of the Thessalonian, Corinthian, and Philippian Churches with Their Wider Civic Communities* (SBLDS, 168; Atlanta: Scholars Press, 1999).

—'Popular Graeco-Roman Responses to Early Christianity', in Philip F. Esler (ed.), *The Early Christian World* (London: Routledge, forthcoming).

—'The Significance of the Change from ΟΙΚΟΣ to ΟΙΚΙΑ in Luke's Account of the Philippian Gaoler (Acts 16.30-4)', *NTS* 41 (1995), pp. 292-96.

Walker, William, 'The Burden of Proof in Identifying Interpolations in the Pauline Letters', *NTS* 33 (1987), pp. 610-18.

—'Text-Critical Evidence for Interpolations in the Letters of Paul', *CBQ* 50 (1988), pp. 622-31.

Walsh, Joseph, 'On Christian Atheism', *VC* 45 (1991), pp. 255-77.

Walton, Steve, 'What Has Aristotle to Do with Paul? Rhetorical Criticism in 1 Thessalonians', *TynBul* 46 (1995), pp. 229-50.

Wanamaker, Charles A., 'Apocalypticism at Thessalonica', *Neot* 21 (1987), pp. 1-10.

—*The Epistles to the Thessalonians: A Commentary on the Greek Text* (NIGTC; Grand Rapids: Eerdmans; Exeter: Paternoster Press, 1990).

Ward, Ronald A., *1 & 2 Thessalonians* (Waco, TX: Word Books, 1973).

Ware, James, 'The Thessalonians as a Missionary Congregation: 1 Thessalonians 1,5-8', *ZNW* 83 (1992), pp. 126-31.

Watson, Francis, *Paul, Judaism and the Gentiles: A Sociological Approach* (SNTMS, 56; Cambridge: Cambridge University Press, 1986).

Weatherly, Jon A., 'The Authenticity of 1 Thessalonians 2.13-16: Additional Evidence', *JSNT* 42 (1991), pp. 79-98.

—*1 & 2 Thessalonians* (CPNIVC; Joplin, MO: College Press, 1996).

Weber, Max, *The Theory of Social and Economic Organization* (New York: Free Press, 1947).

Wedderburn, A.J.M., *The Reasons for Romans* (Minneapolis: Fortress Press, 1991).

Weima, Jeffrey A.D., 'An Apology for the Apologetic Function of 1 Thessalonians 2.1-12', *JSNT* 68 (1997), pp. 73-99.

—*Neglected Endings: The Significance of the Pauline Letter Closings* (JSNTSup, 101; Sheffield: JSOT Press, 1994).

Weima, Jeffrey A.D., and Stanley E. Porter, *1 and 2 Thessalonians: An Annotated Bibliography* (NTTS, 26; Leiden: E.J. Brill, 1998).

Weinstock, S., *Divus Julius* (Oxford: Clarendon Press, 1971).

Wengst, Klaus, *Pax Romana and the Peace of Jesus Christ* (trans. John Bowden; London: SCM Pres, 1987).

West, J.C., 'The Order of 1 and 2 Thessalonians', *JTS* 15 (1913), pp. 66-74.

Whitacre, Rodney A., *Johannine Polemic: The Role of Tradition and Theology* (SBLDS, 67; Chico, CA: Scholars Press, 1982).

White, L. Michael, and O. Larry Yarbrough (eds.), *The Social World of the First Christians: Essays in Honor of Wayne A. Meeks* (Minneapolis: Fortress Press, 1995).

Whiteley, D.E.H., *Thessalonians in the Revised Standard Version, with Introduction and Commentary* (London: Oxford University Press, 1969).

Whittaker, Molly (trans.), *Jews and Christians: Graeco-Roman Views* (CCWJCW, 6; Cambridge: Cambridge University Press, 1984).

—' "Signs and Wonders": The Pagan Background', *SE* 5 (1968), pp. 155-58.

Wick, Peter, 'Ist I Thess 2,13-16 antijüdisch?: Der rhetorische Gesamtzusammenhang des Briefes als Interpretationshilfe für eine einzelne Perikope', *TZ* 50 (1994), pp. 9-23.

Wilken, Robert L., *The Christians as the Romans Saw Them* (New Haven: Yale University Press, 1984).

Williams, David J., *1 and 2 Thessalonians* (NIBC, 12; Peabody, MA: Hendrickson, 1992).

Williams, R.M., Jr, *The Reduction of Intergroup Tensions* (New York: Social Science Research Council, 1947).

Wilson, Stephen G., 'The Apostate Minority', *ST* 49 (1995), pp. 201-11.

—*Related Strangers: Jews and Christians 70–170 C.E.* (Minneapolis: Fortress Press, 1995).

Winter, Bruce W., 'The Entries and Ethics of Orators and Paul (1 Thessalonians 2:1-12)', *TynBul* 44 (1993), pp. 55-74.

—' "If a Man Does not Wish to Work...": A Cultural and Historical Setting for 2 Thessalonians 3:6-16', *TynBul* 40 (1989), pp. 303-15.

—*Seek the Welfare of the City: Christians as Benefactors and Citizens* (FCGRW; Grand Rapids: Eerdmans; Carlisle: Paternoster Press, 1994).

Witt, Rex E., 'The Egyptian Cults in Ancient Macedonia', in Basil Laourdas and Ch. Makaronas (eds.), *Ancient Macedonia* (Thessaloniki: Institute for Balkan Studies, 1970), pp. 324-33.

Wolfson, Harry A., *Philo: Foundations of Religious Philosophy in Judaism, Christianity, and Islam* (2 vols.; Cambridge, MA: Harvard University Press, 1948).

Worchel, Stephen, and William G. Austin (eds.), *Psychology of Intergroup Relations* (Chicago: Nelson–Hall, 2nd edn, 1986).

Wortham, Robert A., 'The Problem of Anti-Judaism in 1 Thess 2:14-16 and Related Pauline Texts', *BTB* 25 (1995), pp. 37-44.

Wrede, William, *Die Echtheit des zweiten Thessalonicherbriefs untersucht* (TU, 24.2; Leipzig: Henrichs, 1903).

Wright, N.T., *Christian Origins and the Question of God*. I. *The New Testament and the People of God* (London: SPCK, 1992).

—*What Saint Paul Really Said: Was Paul of Tarsus the Real Founder of Christianity?* (Grand Rapids: Eerdmans; Cincinnati, OH: Forward Movement Publications, 1997).

Yarbrough, O. Larry, *Not Like the Gentiles: Marriage Rules in the Letters of Paul* (SBLDS, 80; Atlanta: Scholars Press, 1985).

Zeisler, John, *The Epistle to the Galatians* (EC; London: Epworth Press, 1992).

INDEXES

INDEX OF REFERENCES

OLD TESTAMENT

NEW TESTAMENT

JOURNAL FOR THE STUDY OF THE NEW TESTAMENT
SUPPLEMENT SERIES